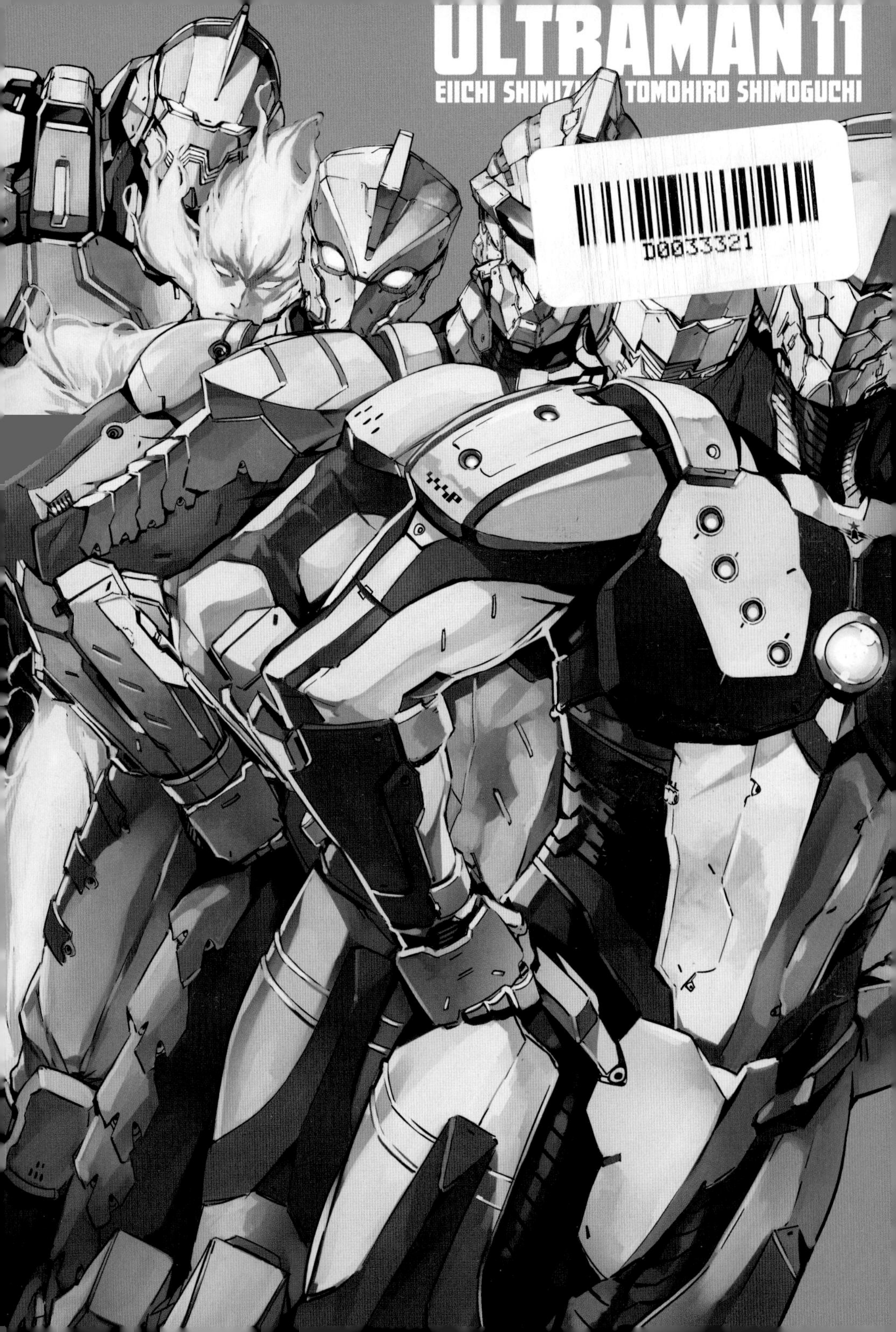
ULTRAMAN 11
EIICHI SHIMIZU TOMOHIRO SHIMOGUCHI

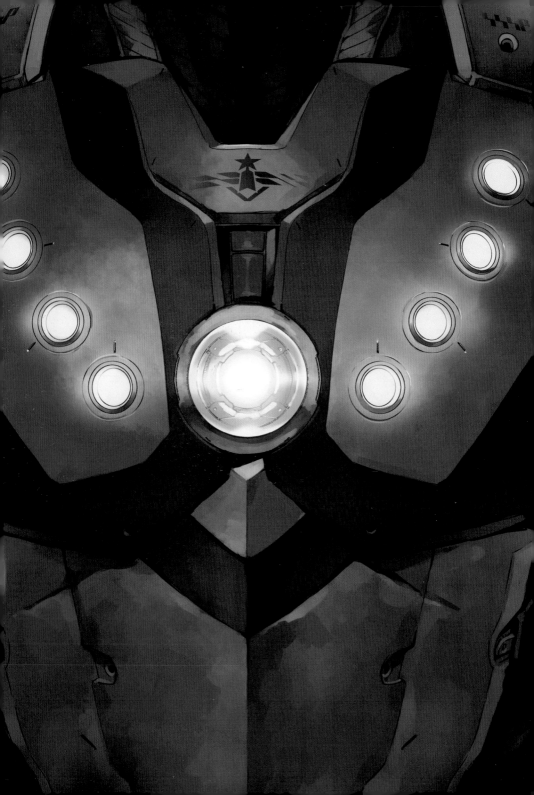

THIS IS THE BEGINNING OF A NEW AGE.

CONTENTS

CHAPTER 66	RIGHTEOUS RETRIBUTION	005
CHAPTER 67	OATH TO FULFILL	041
CHAPTER 68	DEADLY TOUCH	077
CHAPTER 69	AGITATOR	113
CHAPTER 70	THREE LIGHTS	145

ULTRAMAN CHAPTER 66 - RIGHTEOUS RETRIBUTION

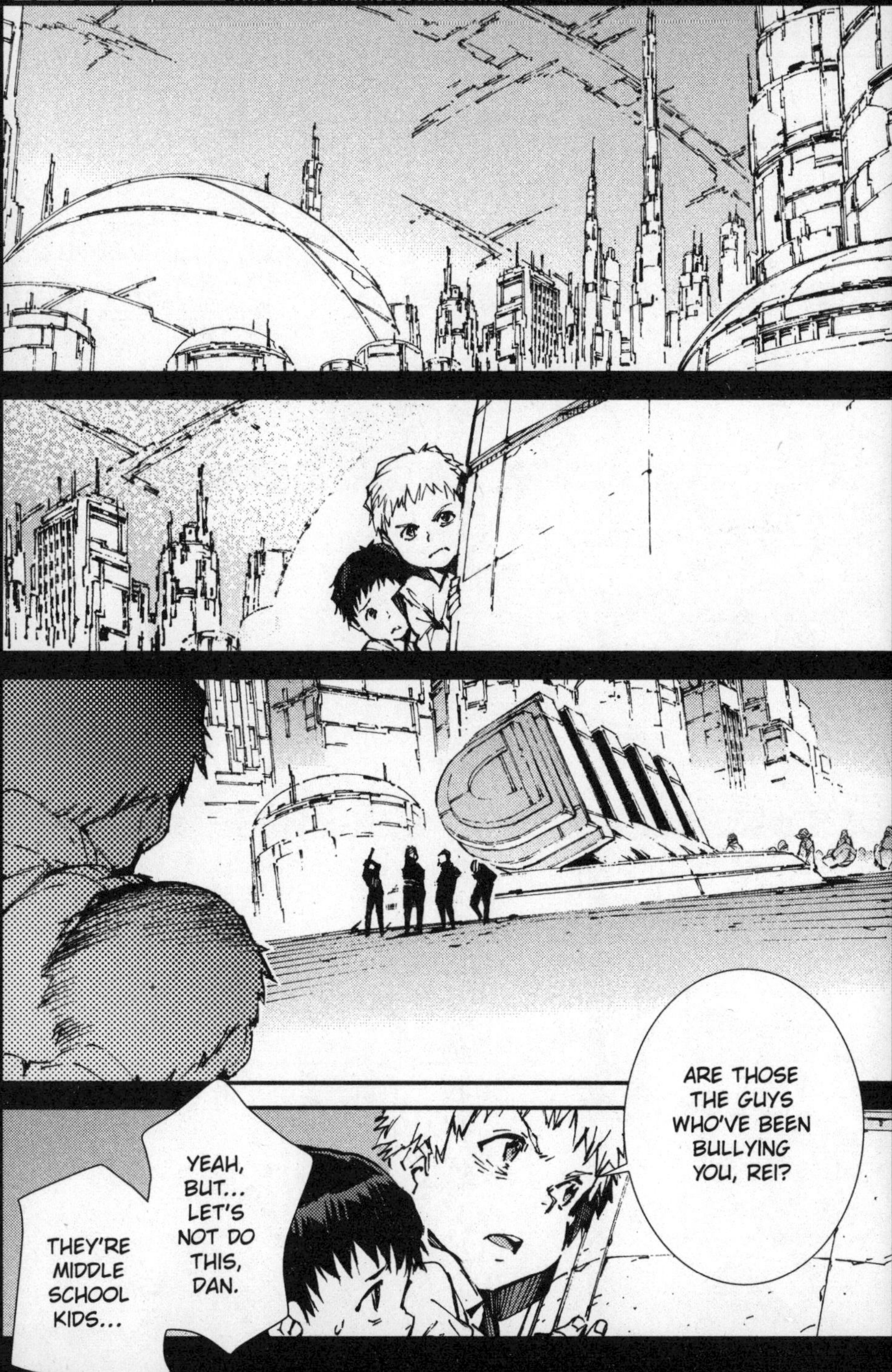
ARE THOSE THE GUYS WHO'VE BEEN BULLYING YOU, REI?
YEAH, BUT... LET'S NOT DO THIS, DAN.
THEY'RE MIDDLE SCHOOL KIDS...

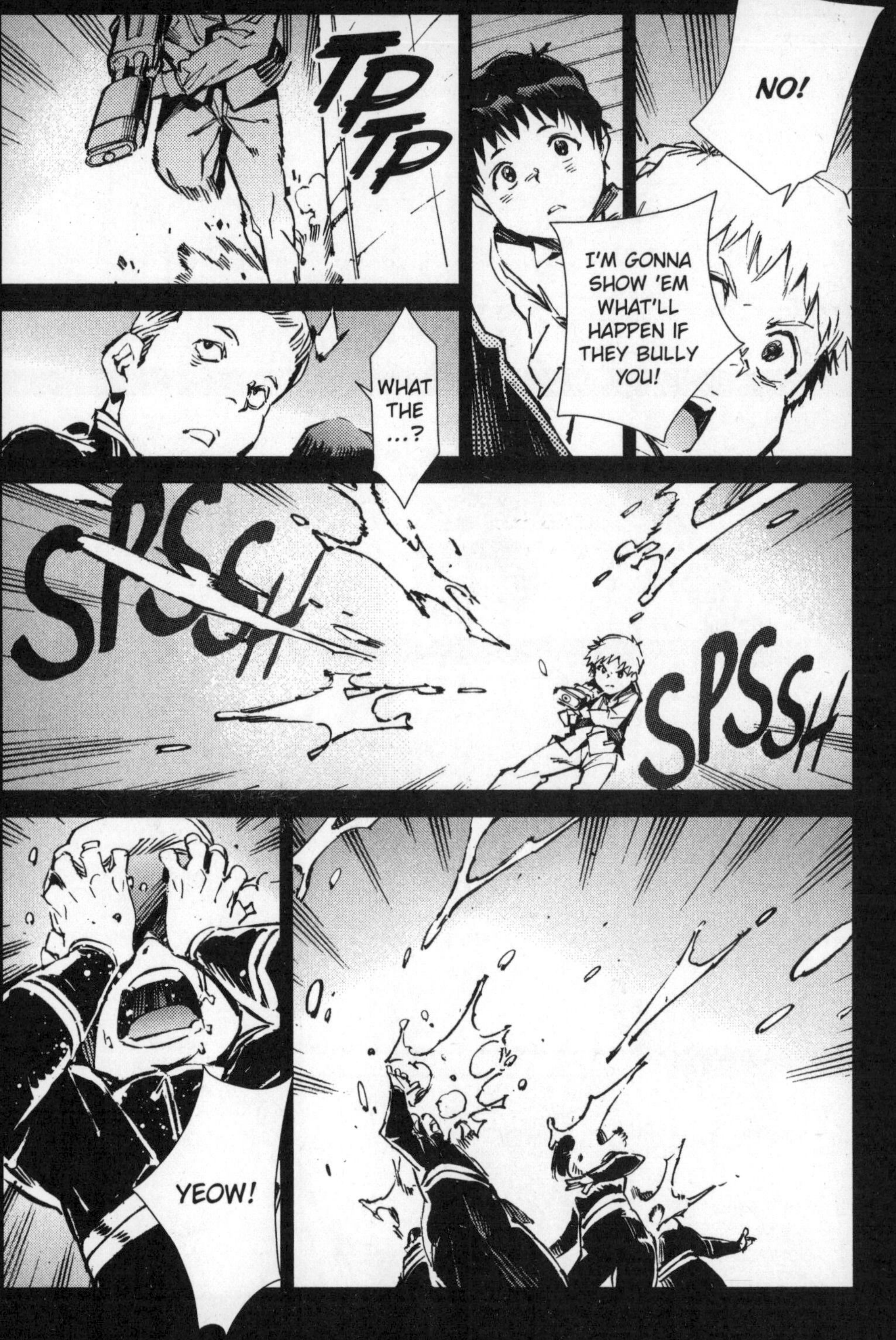
NO!
I'M GONNA SHOW 'EM WHAT'LL HAPPEN IF THEY BULLY YOU!
TP TP
WHAT THE ...?
SPSSH
SPSSH
YEOW!

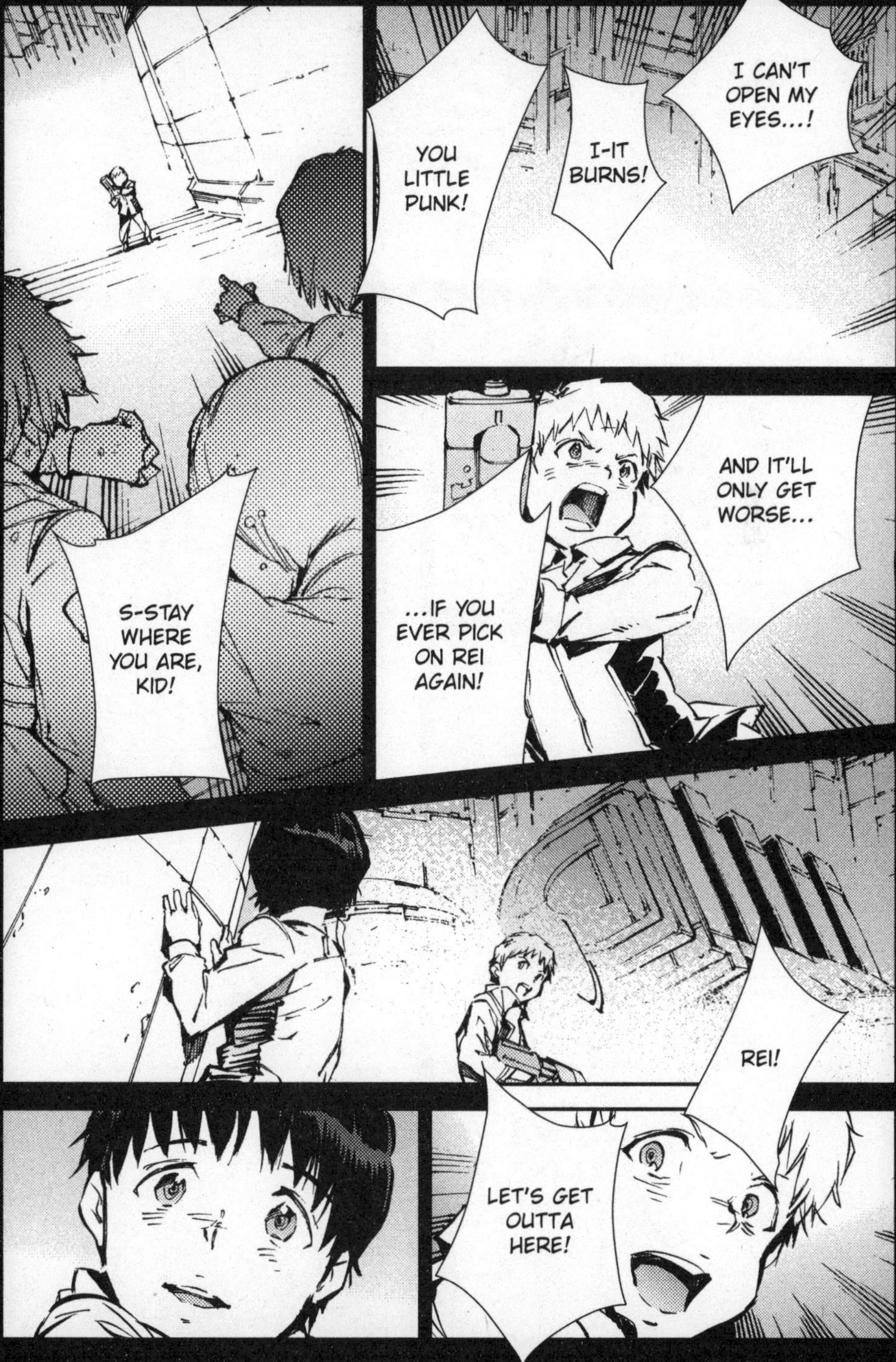
I CAN'T OPEN MY EYES...!
I-IT BURNS!
YOU LITTLE PUNK!
AND IT'LL ONLY GET WORSE...
...IF YOU EVER PICK ON REI AGAIN!
S-STAY WHERE YOU ARE, KID!
REI!
LET'S GET OUTTA HERE!

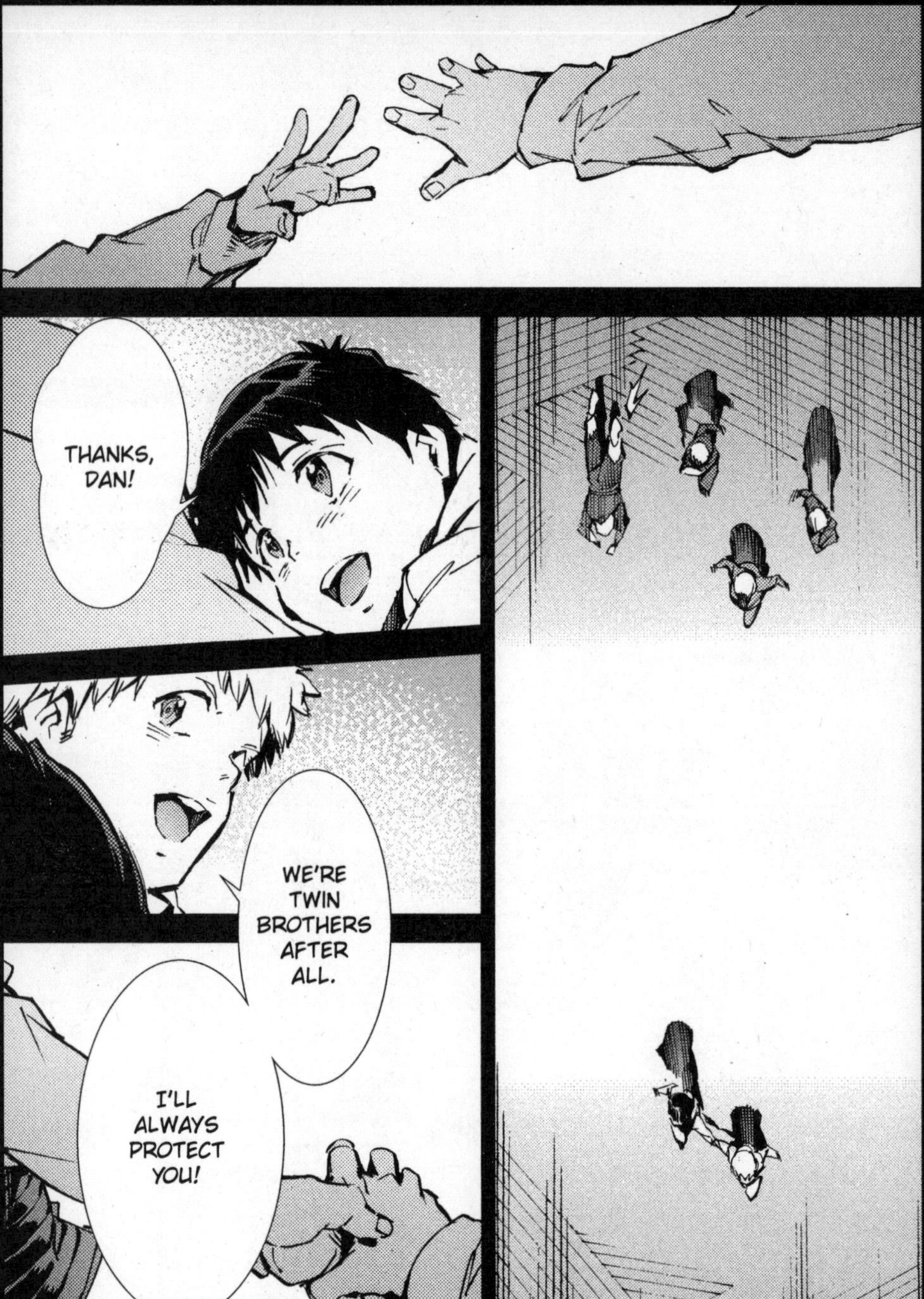
THANKS, DAN!
WE'RE TWIN BROTHERS AFTER ALL.
I'LL ALWAYS PROTECT YOU!

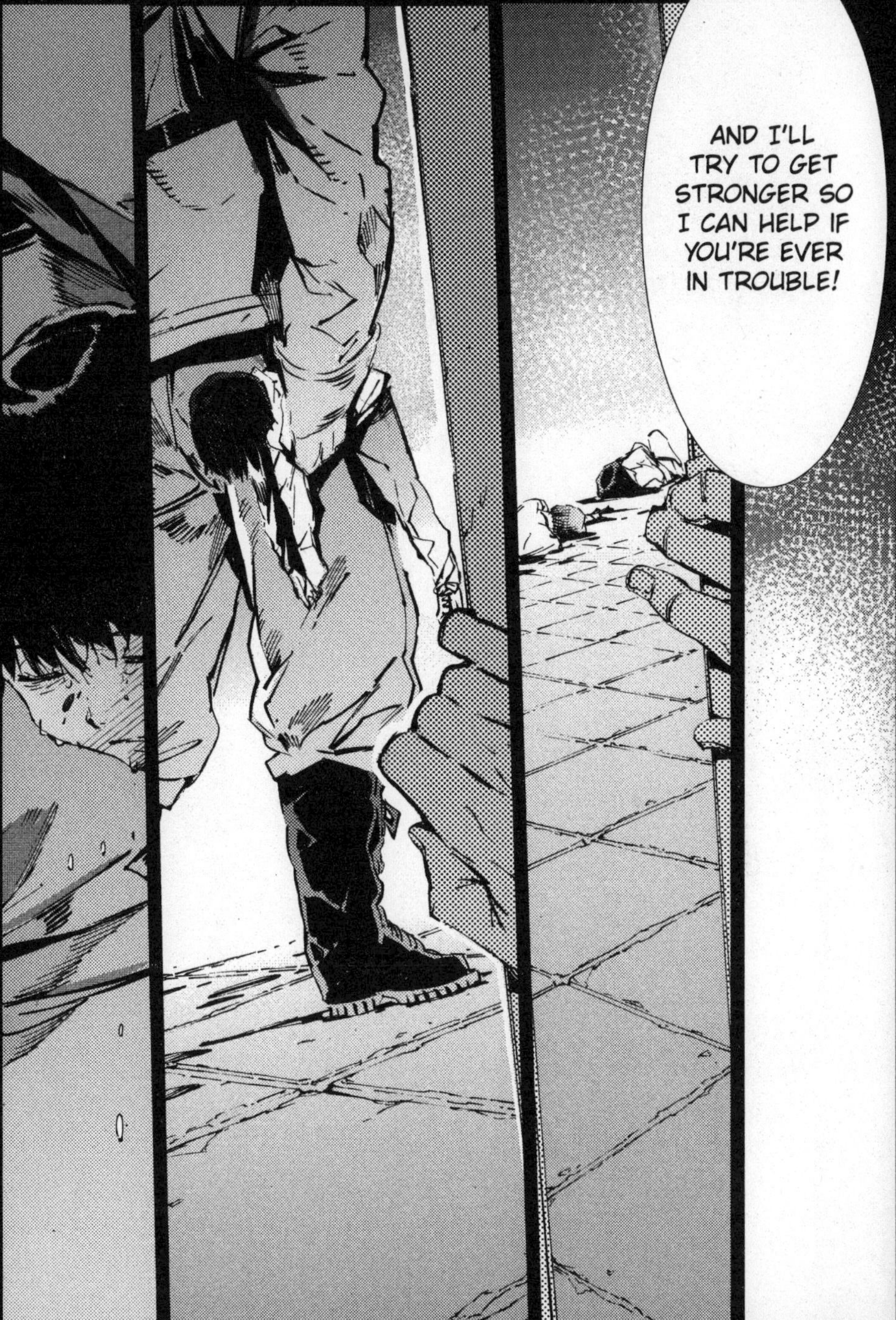
AND I'LL TRY TO GET STRONGER SO I CAN HELP IF YOU'RE EVER IN TROUBLE!

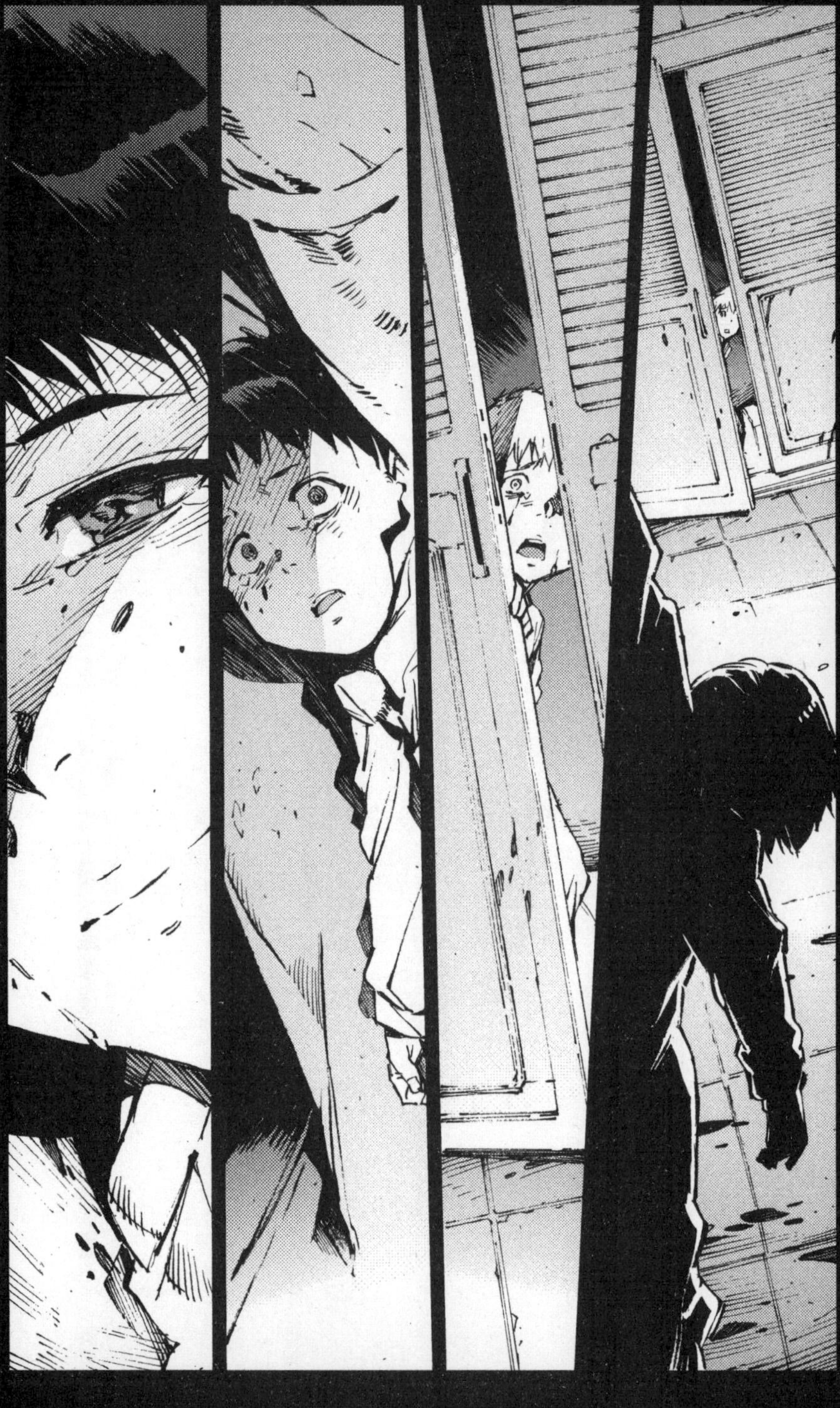

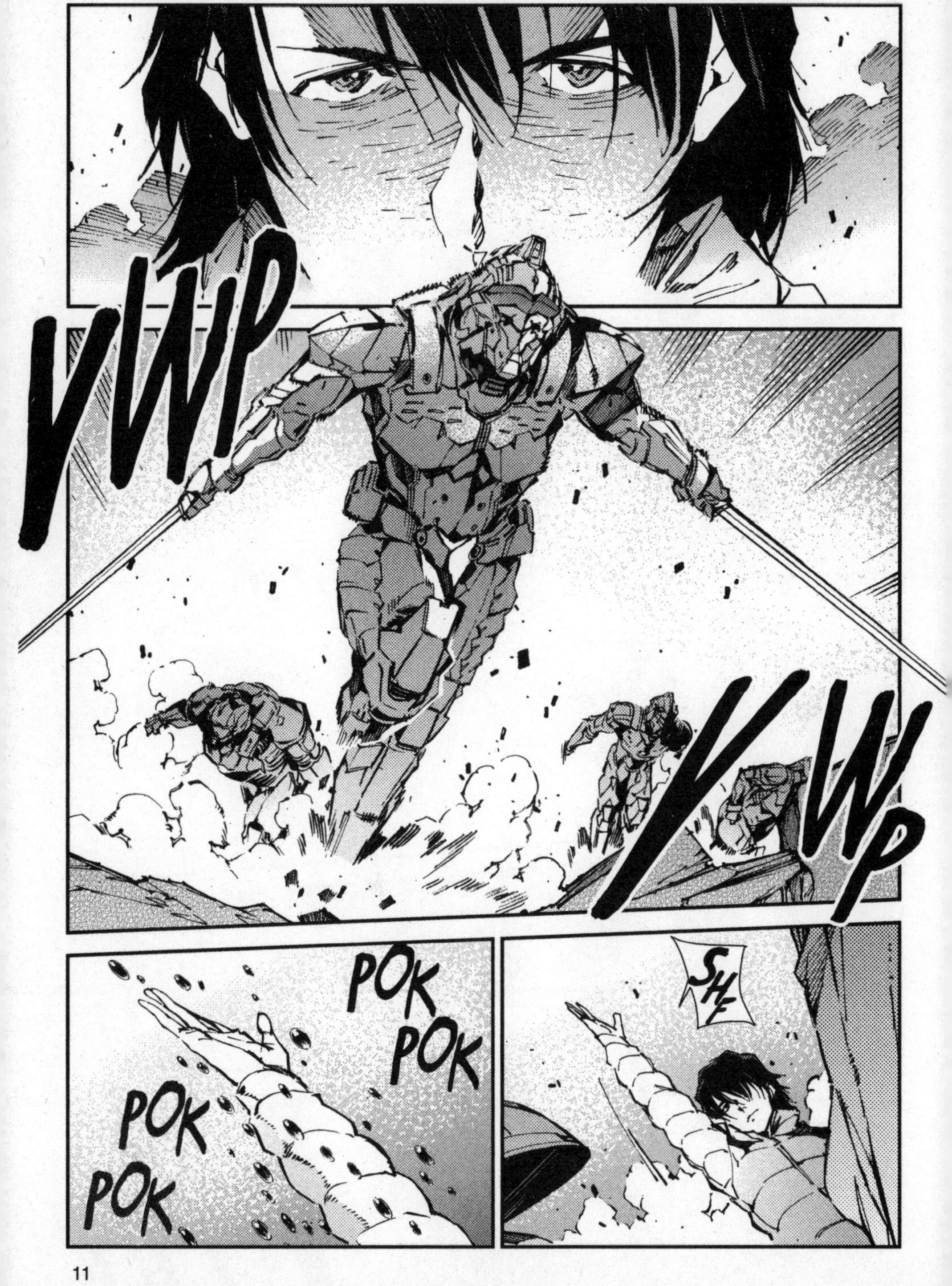
VWP
VWP
SHF
POK
POK
POK
POK

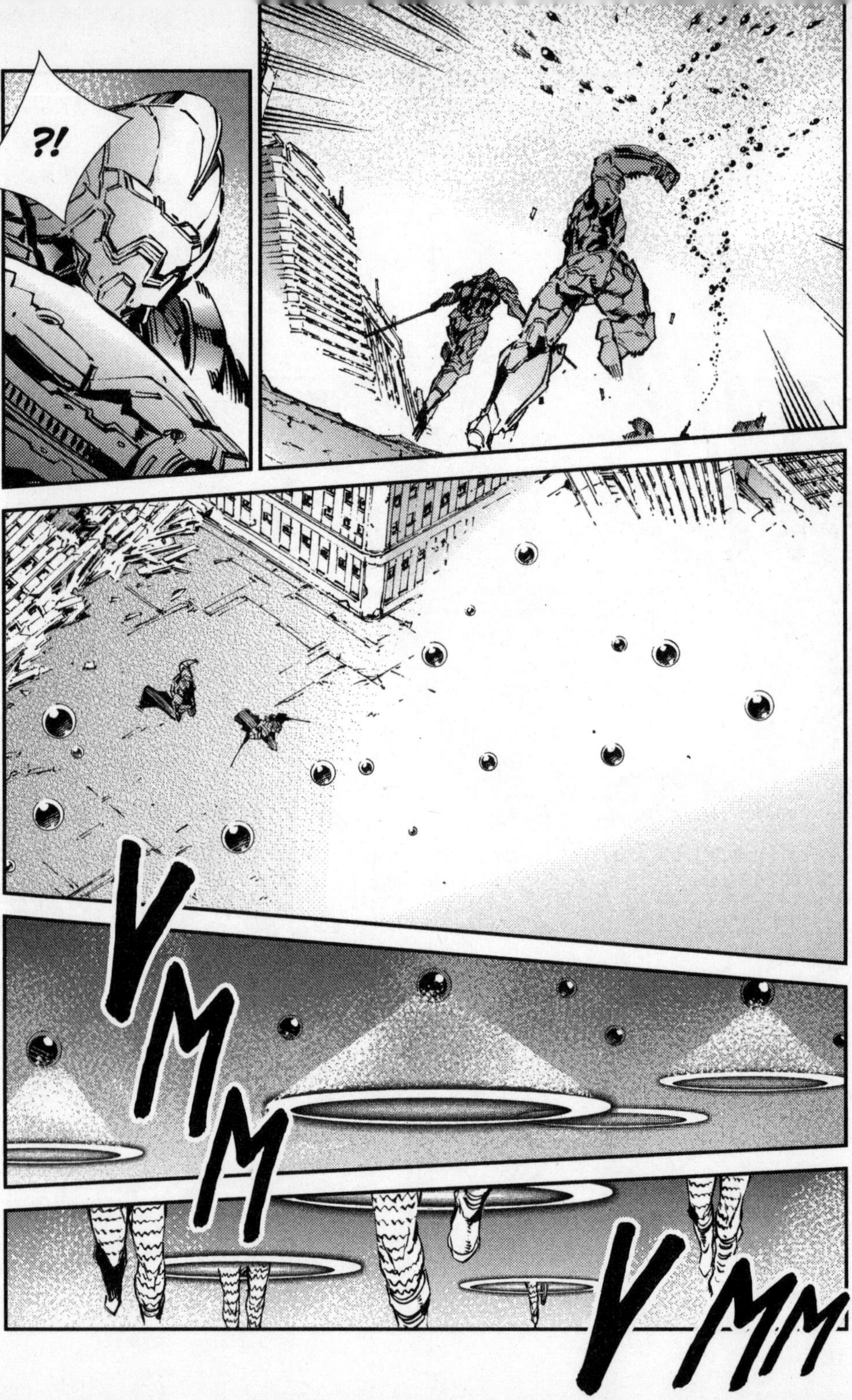
?!
VMM
VMM

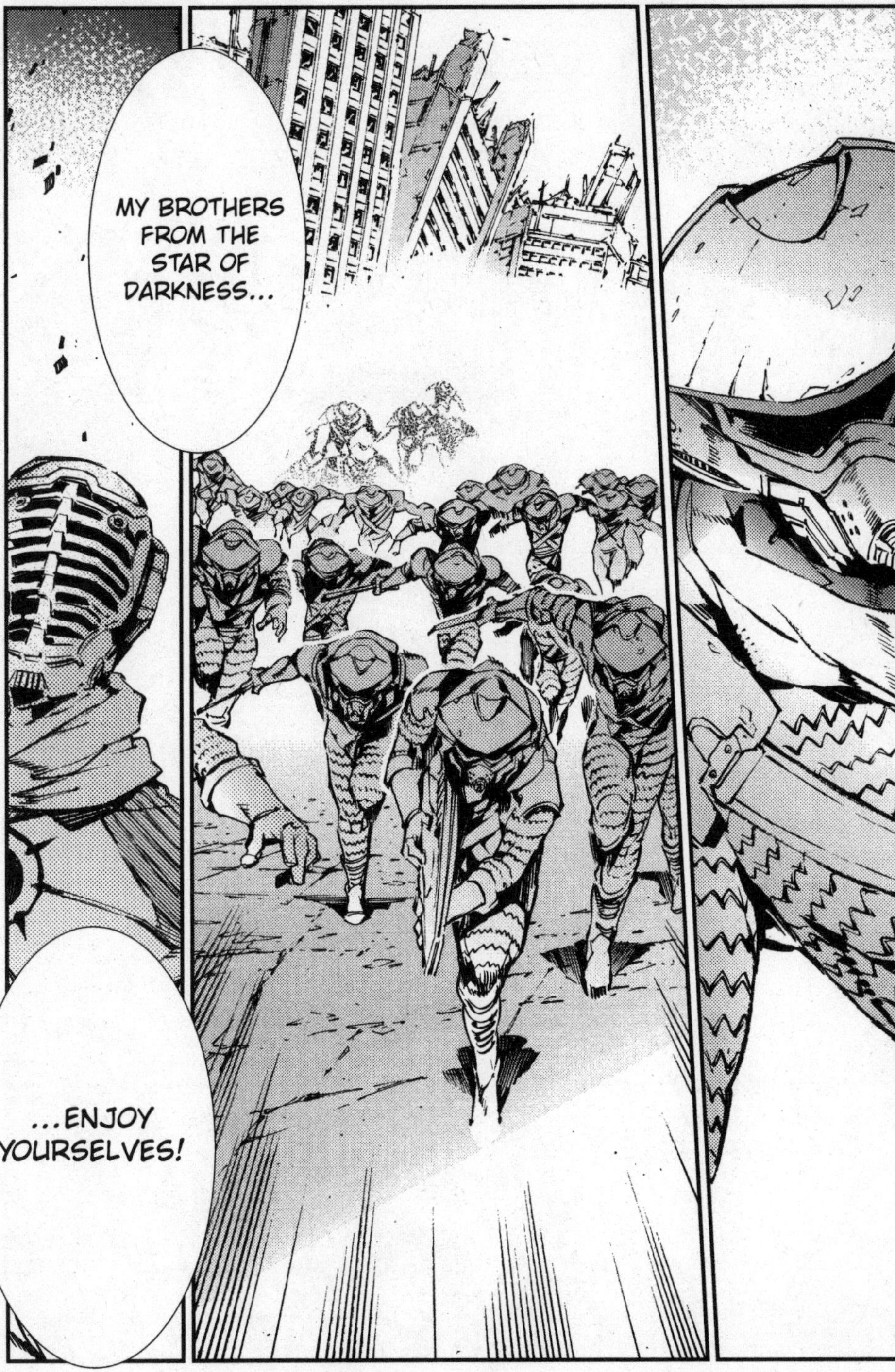
MY BROTHERS FROM THE STAR OF DARKNESS...
...ENJOY YOURSELVES!

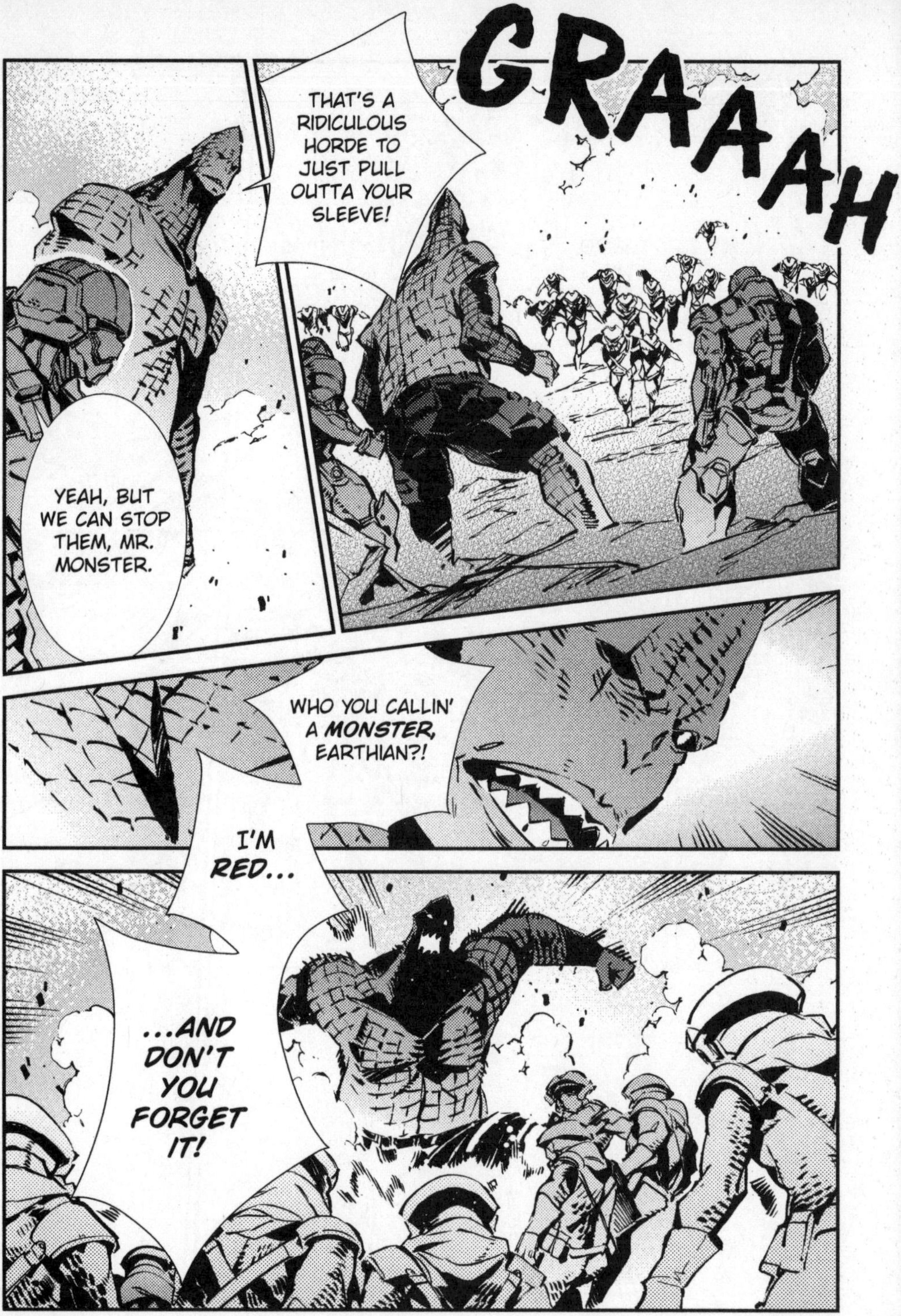
GRAAAH
THAT'S A RIDICULOUS HORDE TO JUST PULL OUTTA YOUR SLEEVE!
YEAH, BUT WE CAN STOP THEM, MR. MONSTER.
WHO YOU CALLIN' A ***MONSTER***, EARTHIAN?!
I'M ***RED...***
...AND DON'T YOU FORGET IT!

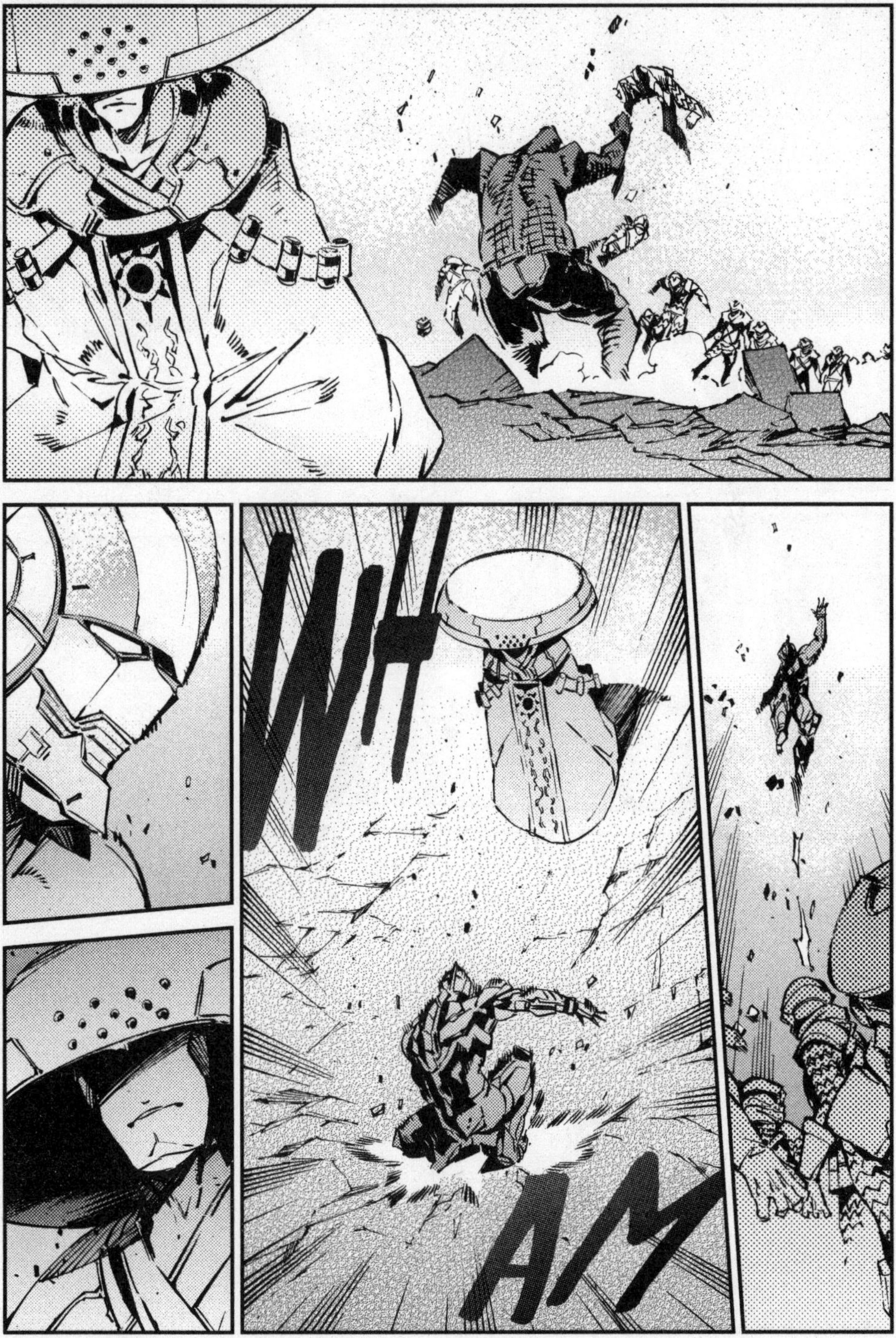
WHAM

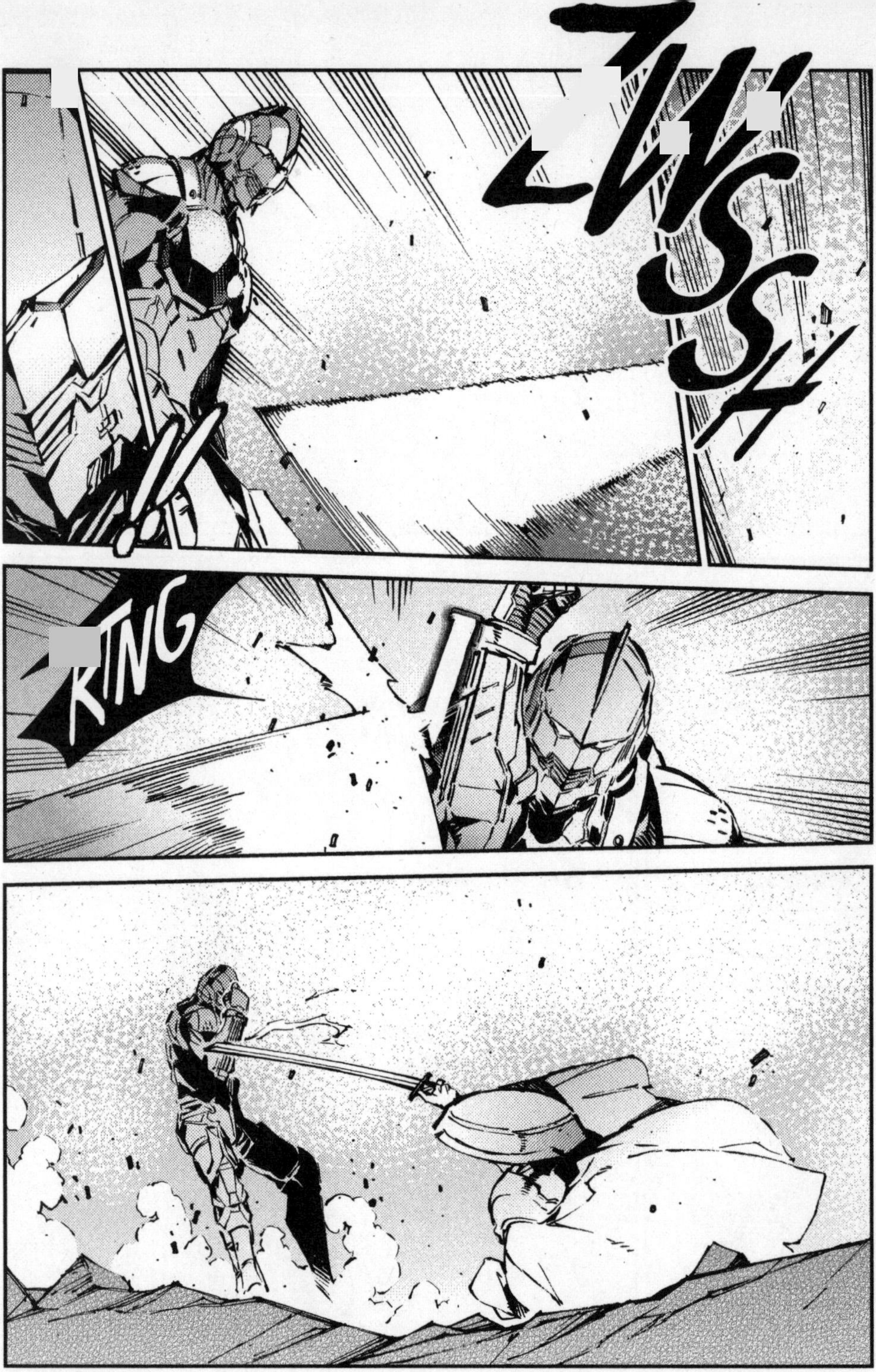
ZWSSH
KTING

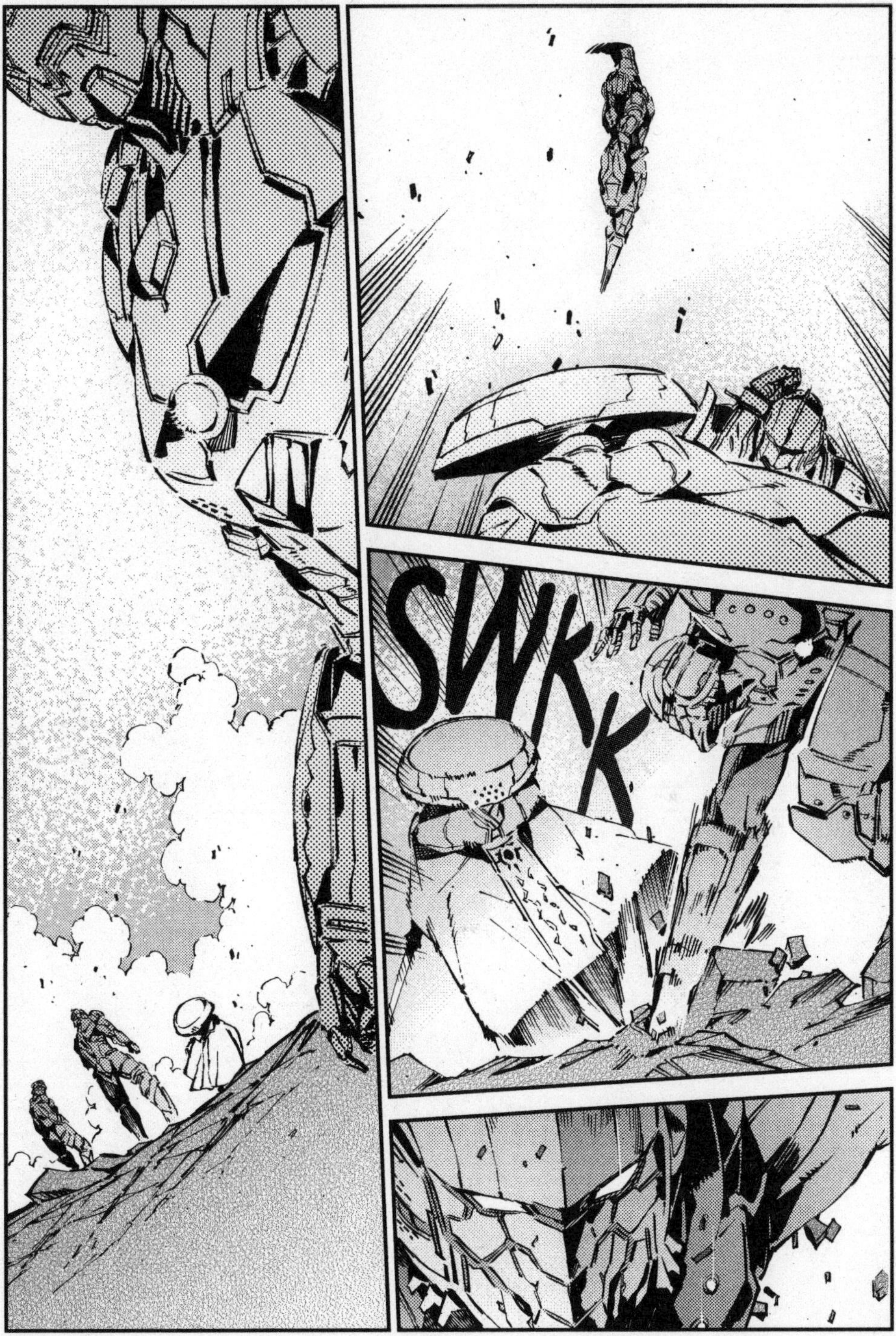
SWK
K

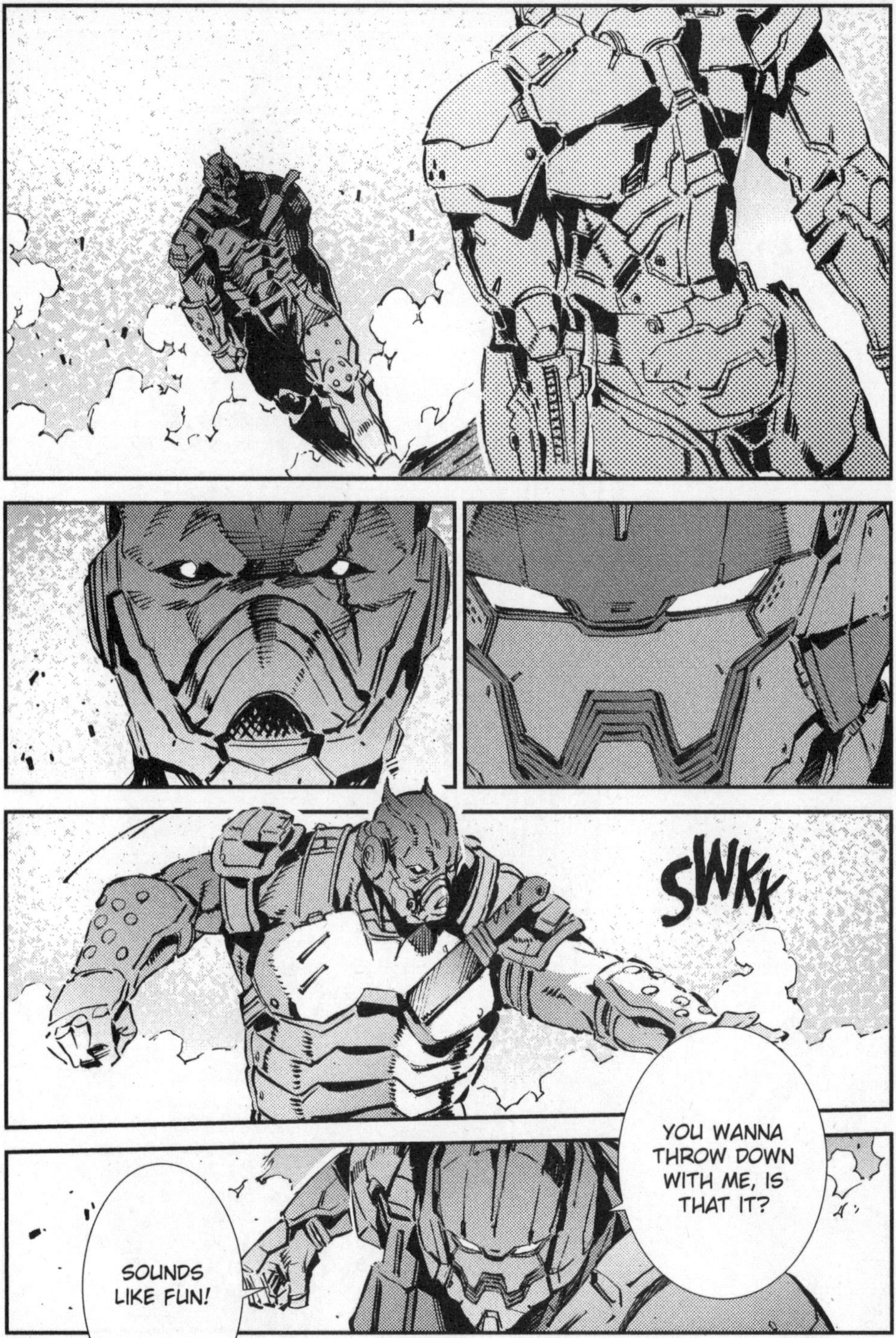
SWKK
YOU WANNA THROW DOWN WITH ME, IS THAT IT?
SOUNDS LIKE FUN!

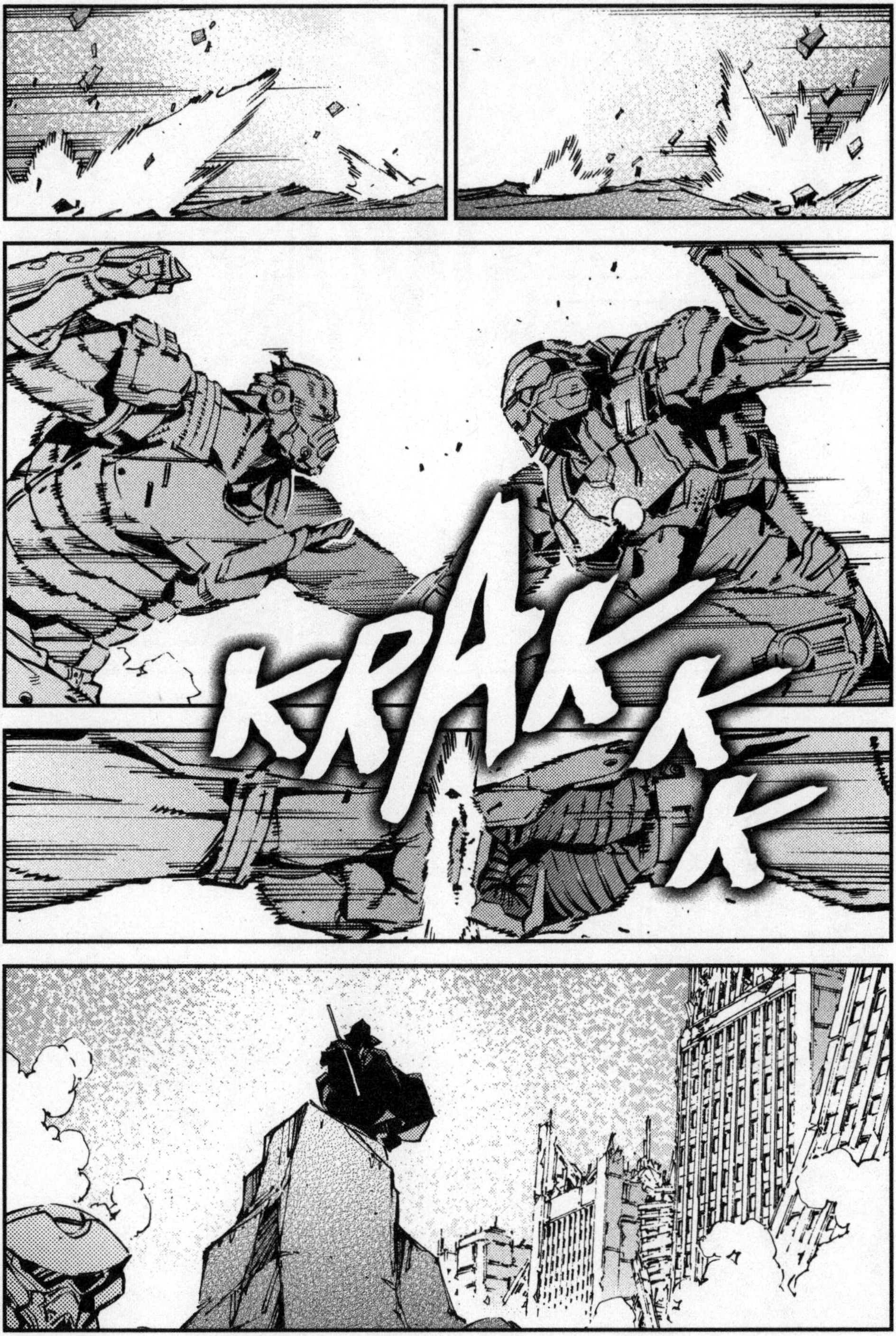
KRAK K K

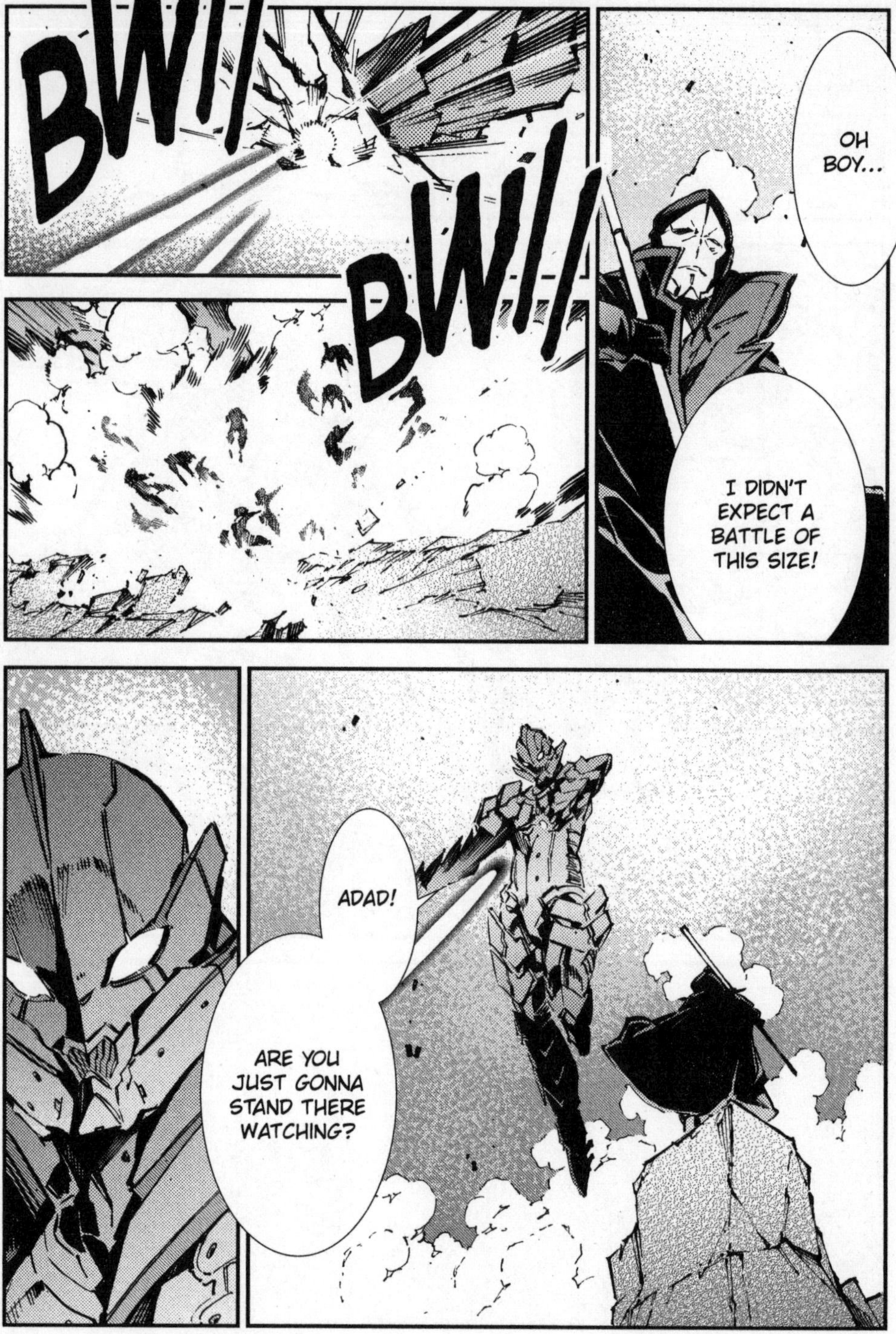
OH BOY...
I DIDN'T EXPECT A BATTLE OF THIS SIZE!
BWII
BWII
ADAD!
ARE YOU JUST GONNA STAND THERE WATCHING?

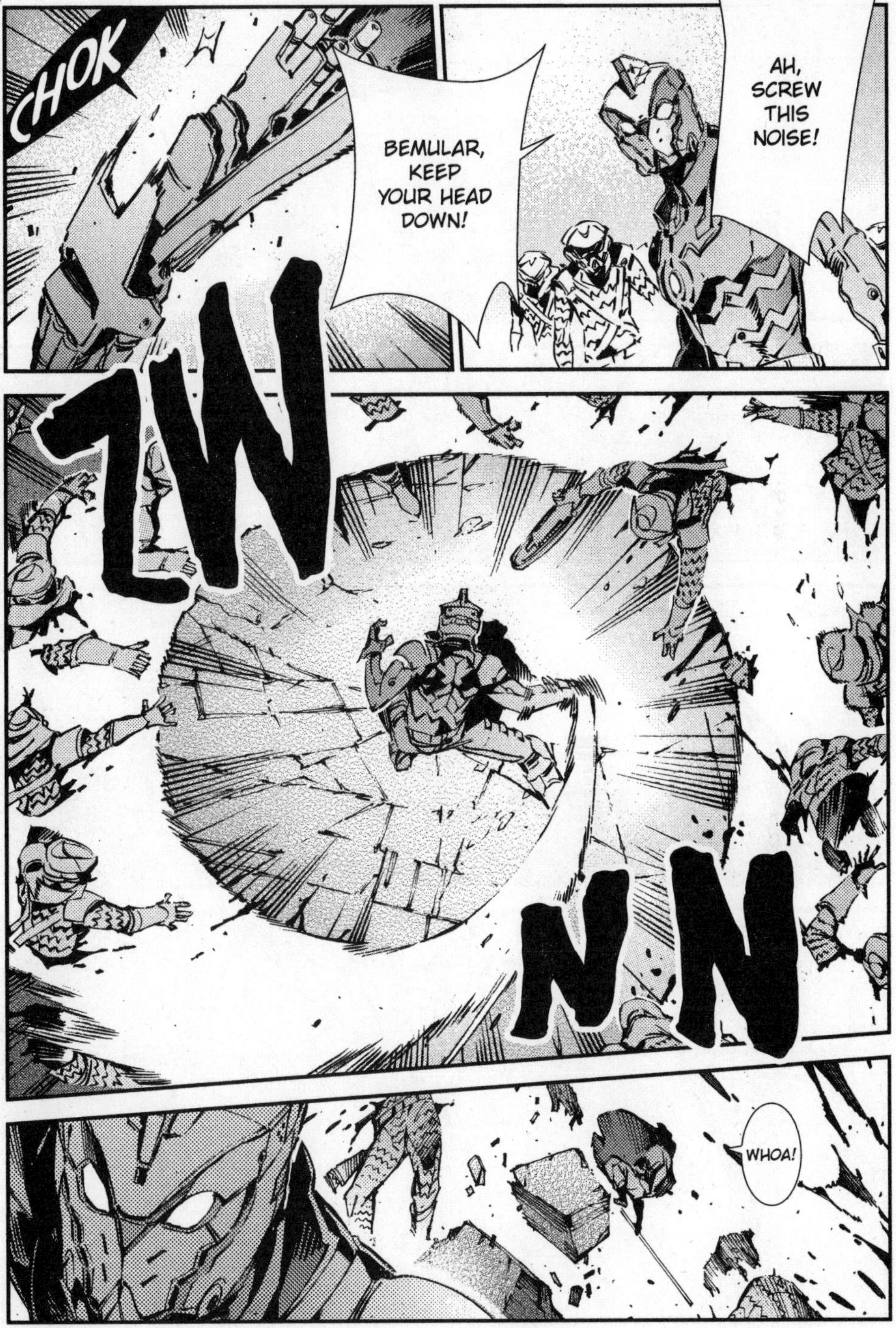
AH, SCREW THIS NOISE!
BEMULAR, KEEP YOUR HEAD DOWN!
CHOK
ZW
NN
WHOA!

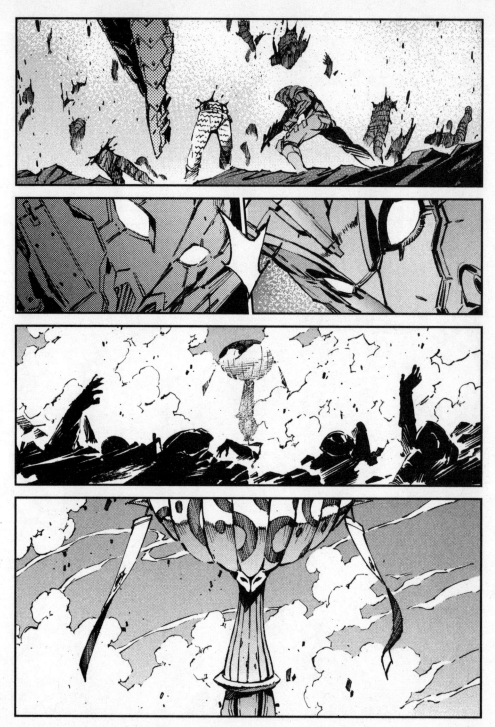

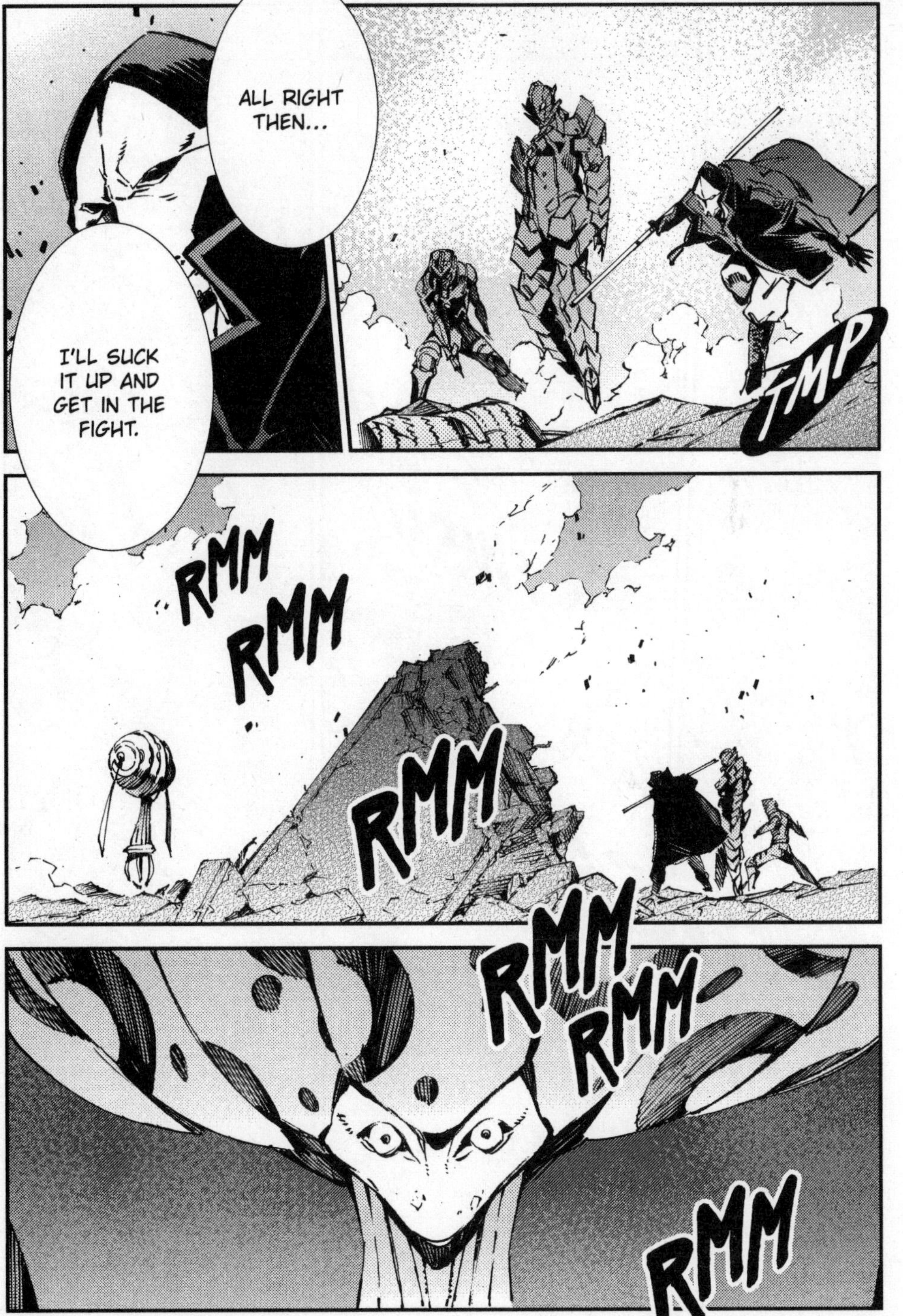
TMP
ALL RIGHT THEN...
I'LL SUCK IT UP AND GET IN THE FIGHT.
RMM
RMM
RMM
RMM
RMM
RMM
RMM

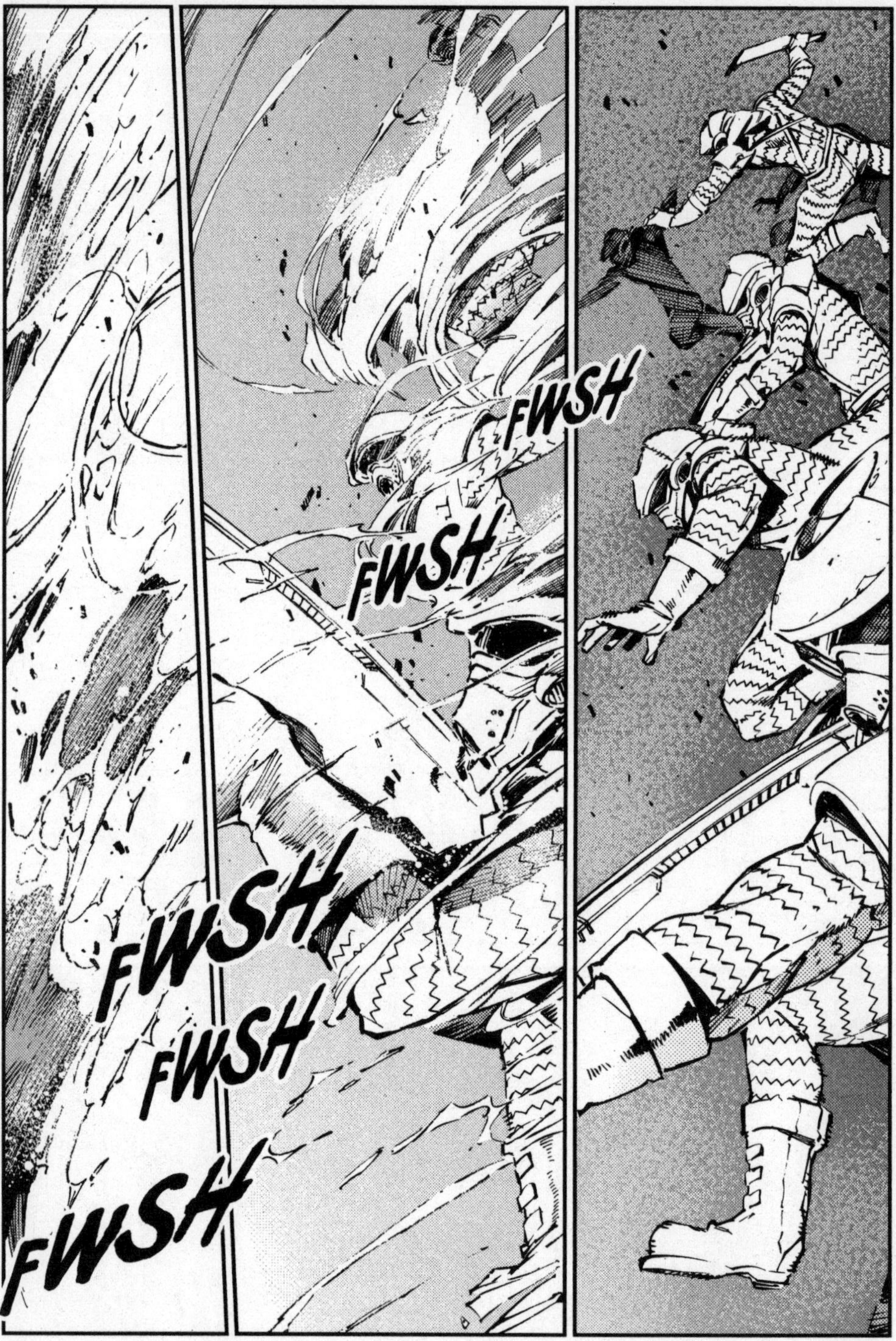
FWSH
FWSH
FWSH
FWSH
FWSH
FWSH

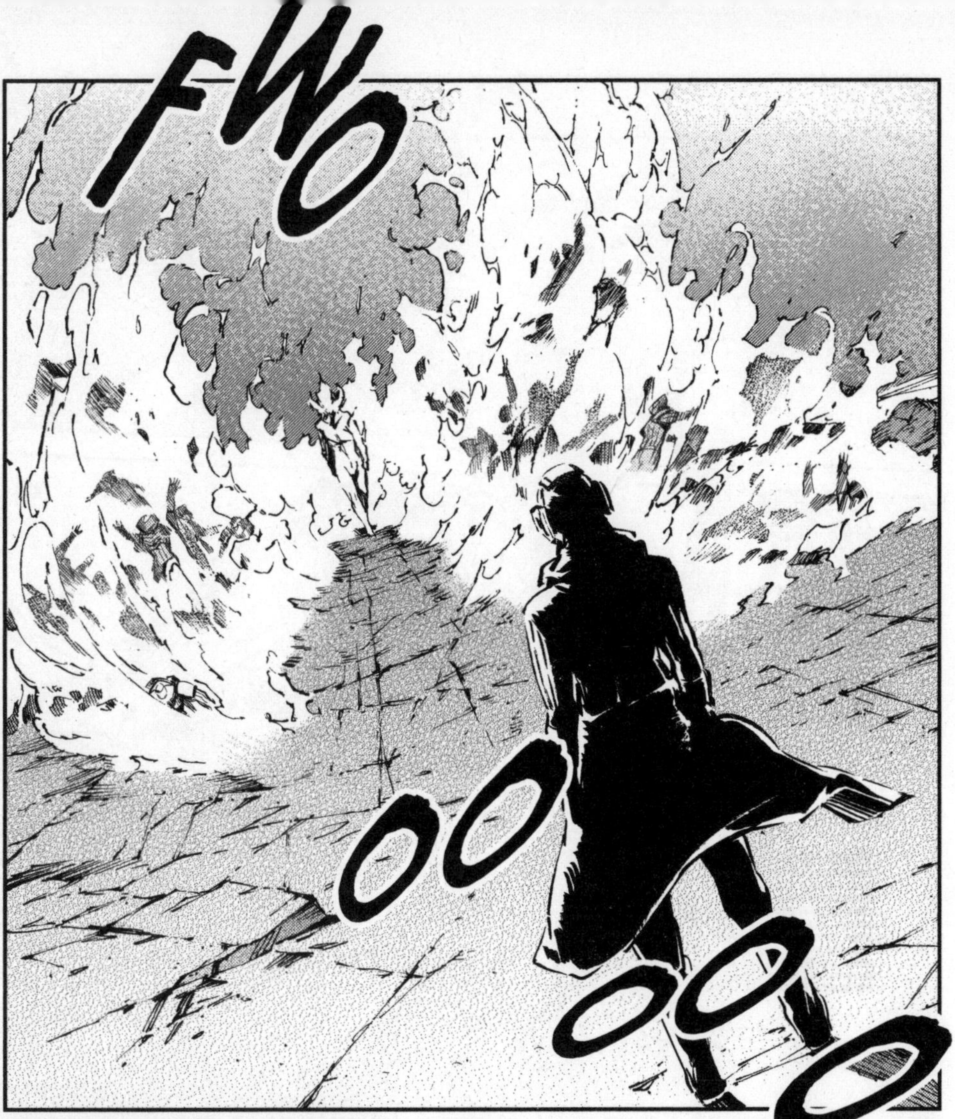
FWOOOOOOO
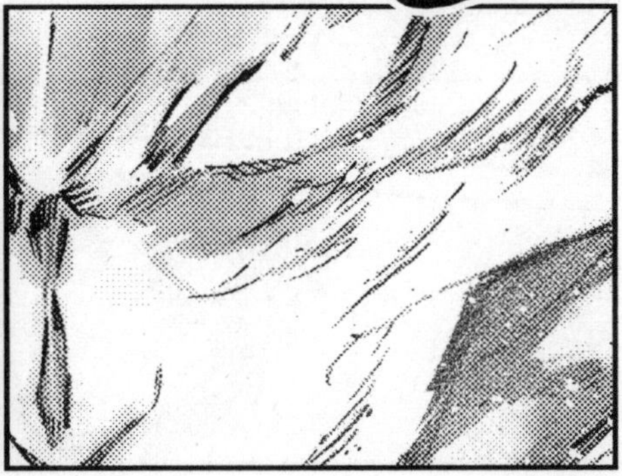
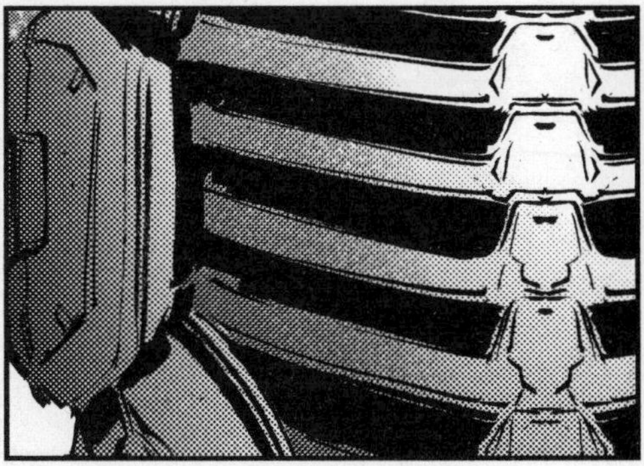

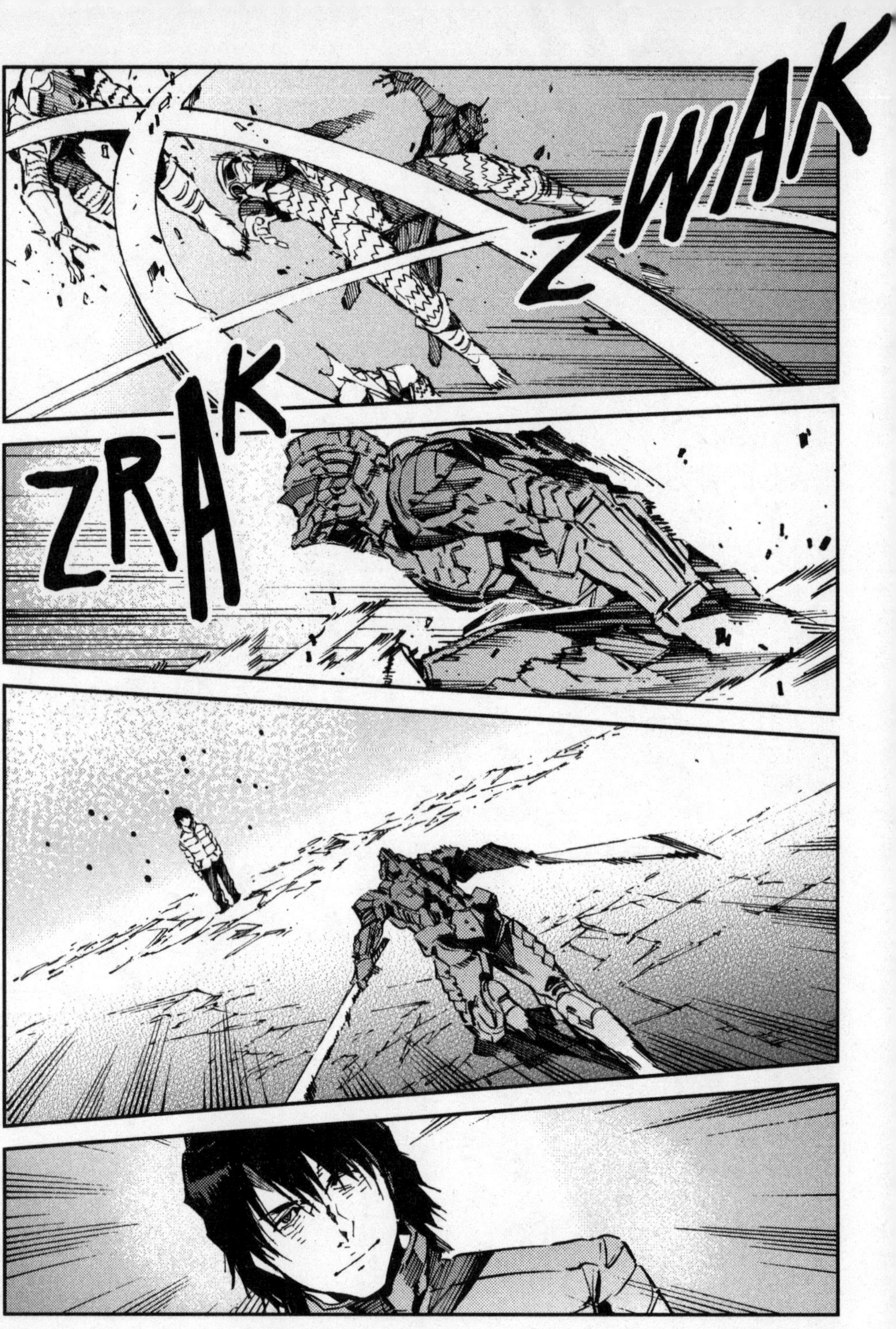
ZWAK
ZRAK

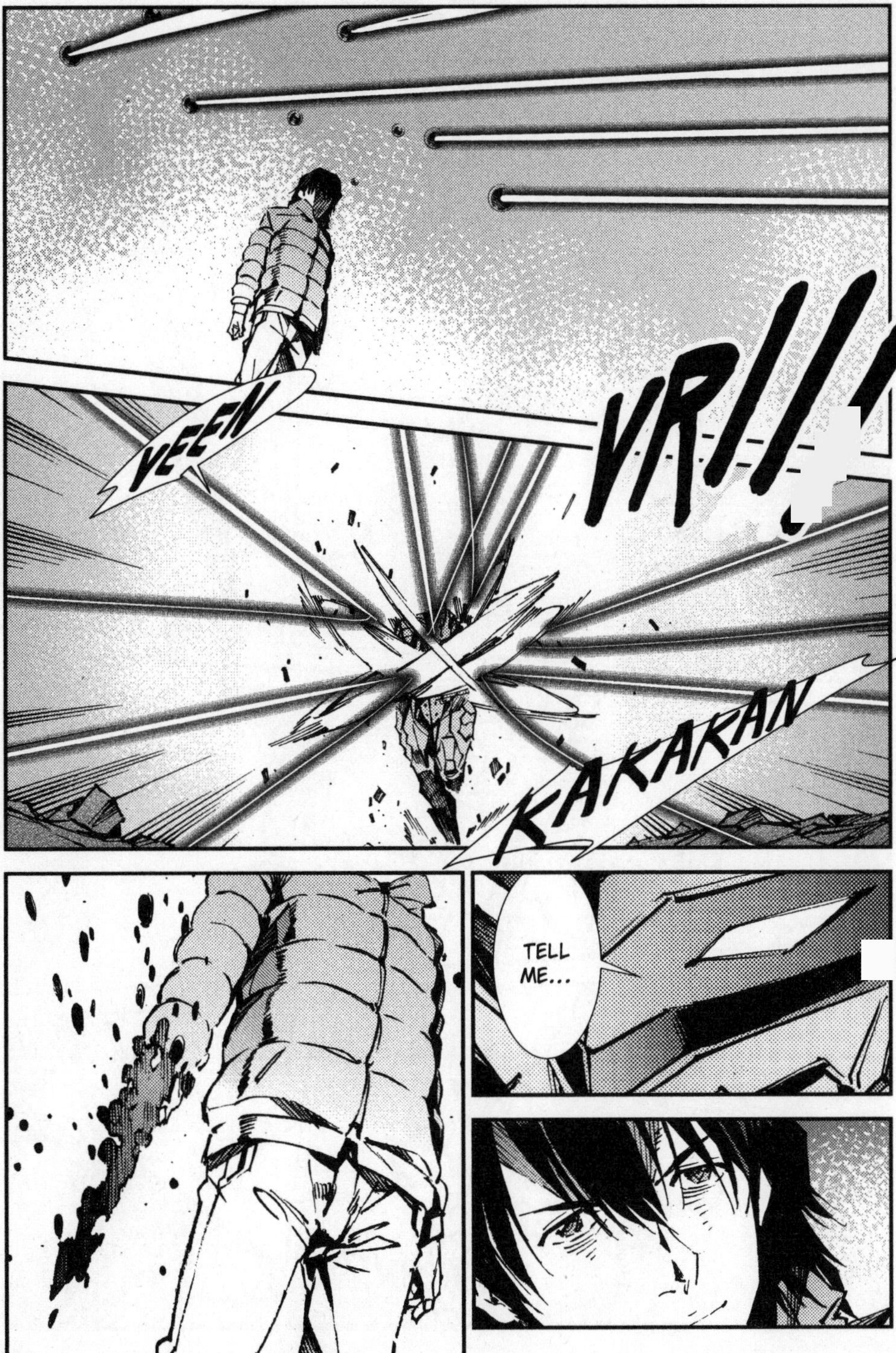
VRIII
VEEN
KAKAKAN
TELL ME...

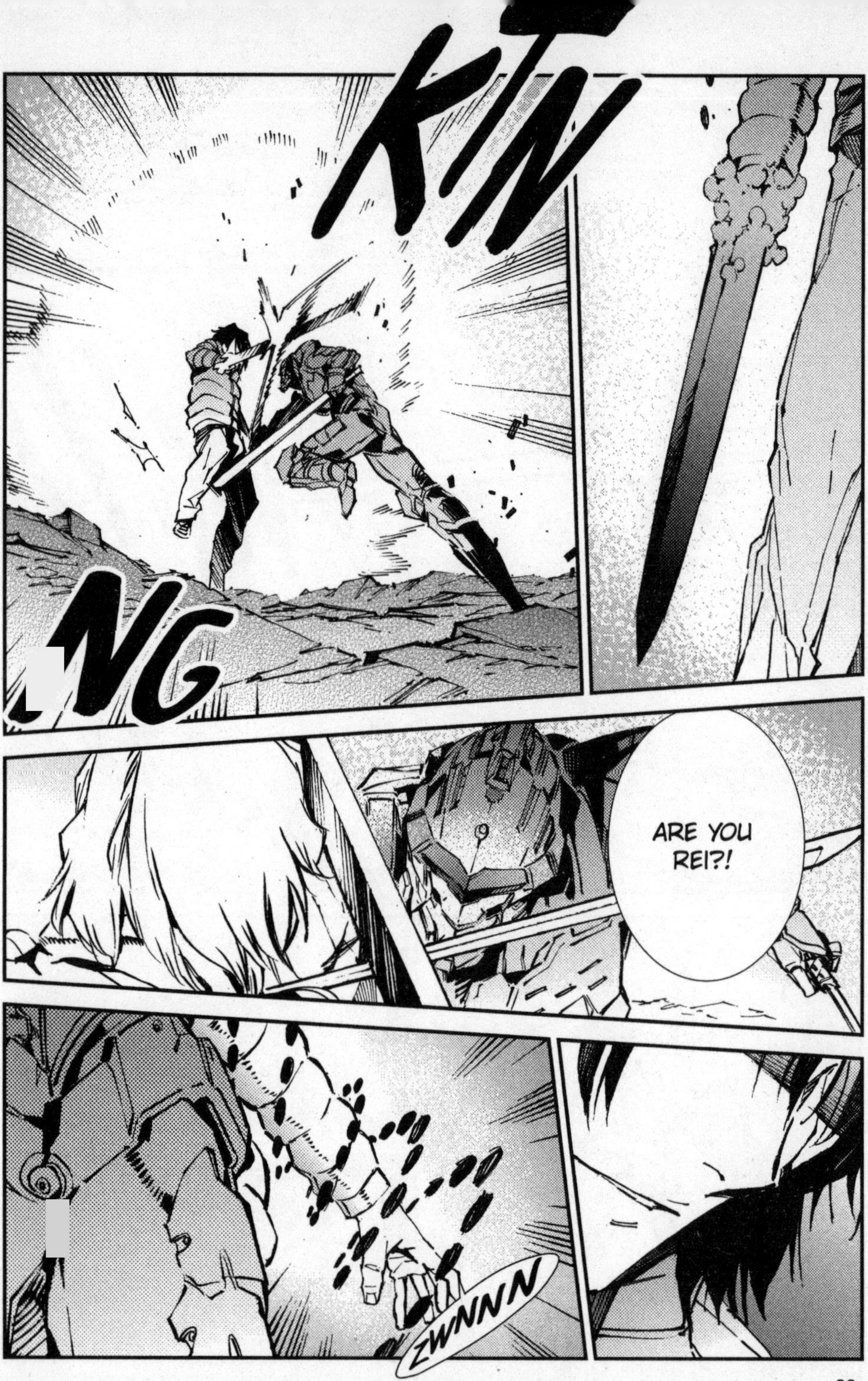
KIN
NG
ARE YOU REI?!
ZWNNN

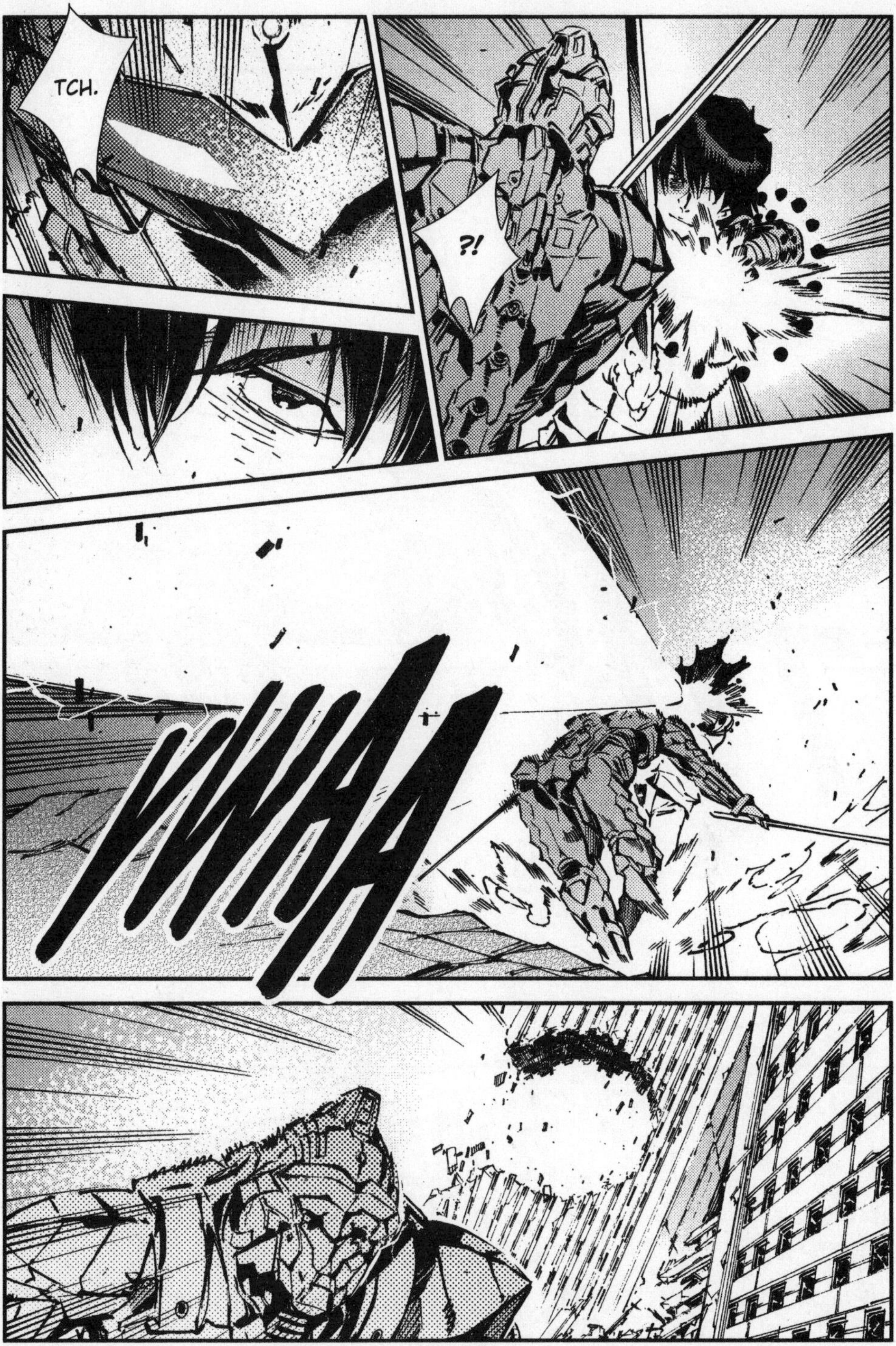
?!
TCH.
WHAM

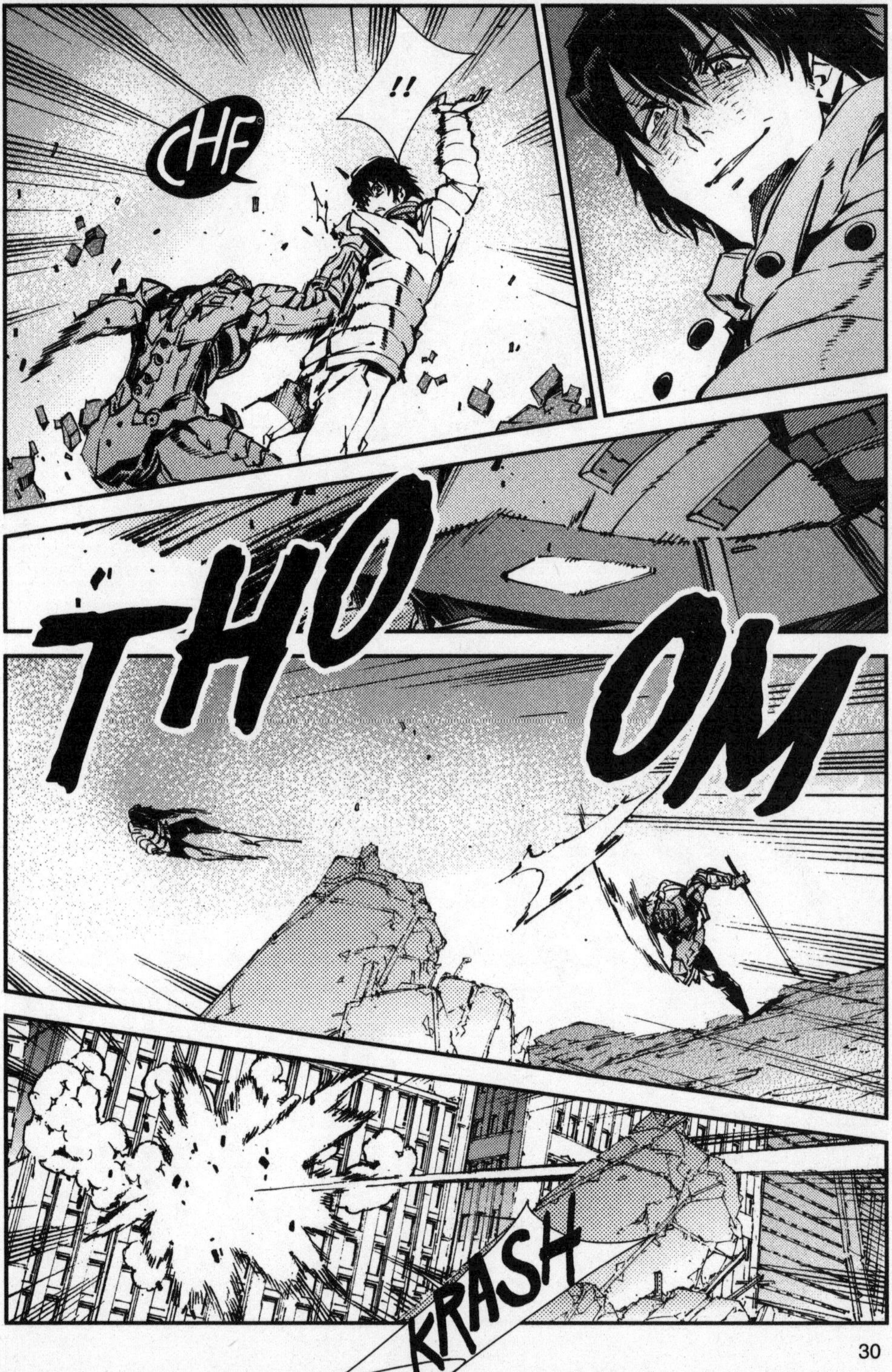
!!
CHF
THOOM
KRASH

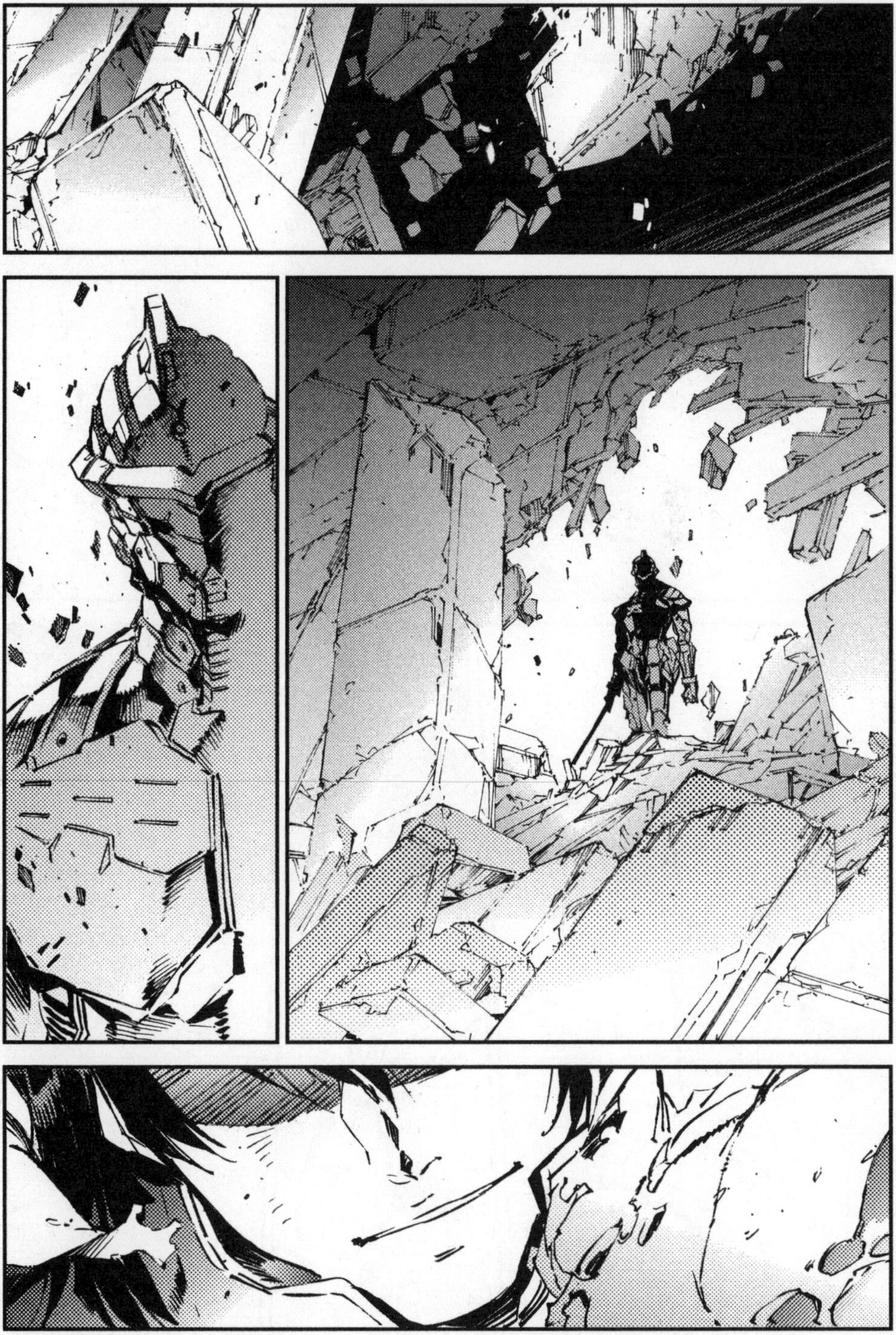

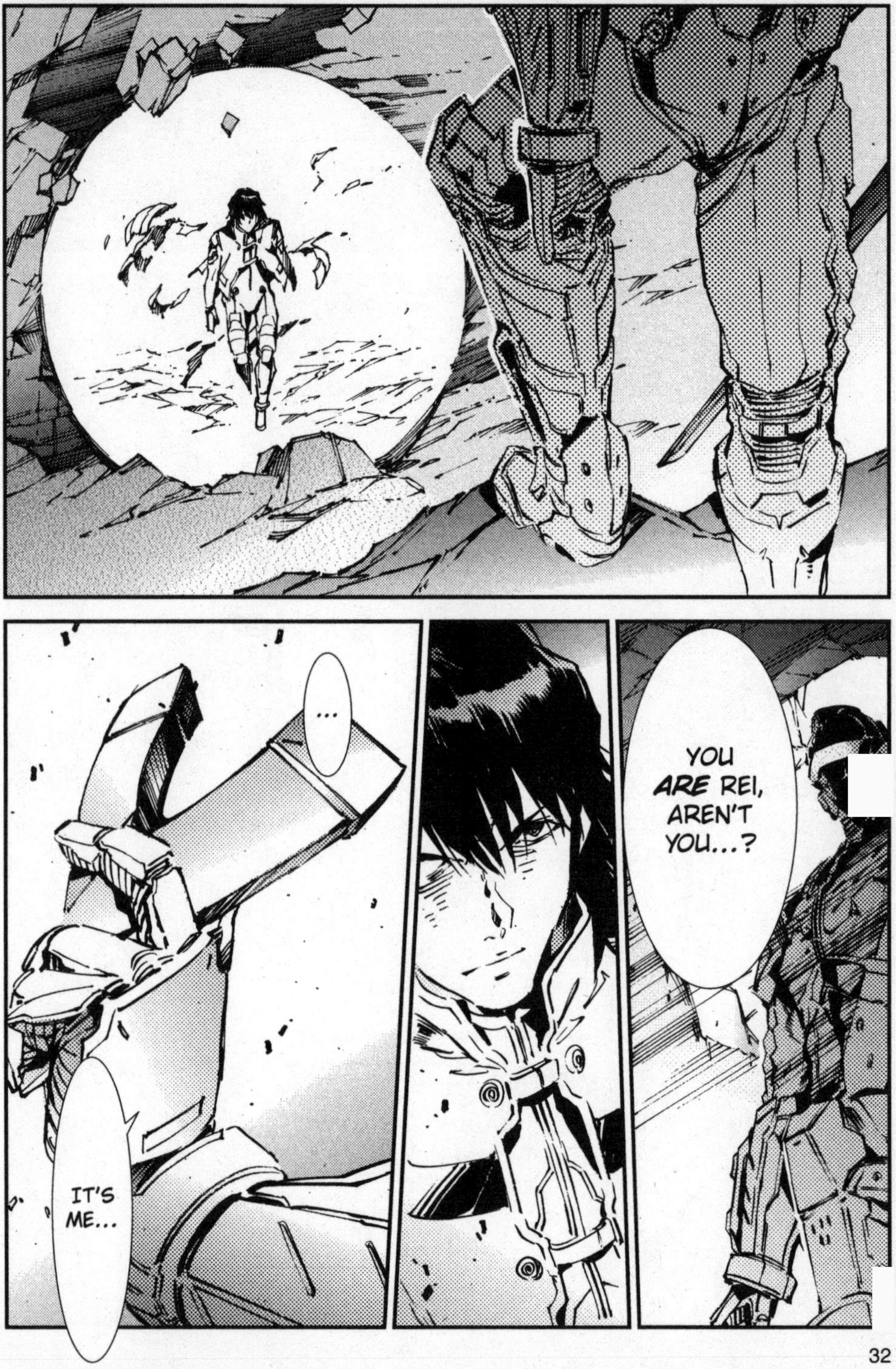
YOU ARE REI, AREN'T YOU...?
...
IT'S ME...

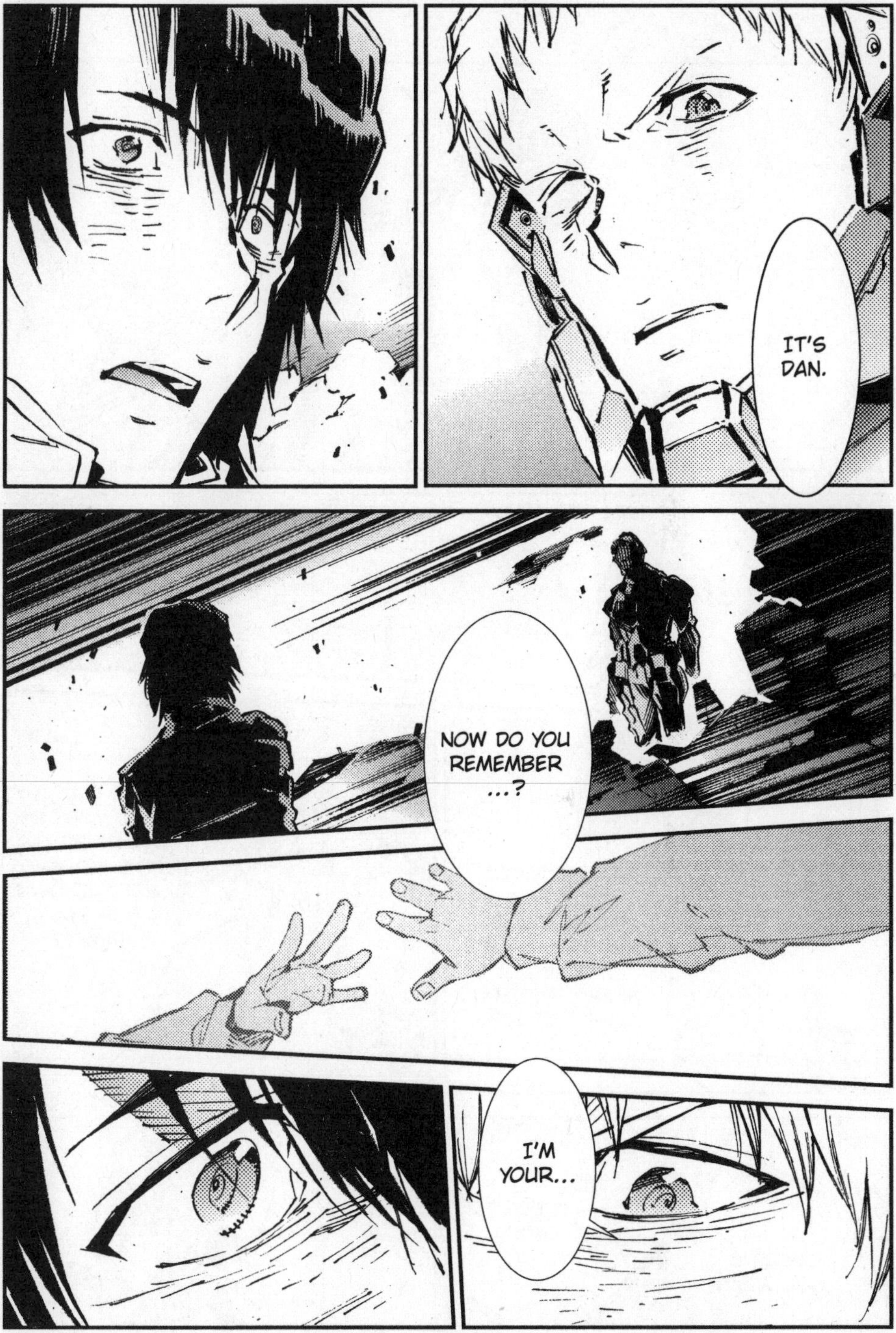
IT'S DAN.
NOW DO YOU REMEMBER ...?
I'M YOUR...

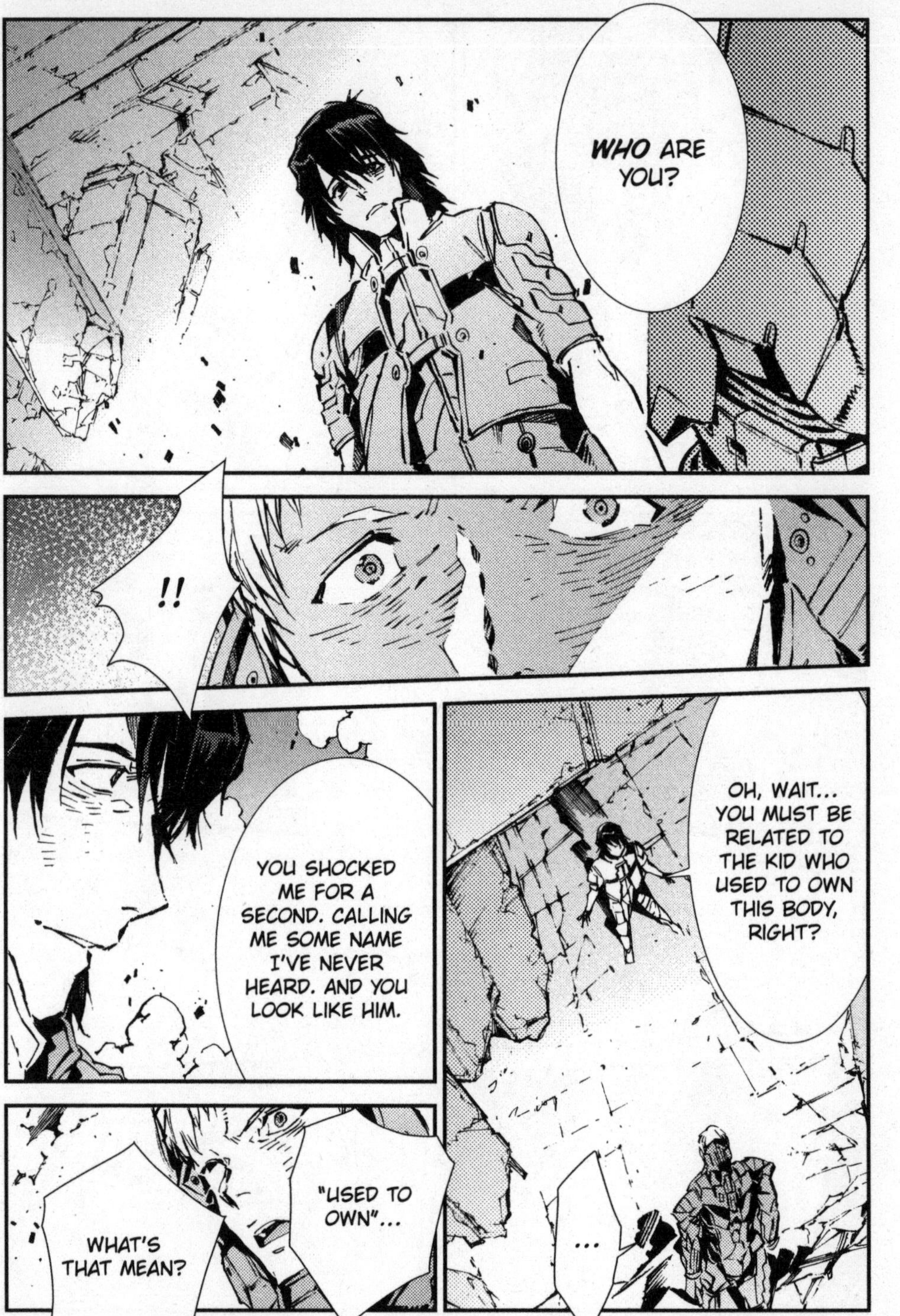
WHO ARE YOU?
!!
YOU SHOCKED ME FOR A SECOND. CALLING ME SOME NAME I'VE NEVER HEARD. AND YOU LOOK LIKE HIM.
OH, WAIT... YOU MUST BE RELATED TO THE KID WHO USED TO OWN THIS BODY, RIGHT?
"USED TO OWN"...
WHAT'S THAT MEAN?
...

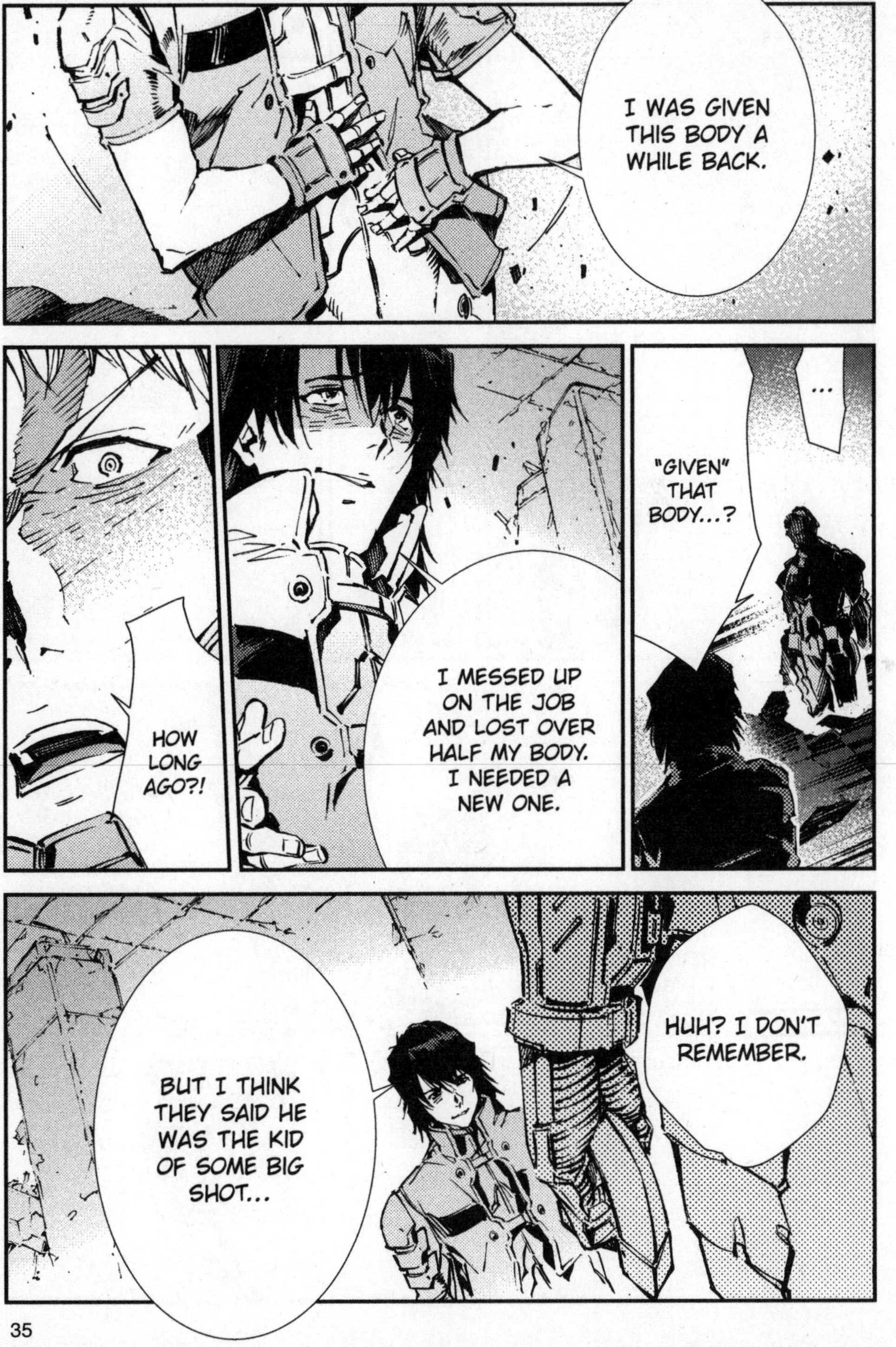
I WAS GIVEN THIS BODY A WHILE BACK.
...
"GIVEN" THAT BODY...?
I MESSED UP ON THE JOB AND LOST OVER HALF MY BODY. I NEEDED A NEW ONE.
HOW LONG AGO?!
HUH? I DON'T REMEMBER.
BUT I THINK THEY SAID HE WAS THE KID OF SOME BIG SHOT...

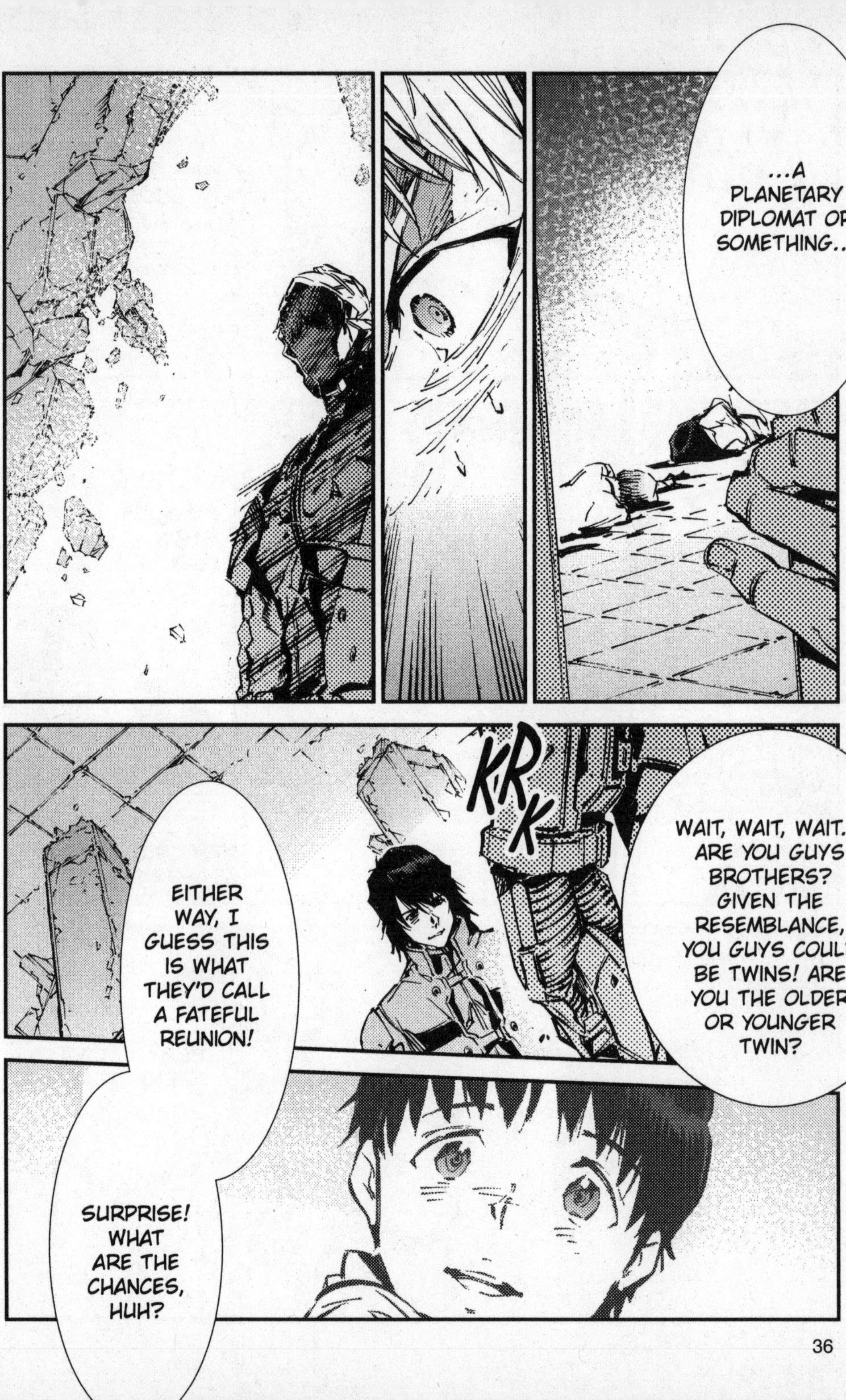
...A PLANETARY DIPLOMAT OR SOMETHING...
KRK
WAIT, WAIT, WAIT... ARE YOU GUYS BROTHERS? GIVEN THE RESEMBLANCE, YOU GUYS COULD BE TWINS! ARE YOU THE OLDER OR YOUNGER TWIN?
EITHER WAY, I GUESS THIS IS WHAT THEY'D CALL A FATEFUL REUNION!
SURPRISE! WHAT ARE THE CHANCES, HUH?

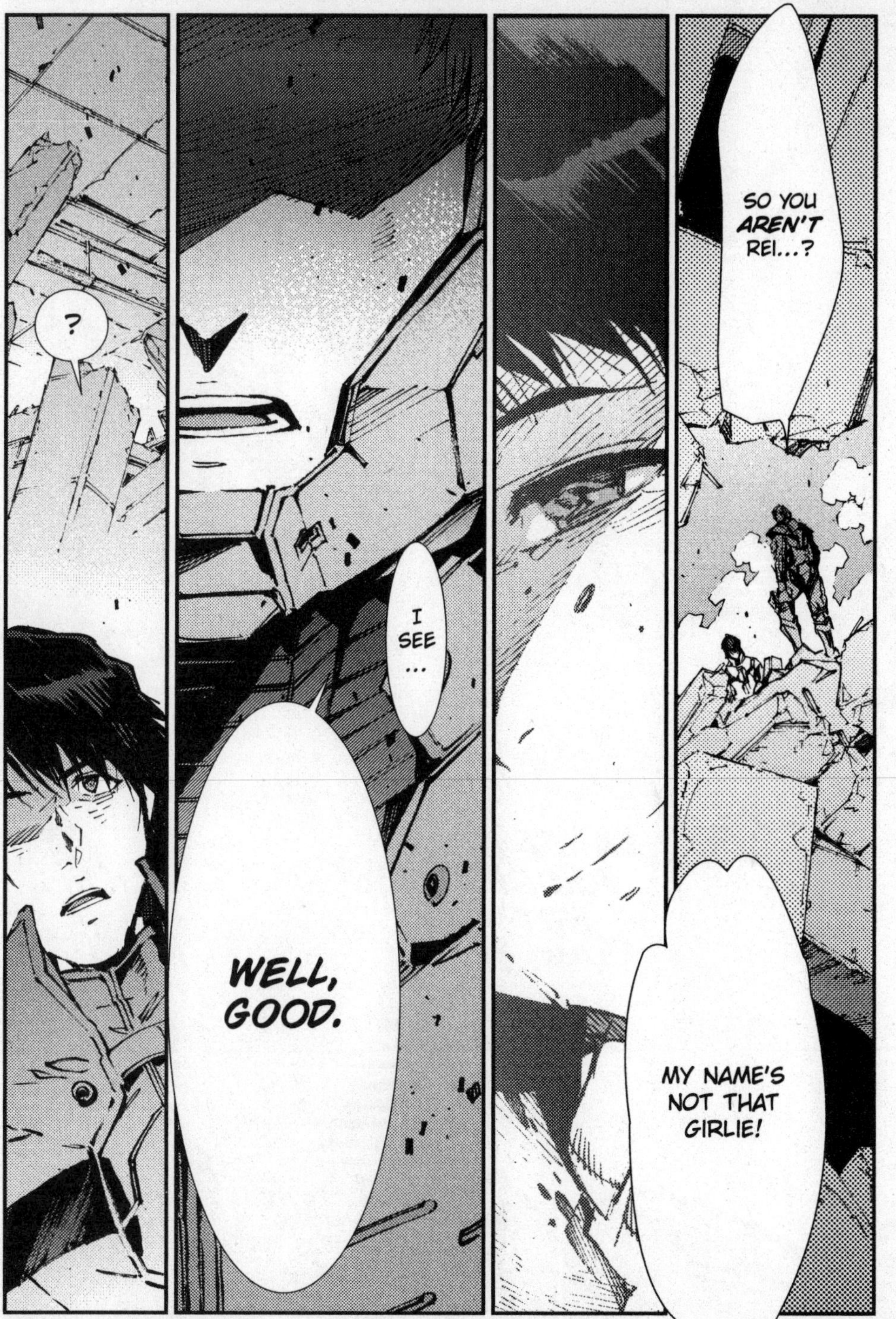
SO YOU AREN'T REI...?
MY NAME'S NOT THAT GIRLIE!
I SEE...
WELL, GOOD.
?

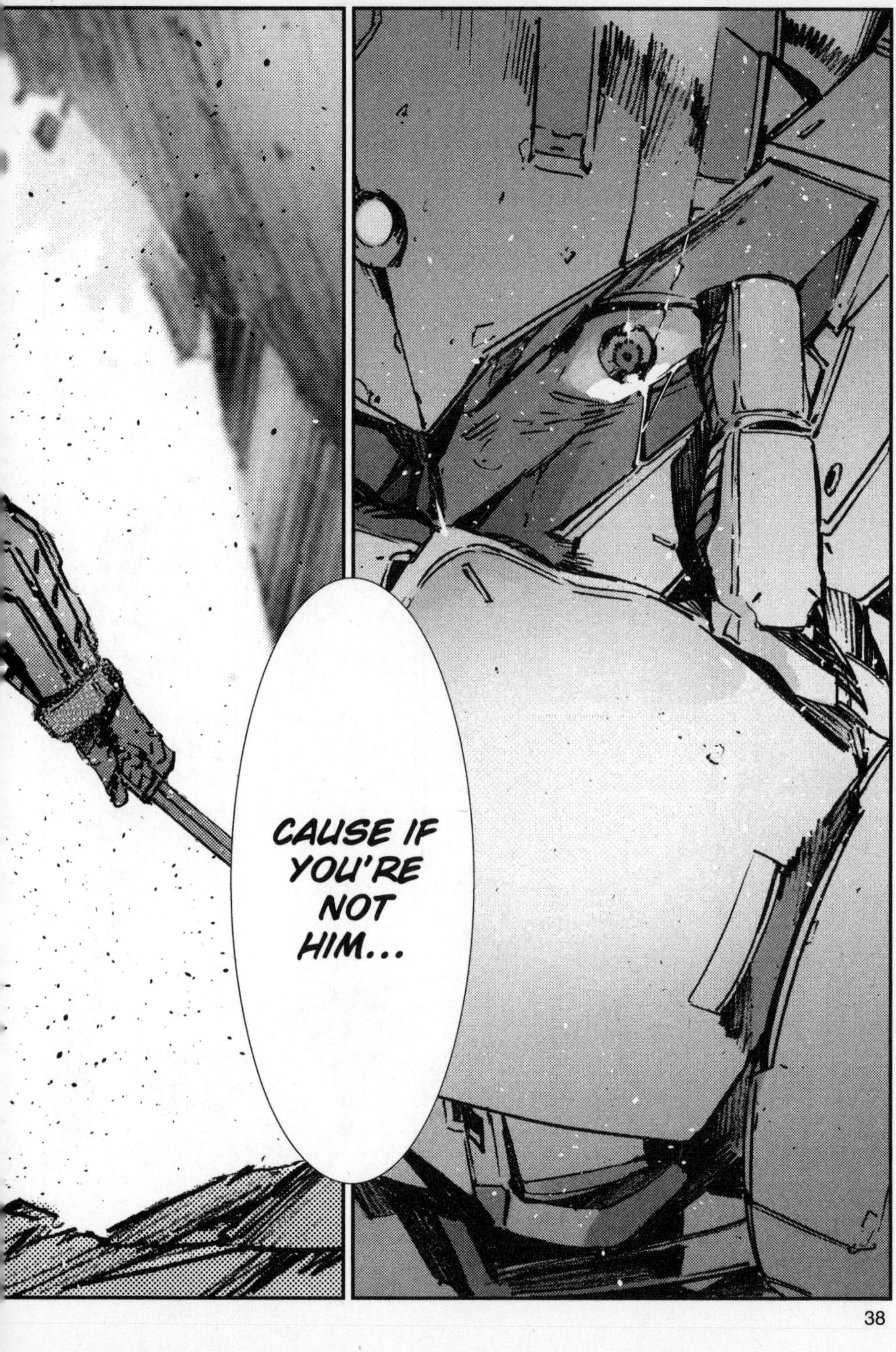
CAUSE IF YOU'RE NOT HIM...

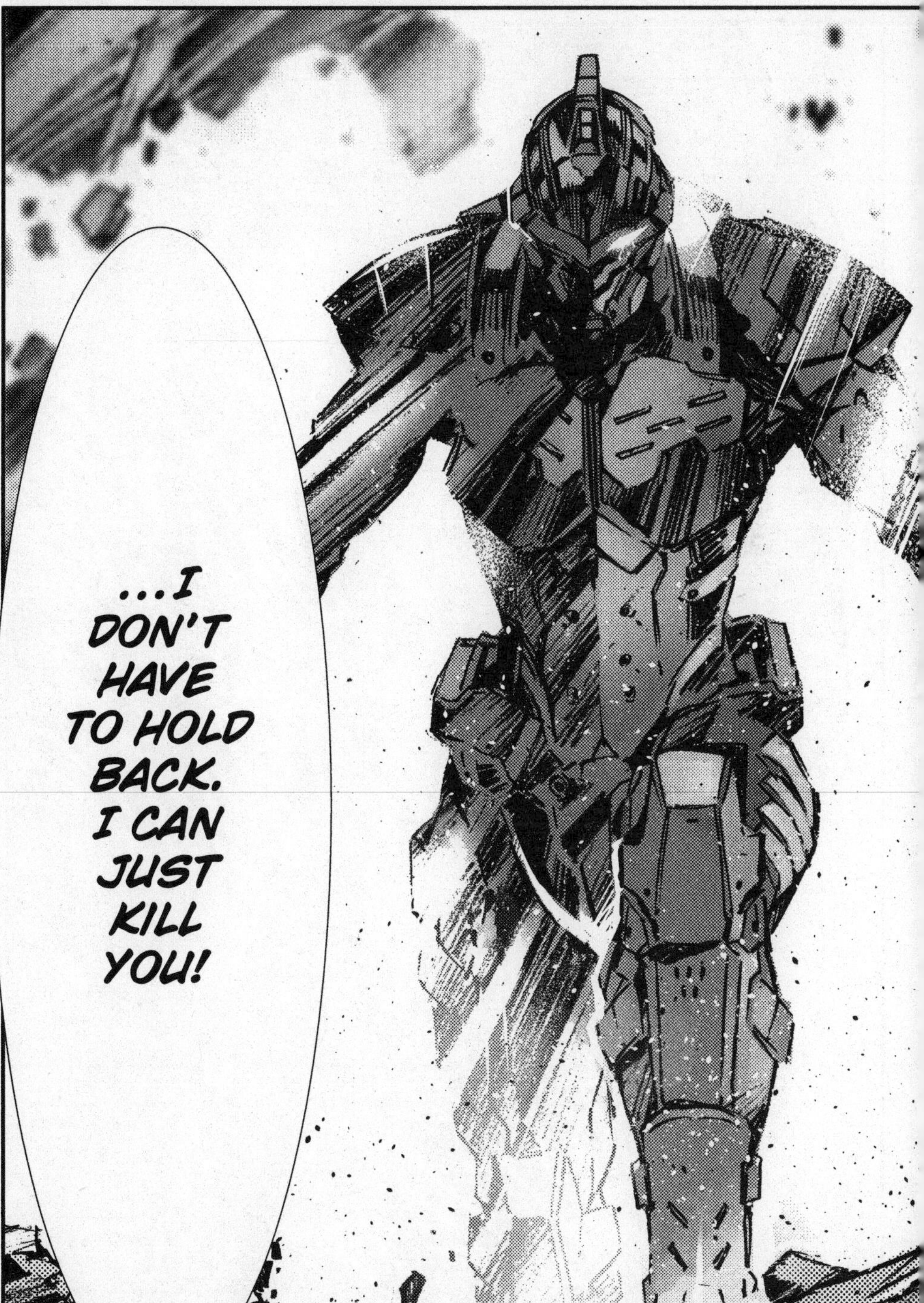
...I DON'T HAVE TO HOLD BACK. I CAN JUST KILL YOU!

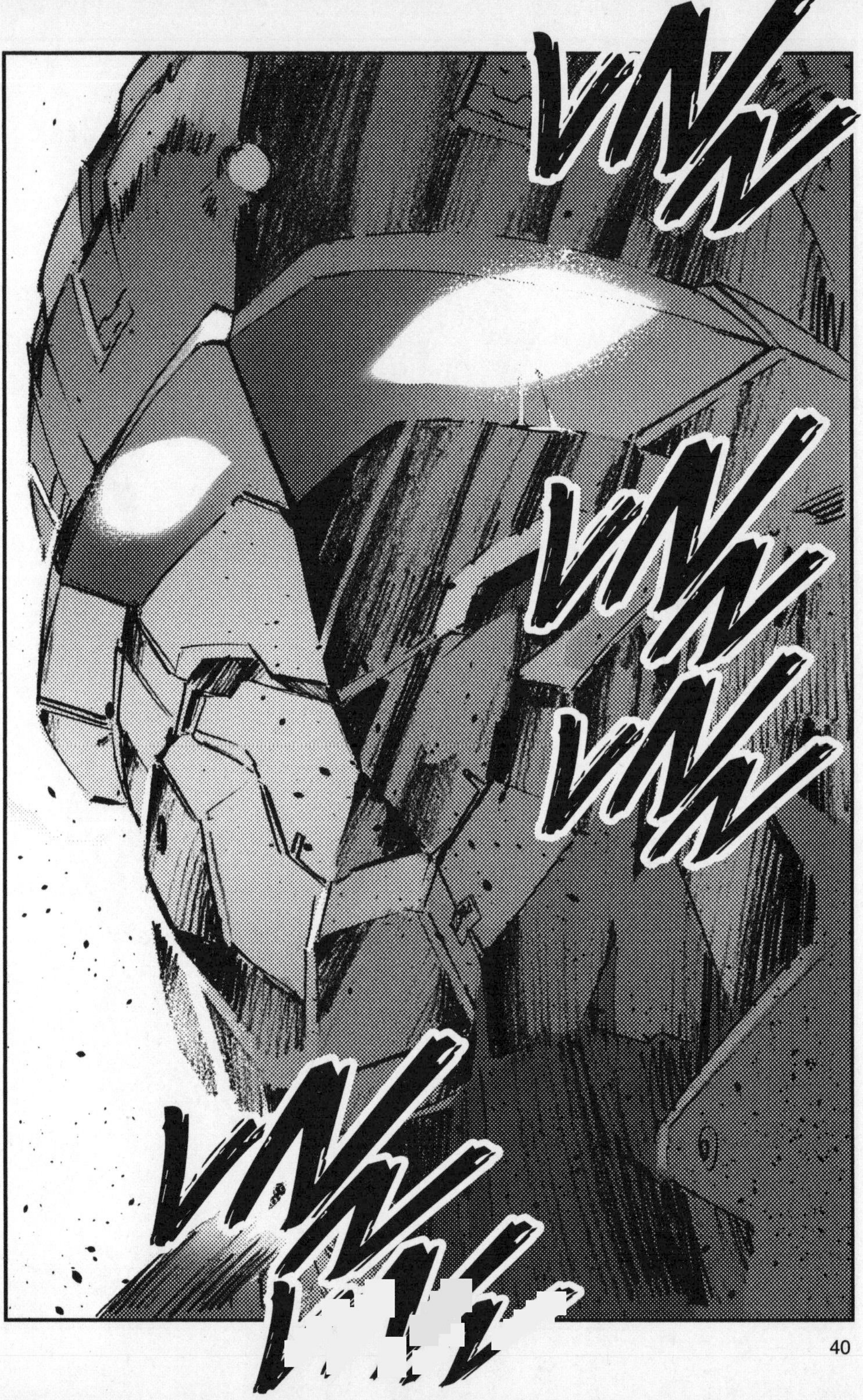

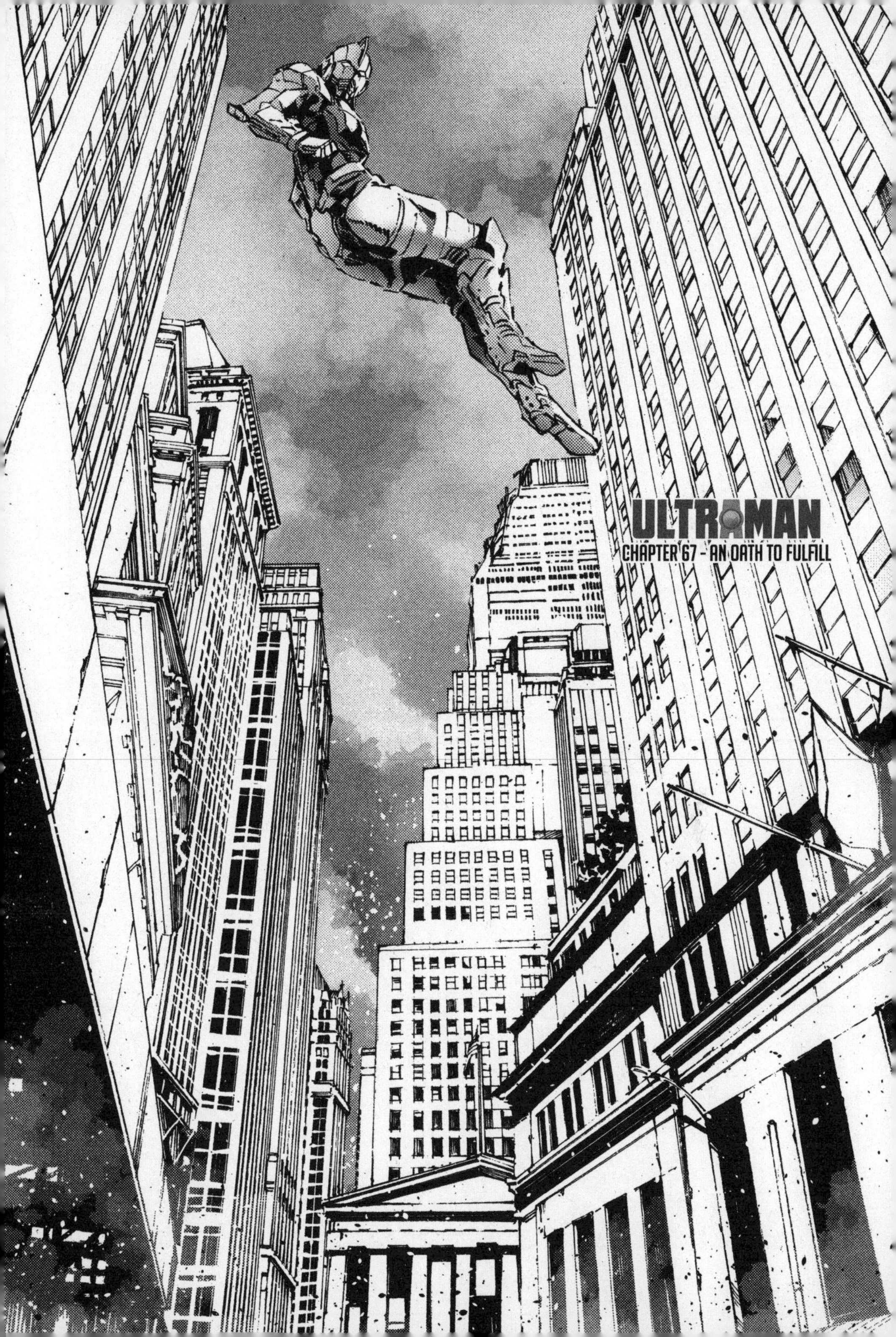
ULTRAMAN
CHAPTER 67 - AN OATH TO FULFILL

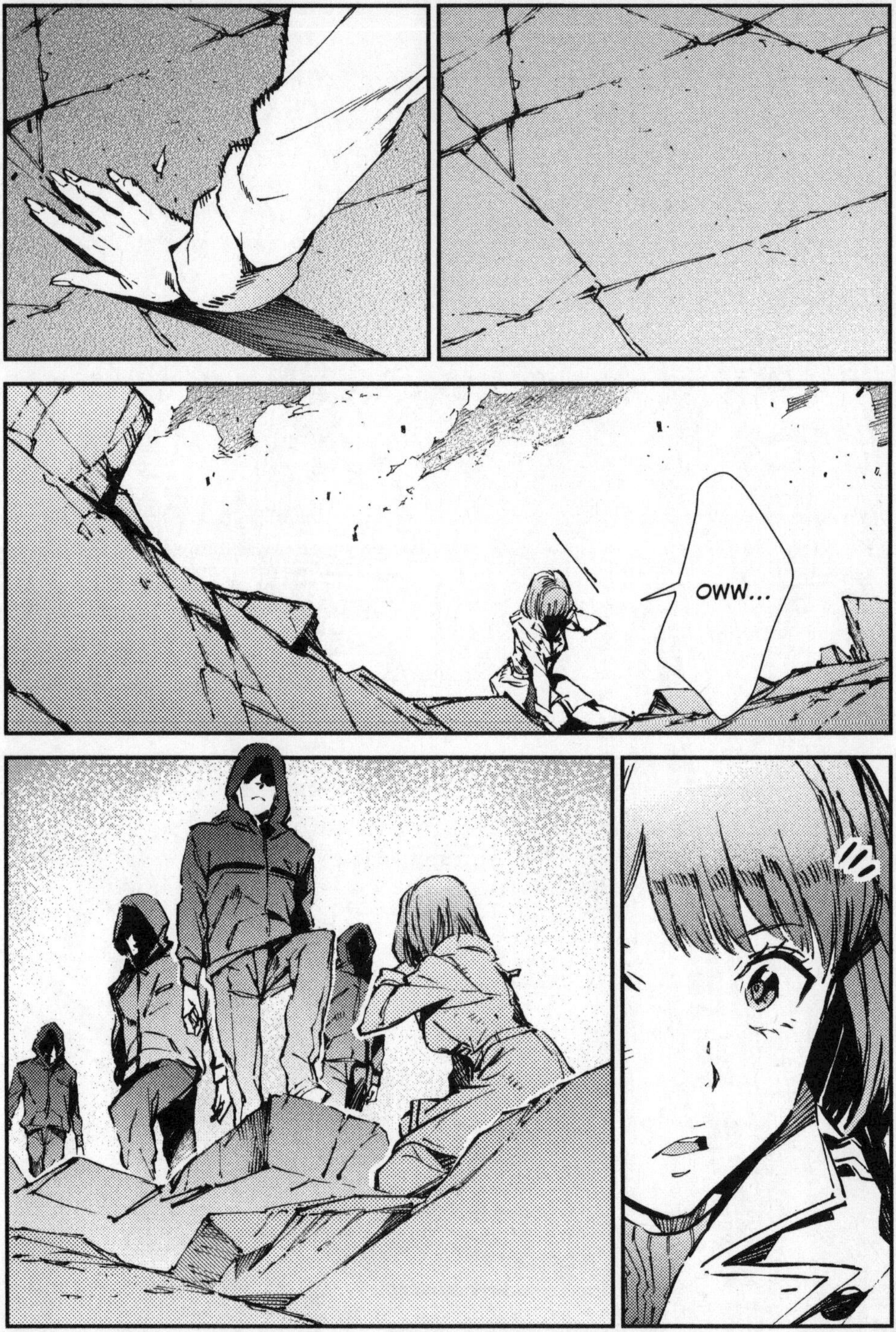
OWW...

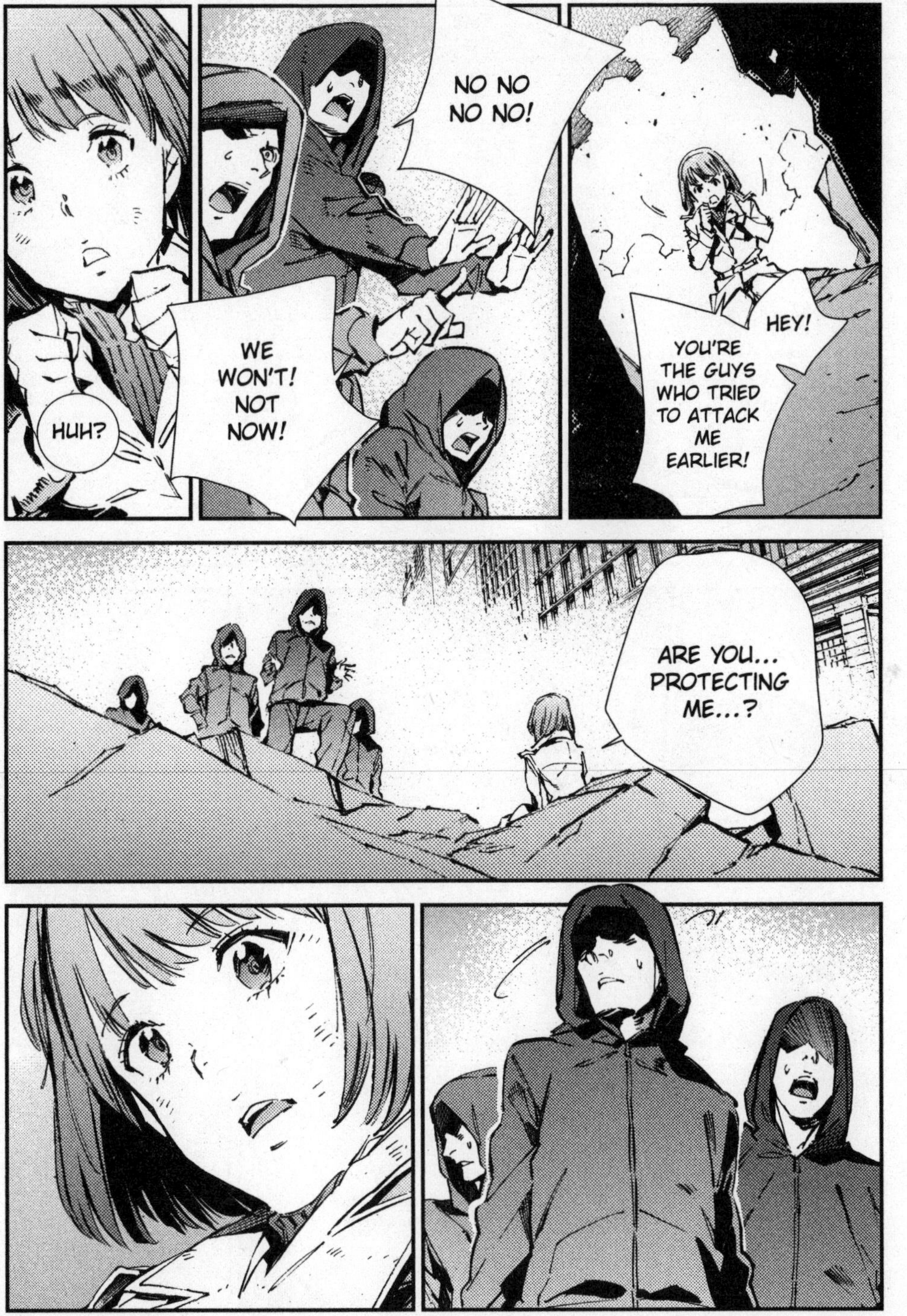
HEY!
YOU'RE THE GUYS WHO TRIED TO ATTACK ME EARLIER!
NO NO NO NO!
WE WON'T! NOT NOW!
HUH?
ARE YOU... PROTECTING ME...?

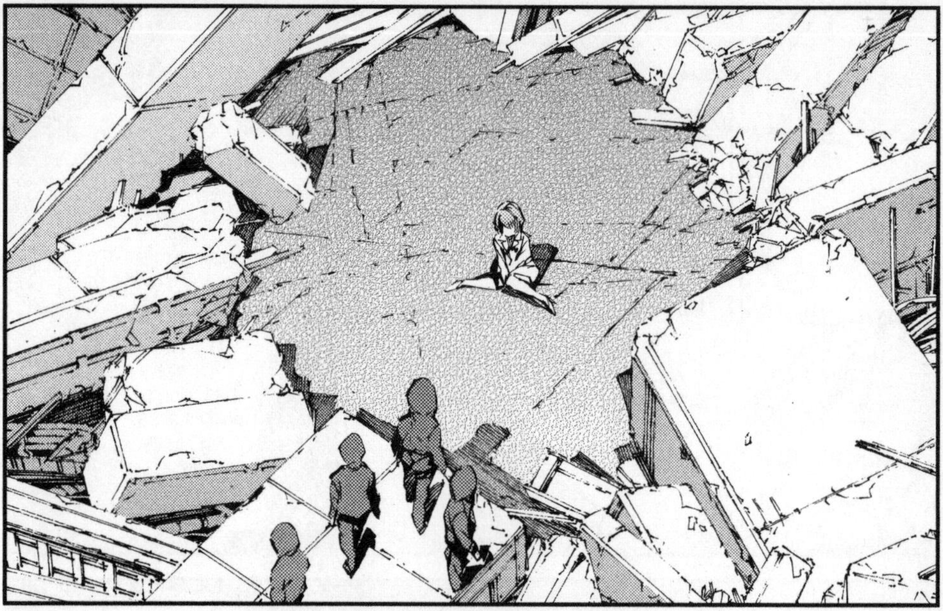

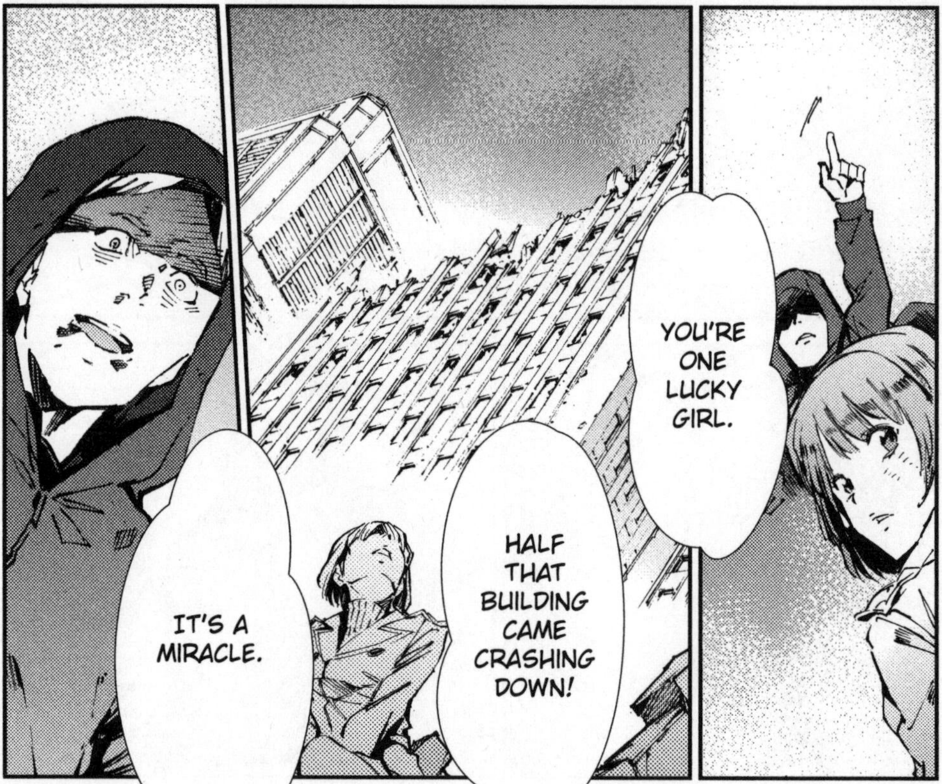
YOU'RE ONE LUCKY GIRL.
HALF THAT BUILDING CAME CRASHING DOWN!
IT'S A MIRACLE.

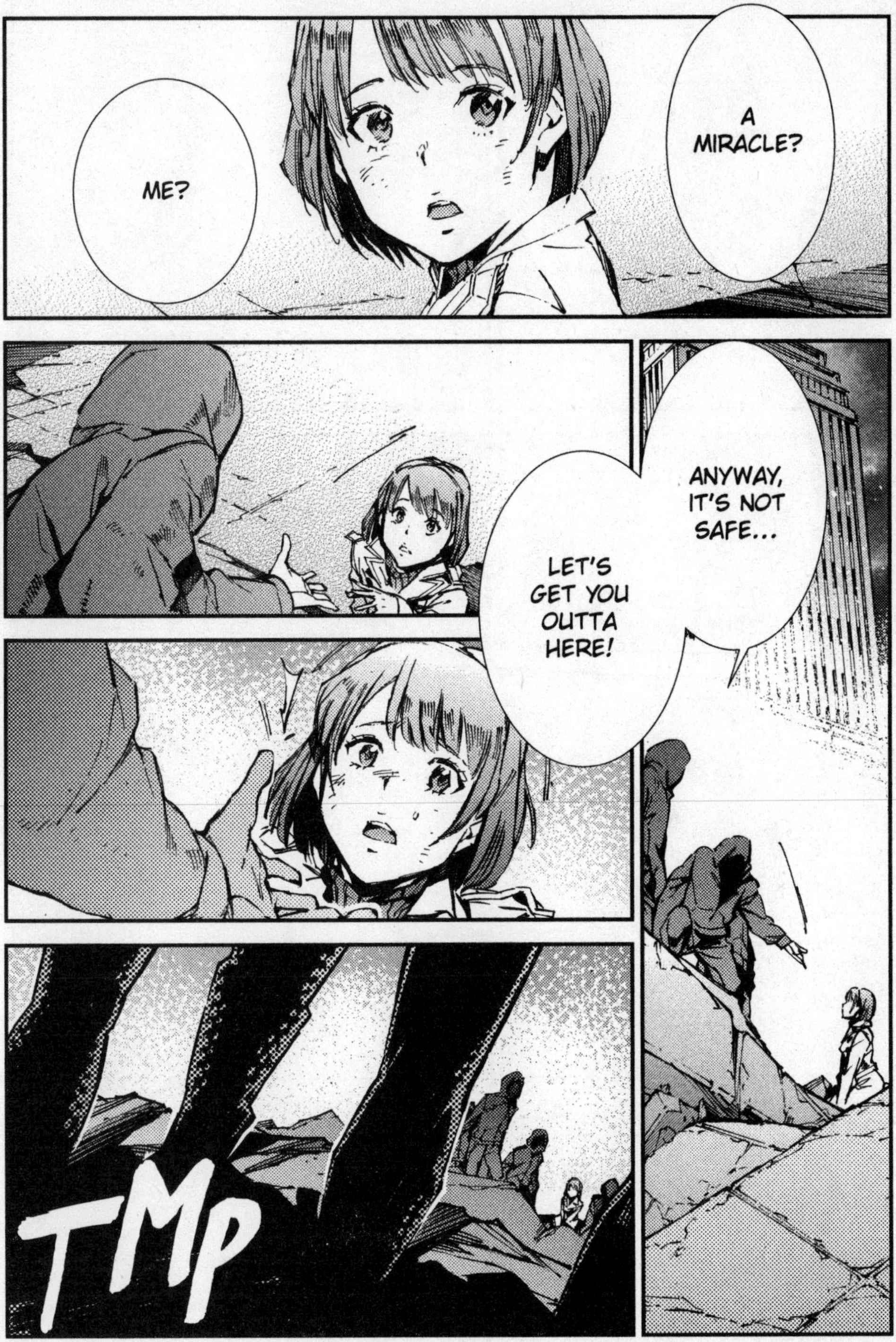
A MIRACLE?
ME?
ANYWAY, IT'S NOT SAFE...
LET'S GET YOU OUTTA HERE!
TMP

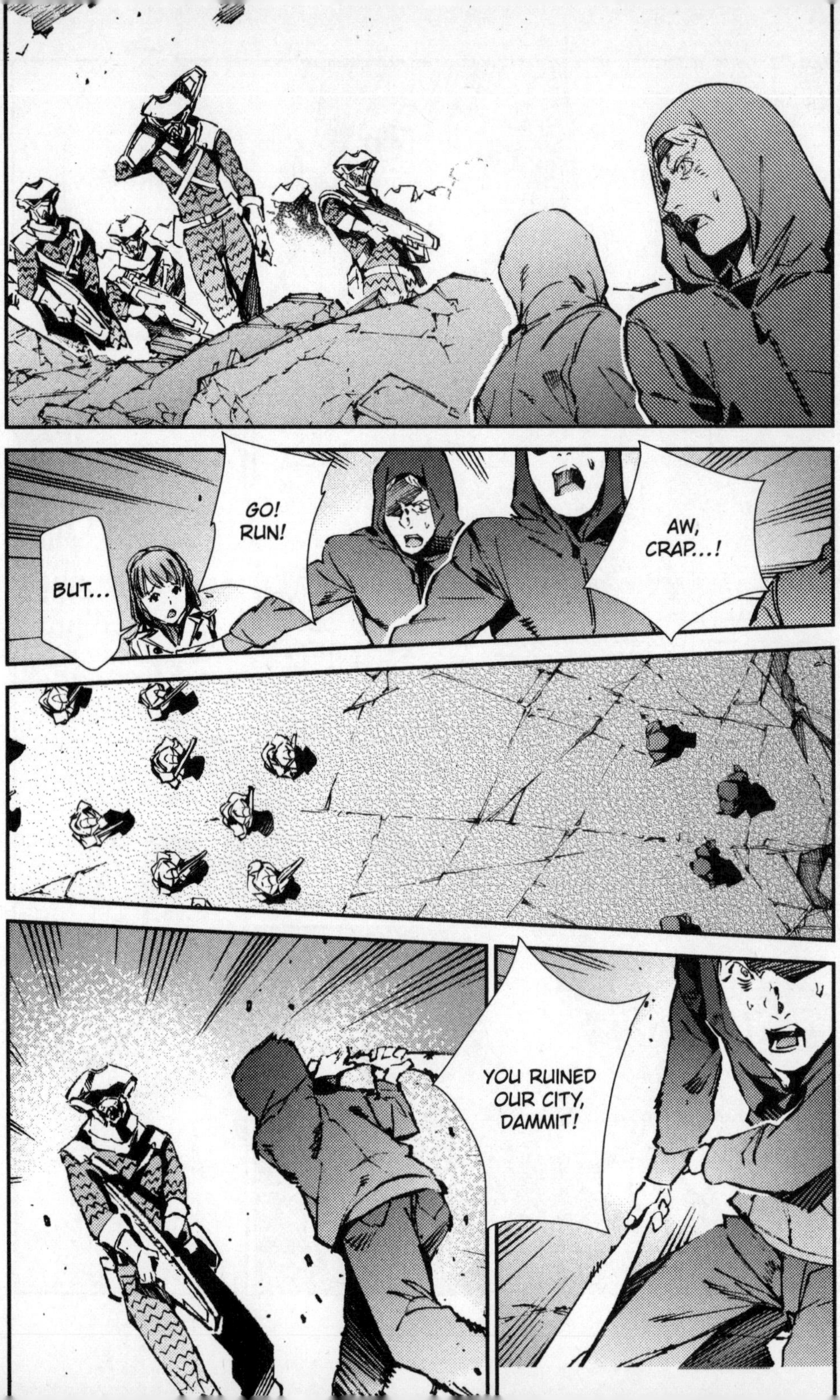
AW, CRAP...!
GO! RUN!
BUT...
YOU RUINED OUR CITY, DAMMIT!

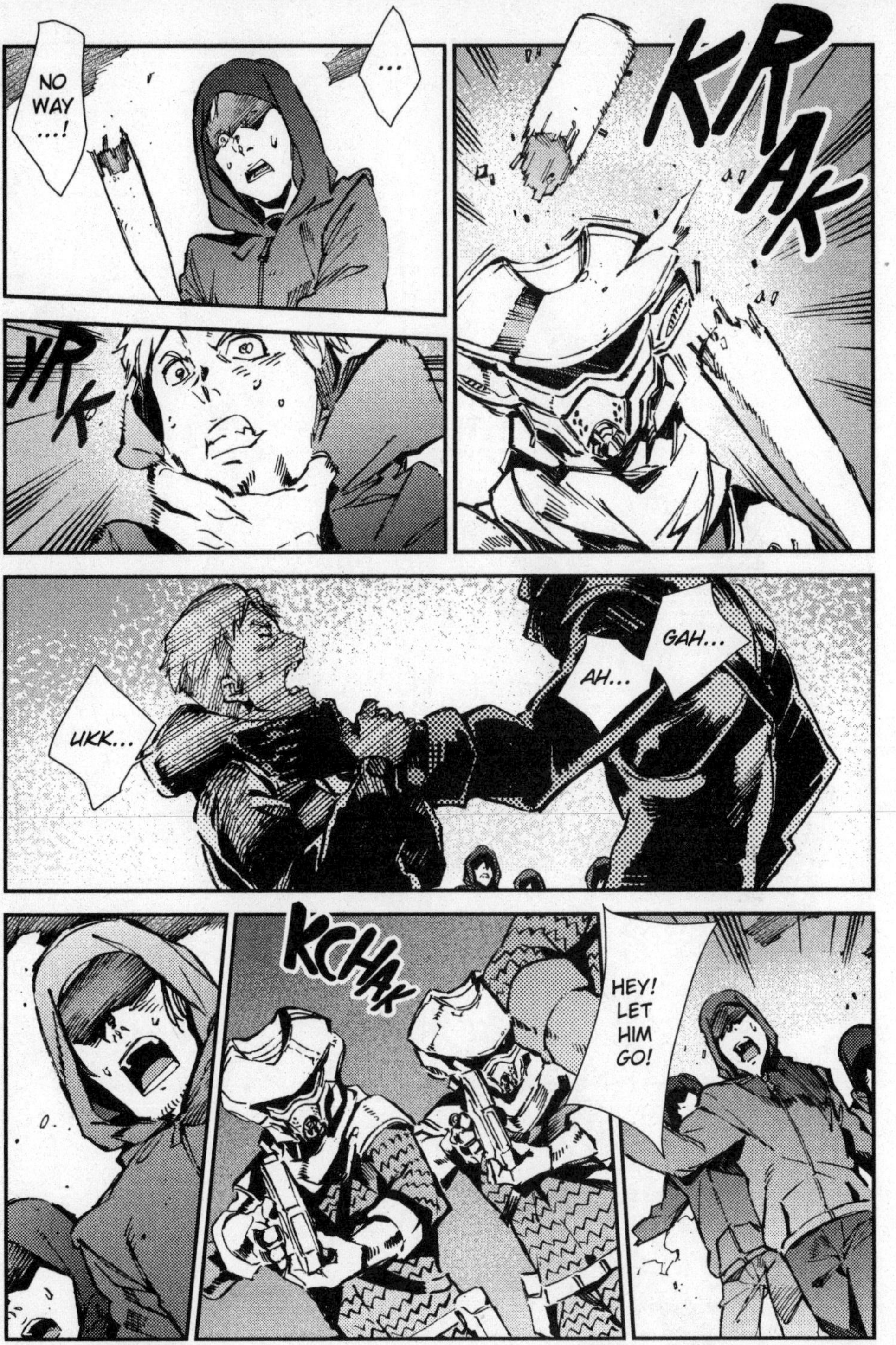
KRAK
...
NO WAY ...!
YRK
GAH...
AH...
UKK...
HEY! LET HIM GO!
KCHAK

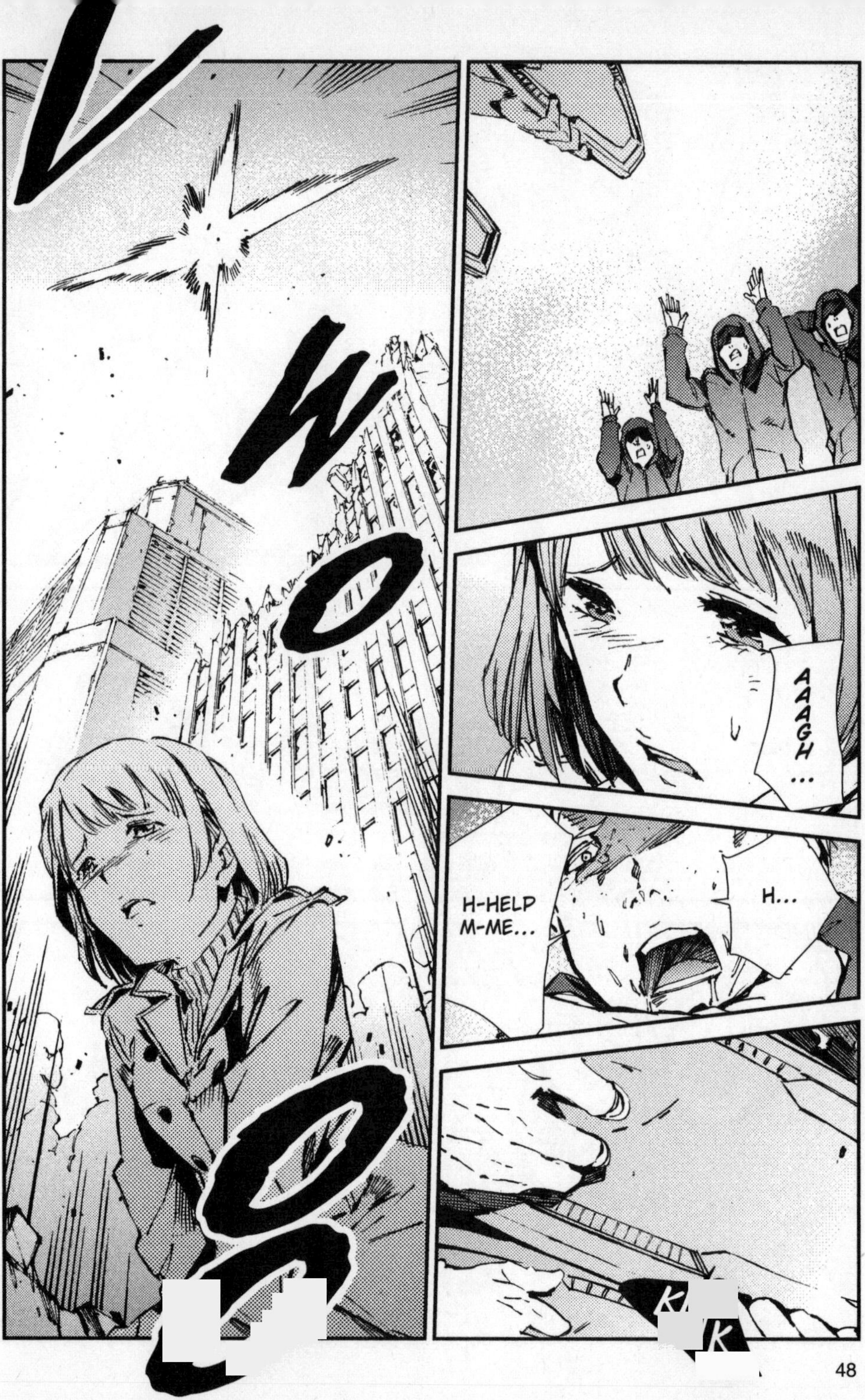
AAAGH...
H...
H-HELP M-ME...
V
W
O
O

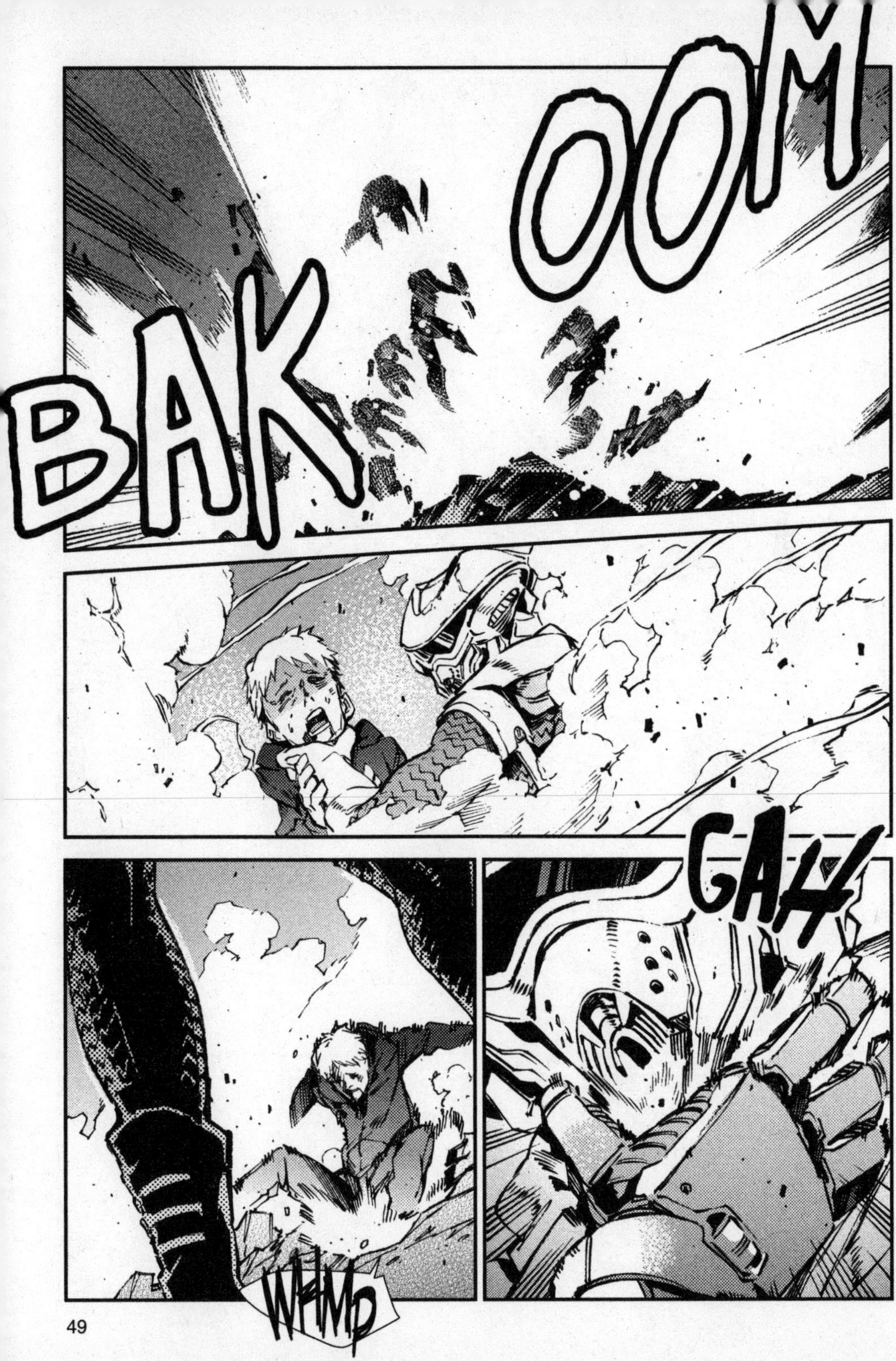
BAK OOM
GAH
WHMP

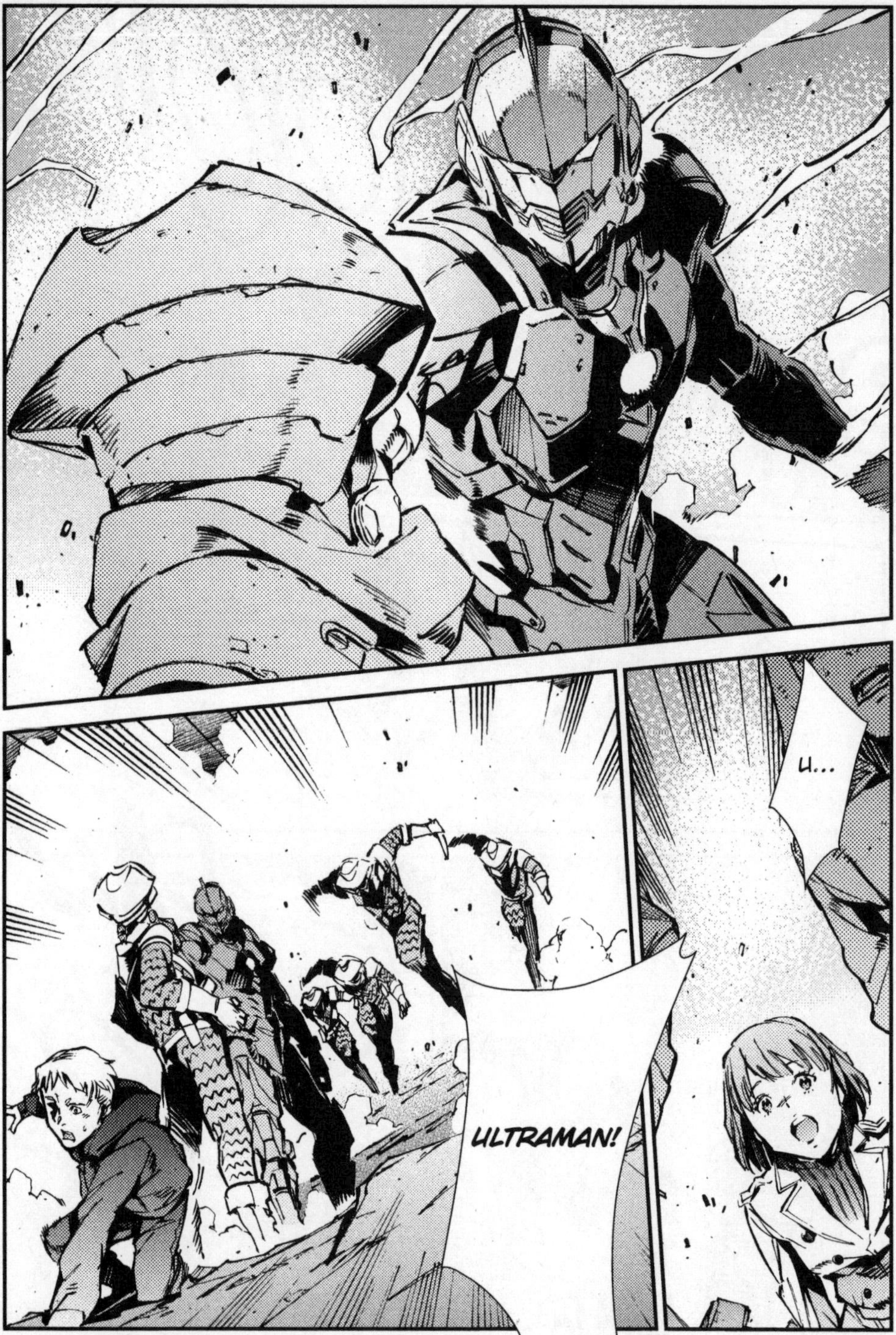
U...
ULTRAMAN!

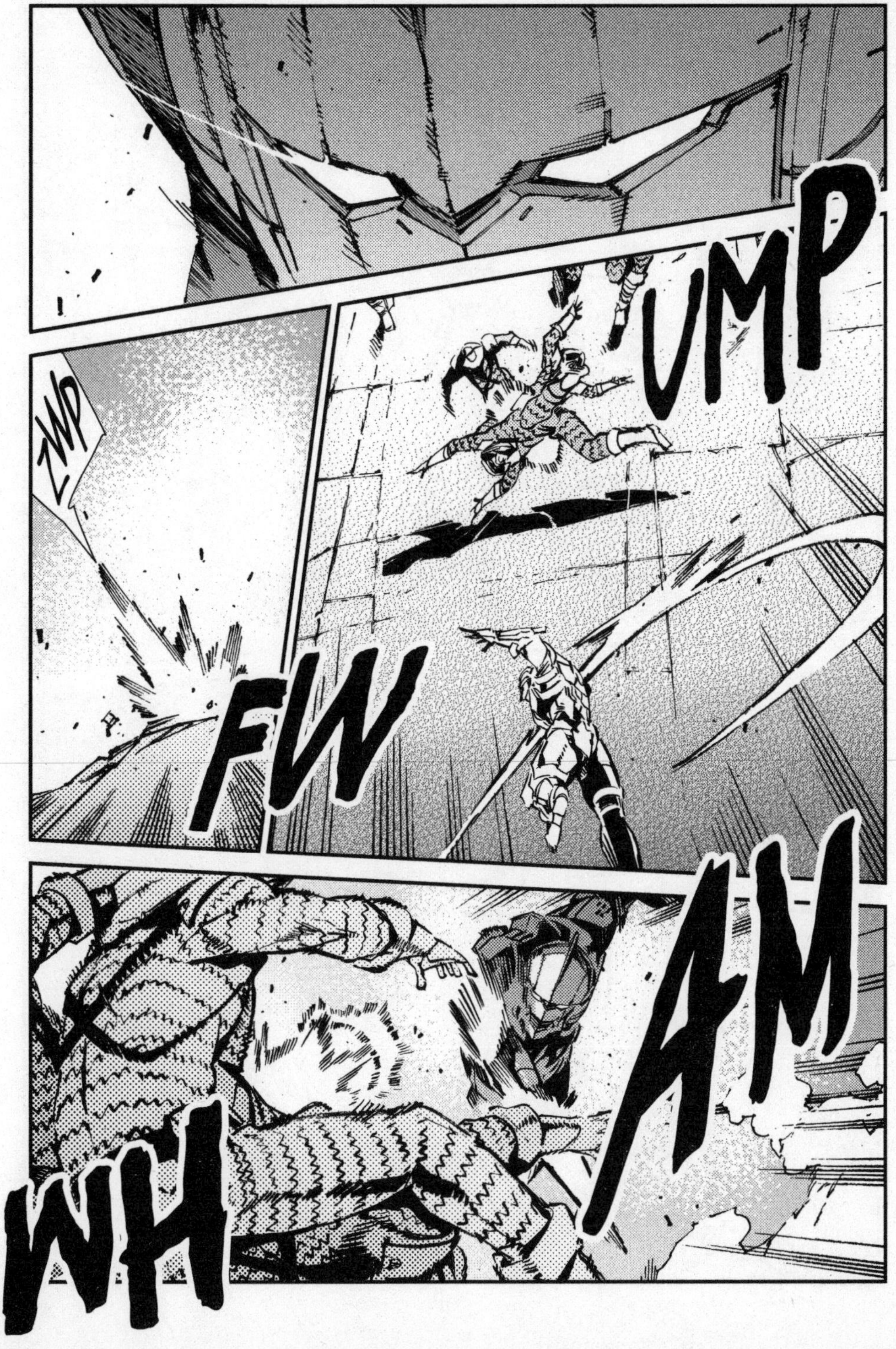
UMP
FW
ZWP
AM
WH

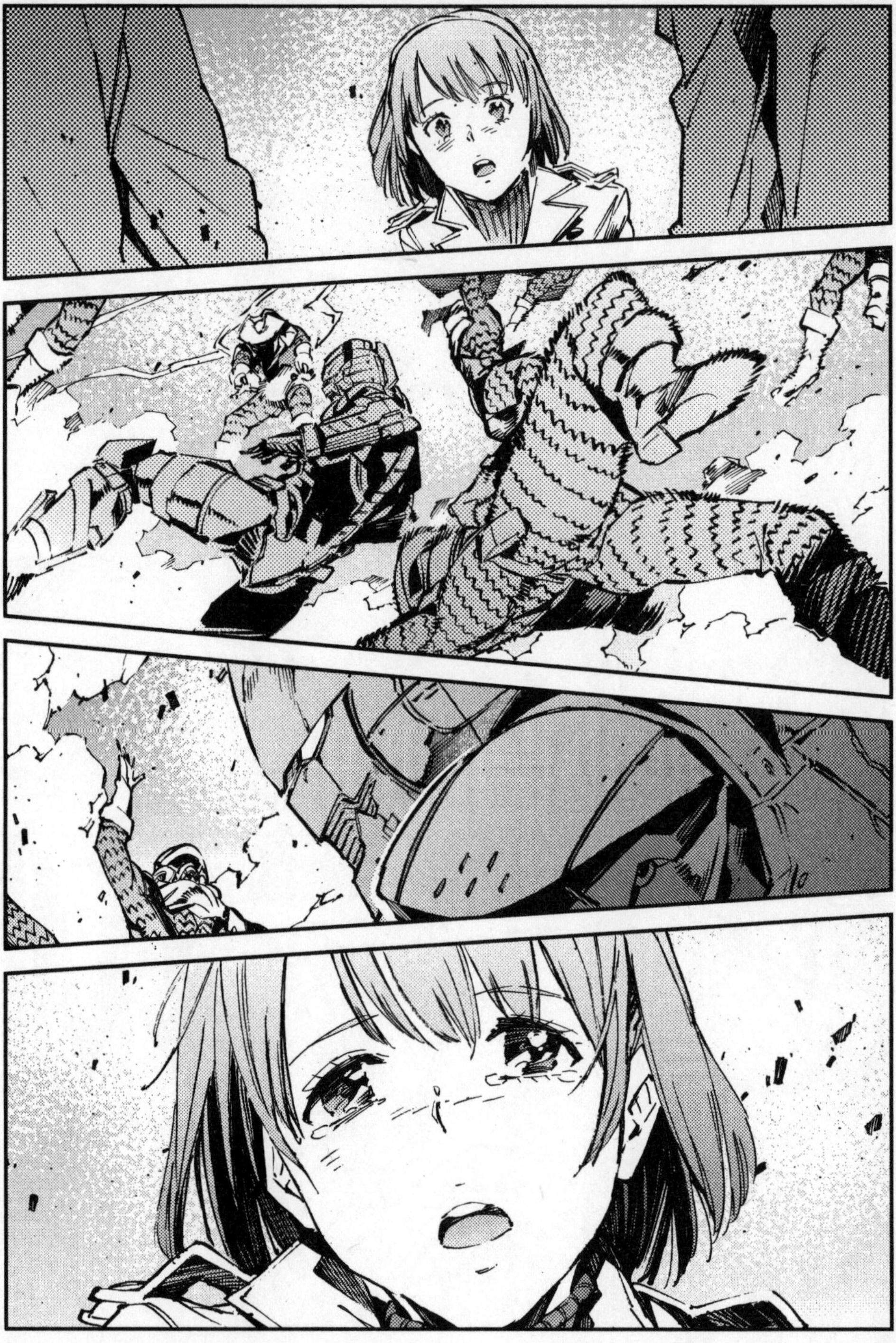

THMP
KRAK

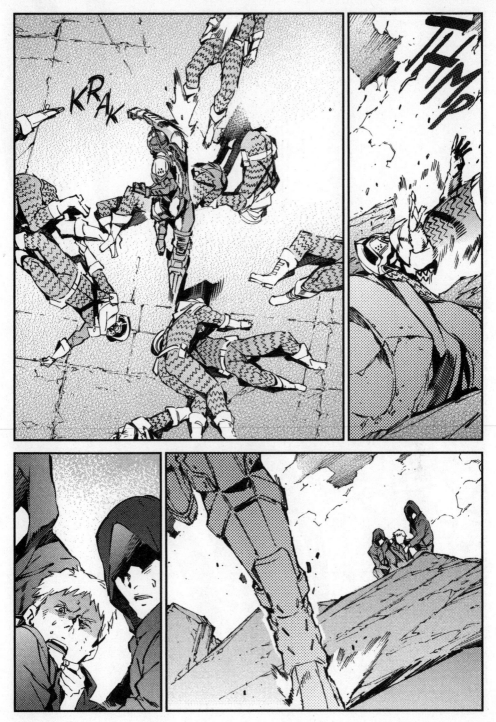

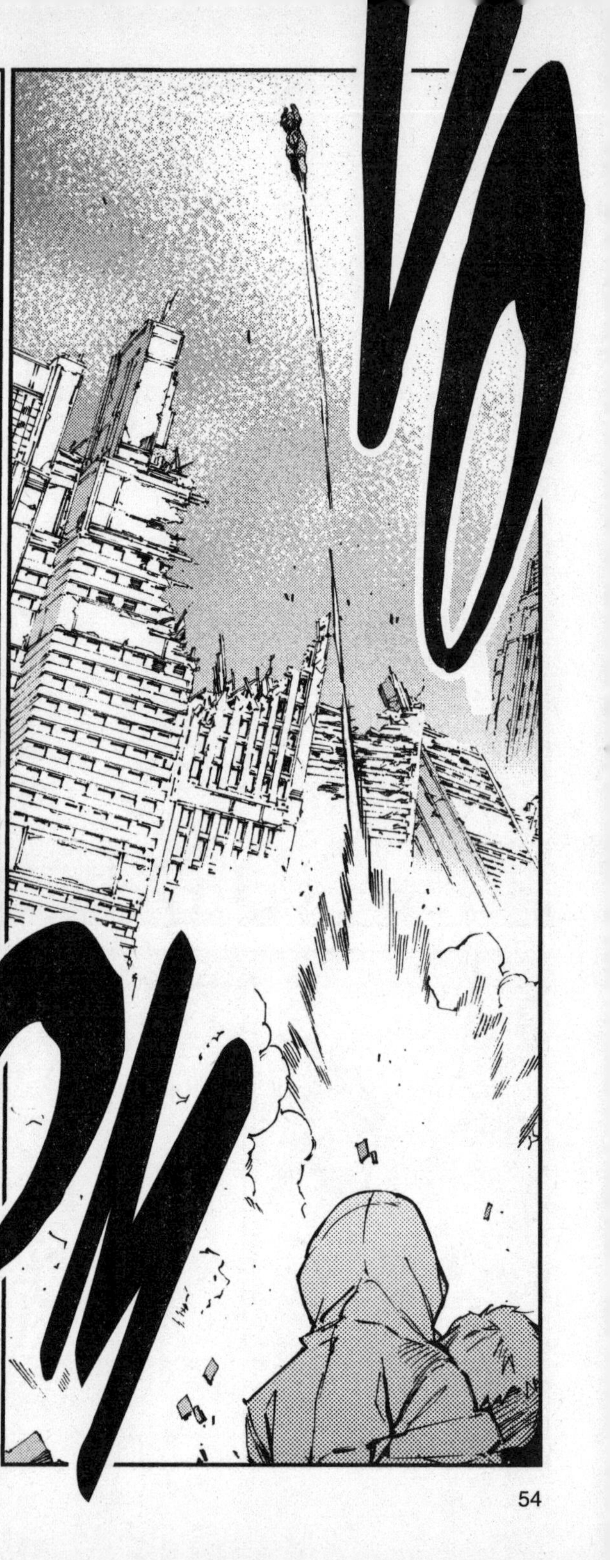

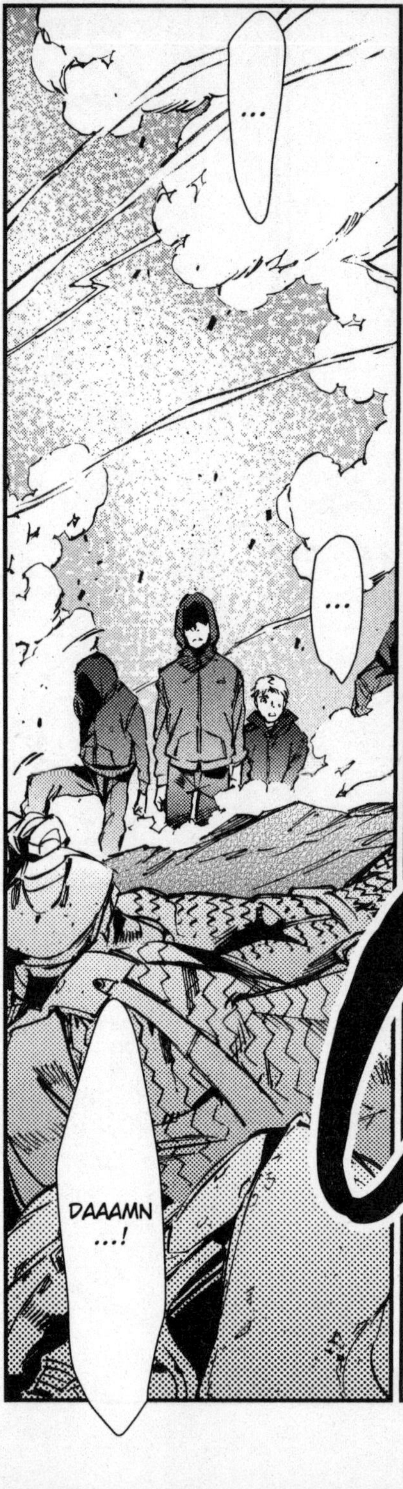
...
...
DAAAMN ...!

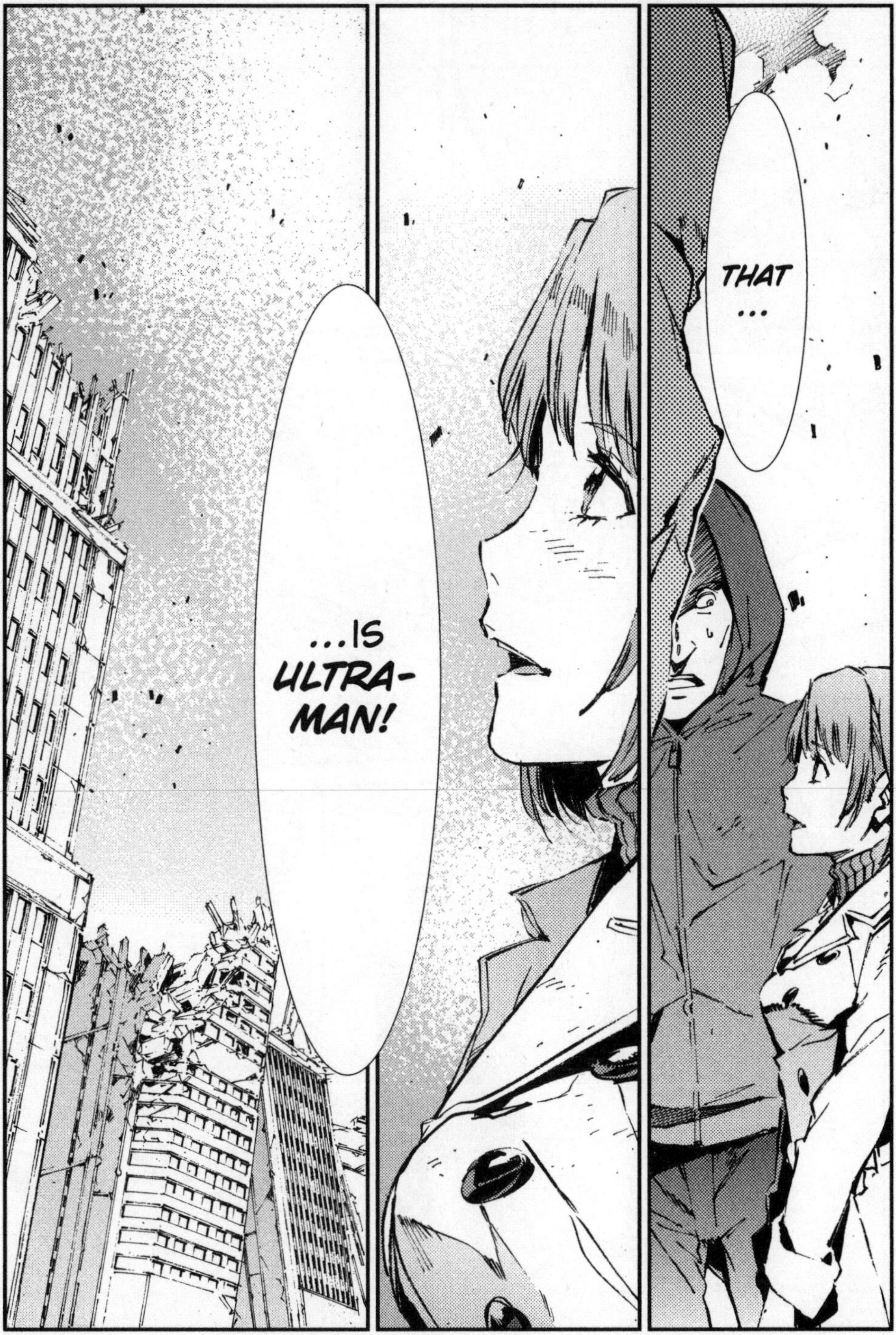
THAT ...
...IS ULTRA-MAN!

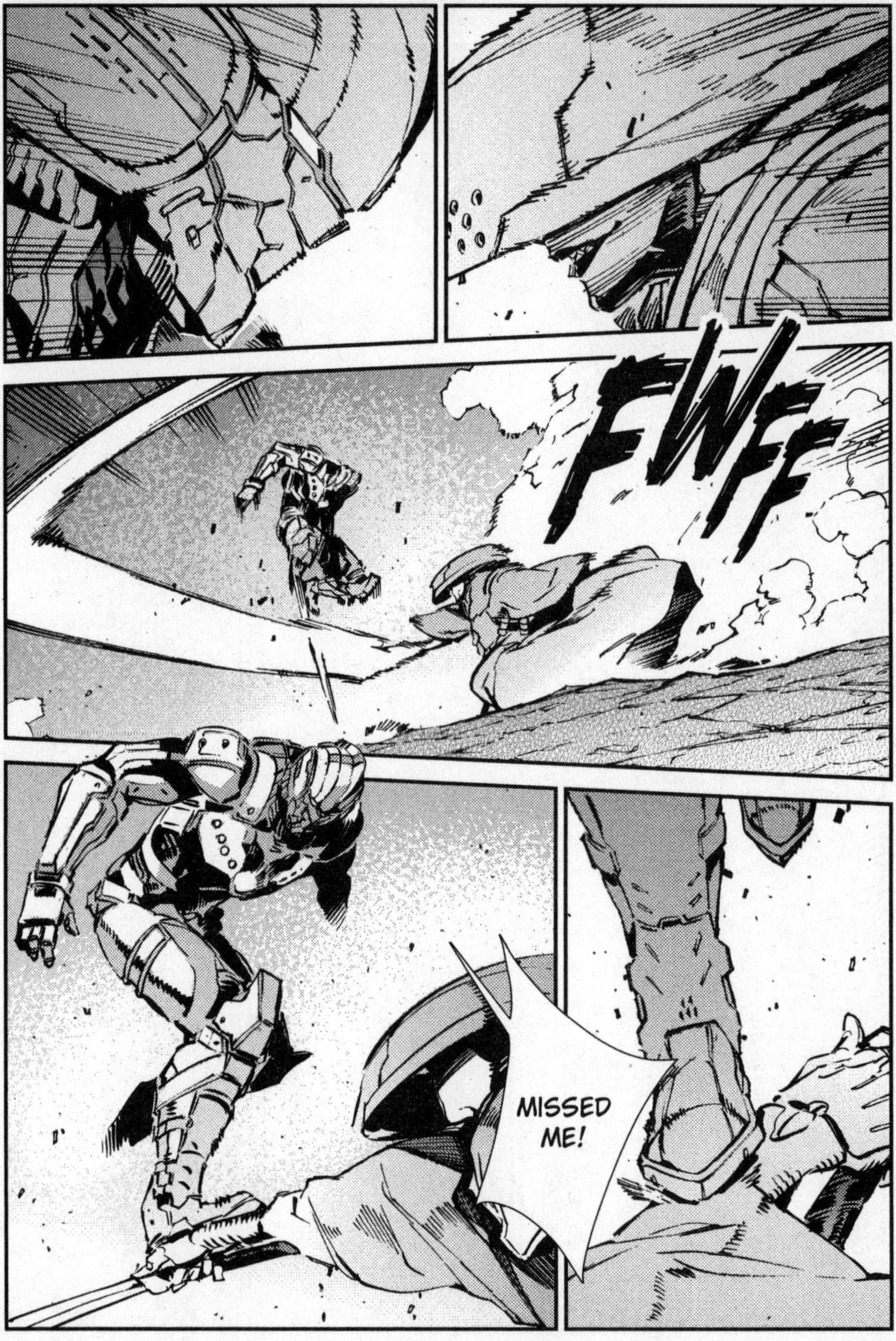
FWFF
MISSED ME!

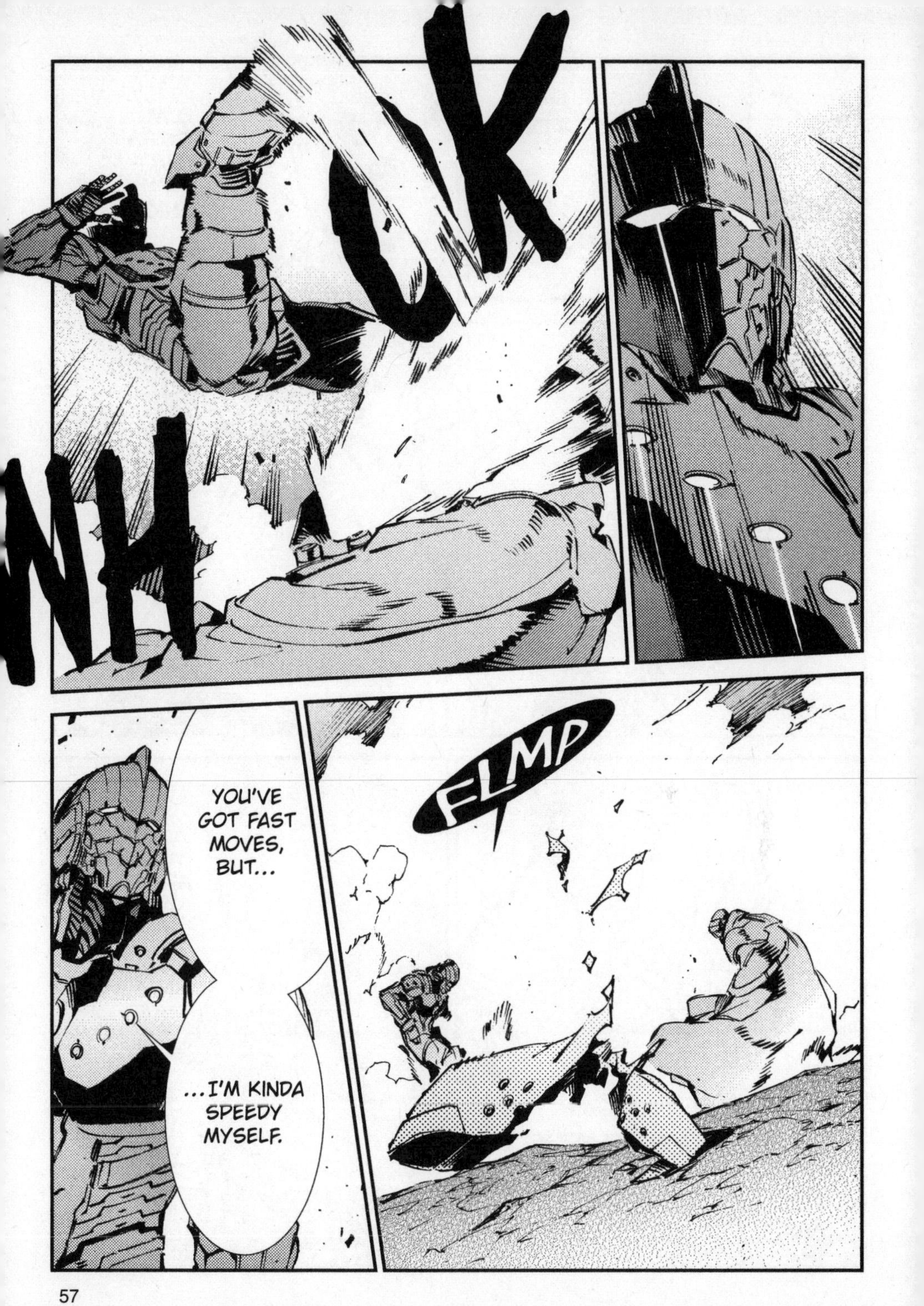
FLMP
YOU'VE GOT FAST MOVES, BUT...
...I'M KINDA SPEEDY MYSELF.

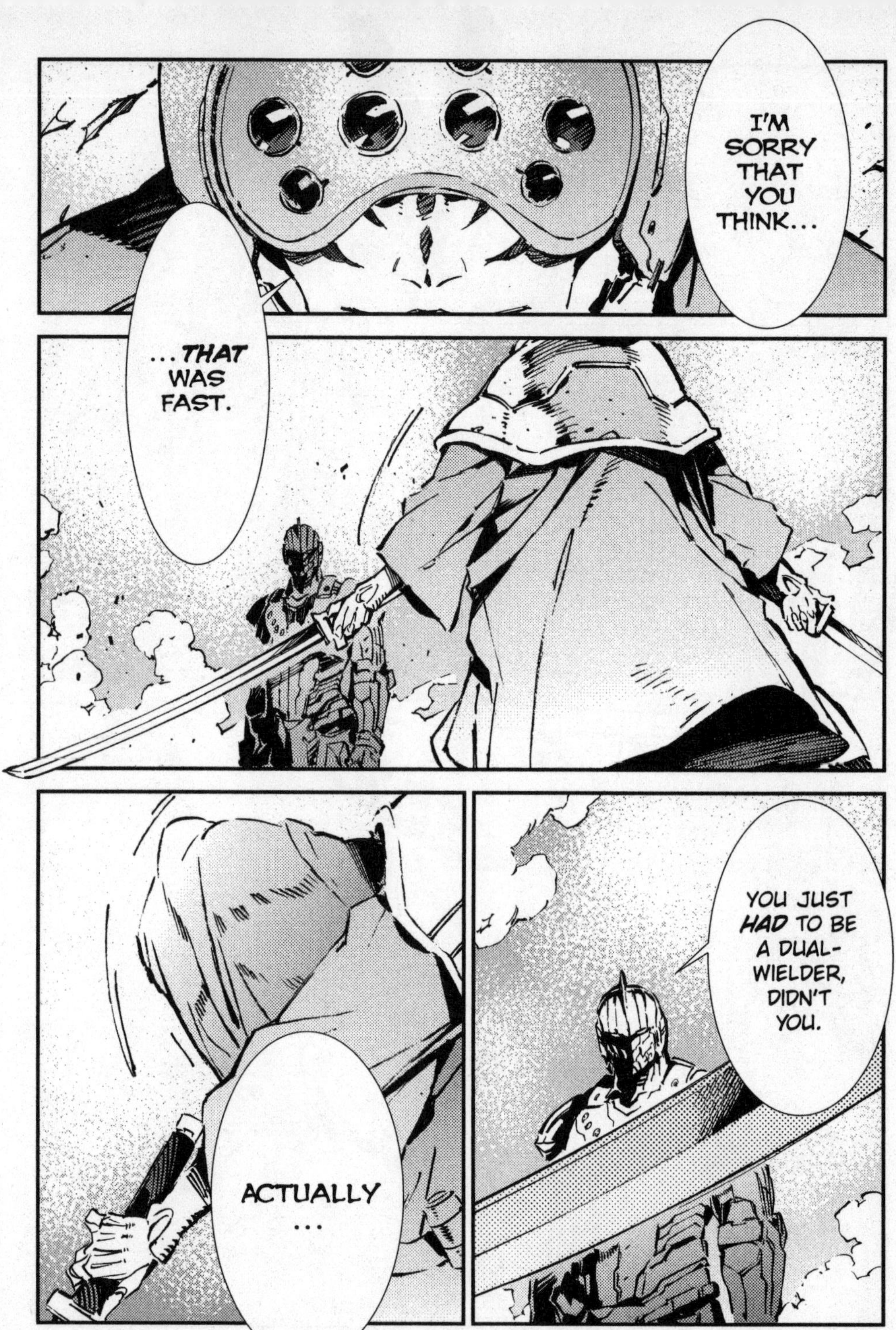
I'M SORRY THAT YOU THINK...
...*THAT* WAS FAST.
YOU JUST *HAD* TO BE A DUAL-WIELDER, DIDN'T YOU.
ACTUALLY ...

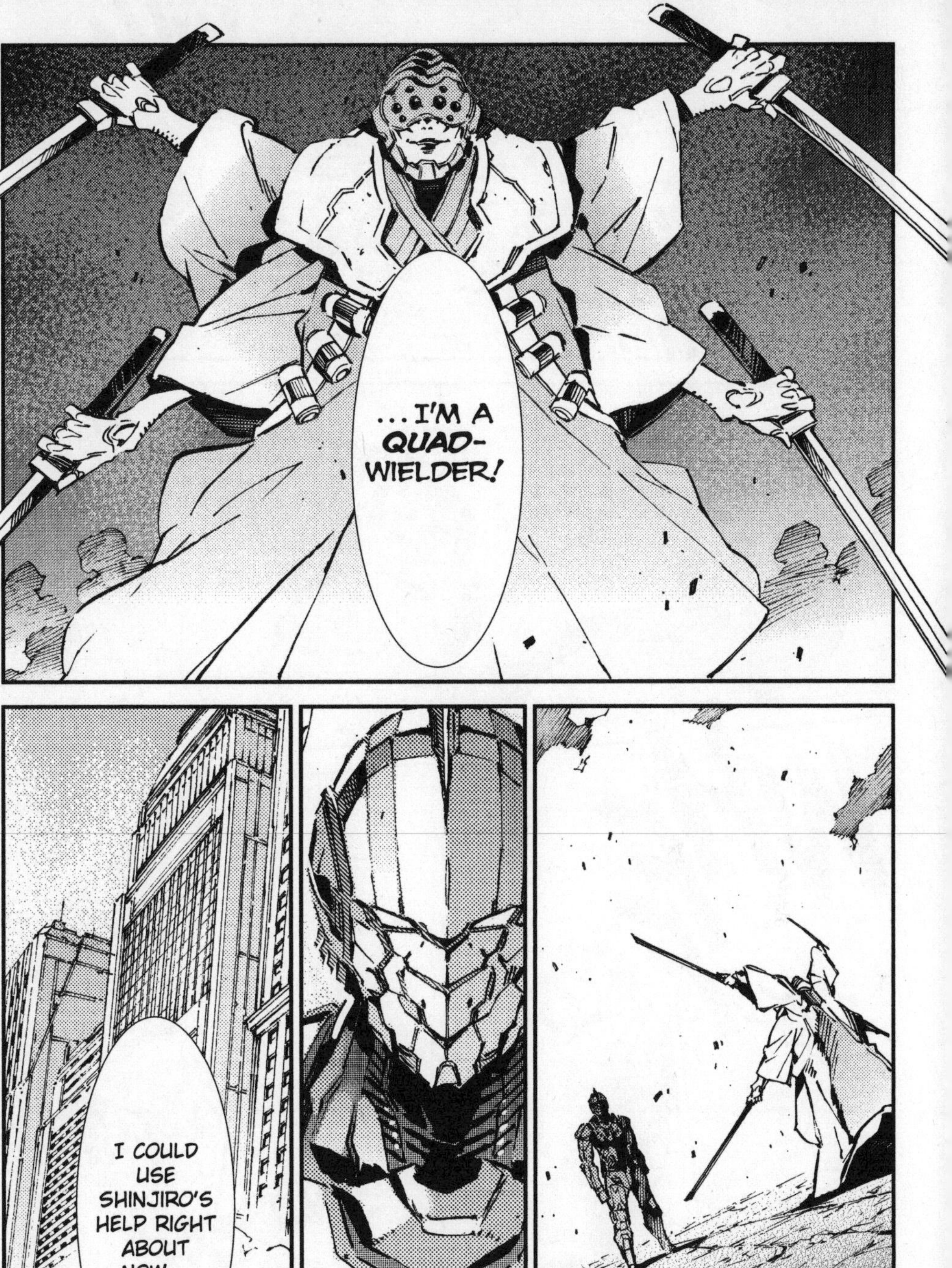
...I'M A QUAD-WIELDER!
I COULD USE SHINJIRO'S HELP RIGHT ABOUT NOW...

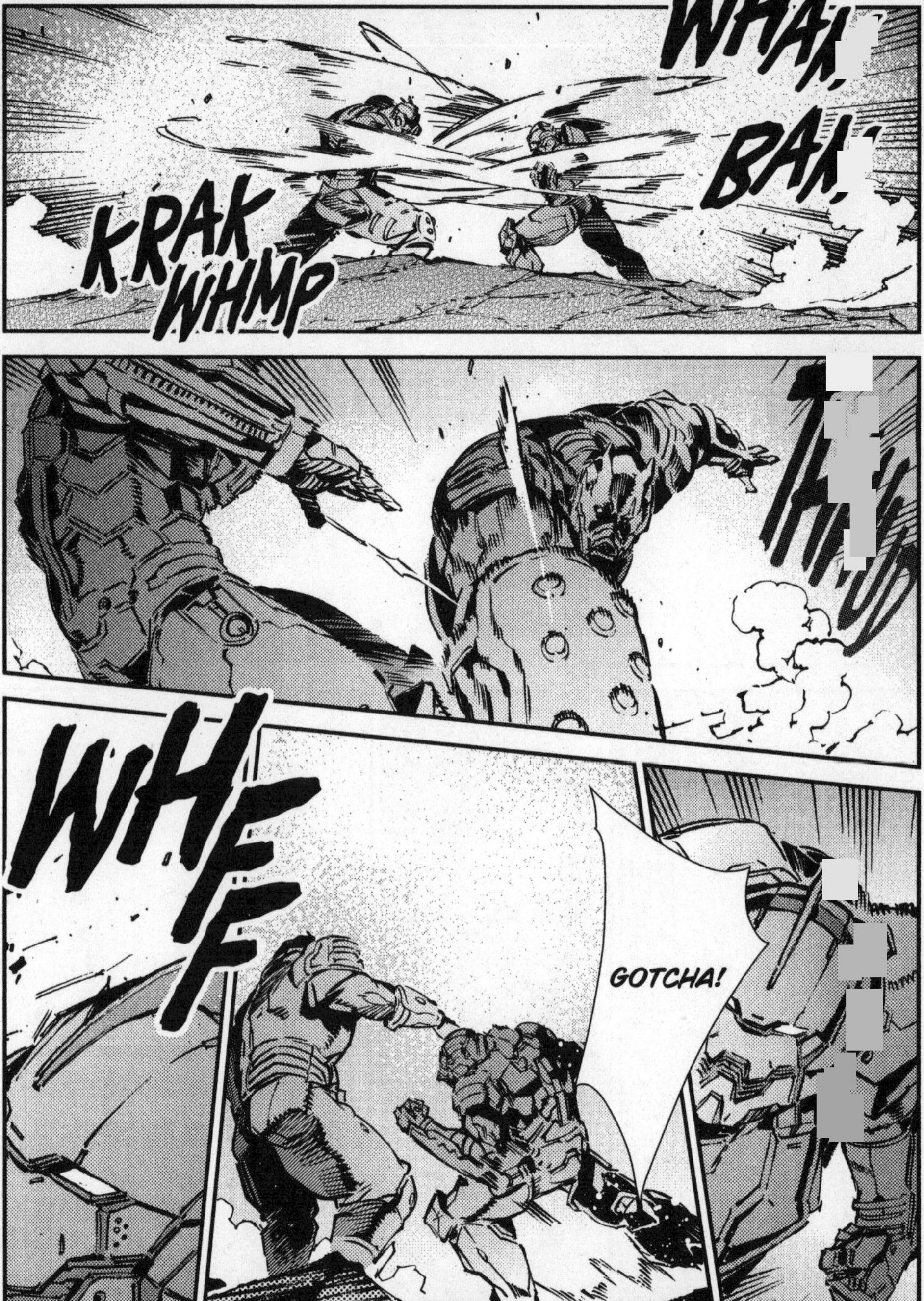
KRAK
WHMP
GOTCHA!
WHFF

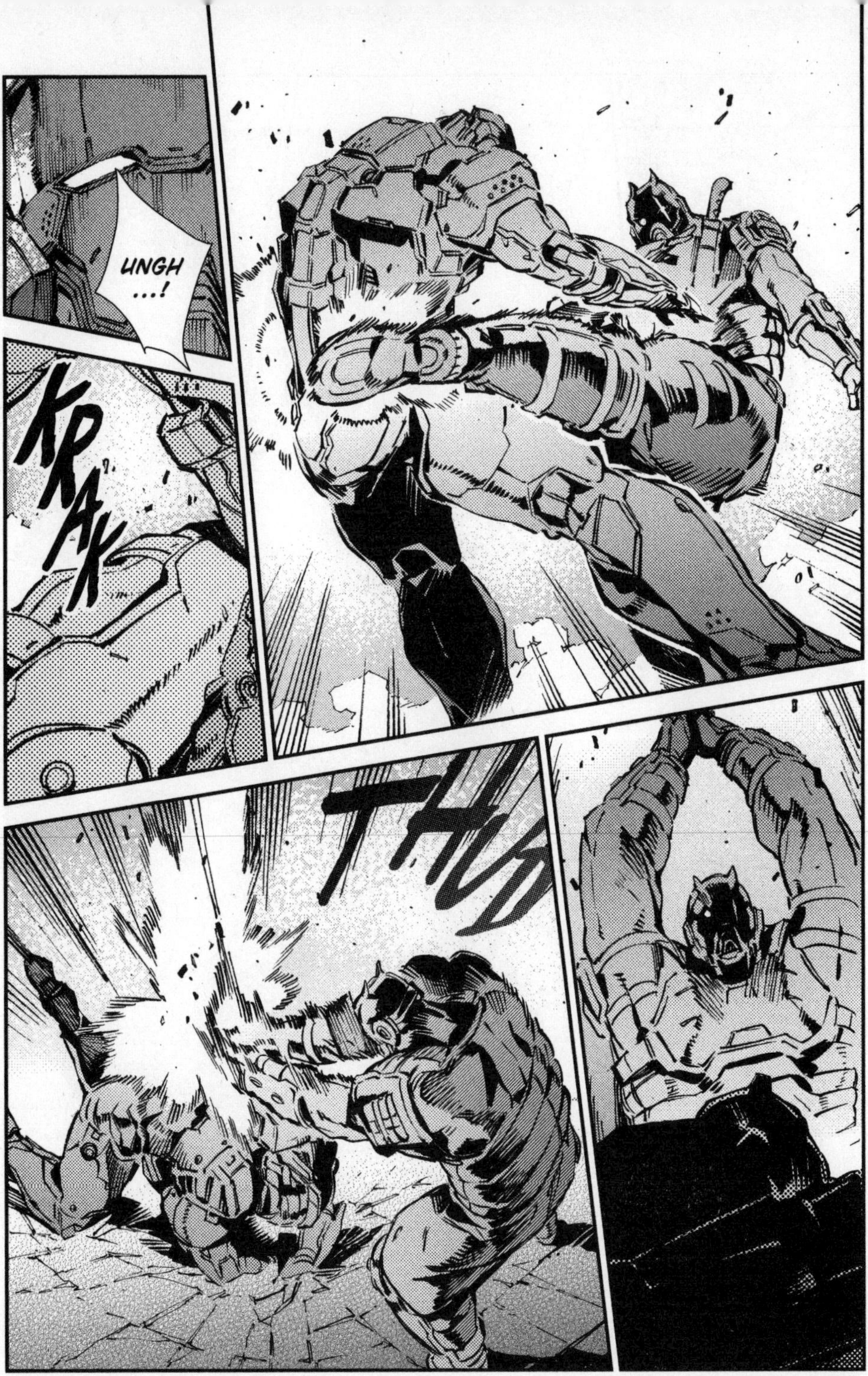
UNGH ...!
KRAK
THUD

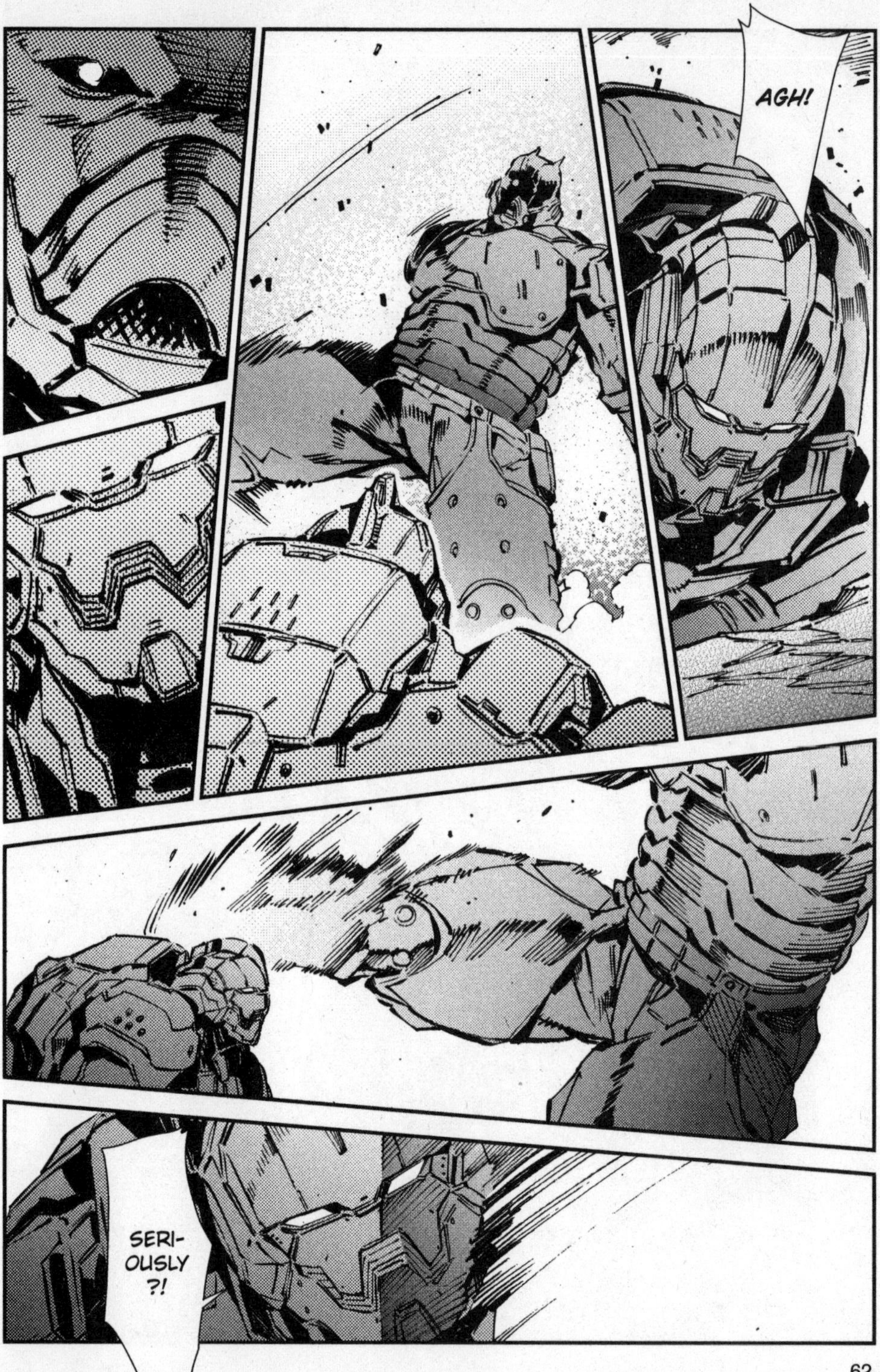
AGH!
SERI-
OUSLY
?!

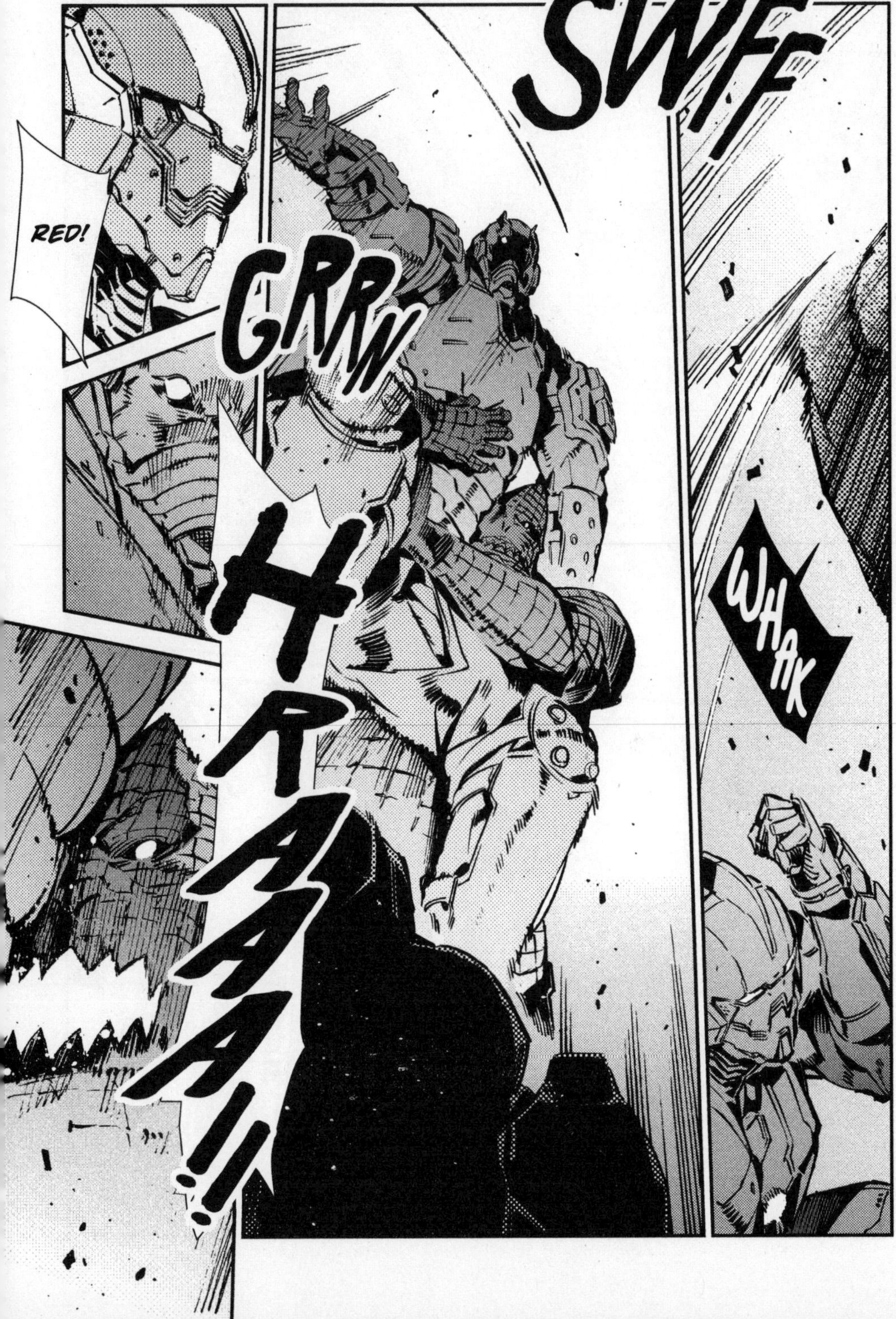
SWFF
WHAK
RED!
GRRW
HRRAAAA!!

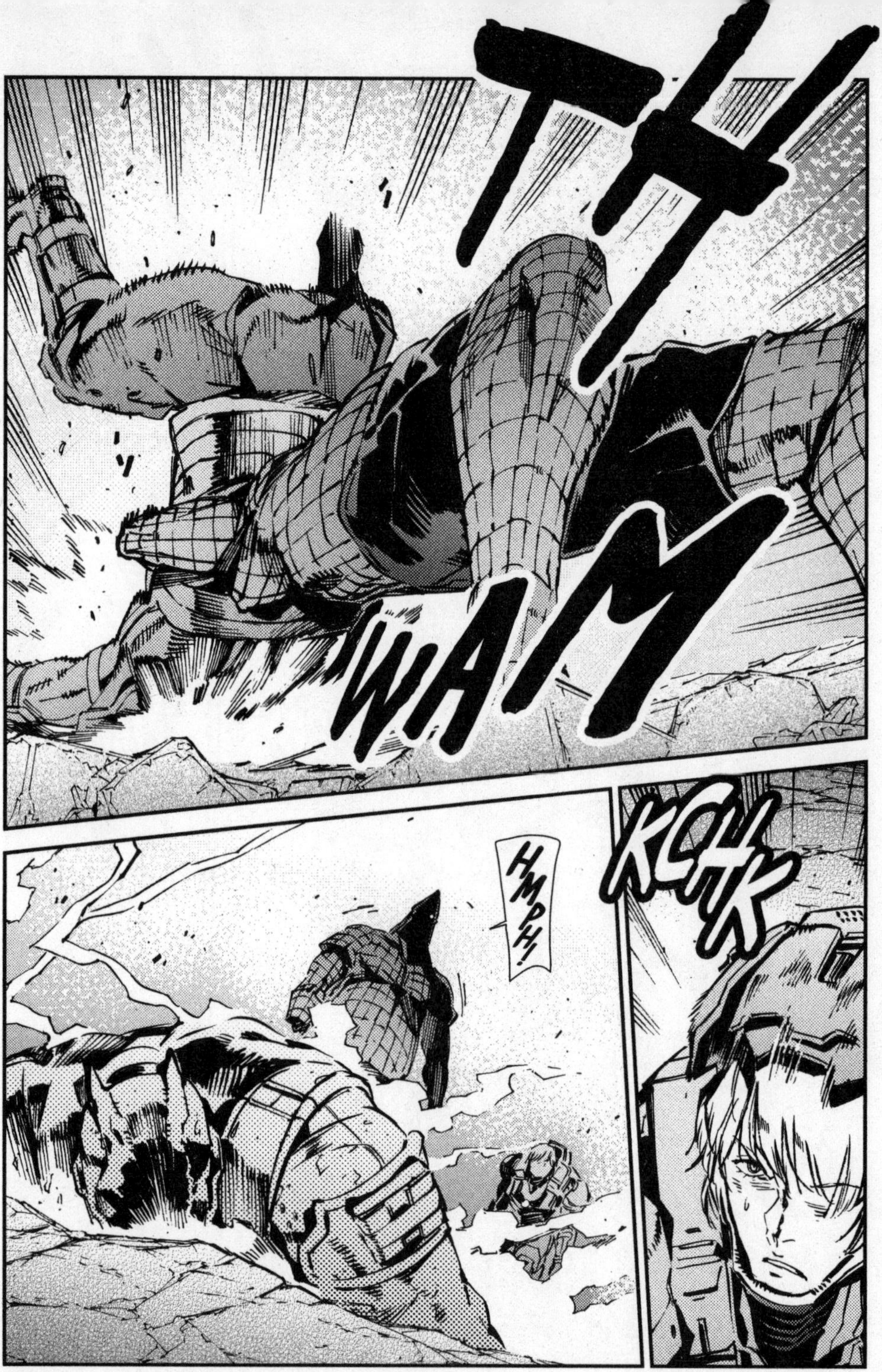
THWAM
KCHK
HMPH!

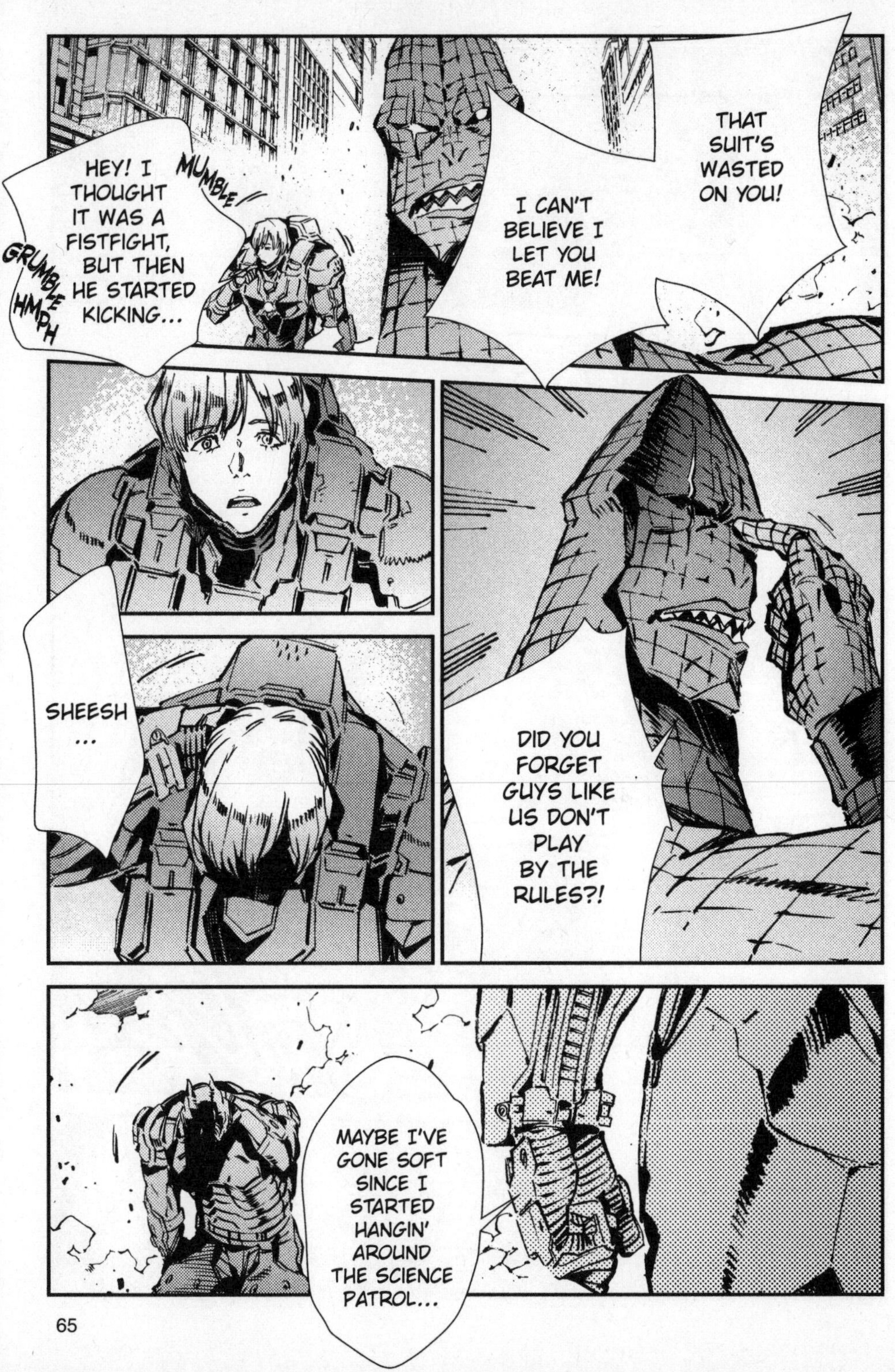
THAT SUIT'S WASTED ON YOU!
I CAN'T BELIEVE I LET YOU BEAT ME!
HEY! I THOUGHT IT WAS A FISTFIGHT, BUT THEN HE STARTED KICKING...
MUMBLE
GRUMBLE
HMPH
DID YOU FORGET GUYS LIKE US DON'T PLAY BY THE RULES?!
SHEESH...
MAYBE I'VE GONE SOFT SINCE I STARTED HANGIN' AROUND THE SCIENCE PATROL...

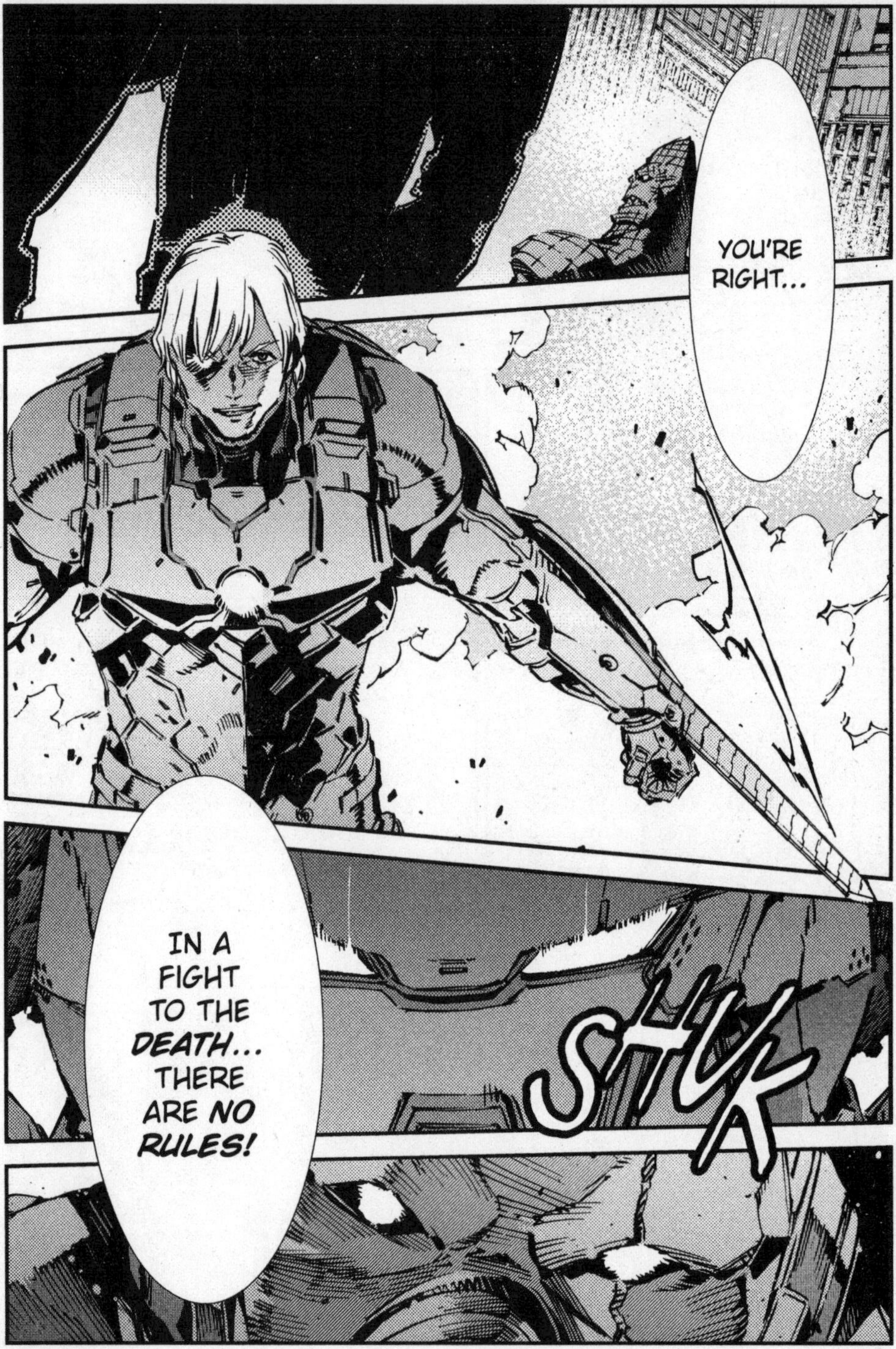
YOU'RE RIGHT...
IN A FIGHT TO THE *DEATH*... THERE ARE *NO RULES!*
SHUK

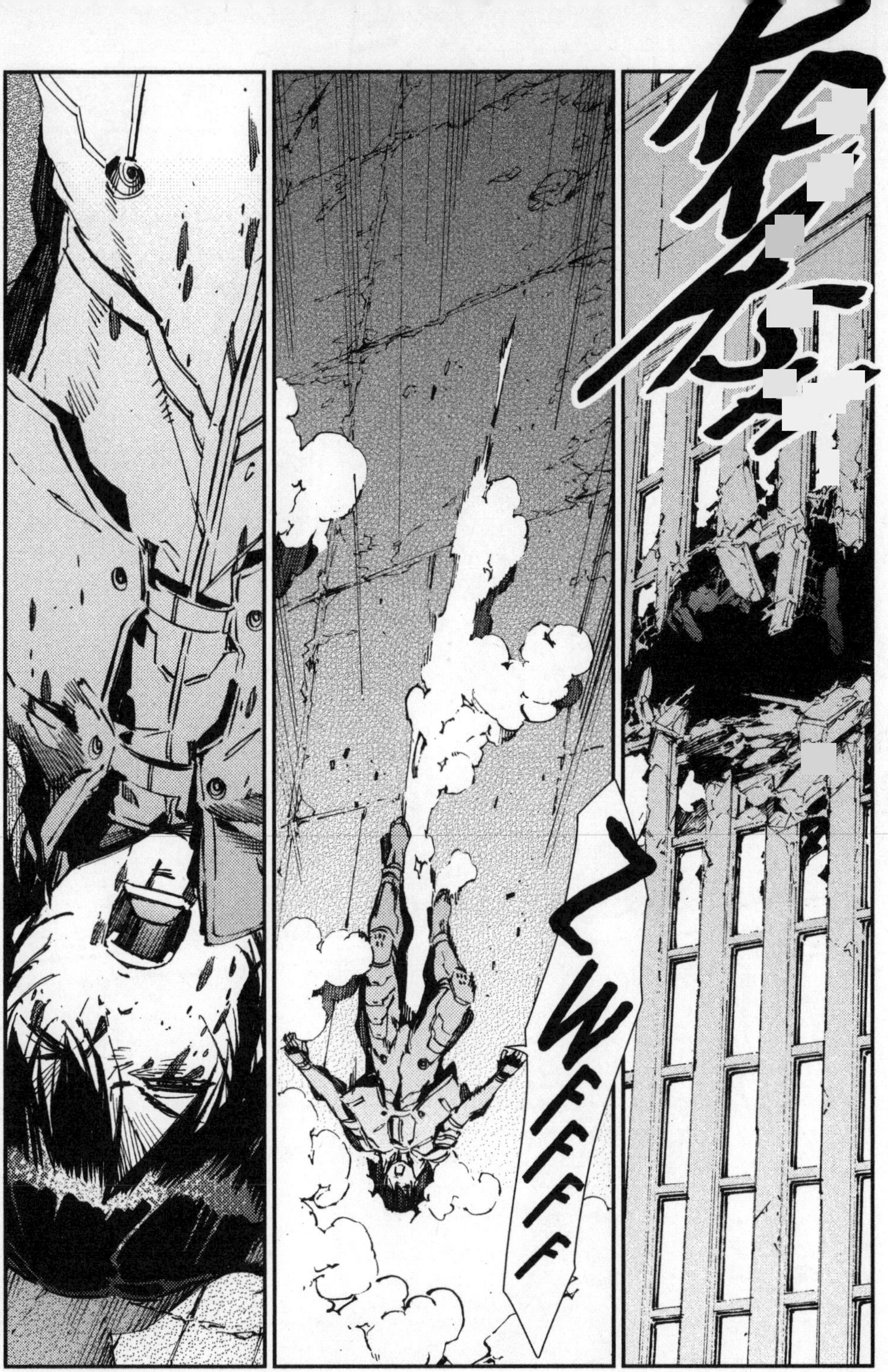
SWFFFF

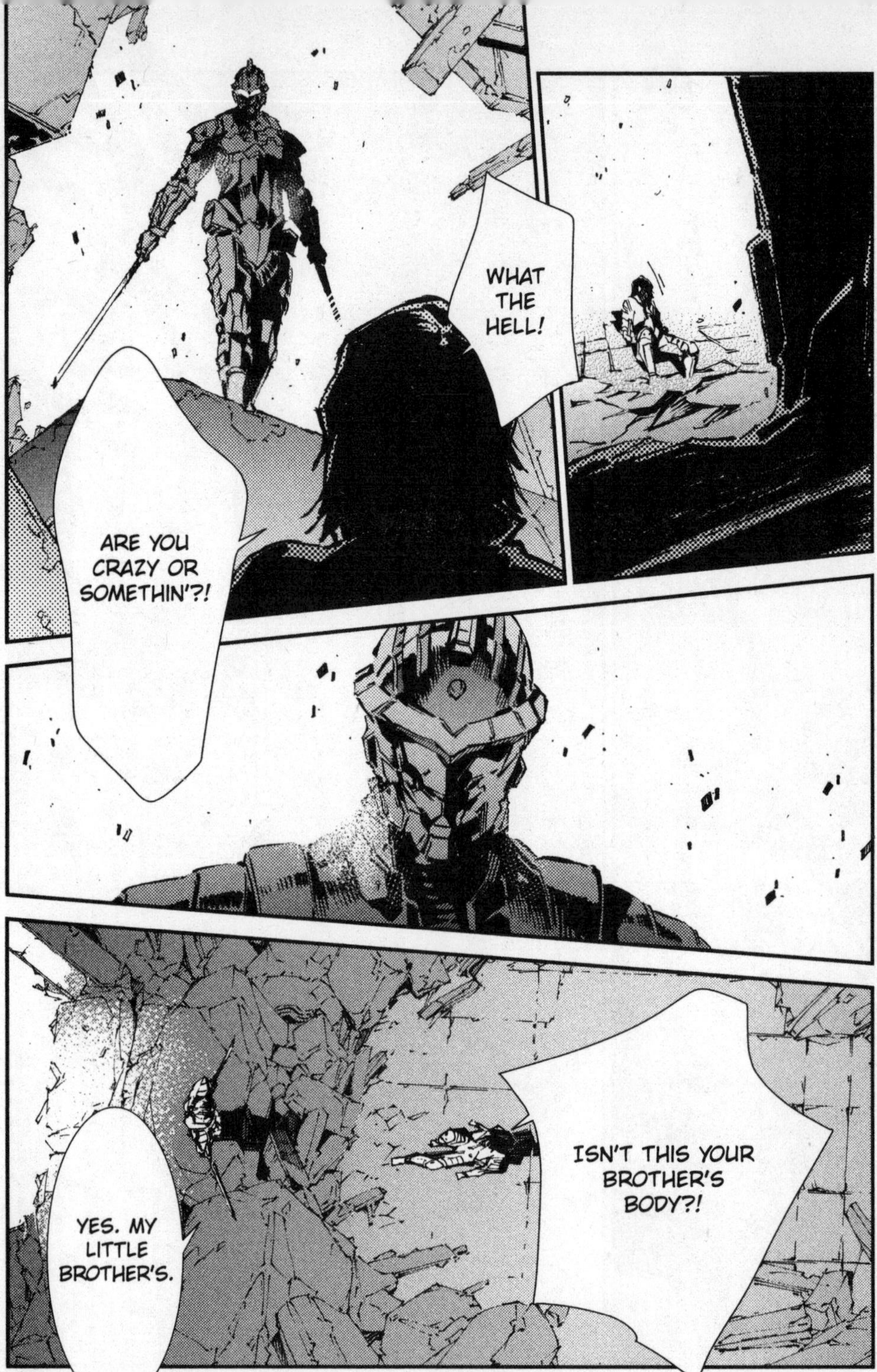
WHAT THE HELL!
ARE YOU CRAZY OR SOMETHIN'?!
ISN'T THIS YOUR BROTHER'S BODY?!
YES. MY LITTLE BROTHER'S.

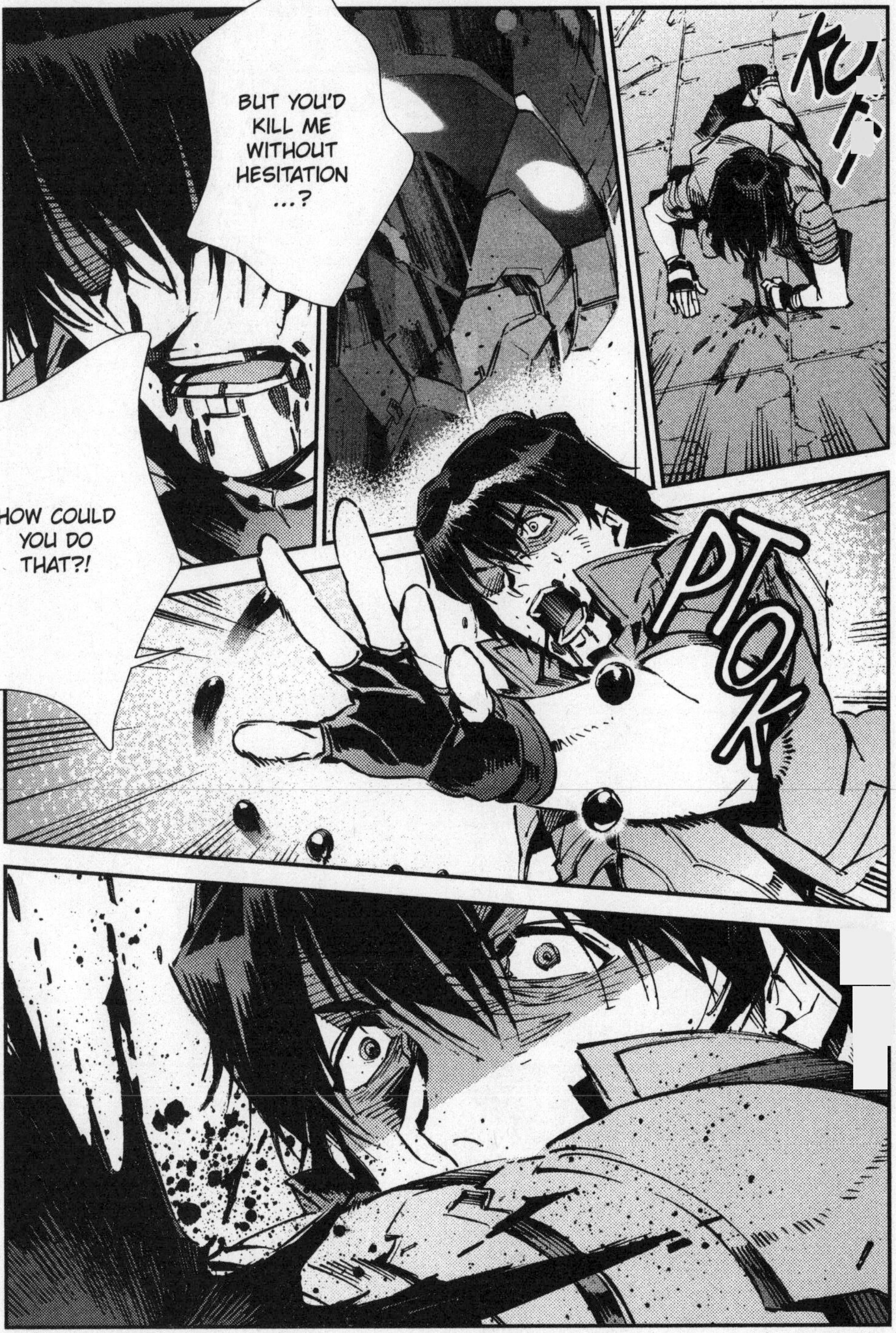
KU
BUT YOU'D KILL ME WITHOUT HESITATION ...?
HOW COULD YOU DO THAT?!
PTOK

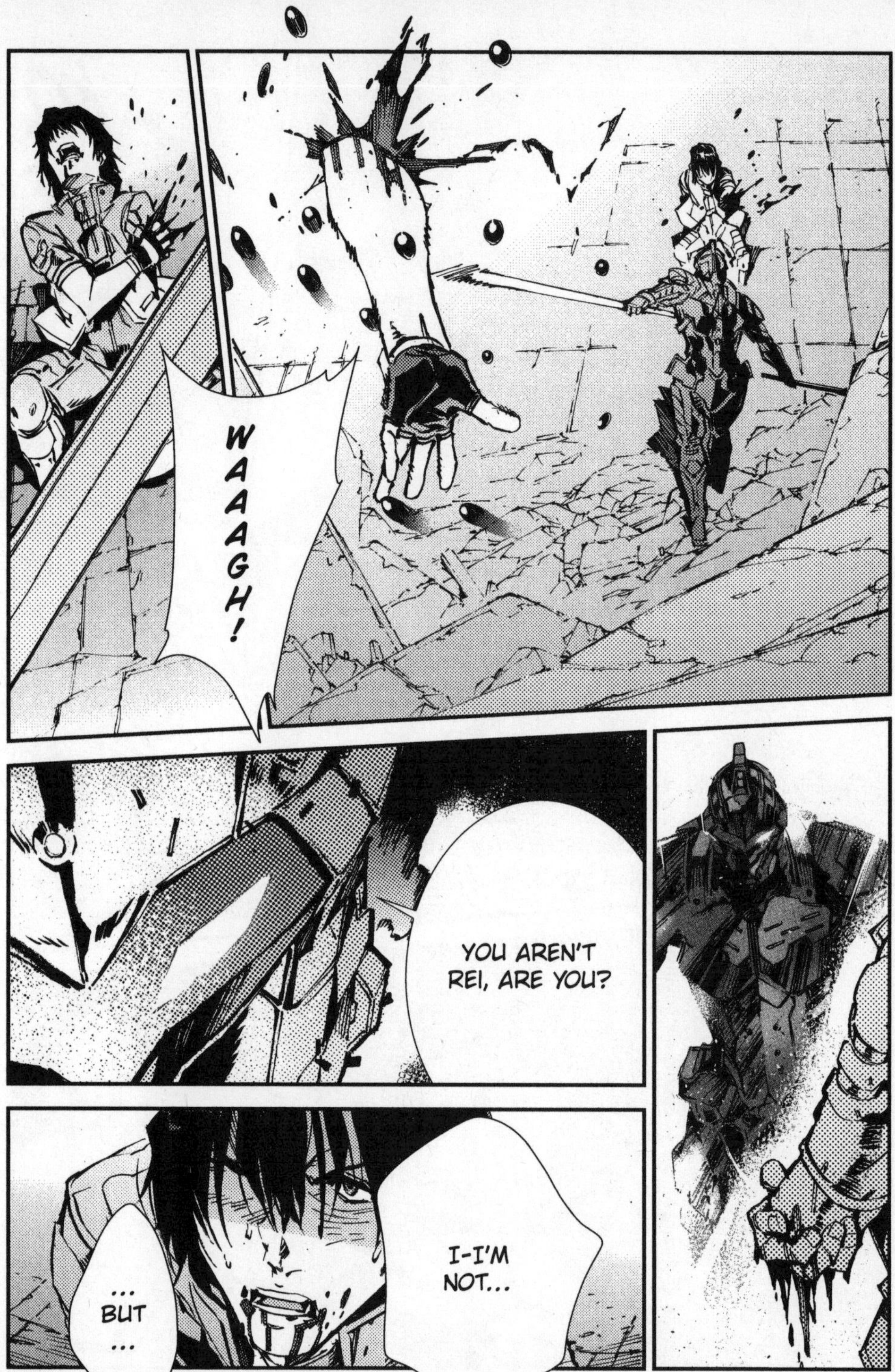
WAAAAGH!
YOU AREN'T REI, ARE YOU?
I-I'M NOT...
... BUT ...

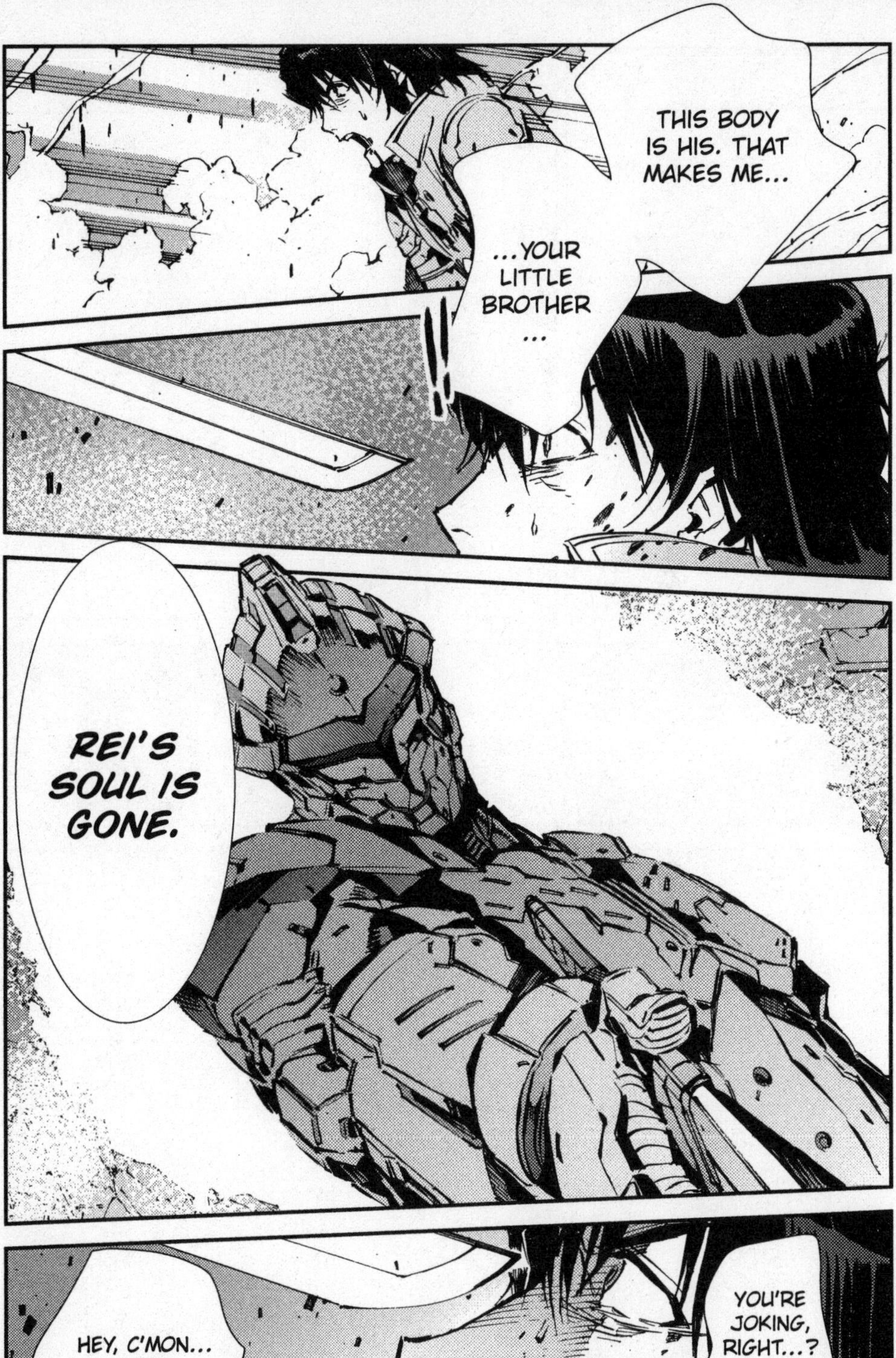
THIS BODY IS HIS. THAT MAKES ME...
...YOUR LITTLE BROTHER ...
!!
REI'S SOUL IS GONE.
YOU'RE JOKING, RIGHT...?
HEY, C'MON... WAIT...

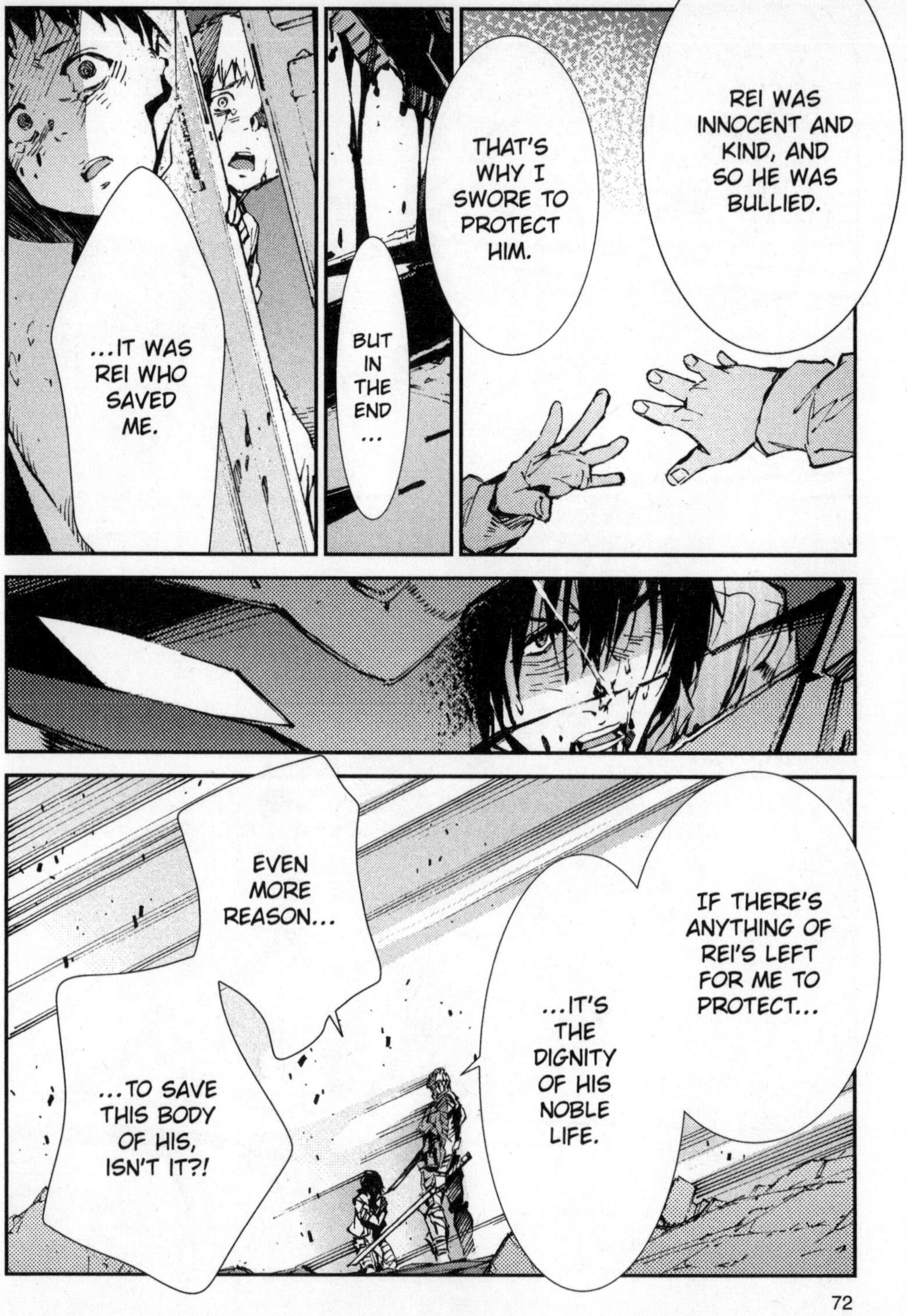
REI WAS INNOCENT AND KIND, AND SO HE WAS BULLIED.
THAT'S WHY I SWORE TO PROTECT HIM.
BUT IN THE END...
...IT WAS REI WHO SAVED ME.
IF THERE'S ANYTHING OF REI'S LEFT FOR ME TO PROTECT...
...IT'S THE DIGNITY OF HIS NOBLE LIFE.
EVEN MORE REASON...
...TO SAVE THIS BODY OF HIS, ISN'T IT?!

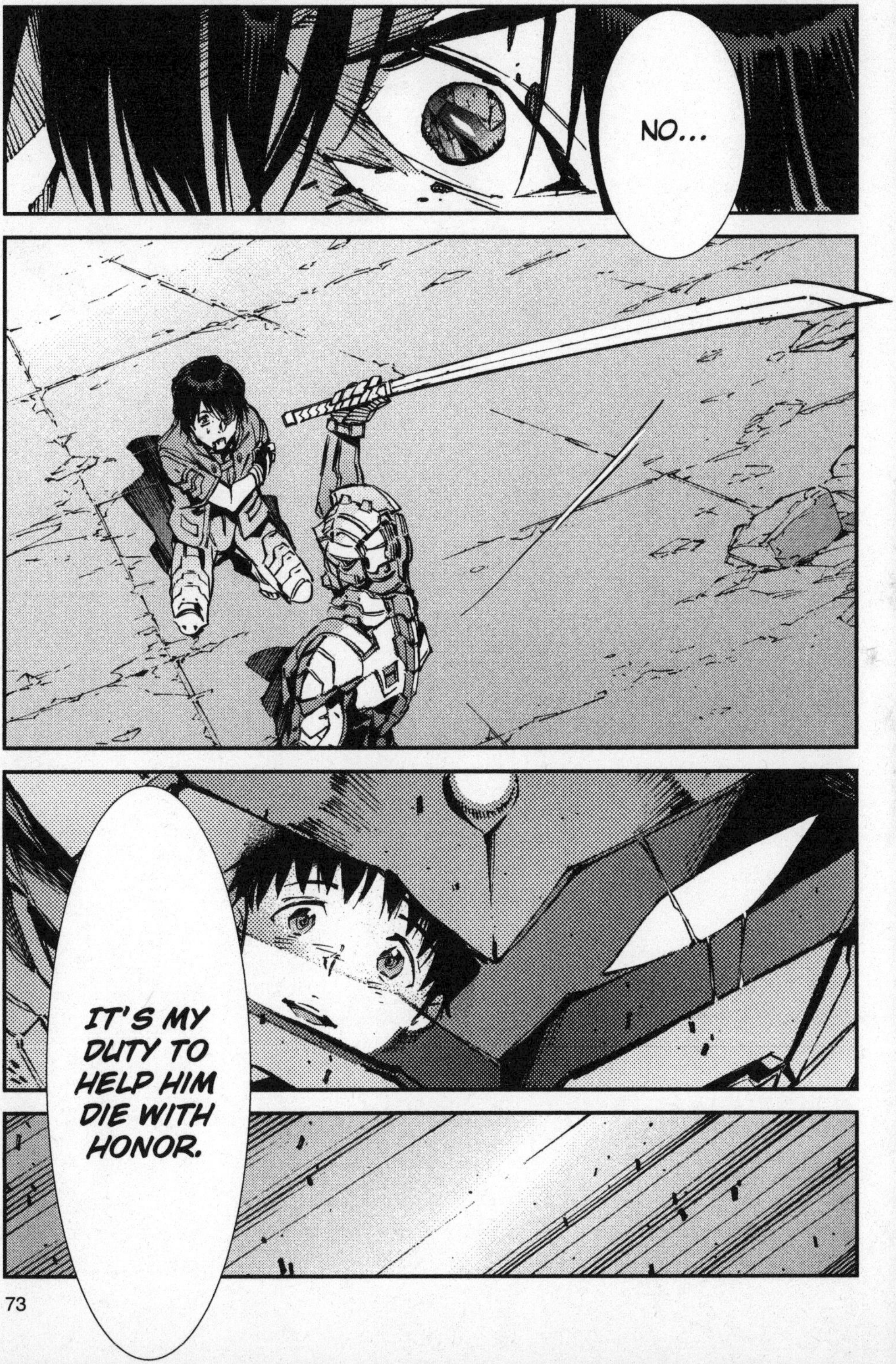
NO...
IT'S MY DUTY TO HELP HIM DIE WITH HONOR.

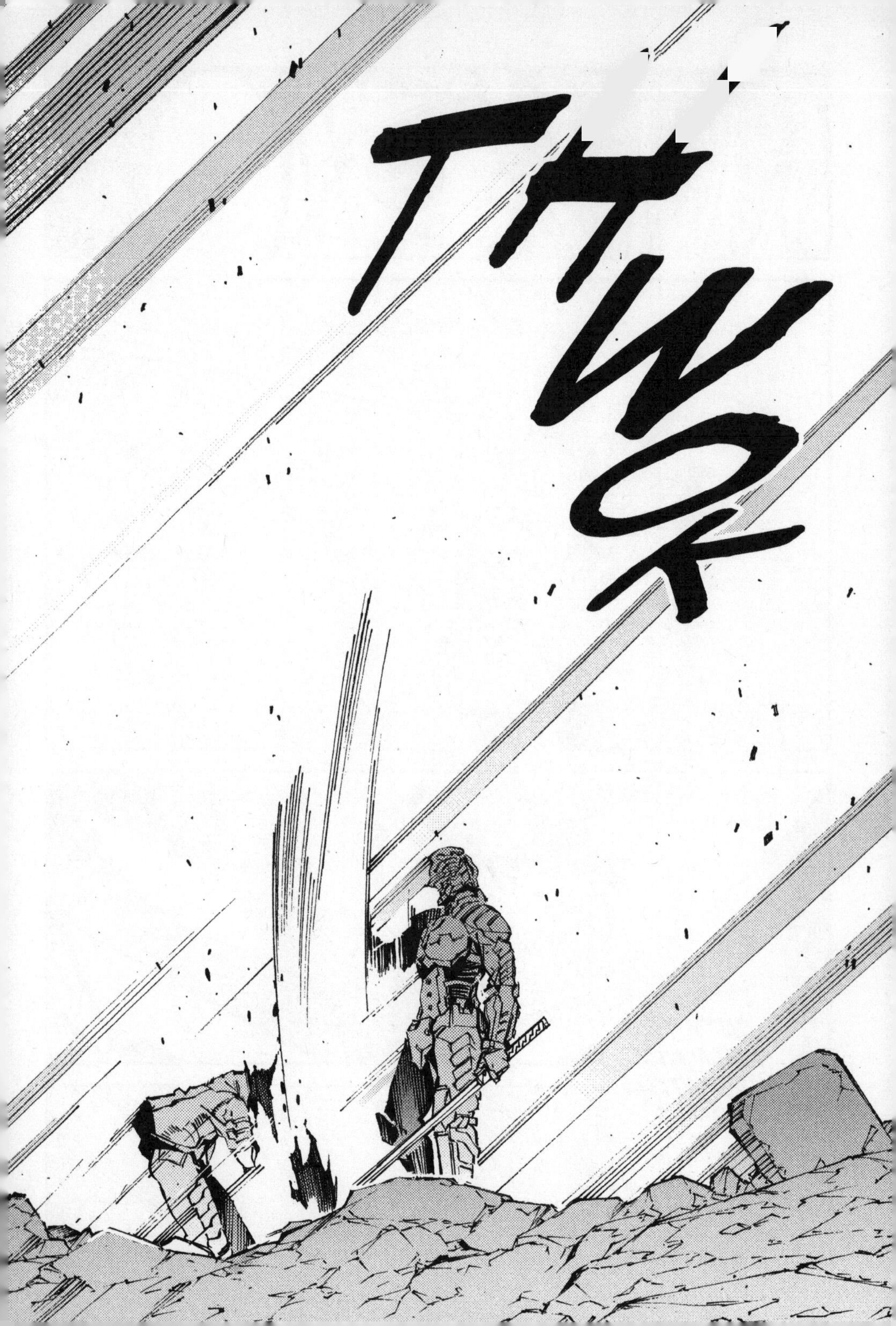
THWOK

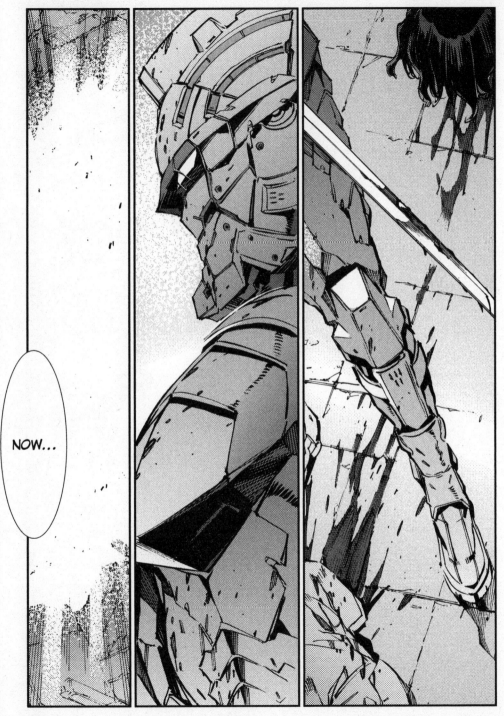

NOW...

75

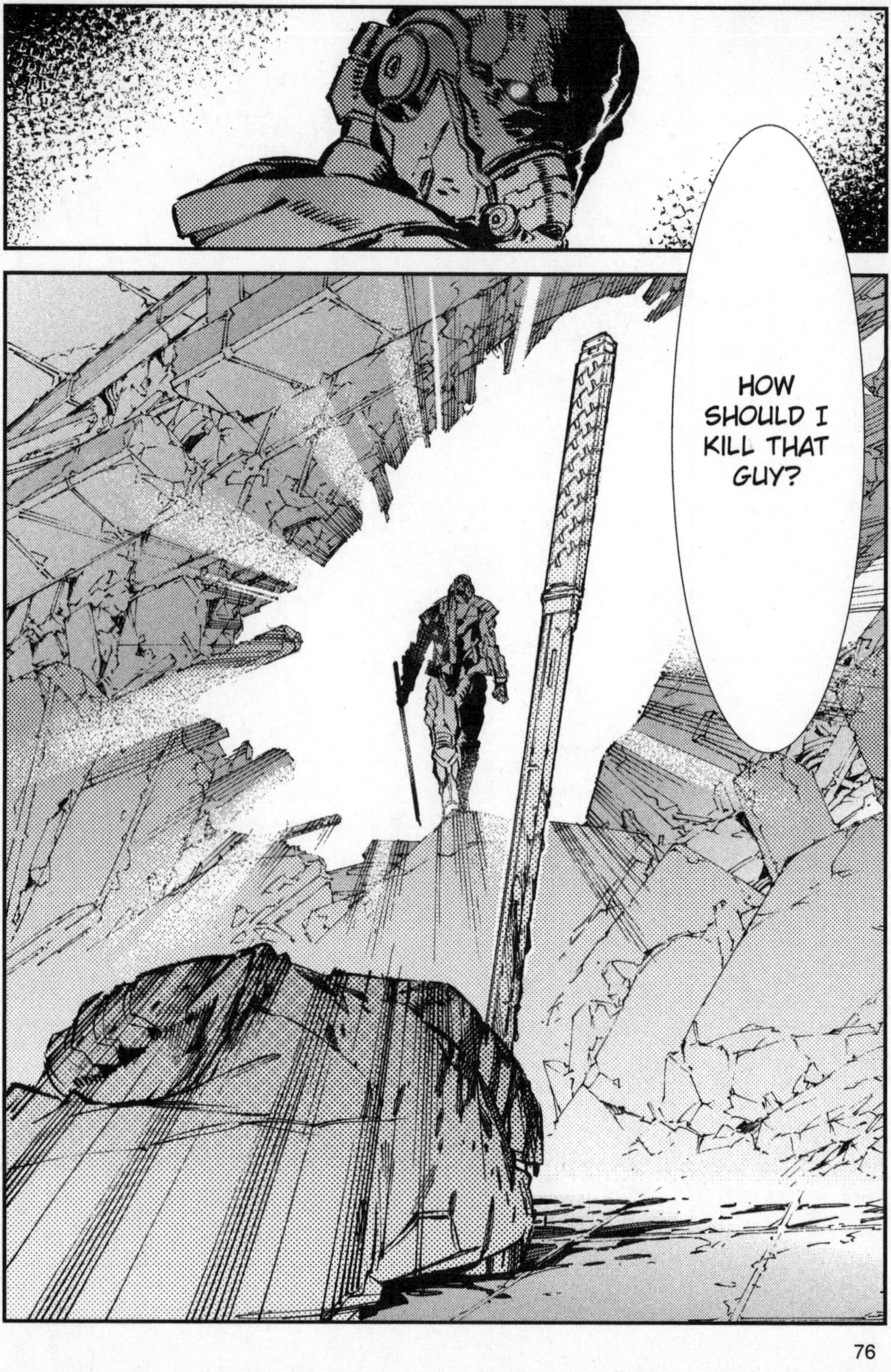
HOW SHOULD I KILL THAT GUY?

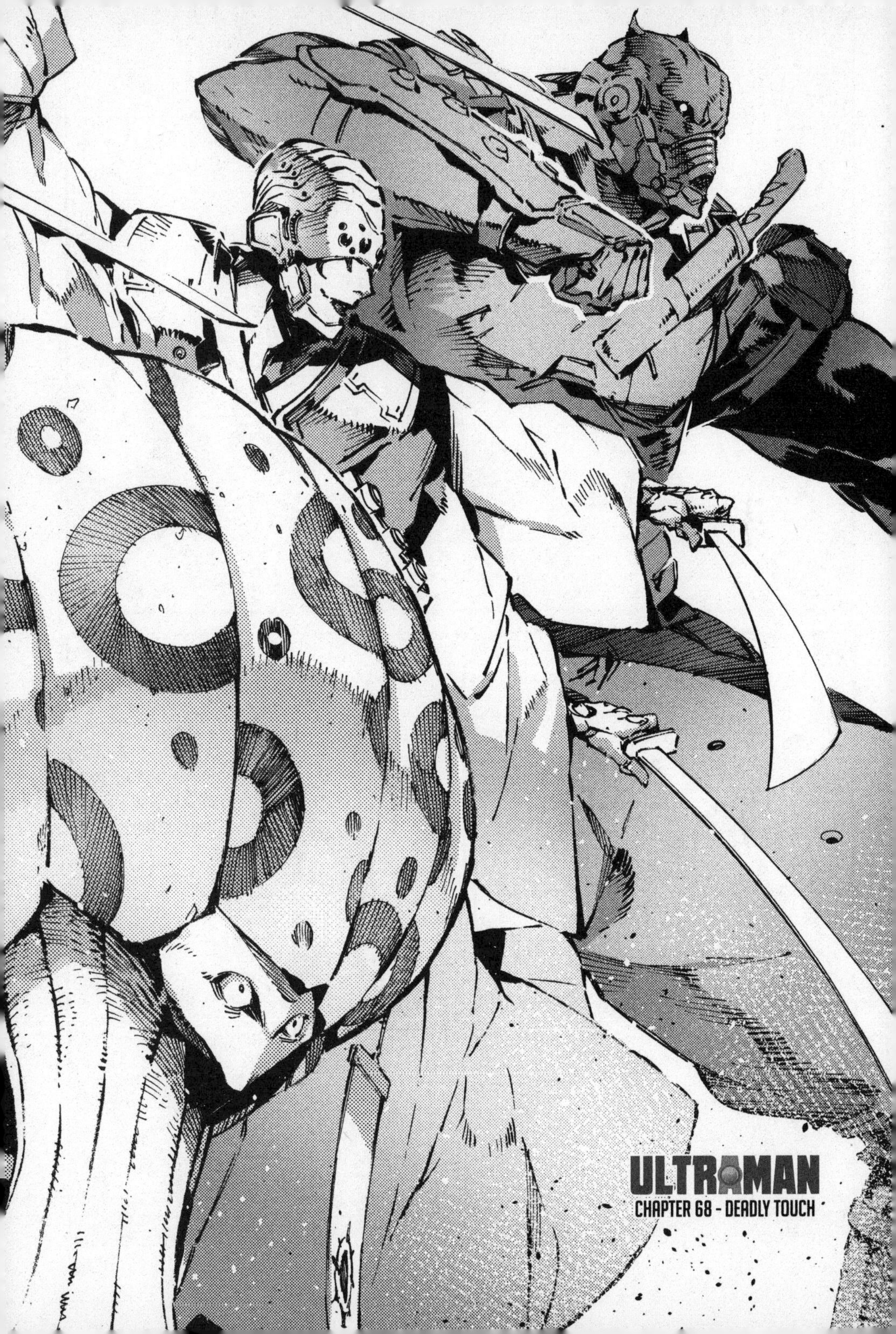
ULTRAMAN
CHAPTER 68 - DEADLY TOUCH

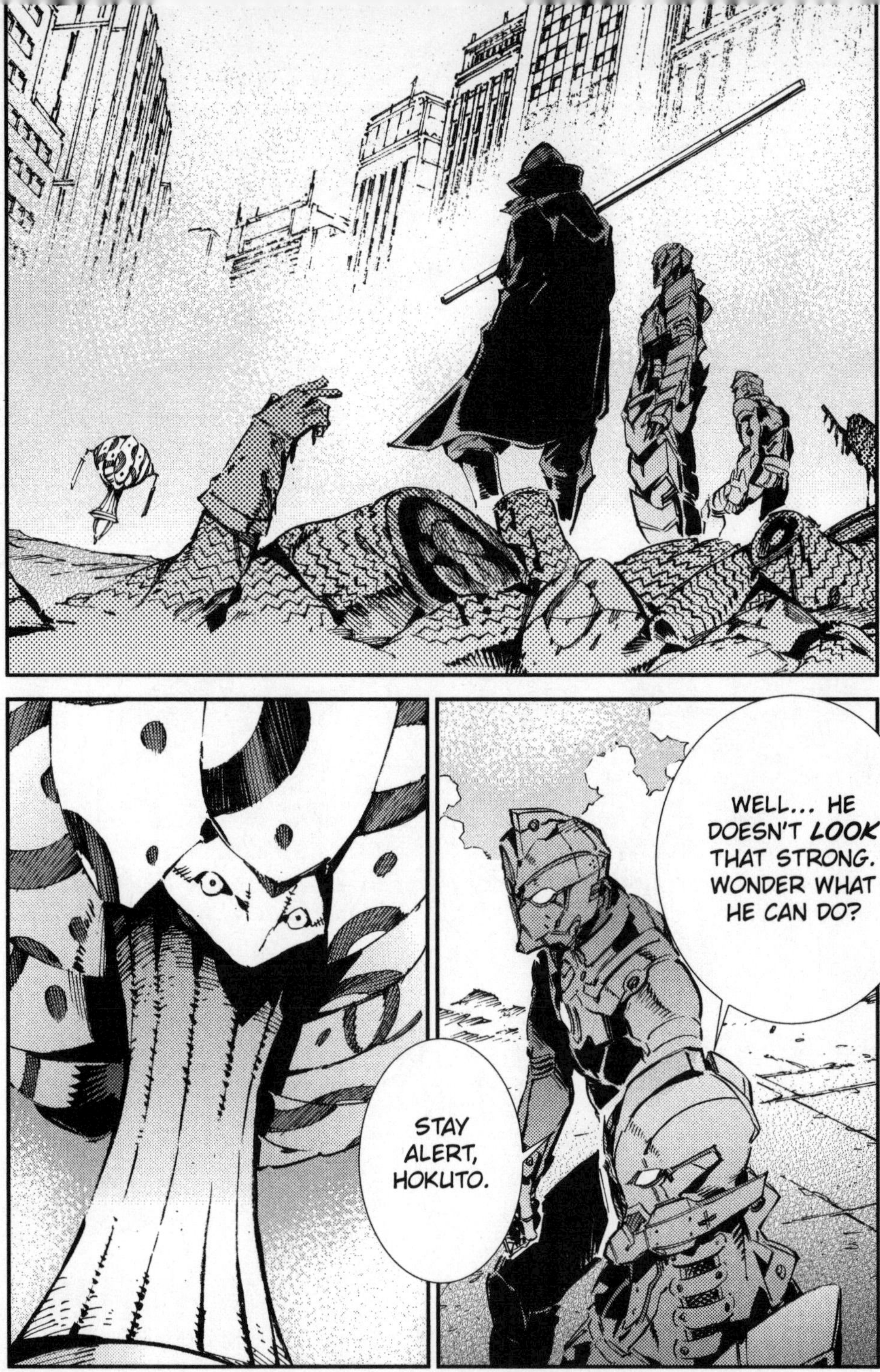
WELL... HE DOESN'T **LOOK** THAT STRONG. WONDER WHAT HE CAN DO?
STAY ALERT, HOKUTO.

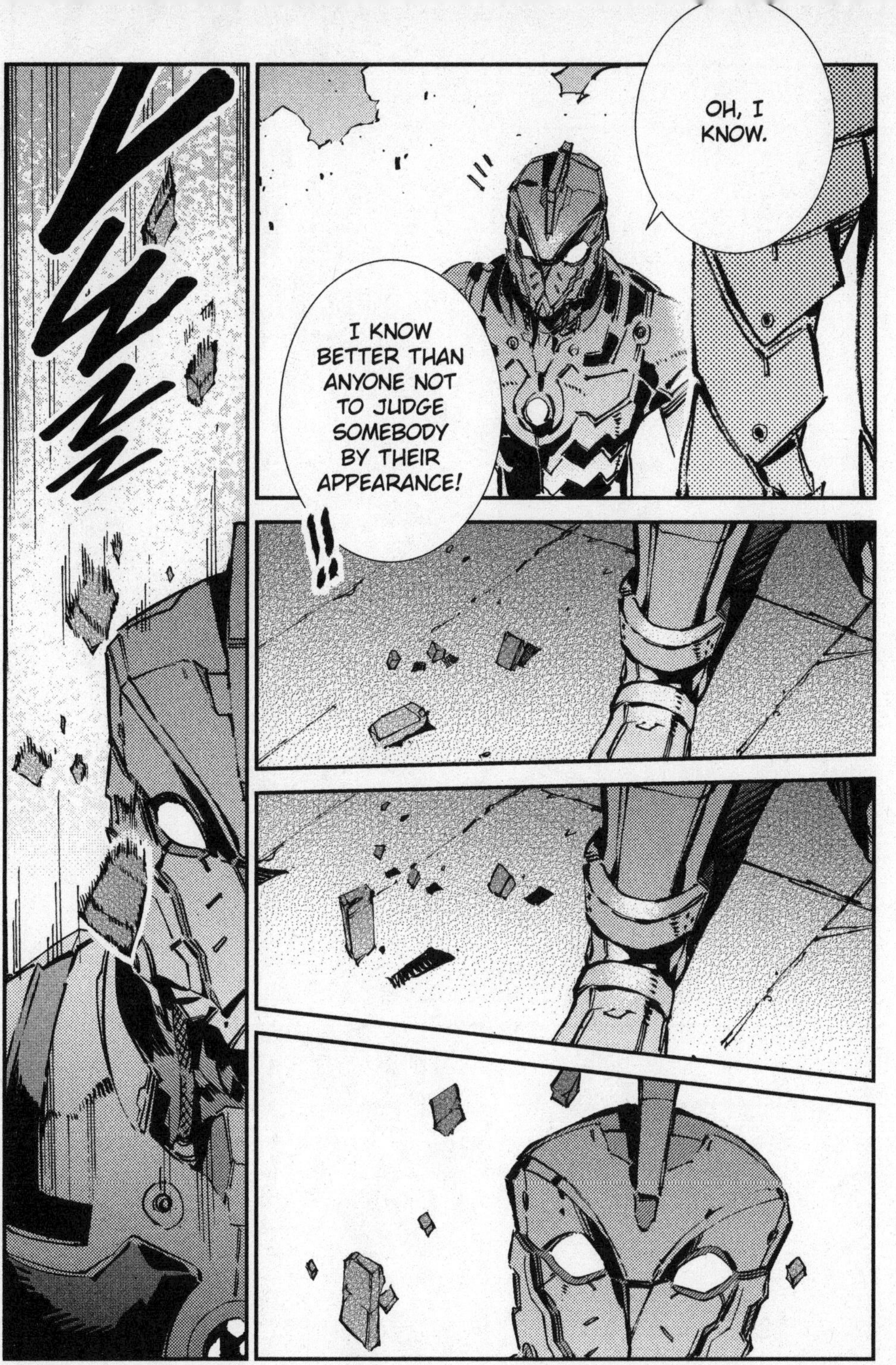
OH, I KNOW.
I KNOW BETTER THAN ANYONE NOT TO JUDGE SOMEBODY BY THEIR APPEARANCE!
VWNN
!!
!!

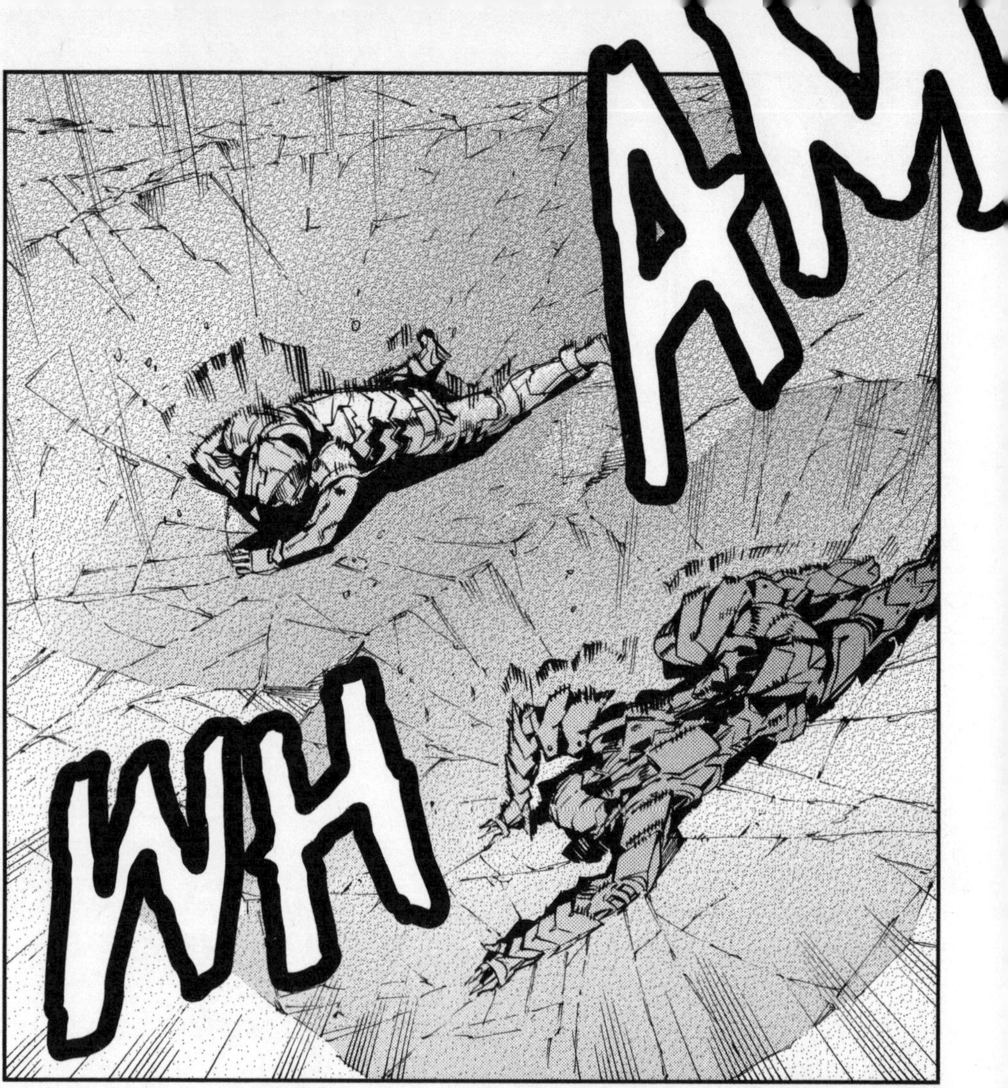
WHAM
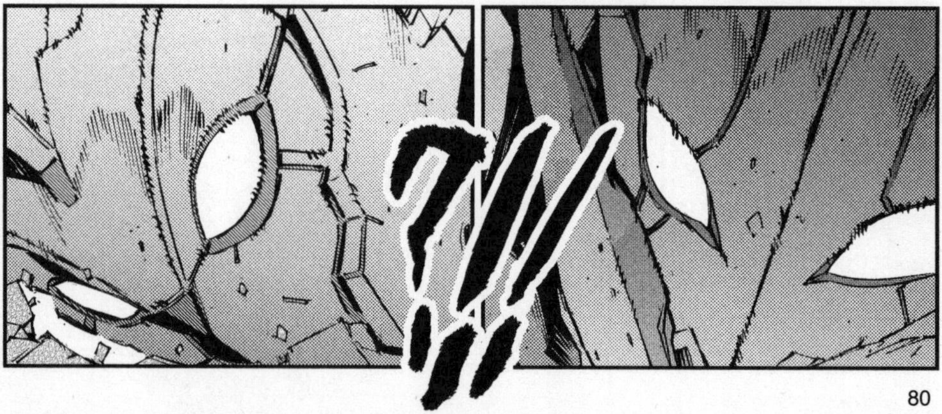
?!!

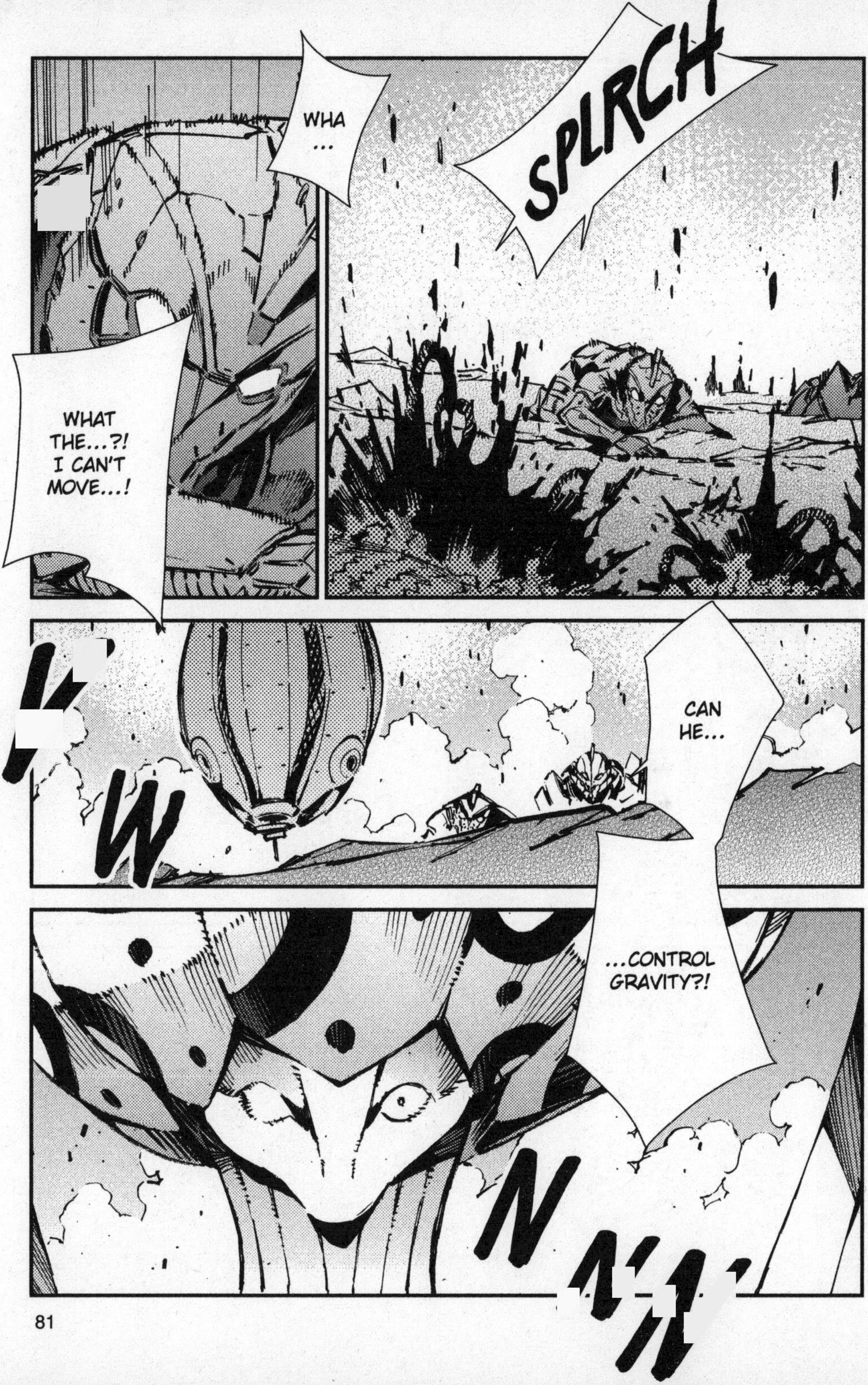
SPLRCH
WHA ...
WHAT THE...?! I CAN'T MOVE...!
CAN HE...
...CONTROL GRAVITY?!

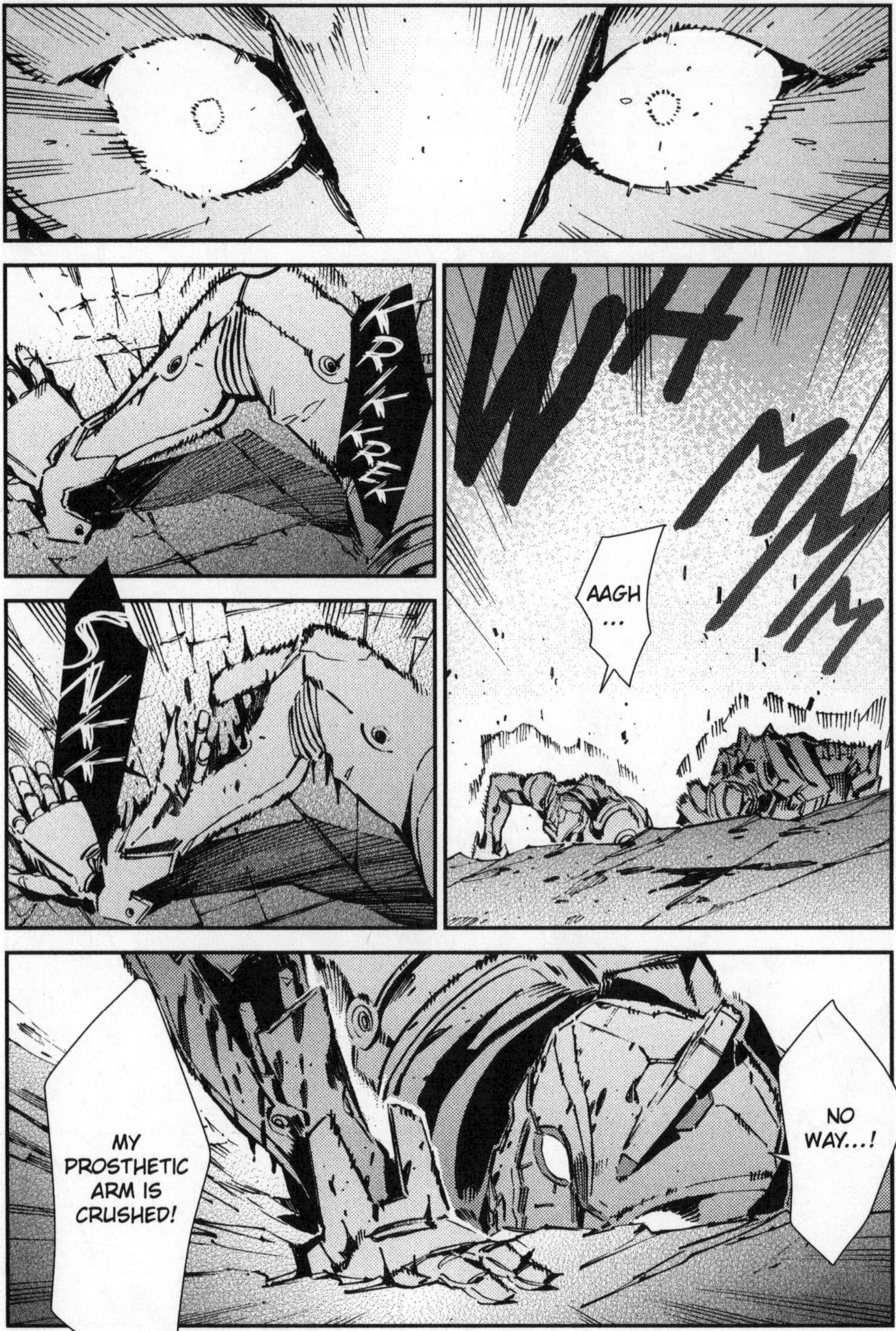
WHMMMM
AAGH ...
KRIK KREK
NO WAY...!
MY PROSTHETIC ARM IS CRUSHED!

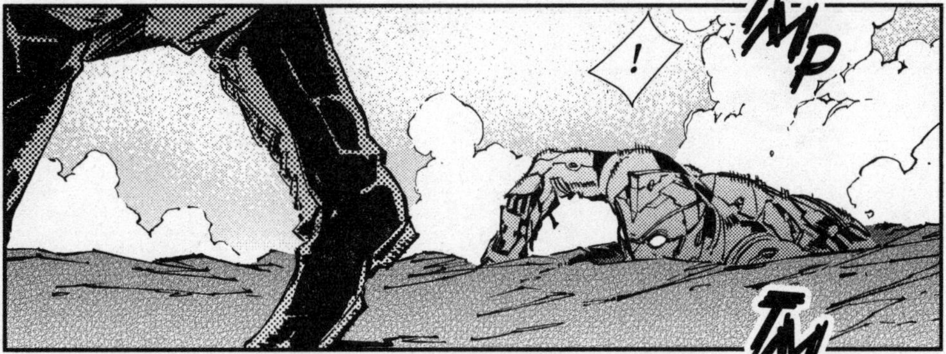
TMP
!
TMP
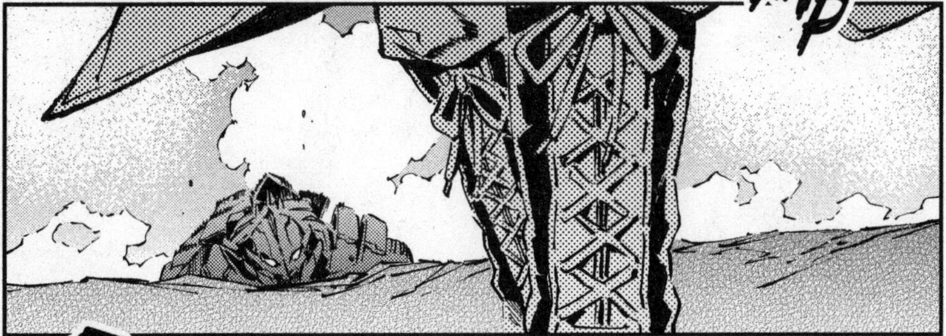
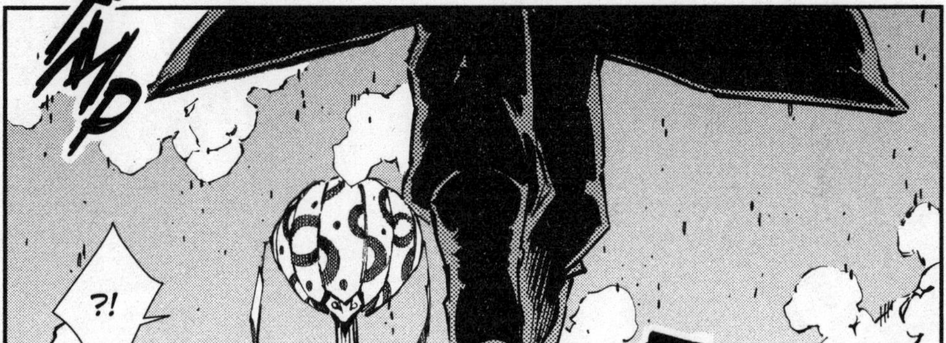
TMP
?!
TMP
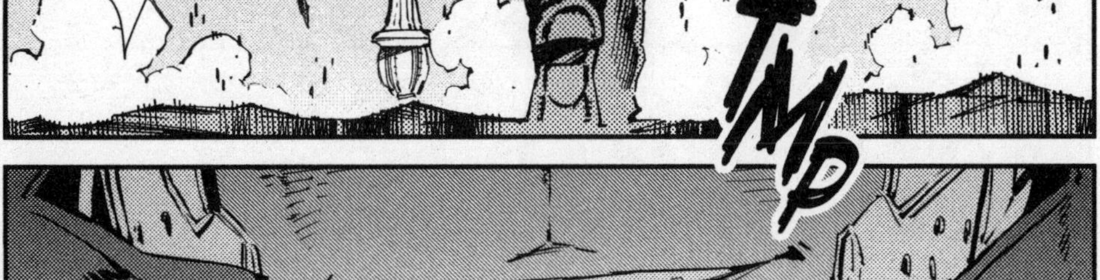

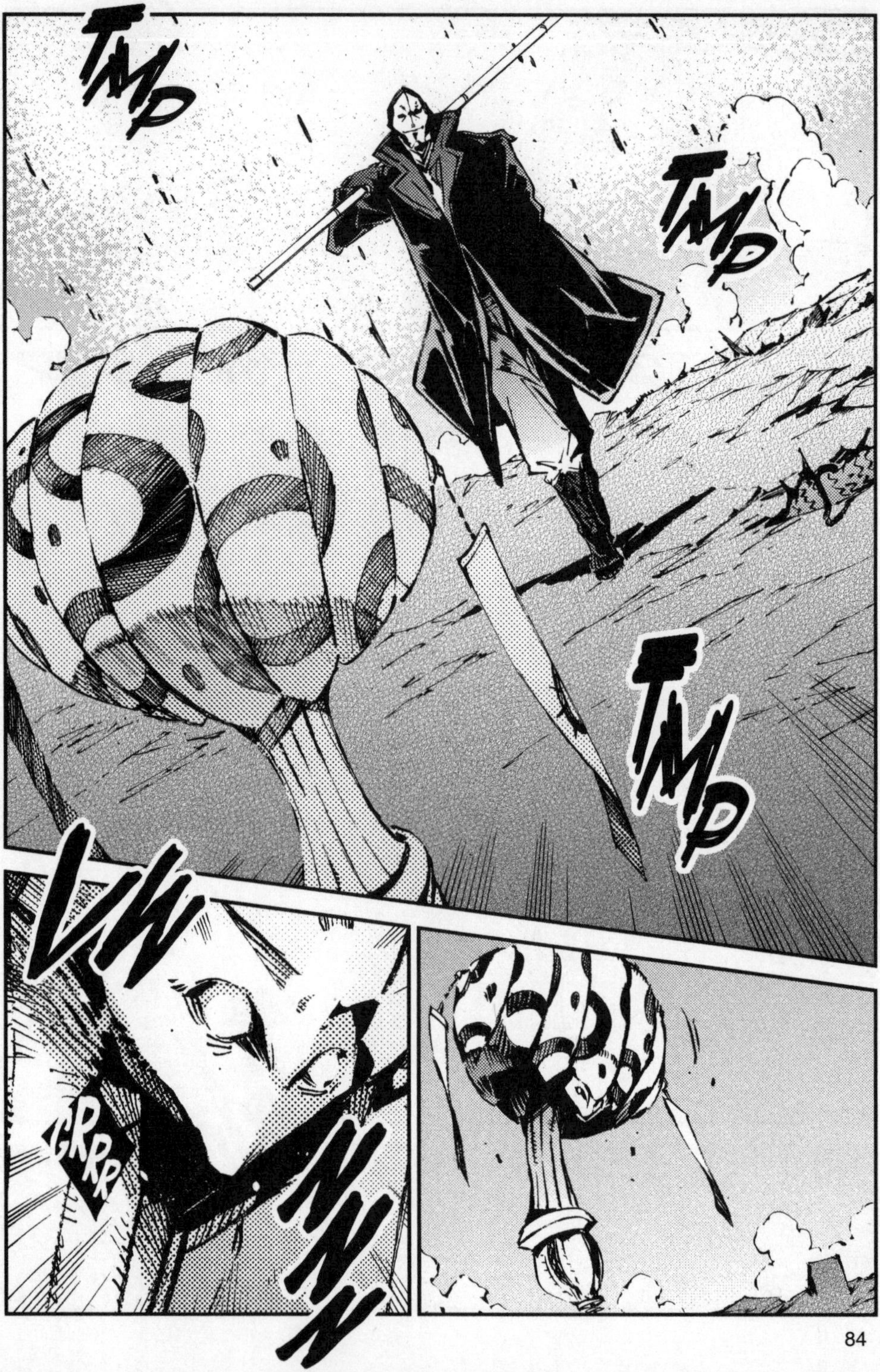
TMP
TMP
TMP
VWNNNN
GRRR

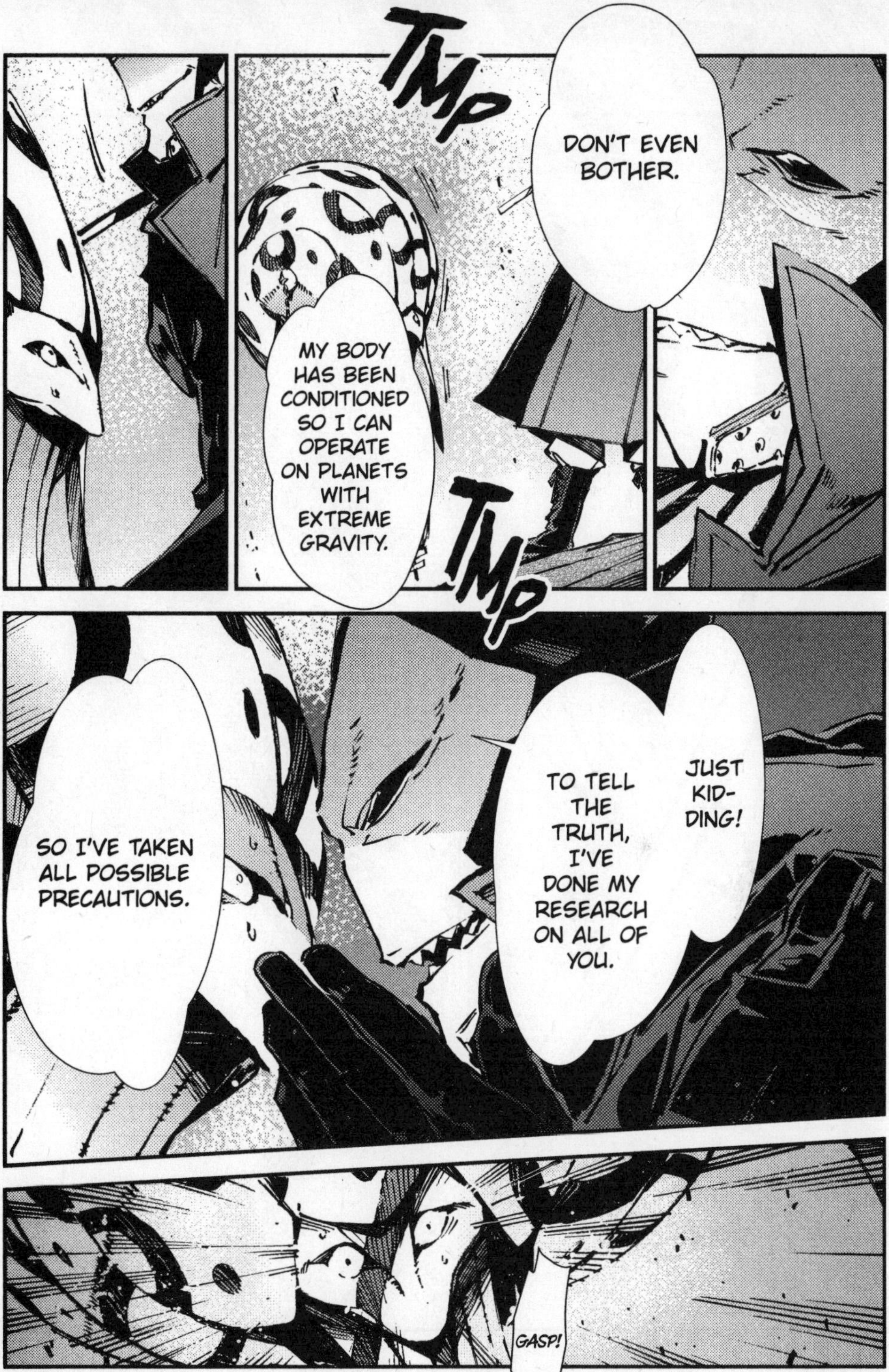
TMP
DON'T EVEN BOTHER.
MY BODY HAS BEEN CONDITIONED SO I CAN OPERATE ON PLANETS WITH EXTREME GRAVITY.
TMP
JUST KID-DING!
TO TELL THE TRUTH, I'VE DONE MY RESEARCH ON ALL OF YOU.
SO I'VE TAKEN ALL POSSIBLE PRECAUTIONS.
GASP!

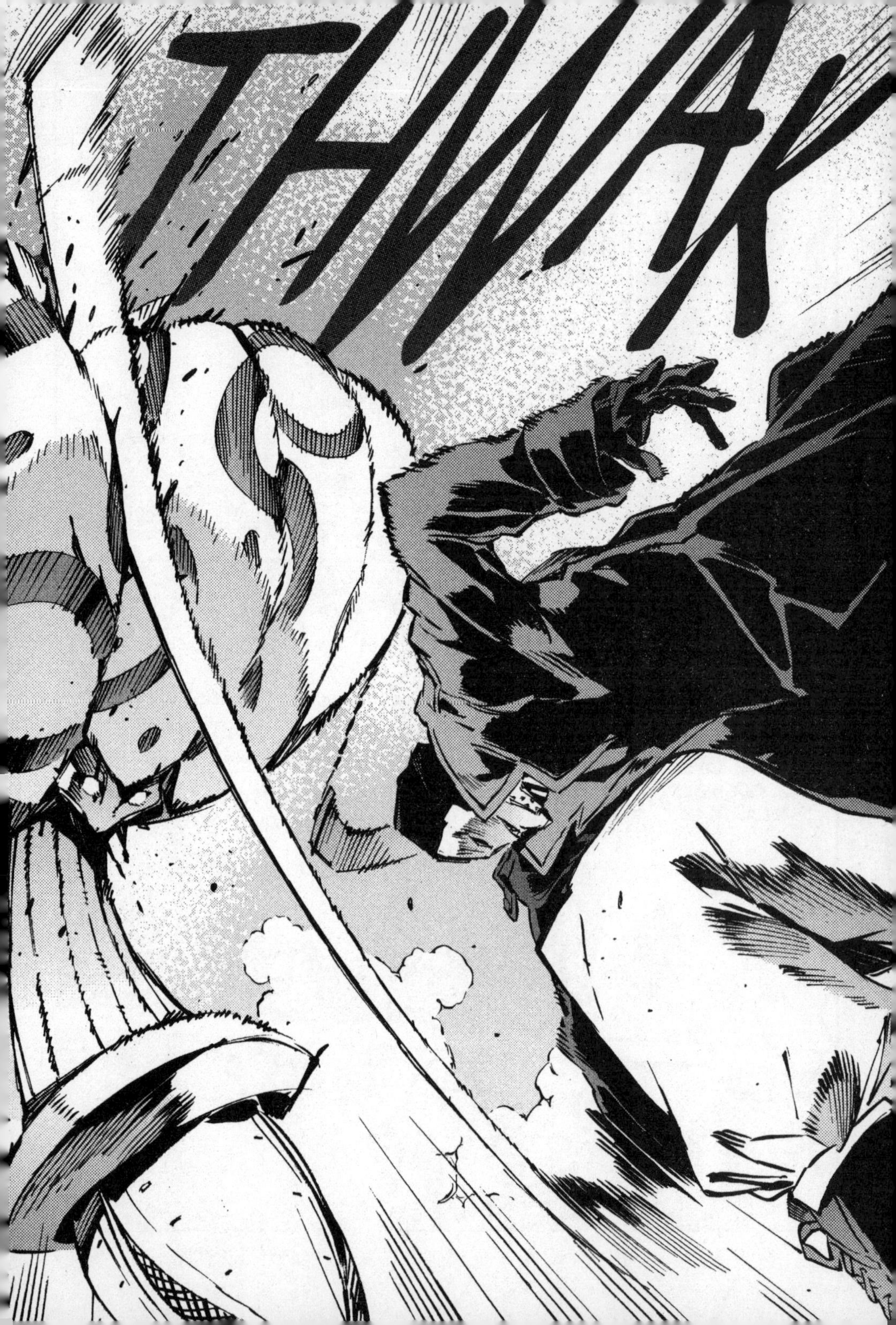
THWAK

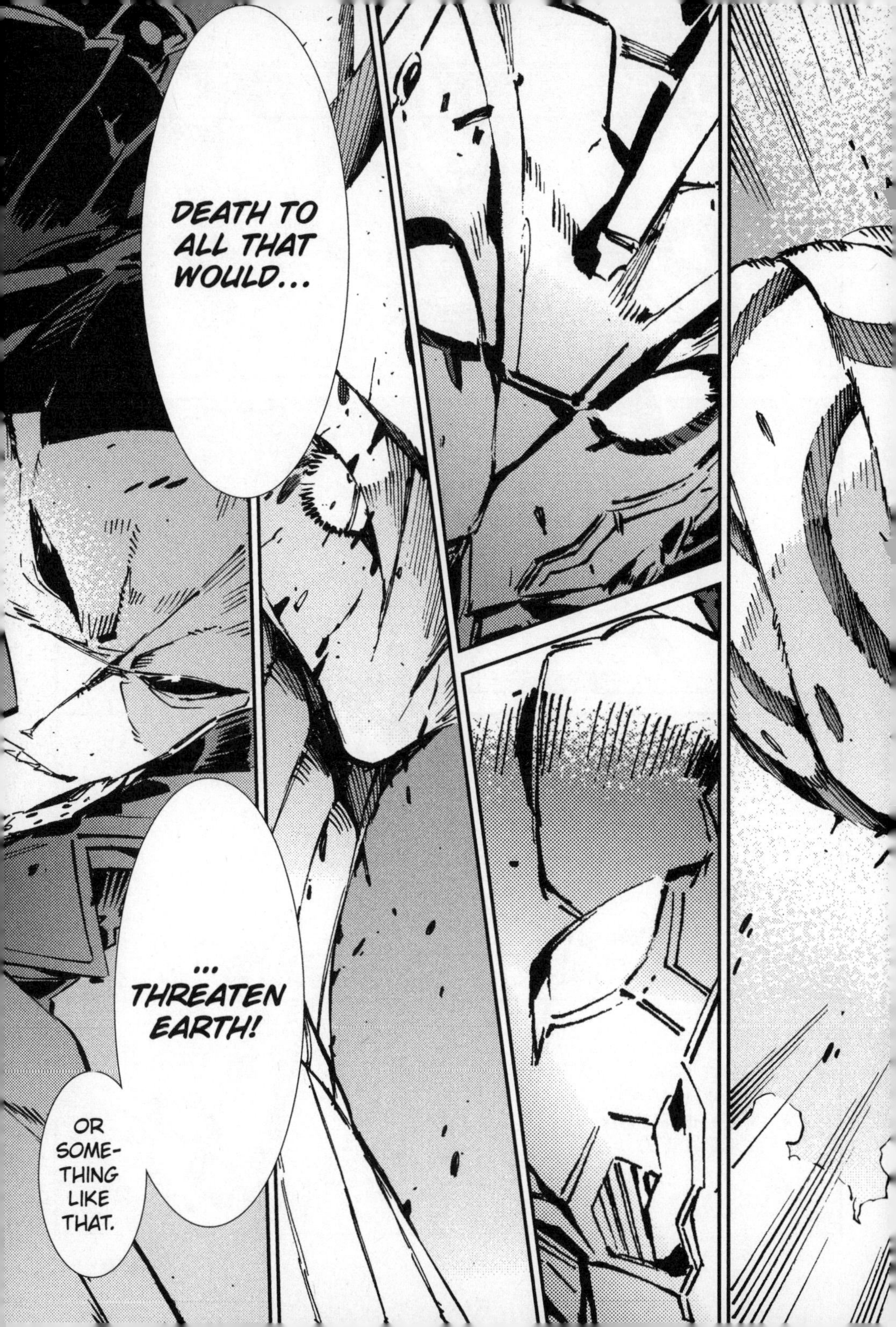
DEATH TO ALL THAT WOULD...
... THREATEN EARTH!
OR SOME-THING LIKE THAT.

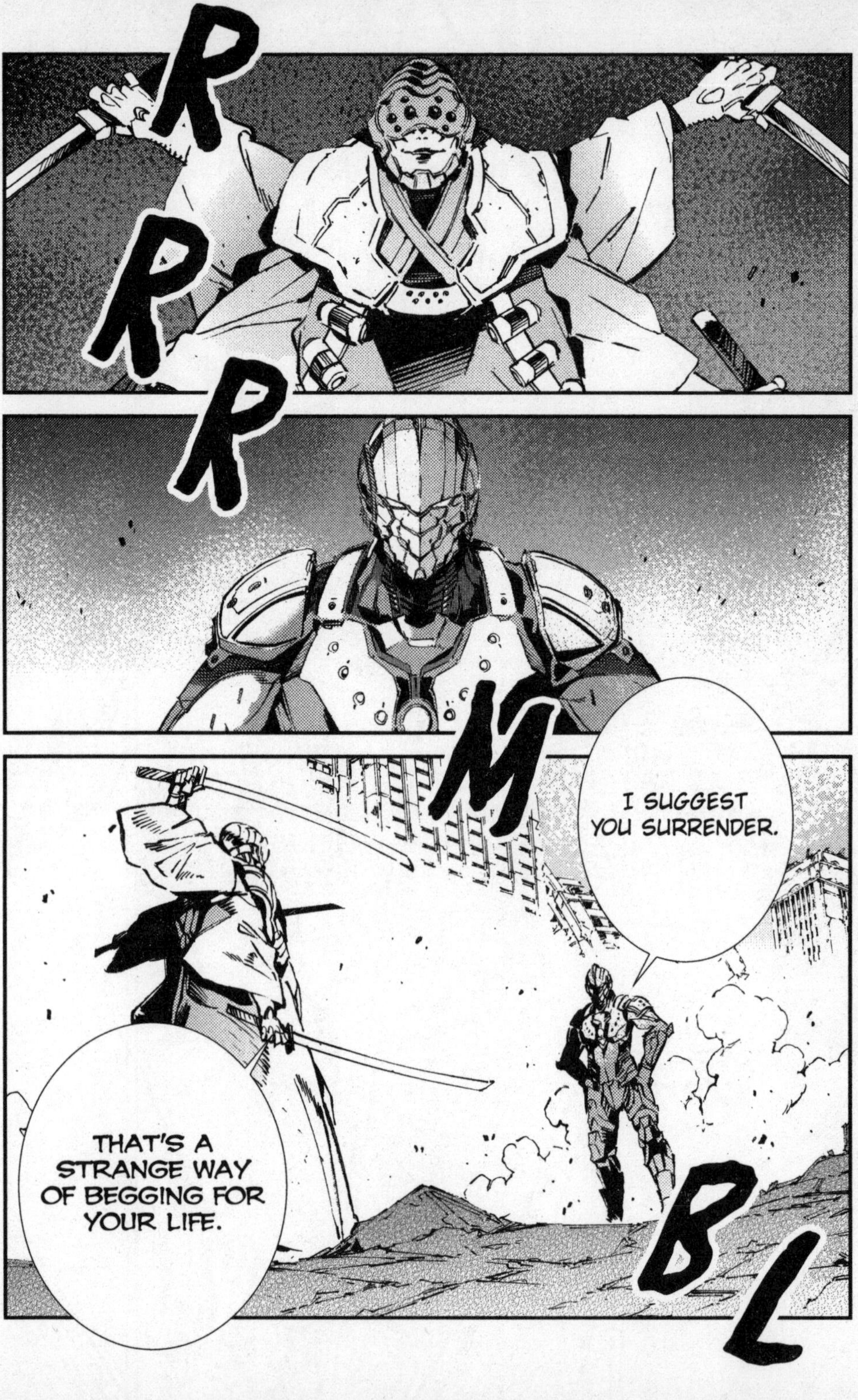
RRR
M
I SUGGEST YOU SURRENDER.
THAT'S A STRANGE WAY OF BEGGING FOR YOUR LIFE.
BL

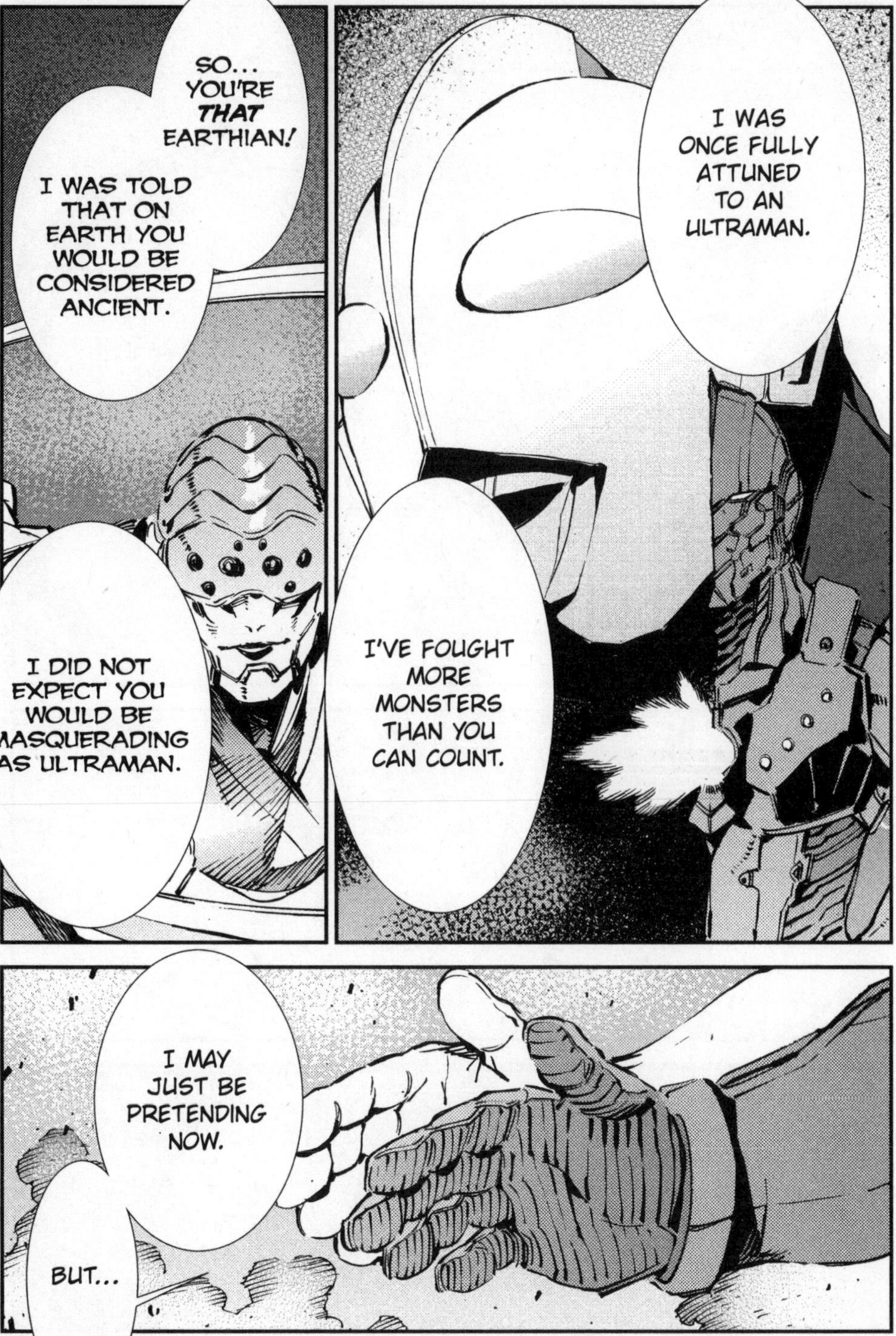
SO... YOU'RE *THAT* EARTHIAN!
I WAS TOLD THAT ON EARTH YOU WOULD BE CONSIDERED ANCIENT.
I DID NOT EXPECT YOU WOULD BE MASQUERADING AS ULTRAMAN.
I WAS ONCE FULLY ATTUNED TO AN ULTRAMAN.
I'VE FOUGHT MORE MONSTERS THAN YOU CAN COUNT.
I MAY JUST BE PRETENDING NOW.
BUT...

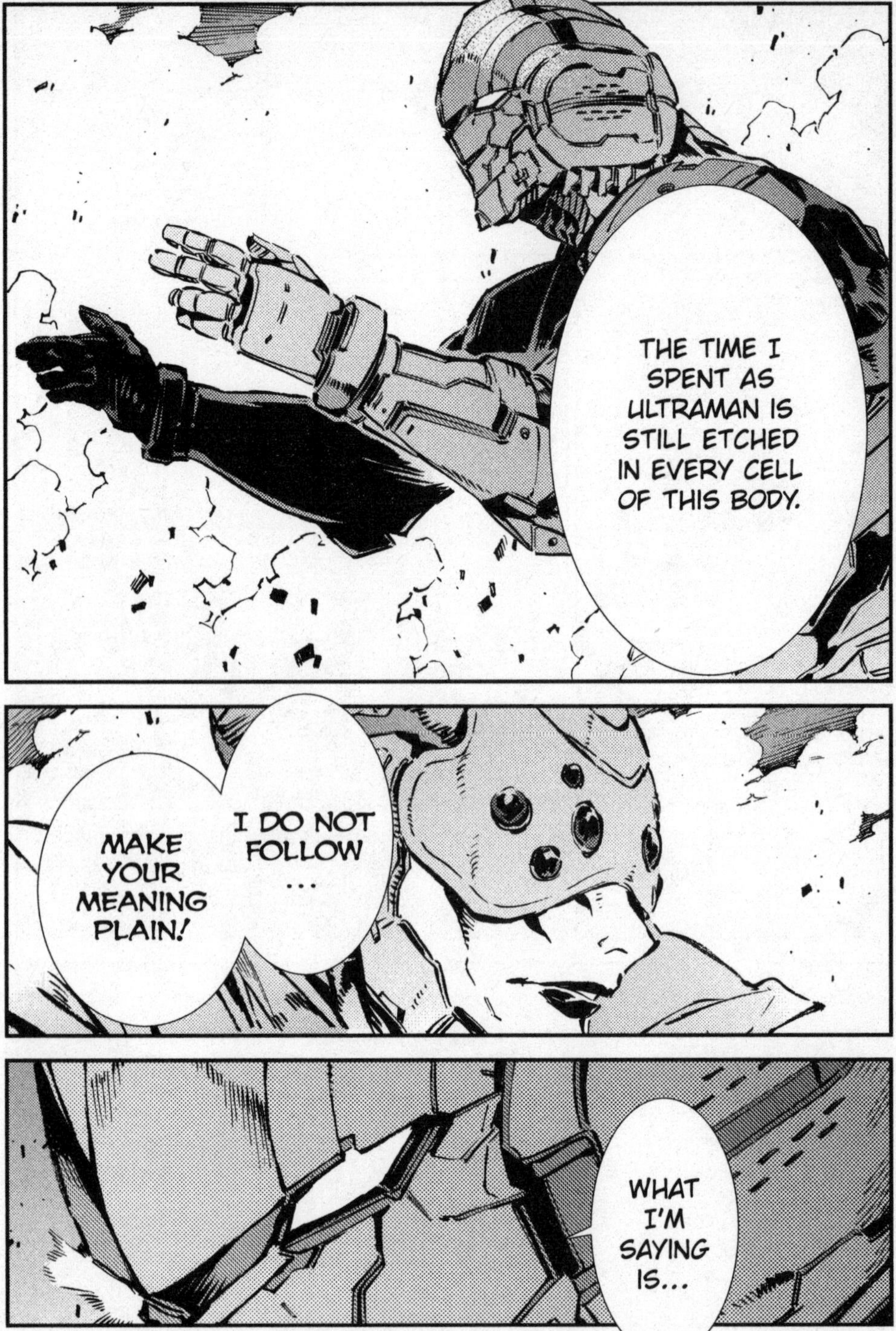
THE TIME I SPENT AS ULTRAMAN IS STILL ETCHED IN EVERY CELL OF THIS BODY.
I DO NOT FOLLOW...
MAKE YOUR MEANING PLAIN!
WHAT I'M SAYING IS...

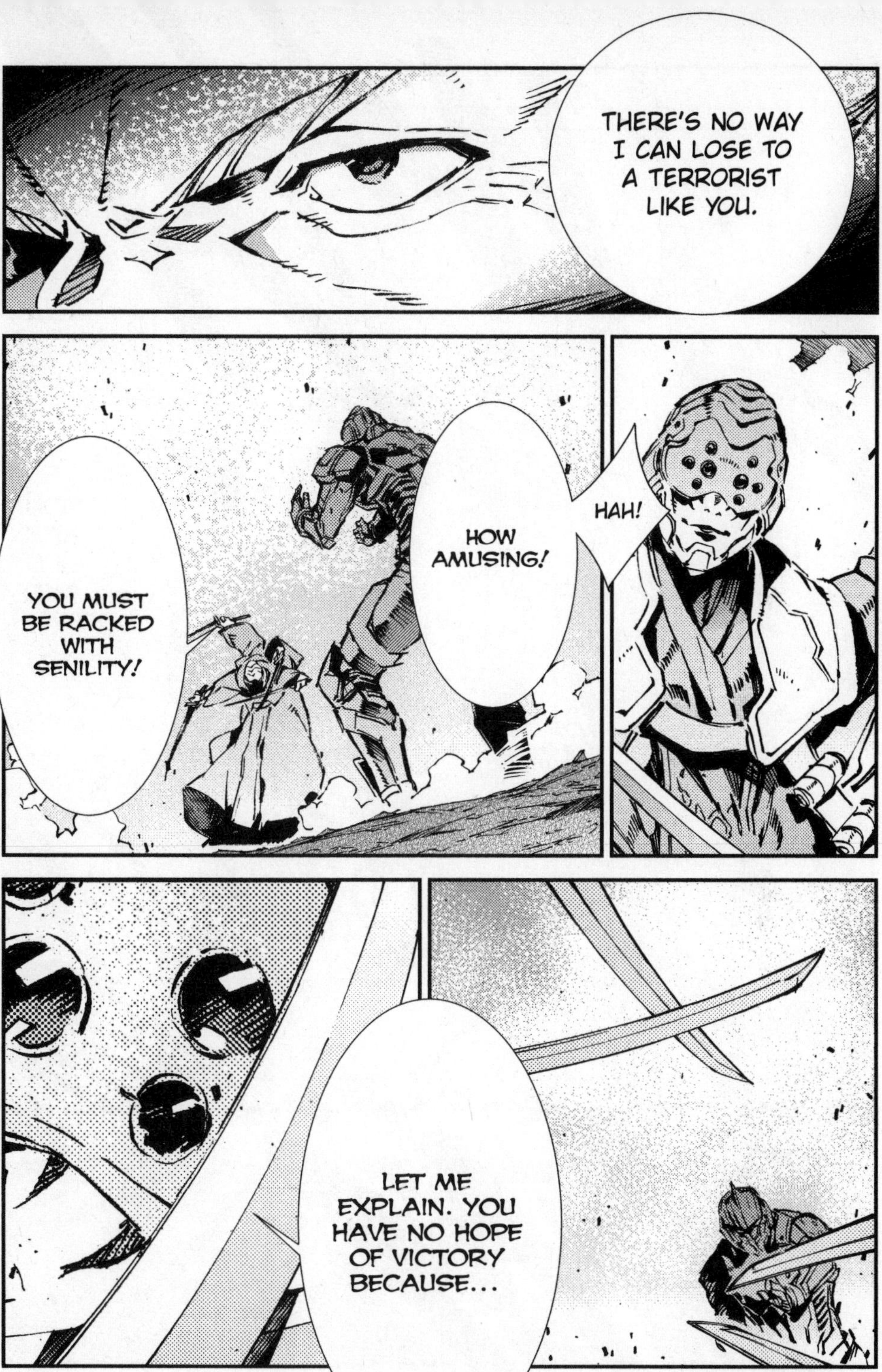
THERE'S NO WAY I CAN LOSE TO A TERRORIST LIKE YOU.
HAH!
HOW AMUSING!
YOU MUST BE RACKED WITH SENILITY!
LET ME EXPLAIN. YOU HAVE NO HOPE OF VICTORY BECAUSE...

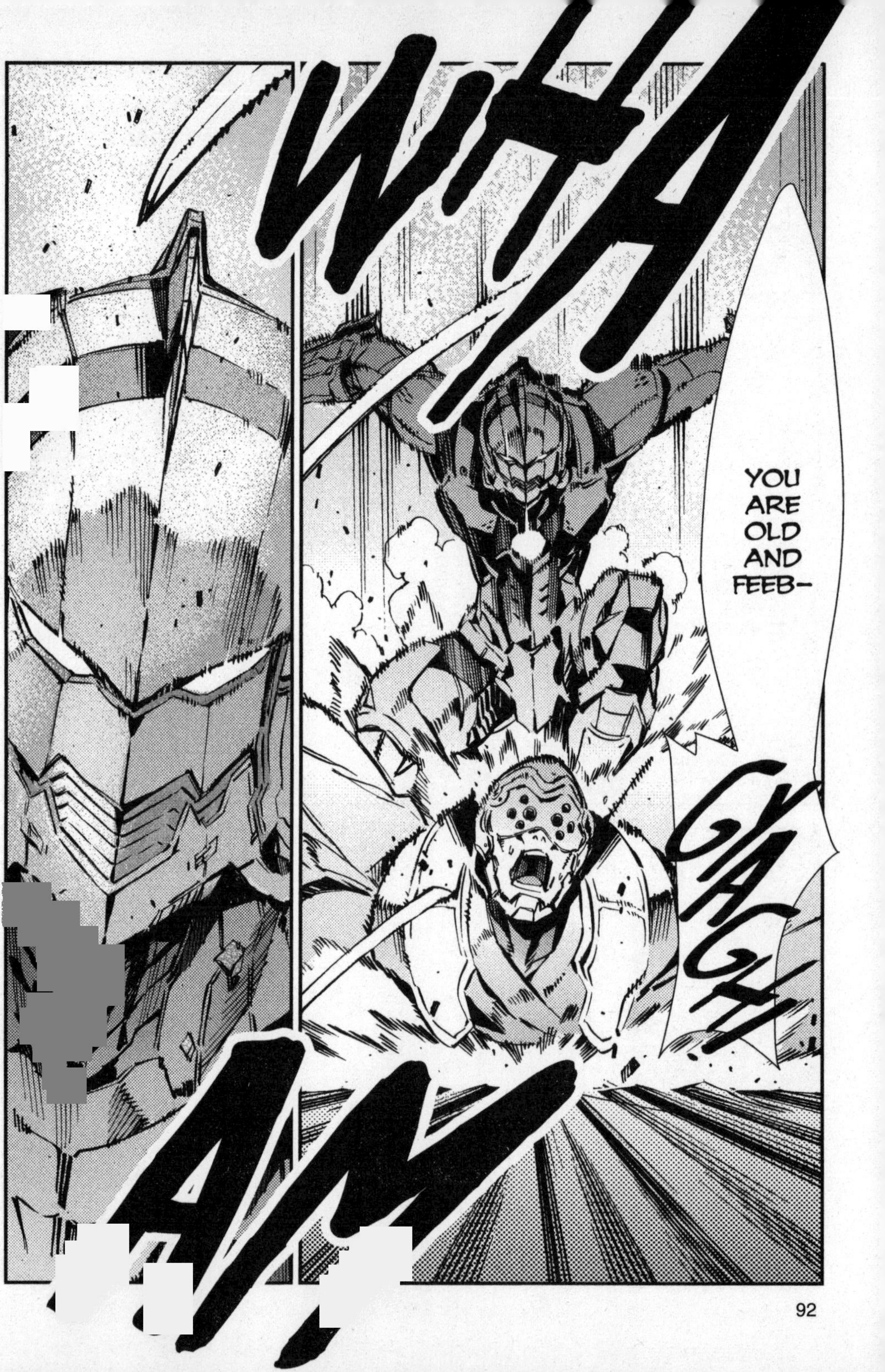
YOU ARE OLD AND FEEB–
GYAGH!!

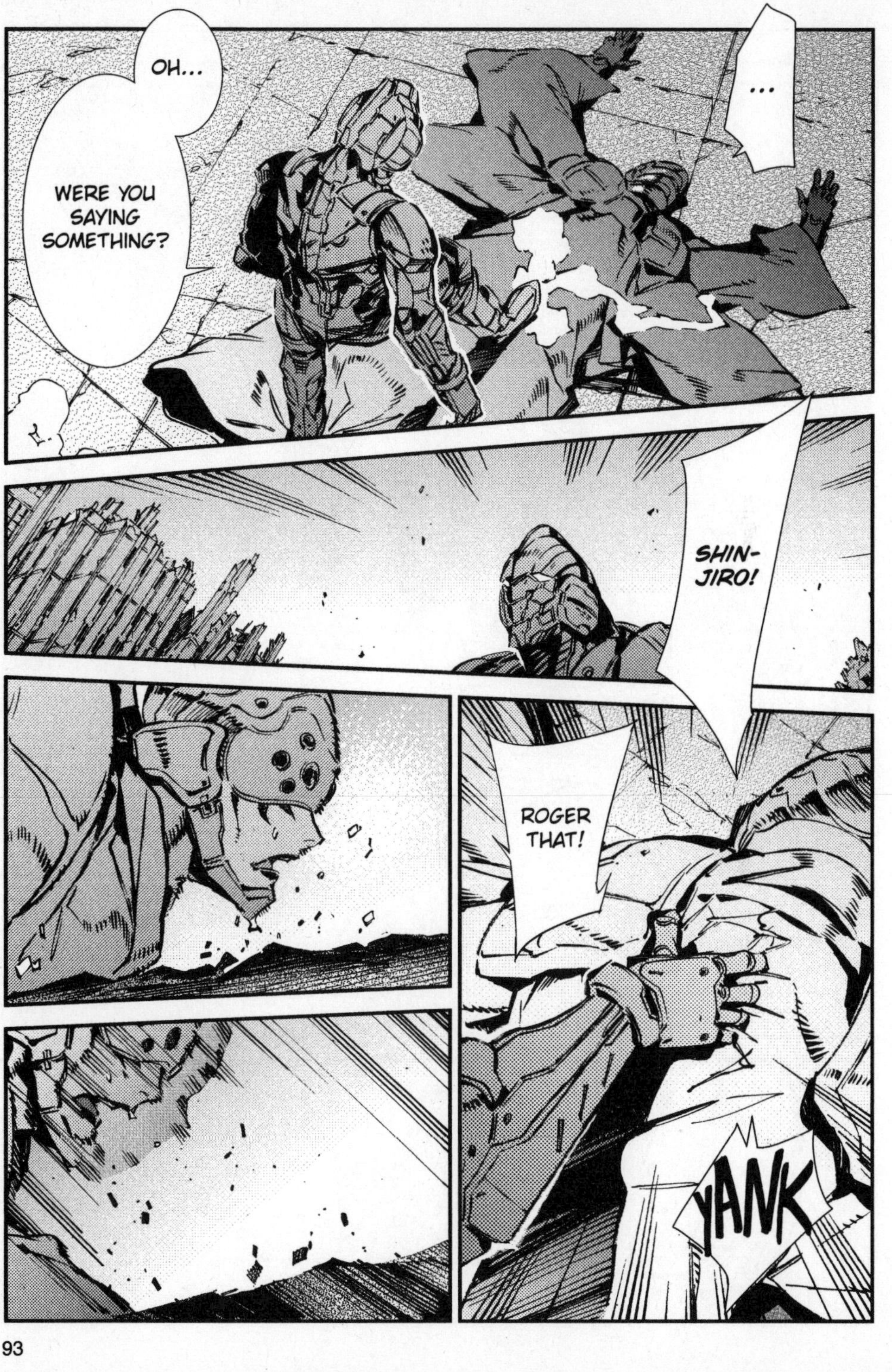
...
OH...
WERE YOU SAYING SOMETHING?
SHIN-JIRO!
ROGER THAT!
YANK

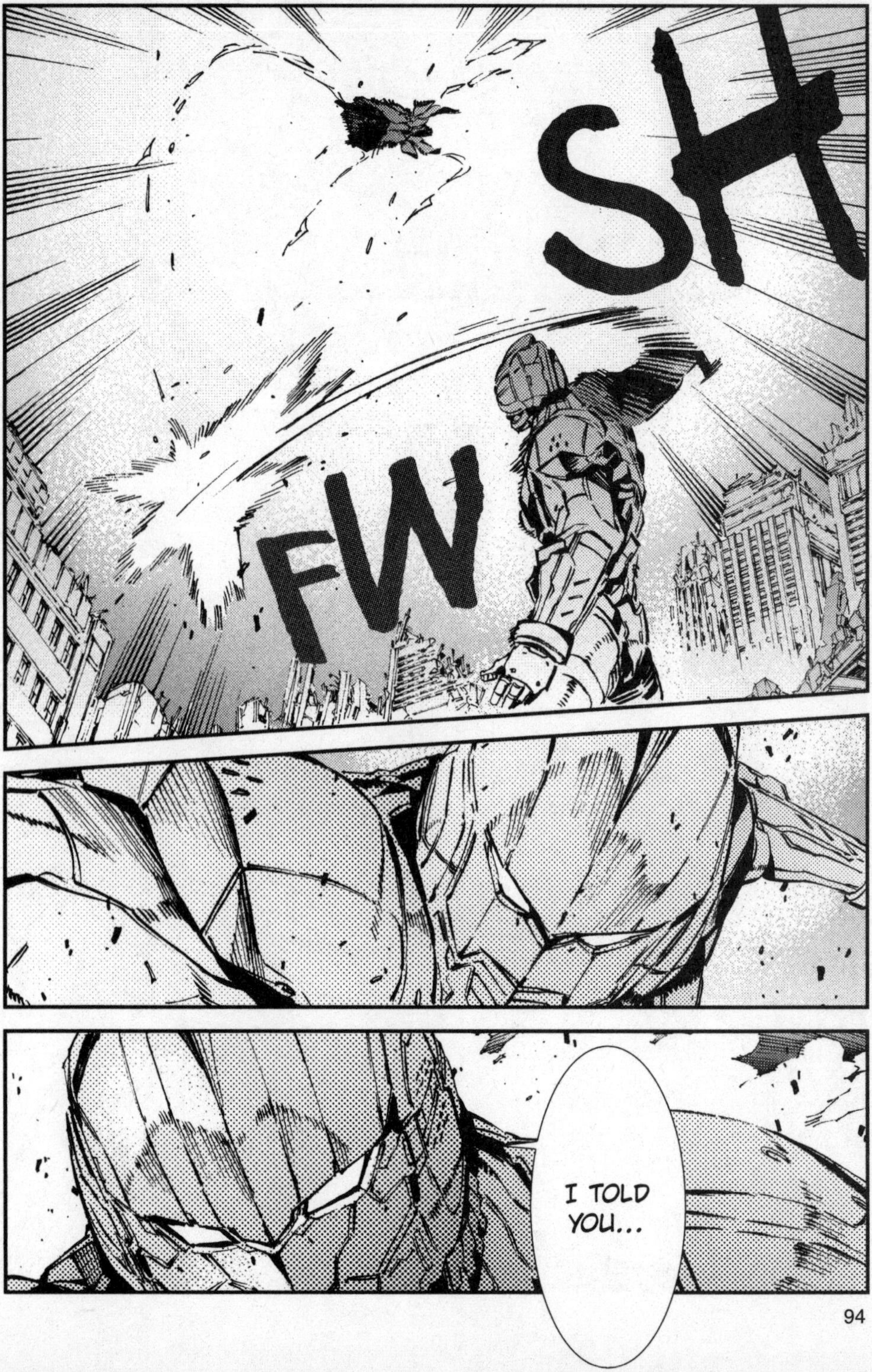
SH
FW
I TOLD YOU...

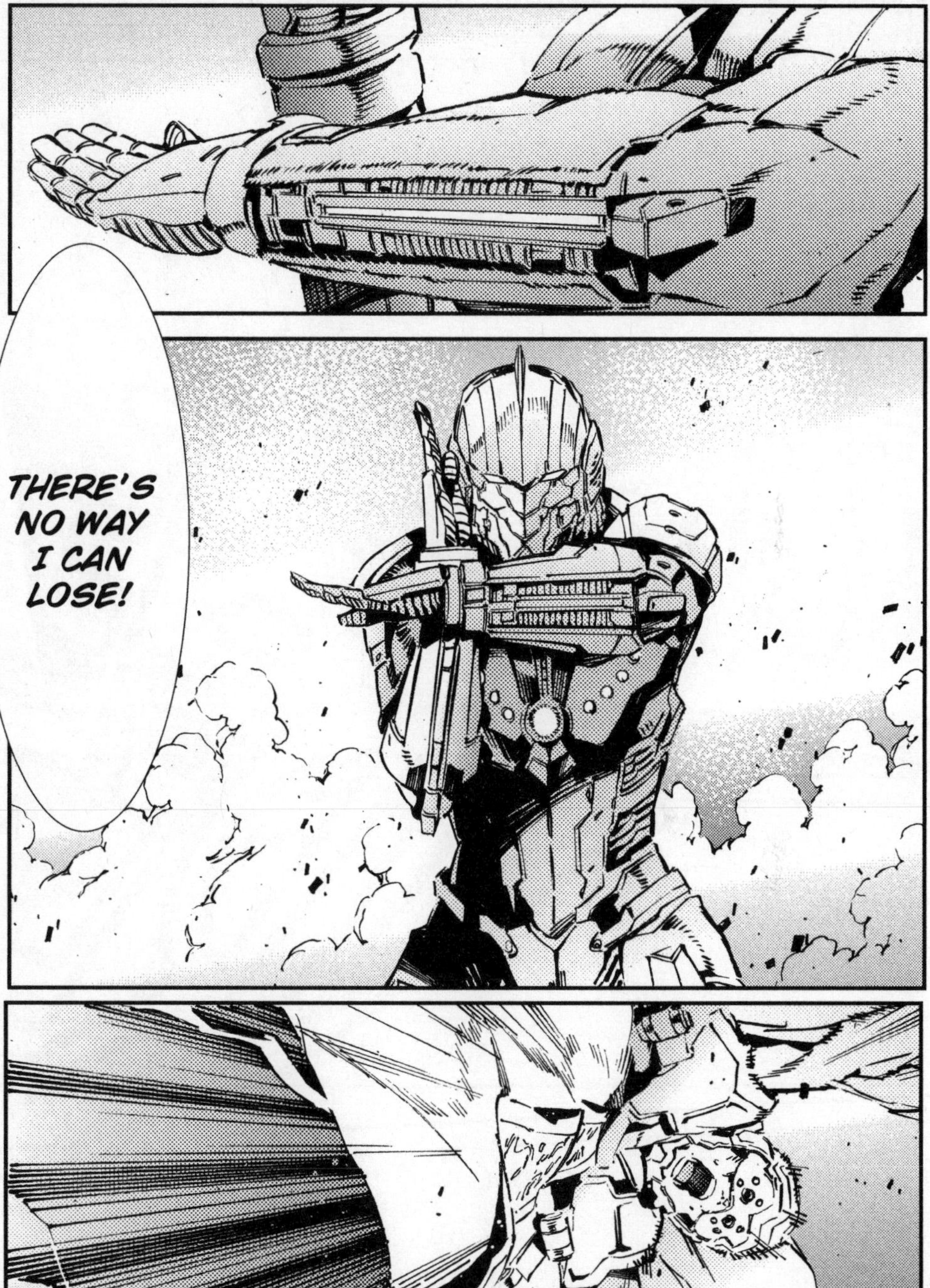
THERE'S NO WAY I CAN LOSE!

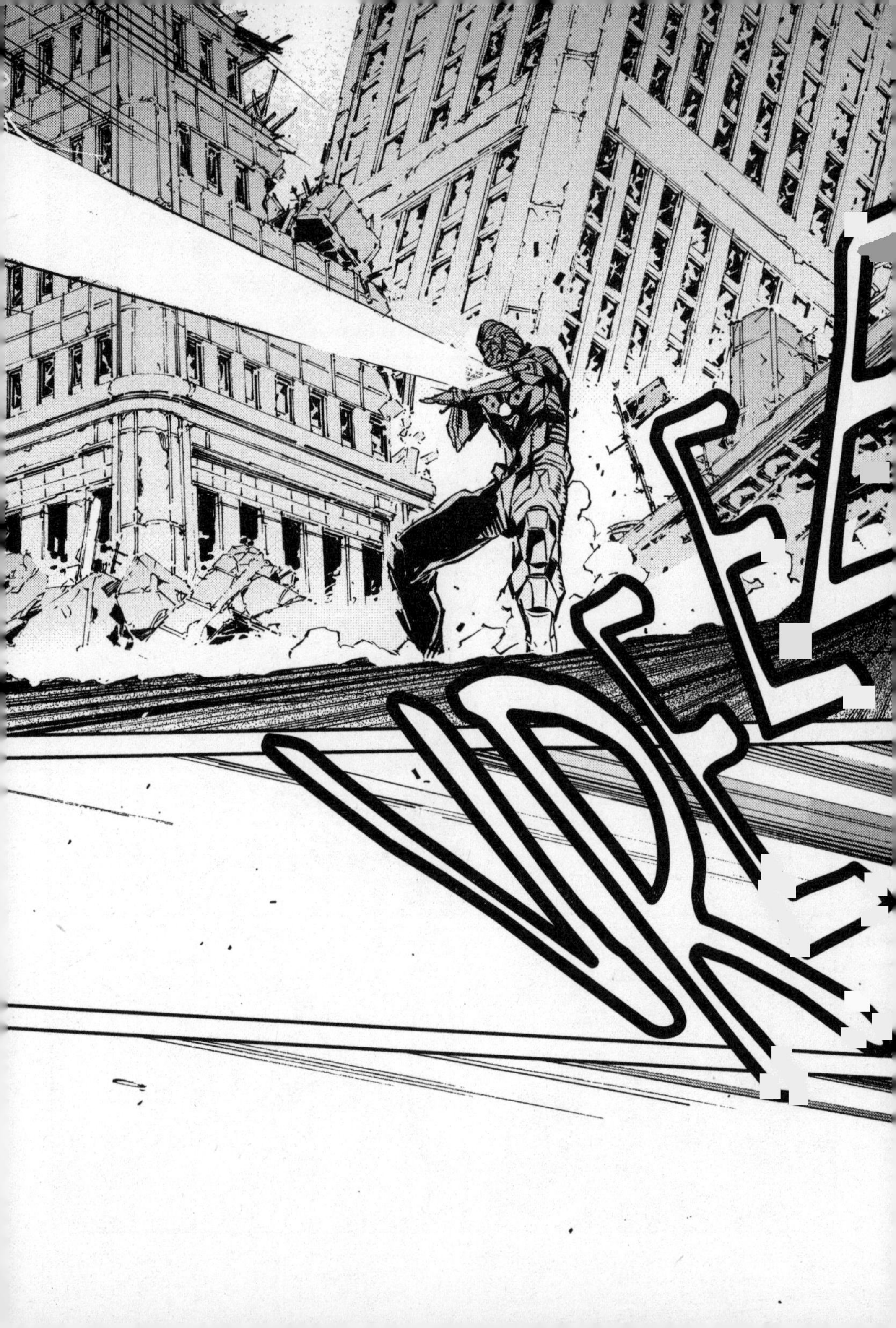

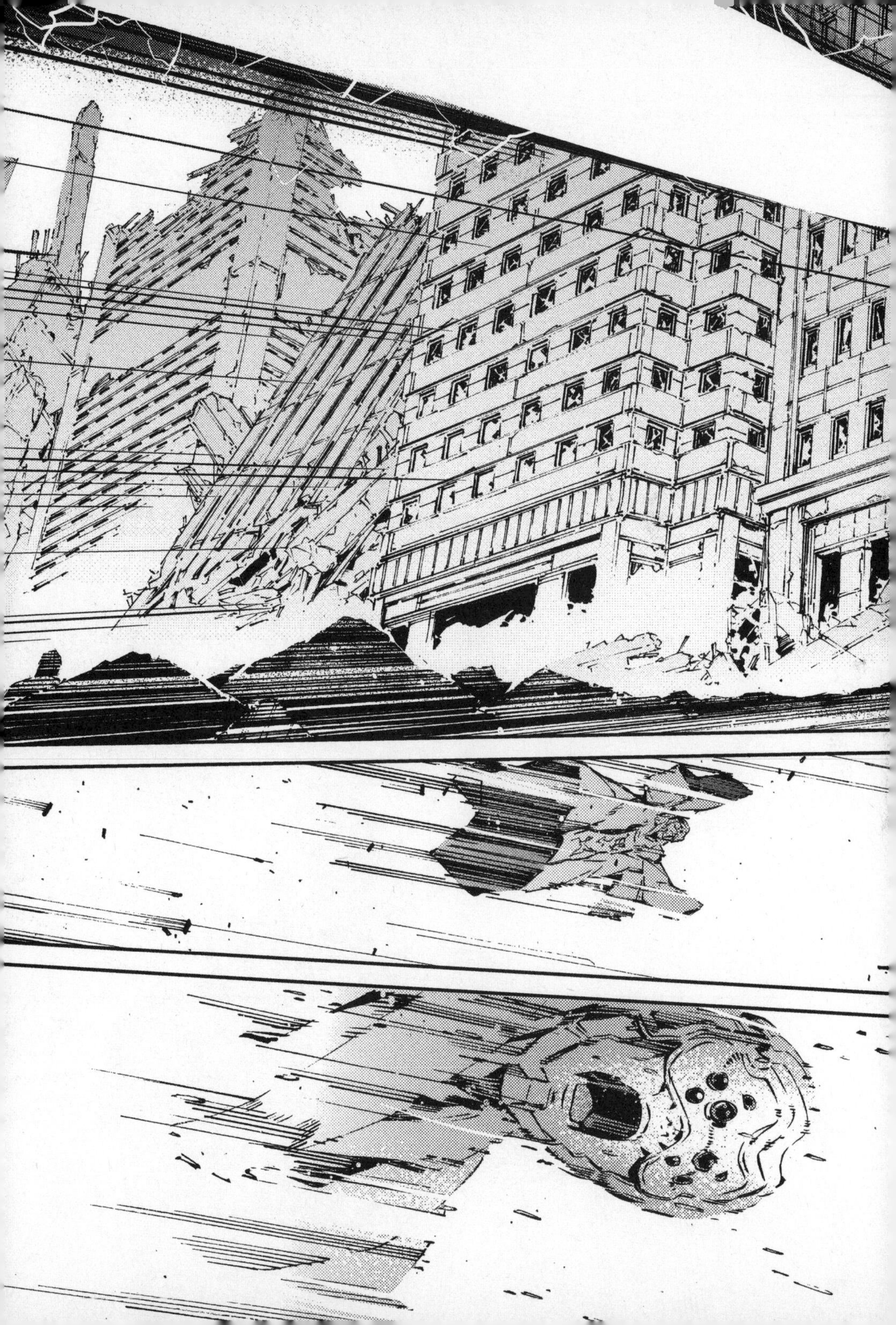

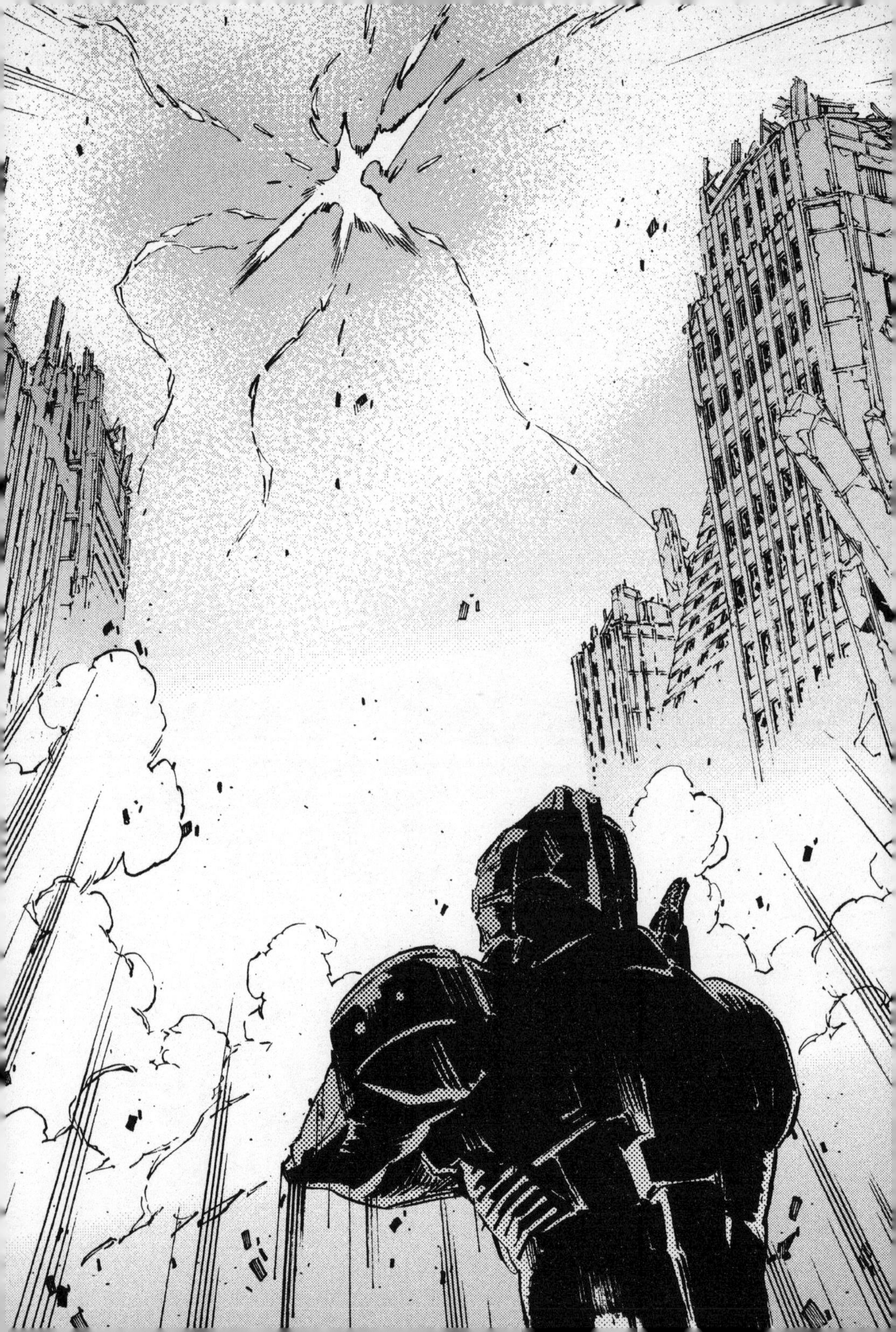

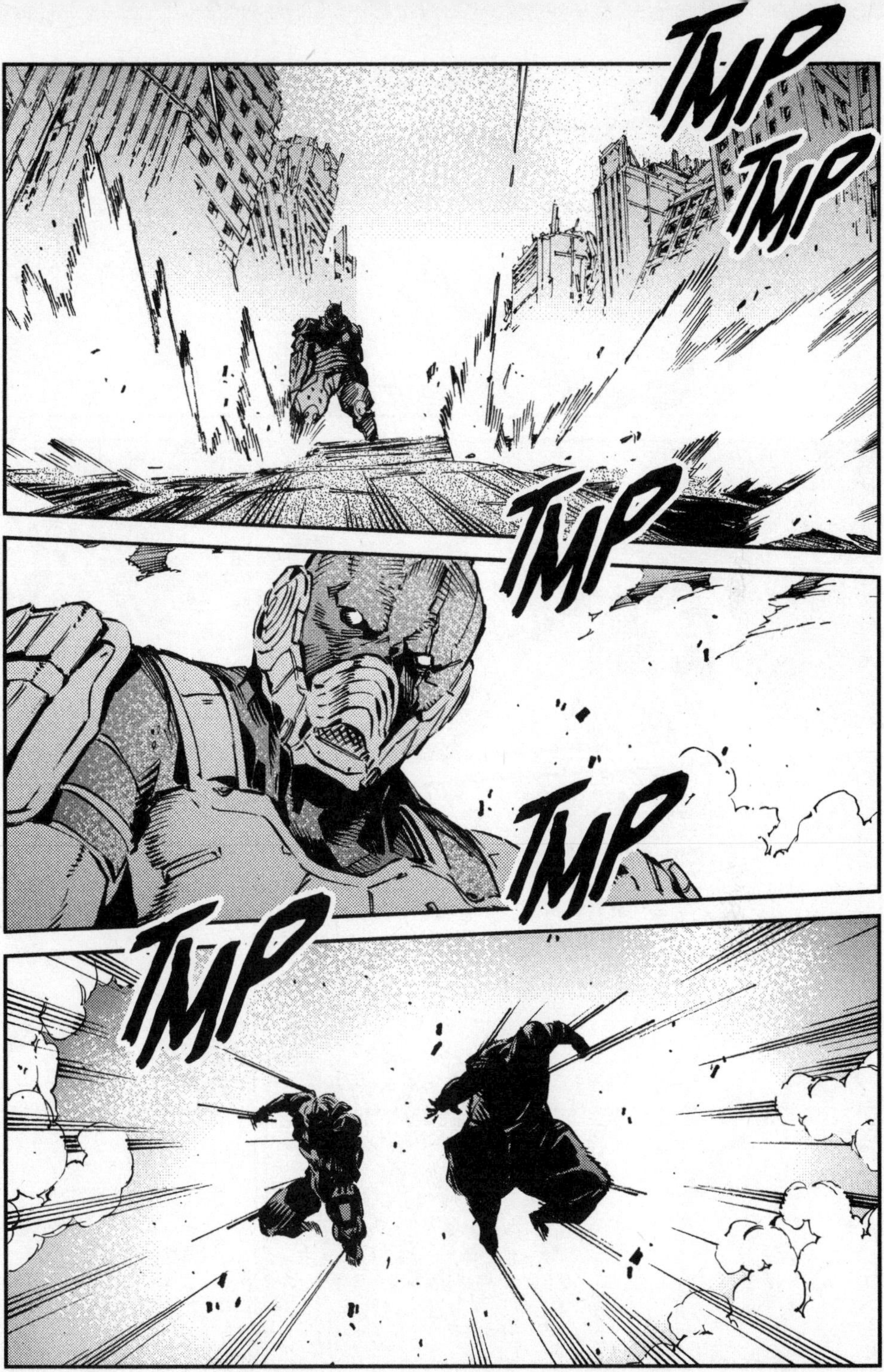
TMP
TMP
TMP
TMP
TMP

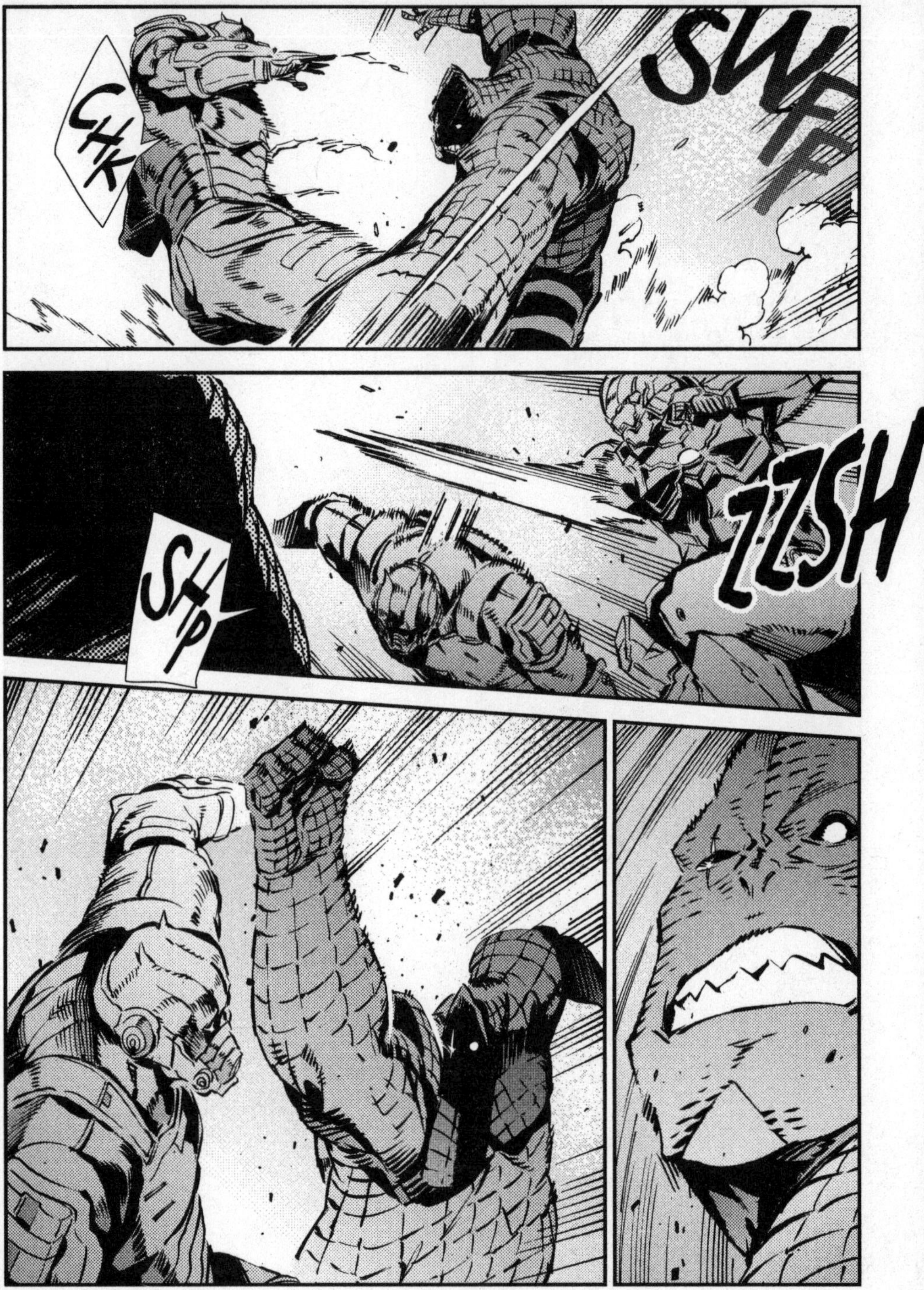
SWFF
CHK
ZZSH
SHIP

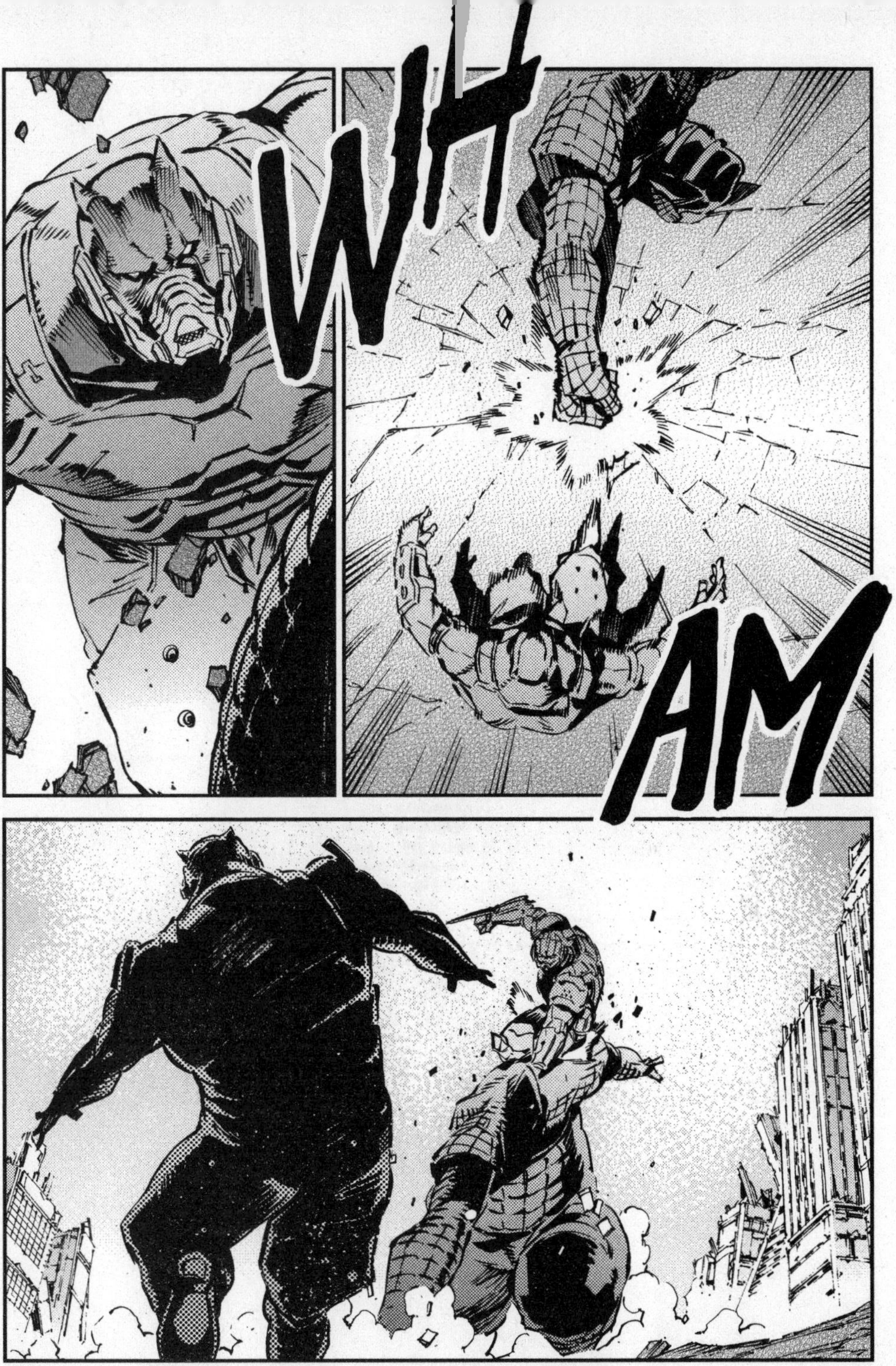
WHAM

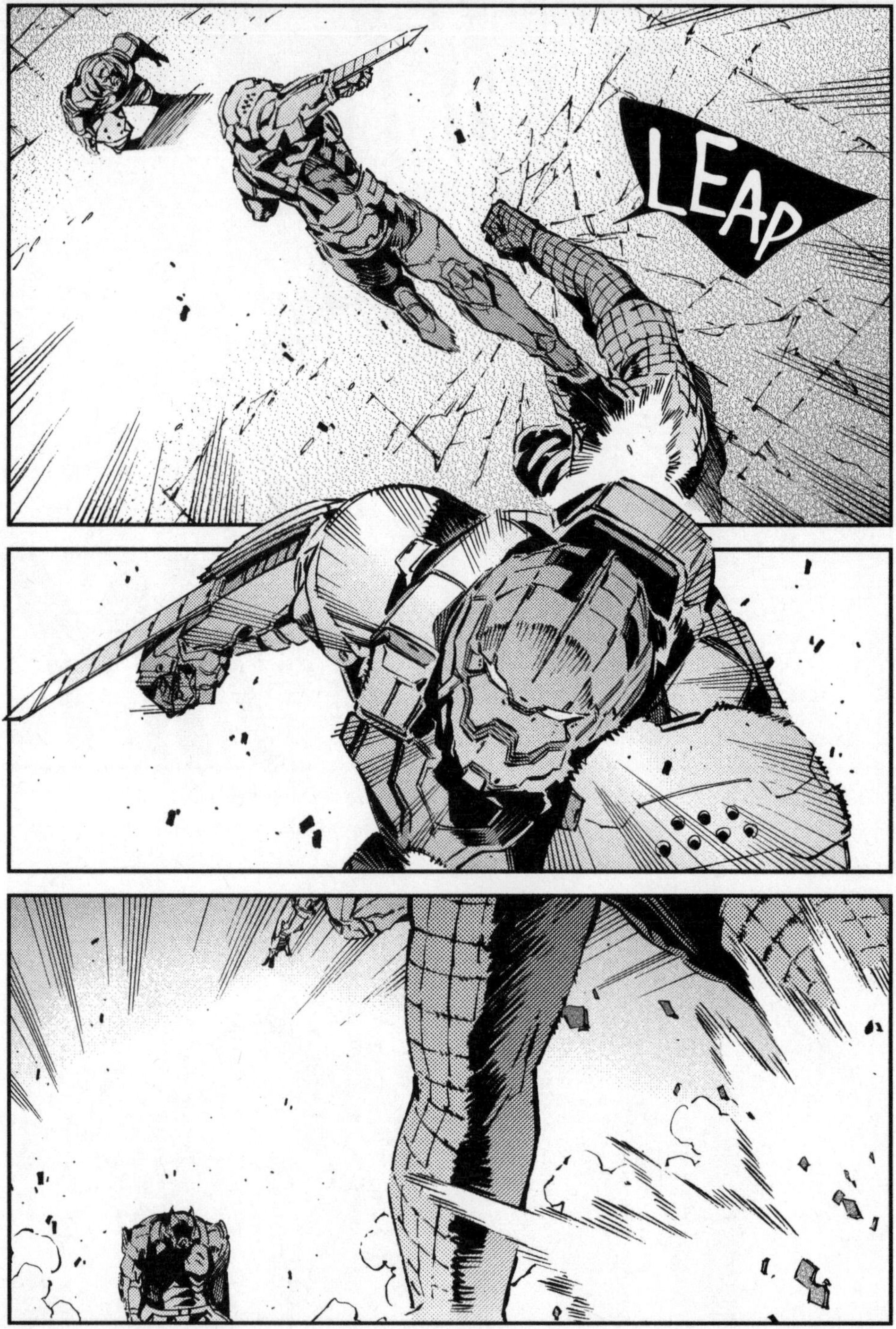
LEAP

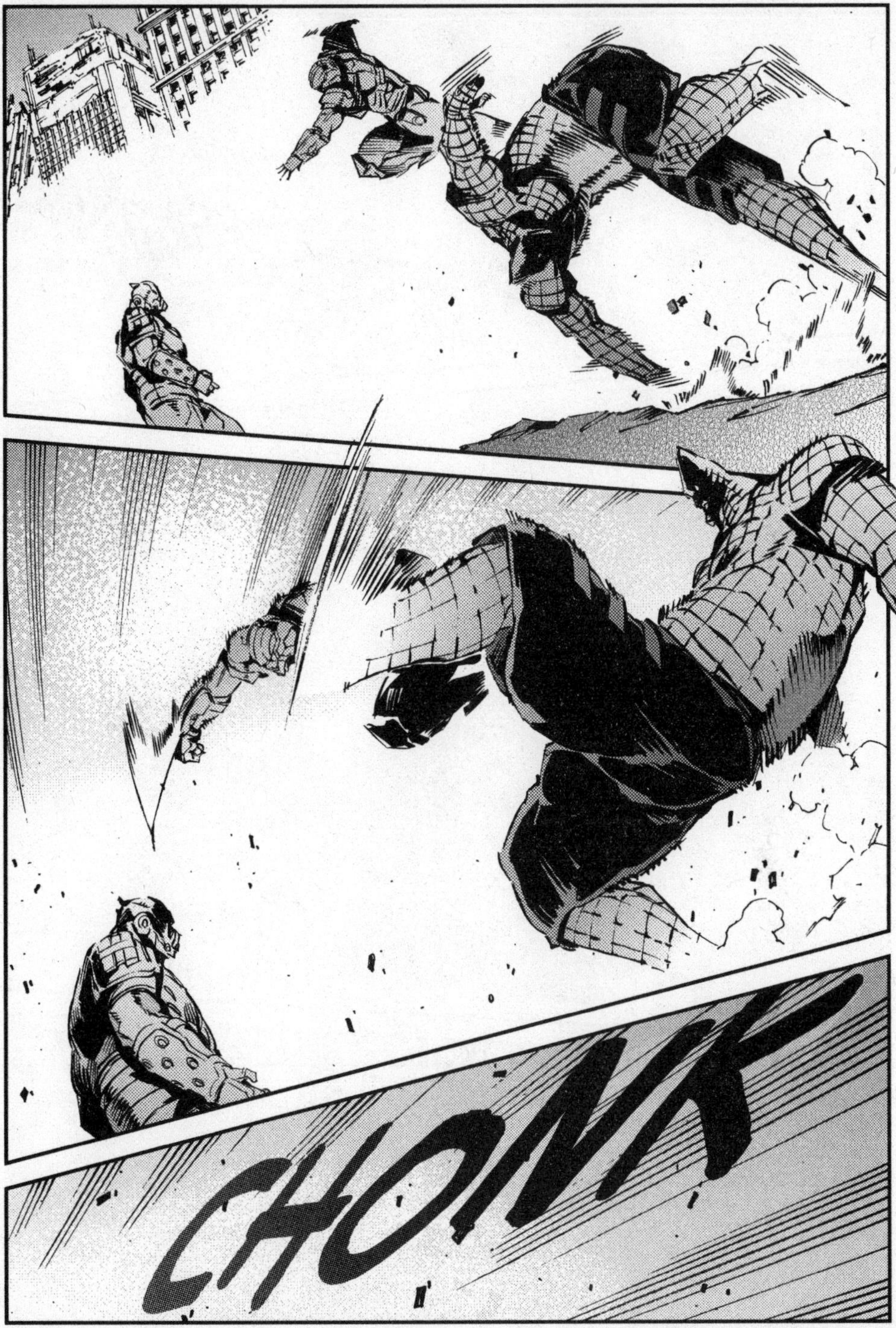
CHOMP

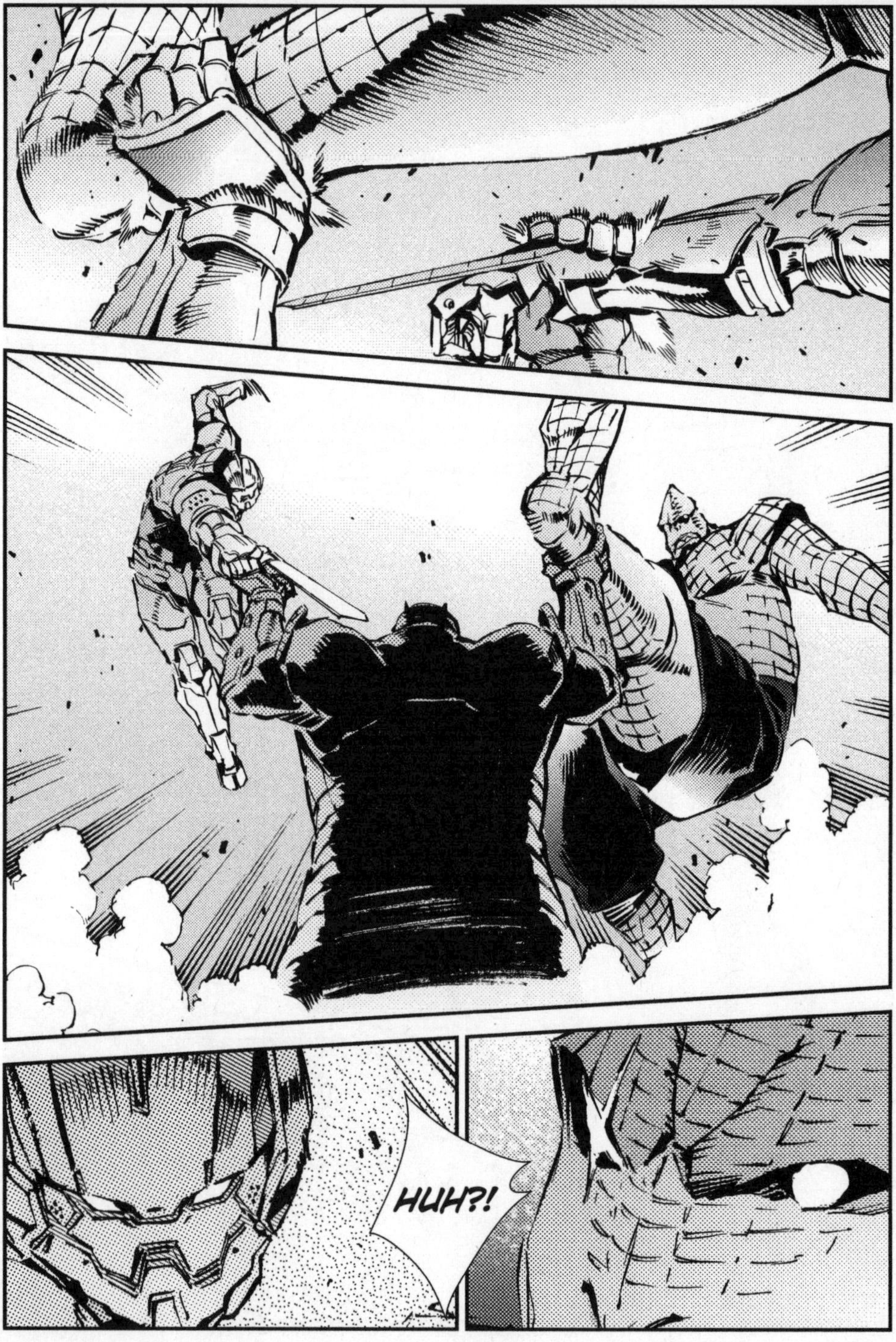
HUH?!

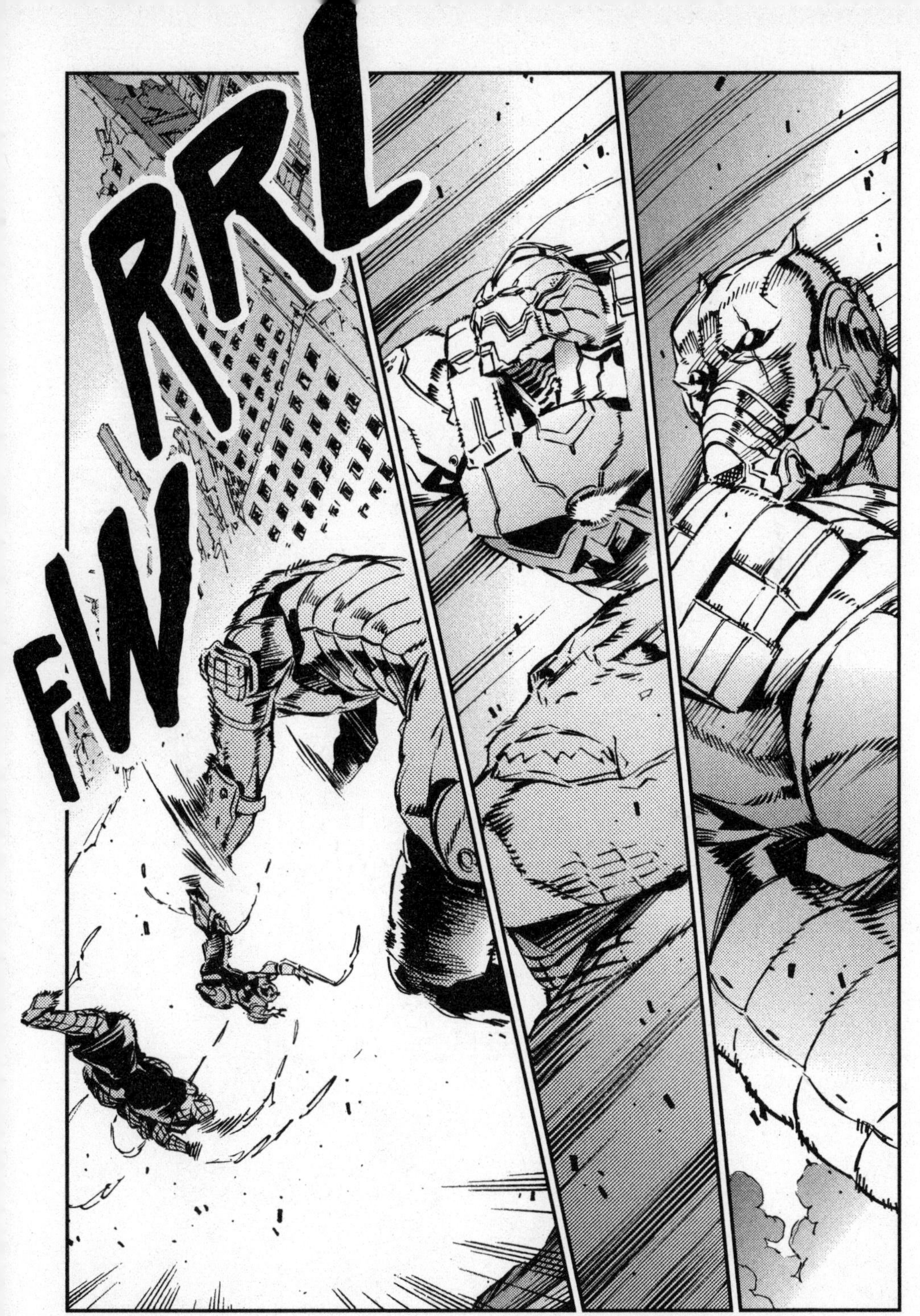
FWRRL

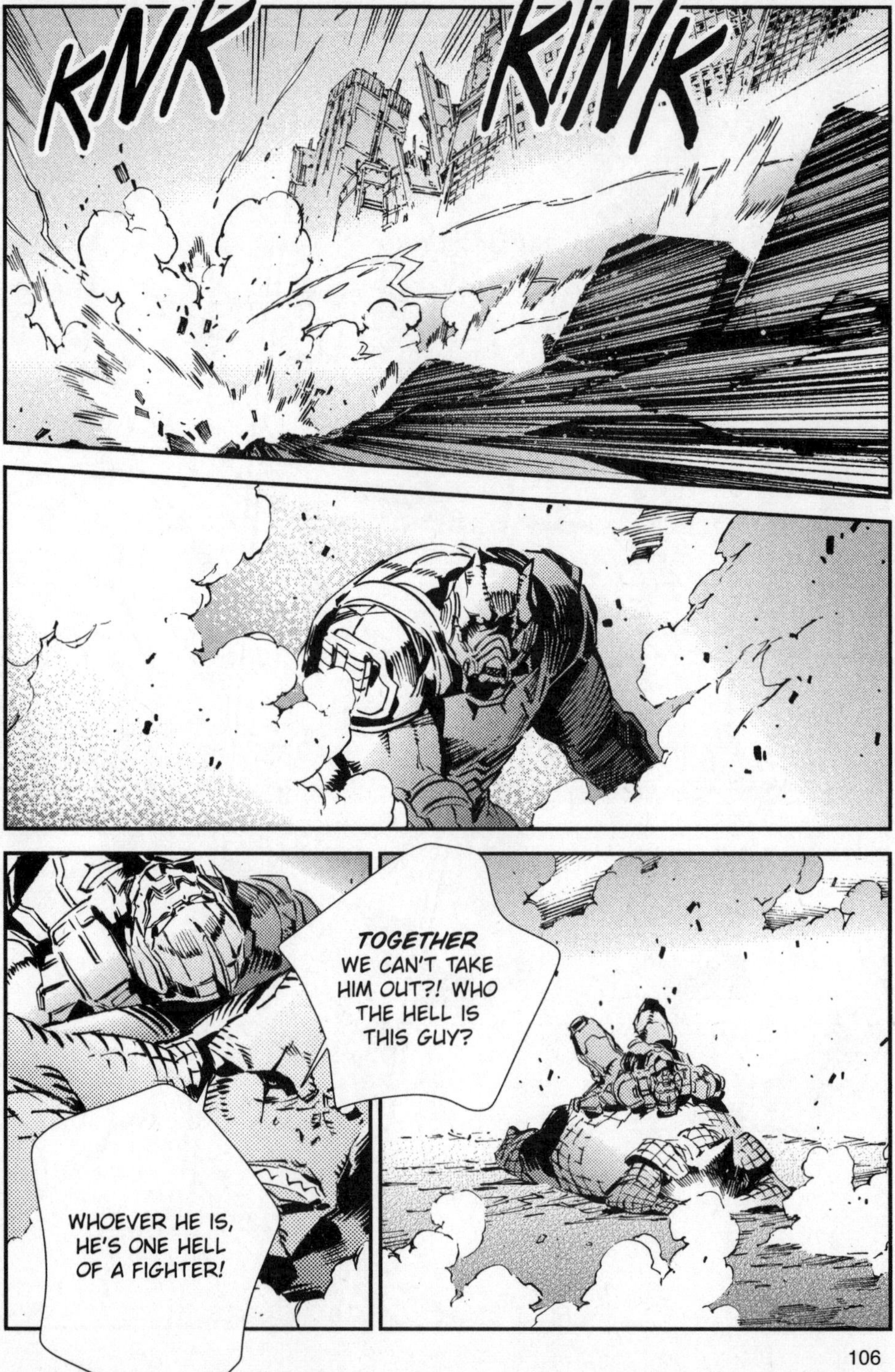
KTINK
KNK
TOGETHER WE CAN'T TAKE HIM OUT?! WHO THE HELL IS THIS GUY?
WHOEVER HE IS, HE'S ONE HELL OF A FIGHTER!

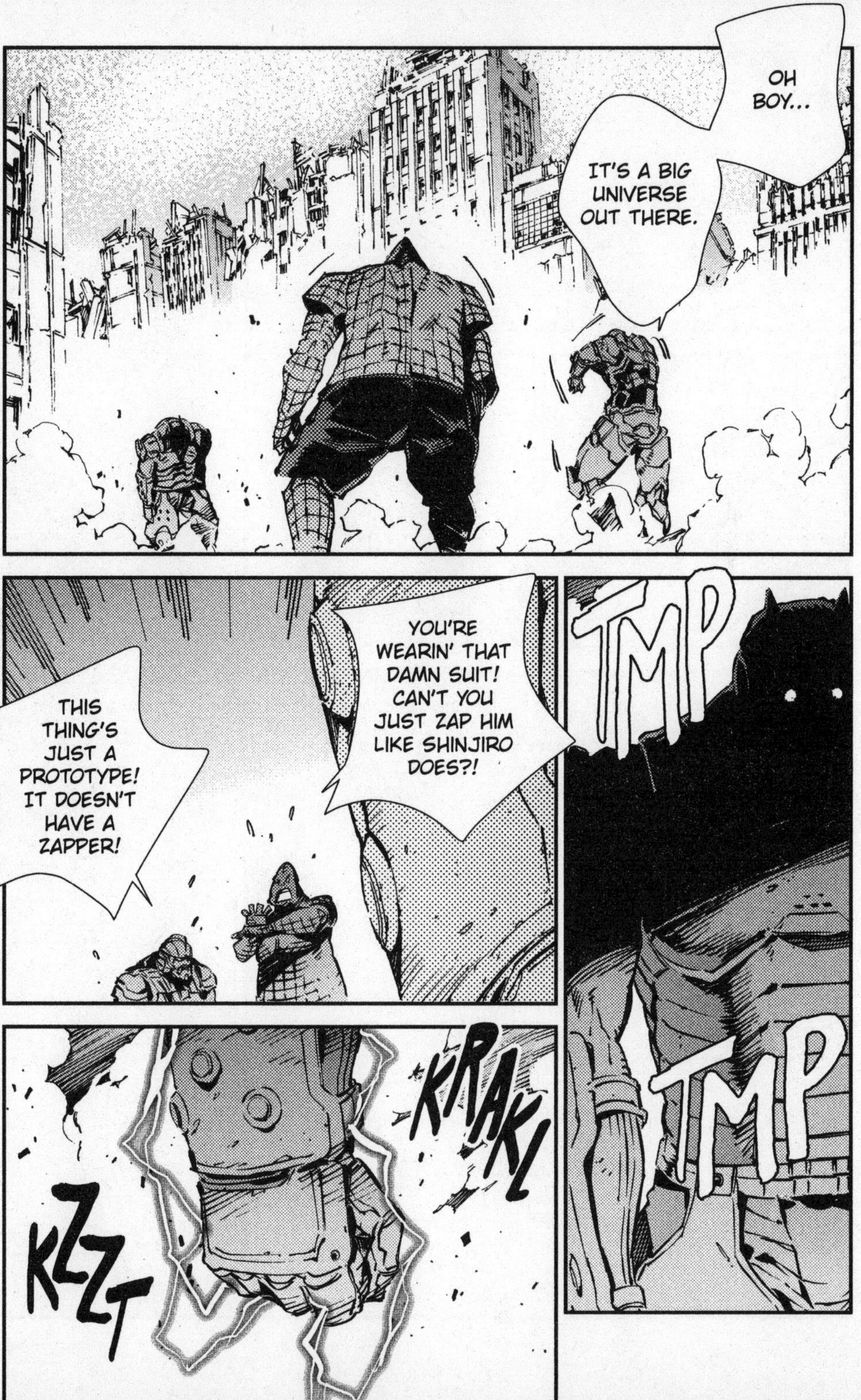
OH BOY...
IT'S A BIG UNIVERSE OUT THERE.
TMP
TMP
YOU'RE WEARIN' THAT DAMN SUIT! CAN'T YOU JUST ZAP HIM LIKE SHINJIRO DOES?!
THIS THING'S JUST A PROTOTYPE! IT DOESN'T HAVE A ZAPPER!
KRAK!
KZZT

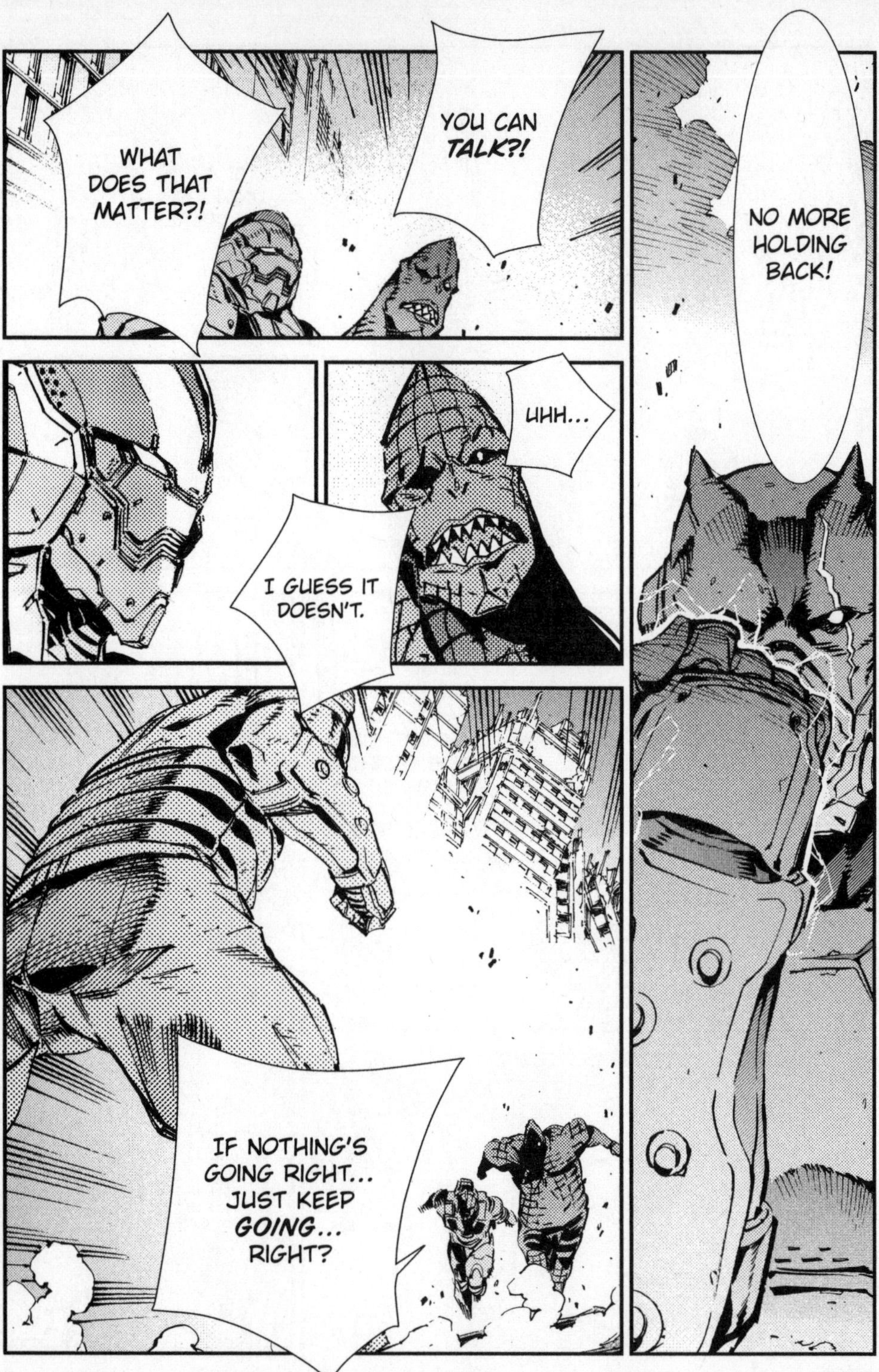
NO MORE HOLDING BACK!
YOU CAN TALK?!
WHAT DOES THAT MATTER?!
UHH...
I GUESS IT DOESN'T.
IF NOTHING'S GOING RIGHT... JUST KEEP GOING... RIGHT?

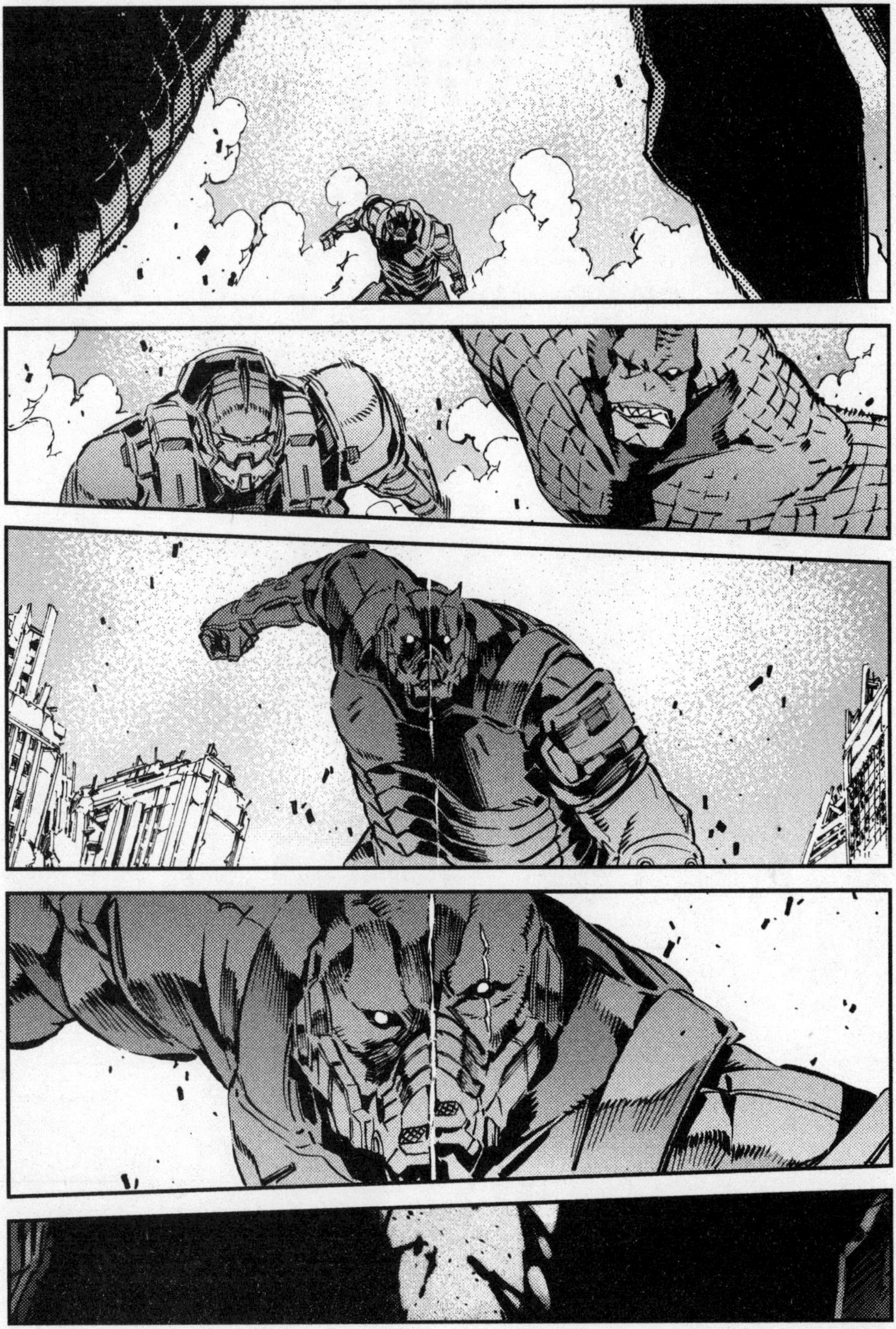

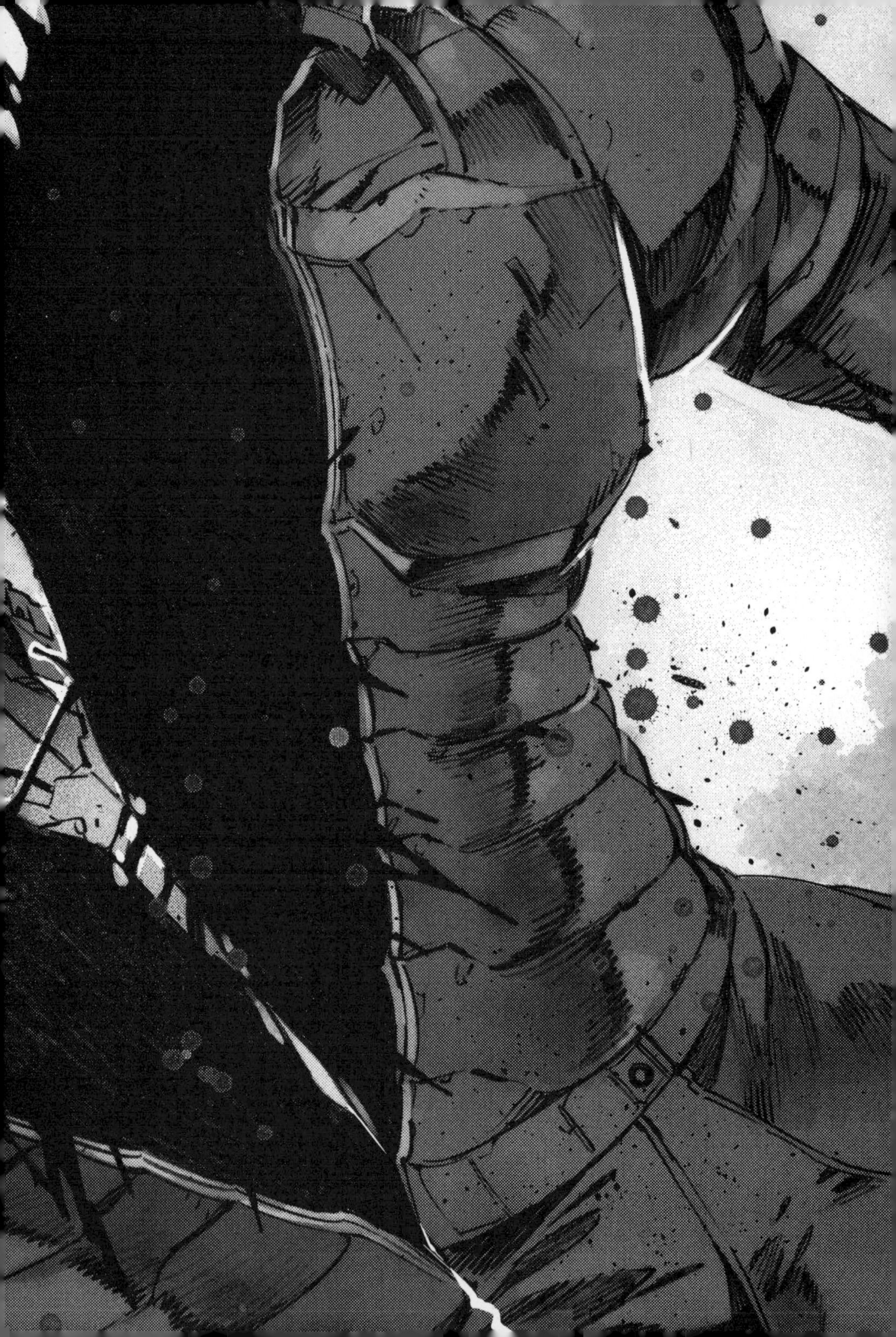

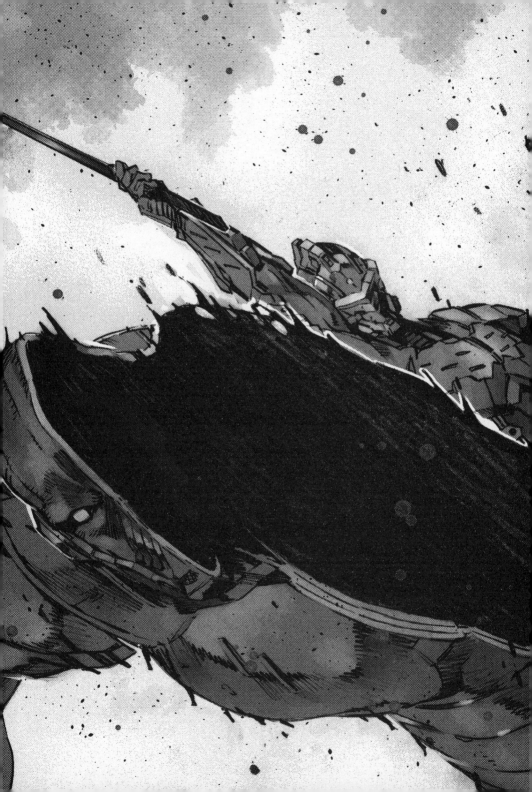

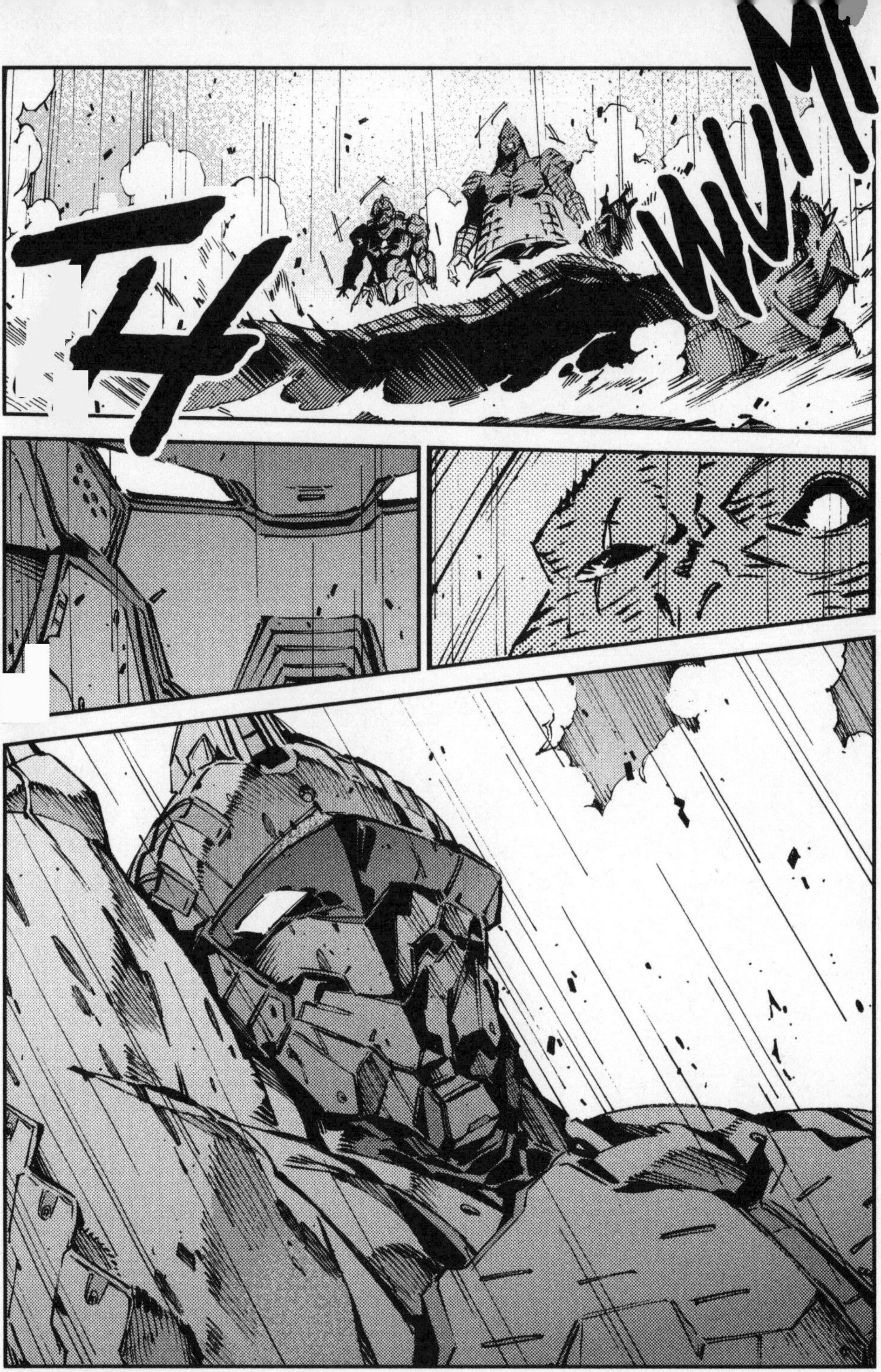
FWUM

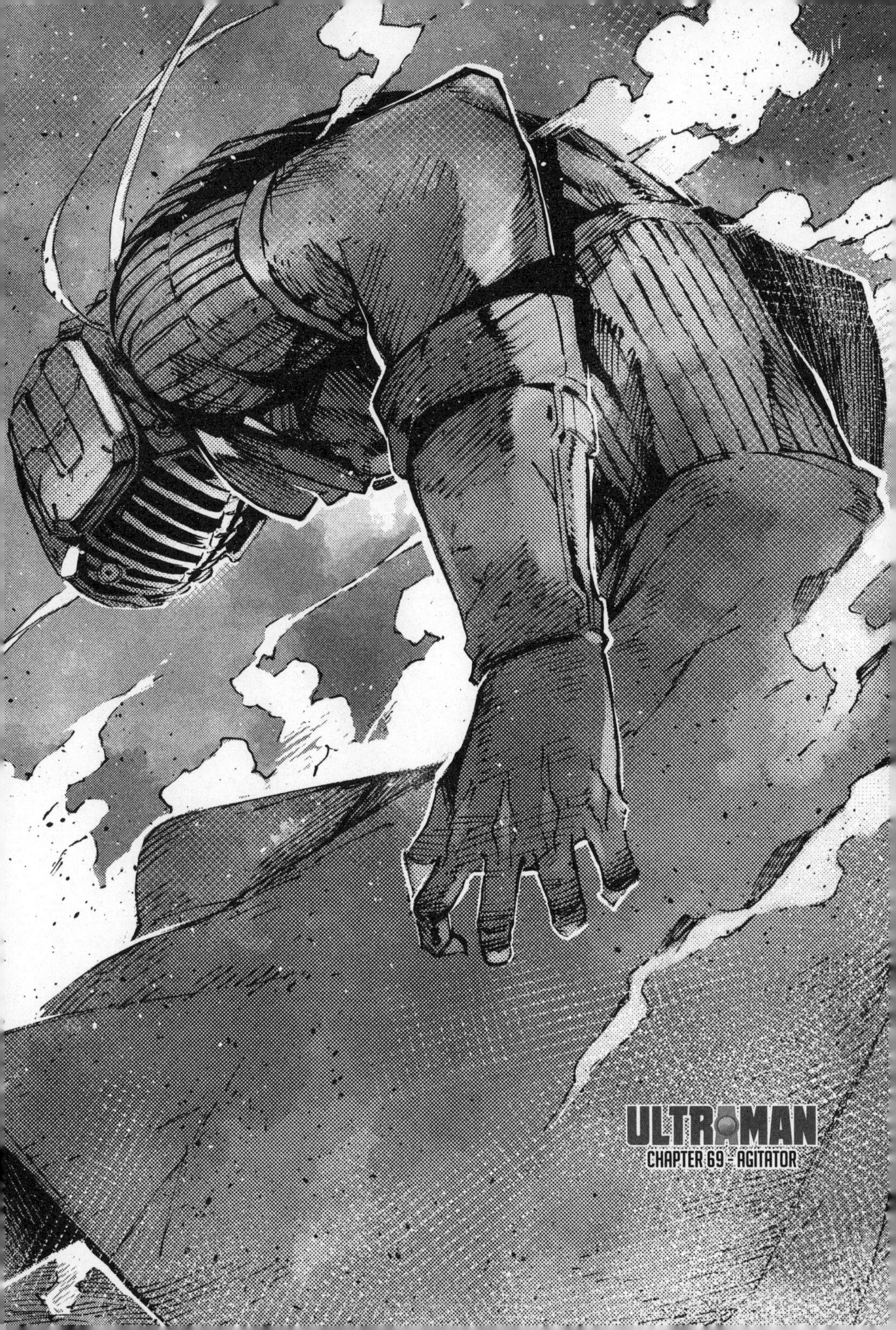
ULTRAMAN
CHAPTER 69 - AGITATOR

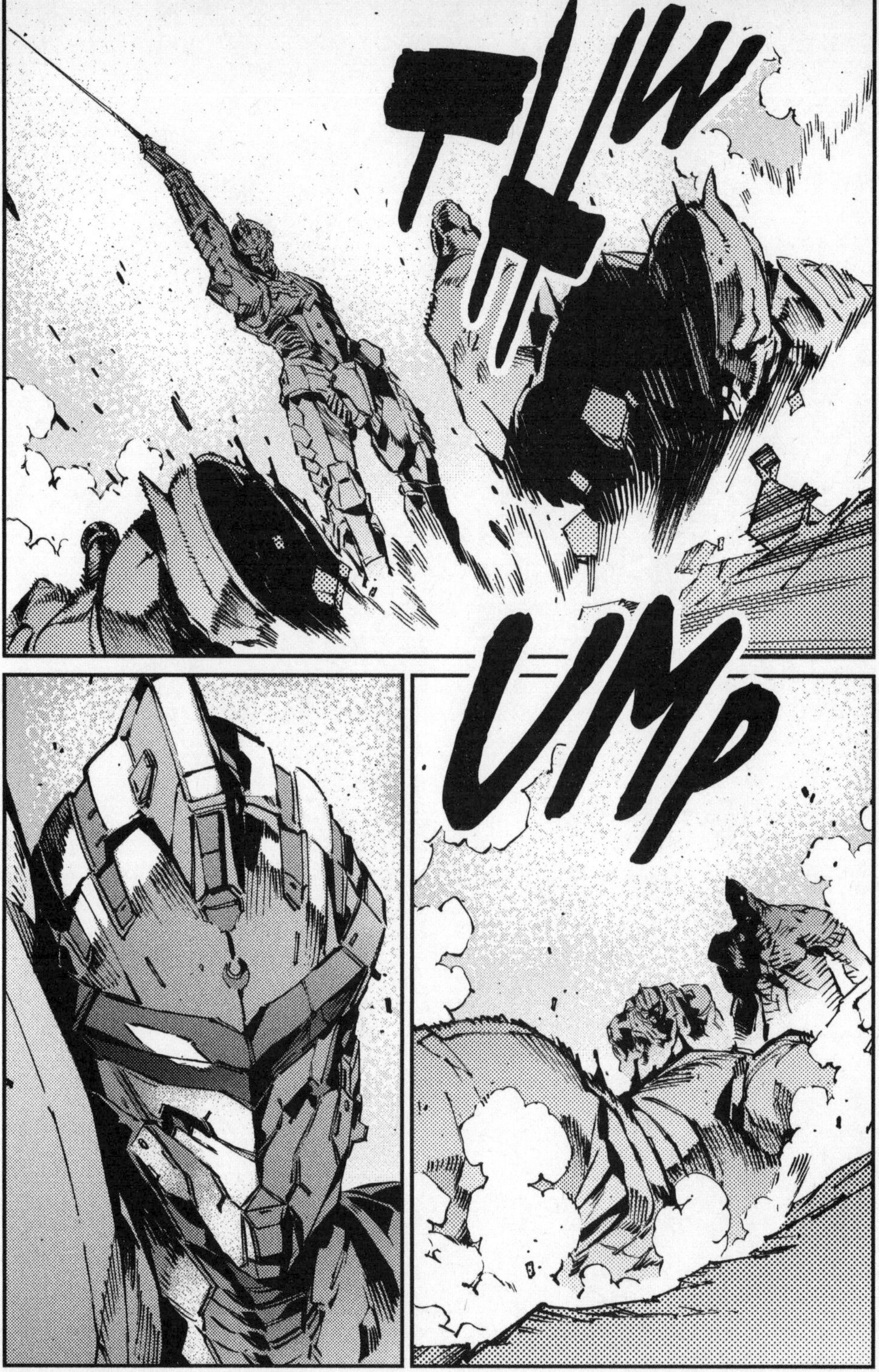
THWUMP

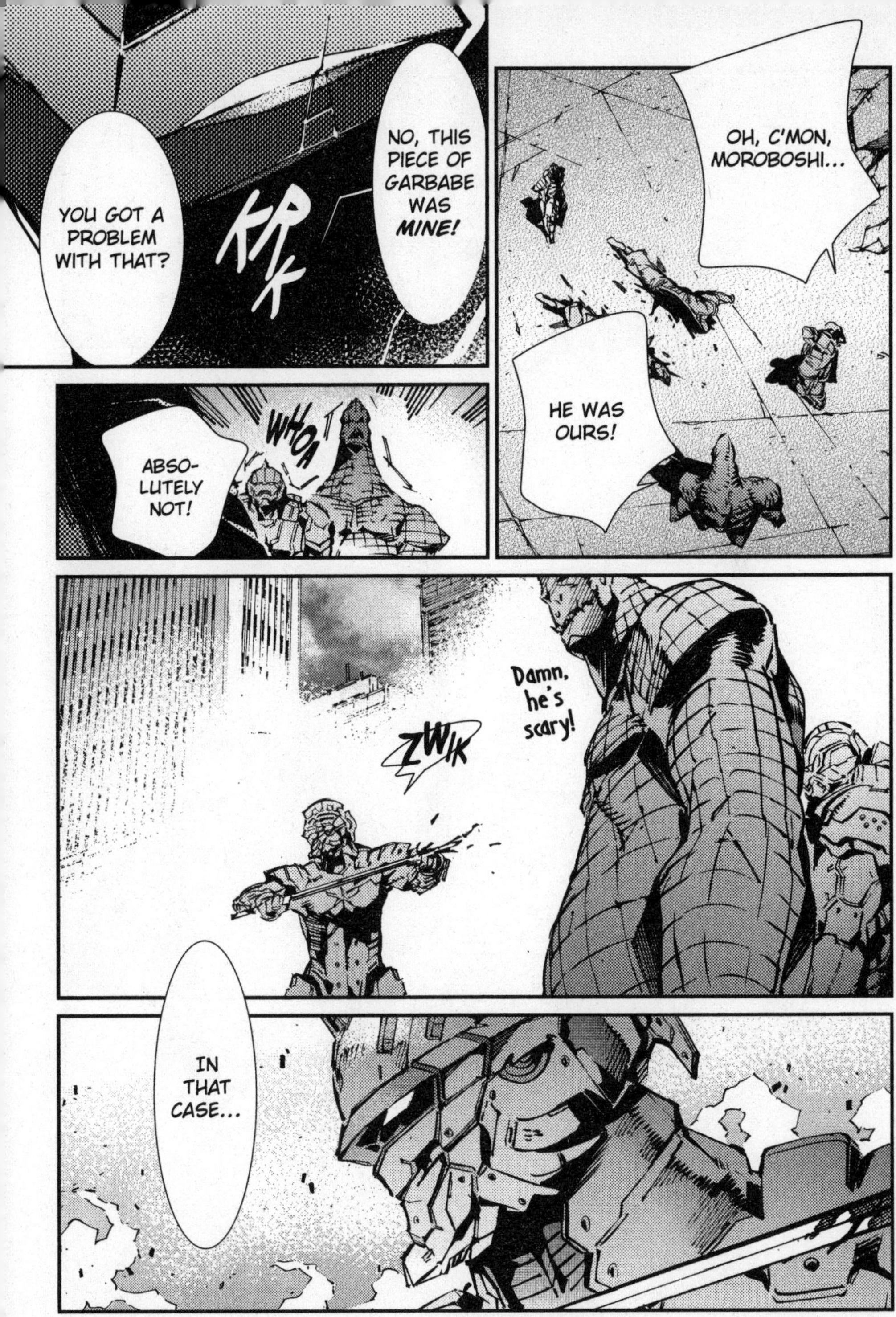
OH, C'MON, MOROBOSHI...
HE WAS OURS!
NO, THIS PIECE OF GARBABE WAS *MINE!*
KRK
YOU GOT A PROBLEM WITH THAT?
WHOA
ABSO-LUTELY NOT!
Damn, he's scary!
ZWIK
IN THAT CASE...

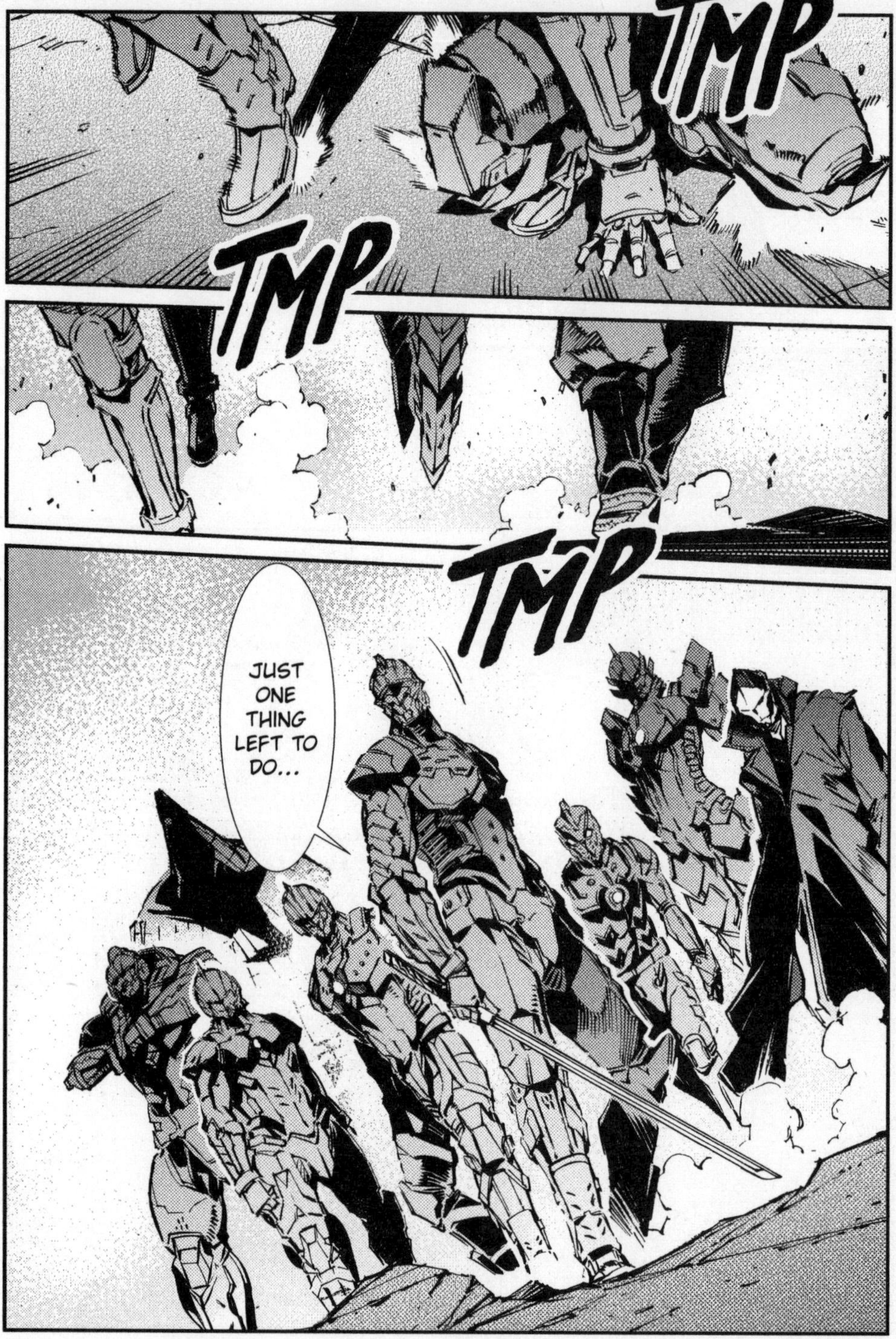
TMP
TMP
TMP
JUST ONE THING LEFT TO DO...

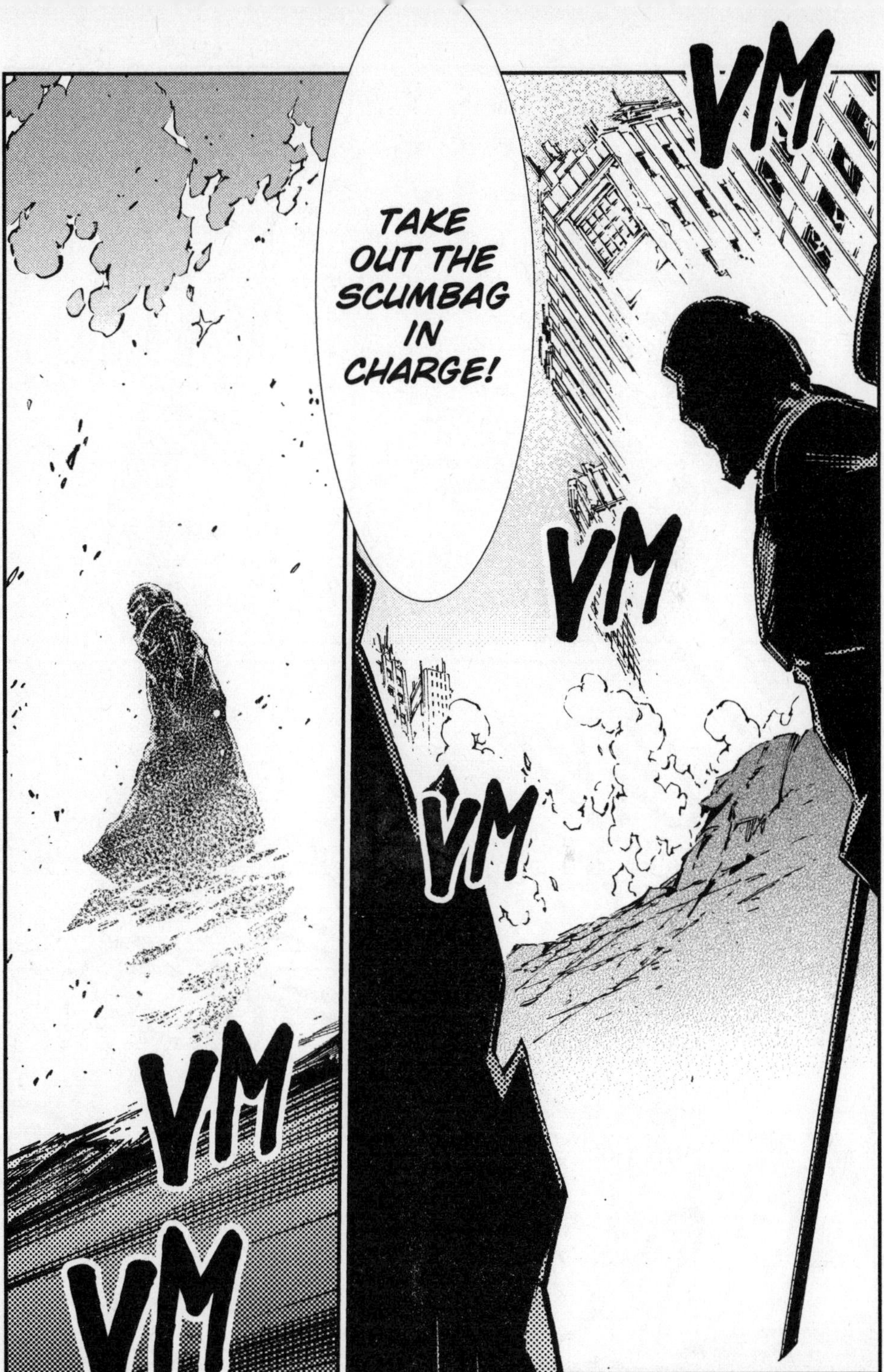
VM
TAKE OUT THE SCUMBAG IN CHARGE!
VM
VM
VM
VM

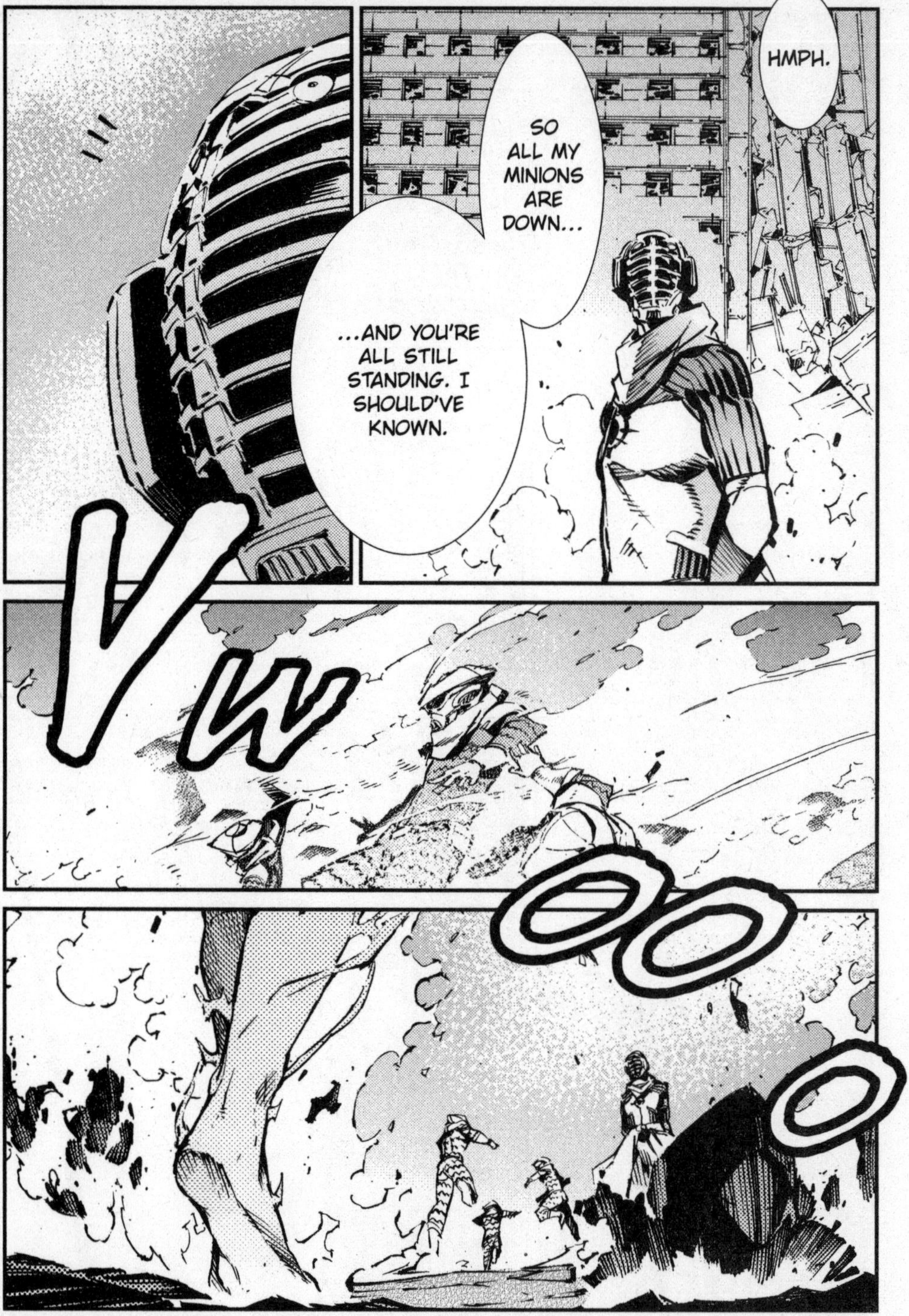
HMPH.
SO ALL MY MINIONS ARE DOWN...
...AND YOU'RE ALL STILL STANDING. I SHOULD'VE KNOWN.
VWOOOO

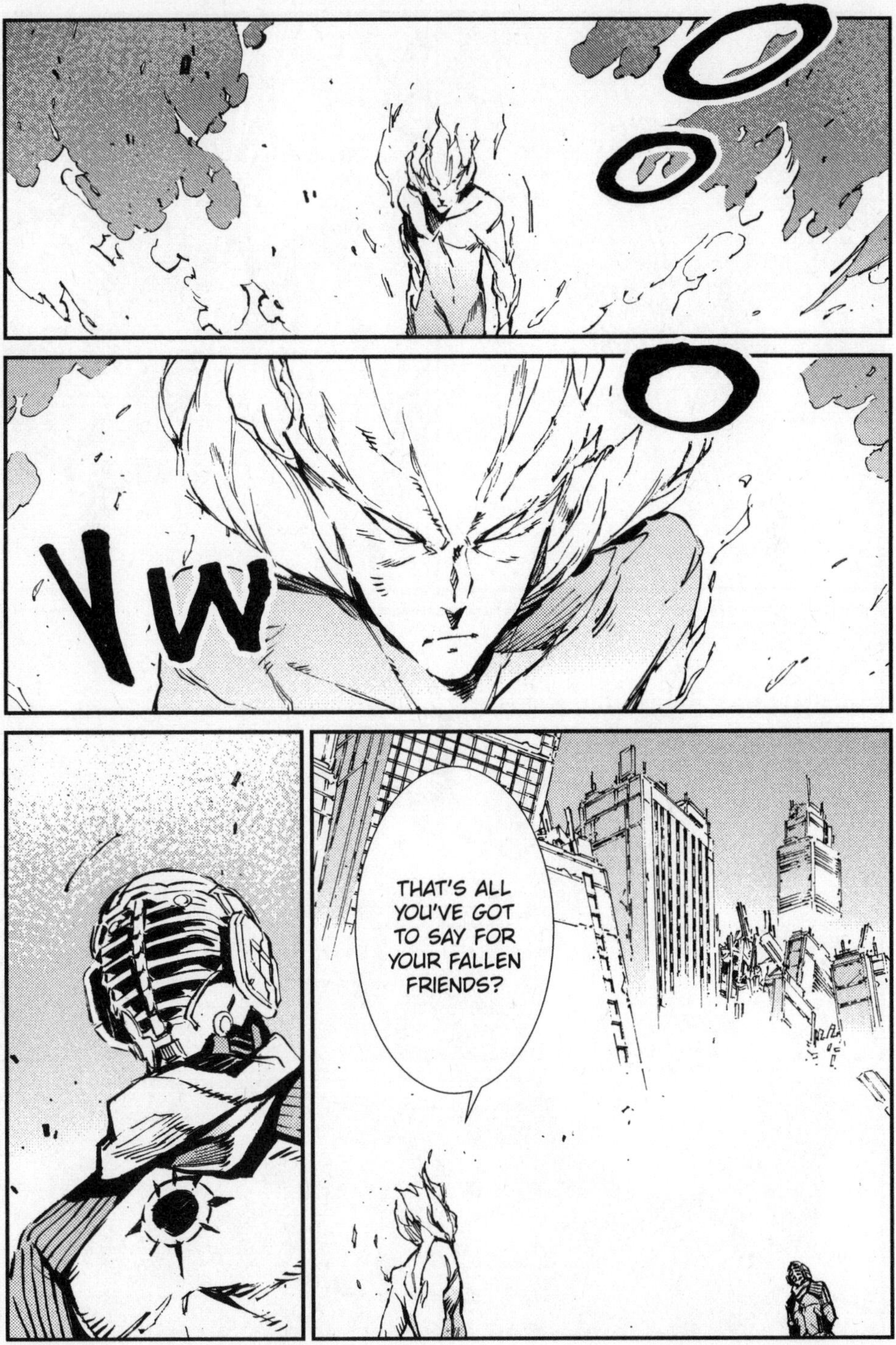
THAT'S ALL YOU'VE GOT TO SAY FOR YOUR FALLEN FRIENDS?

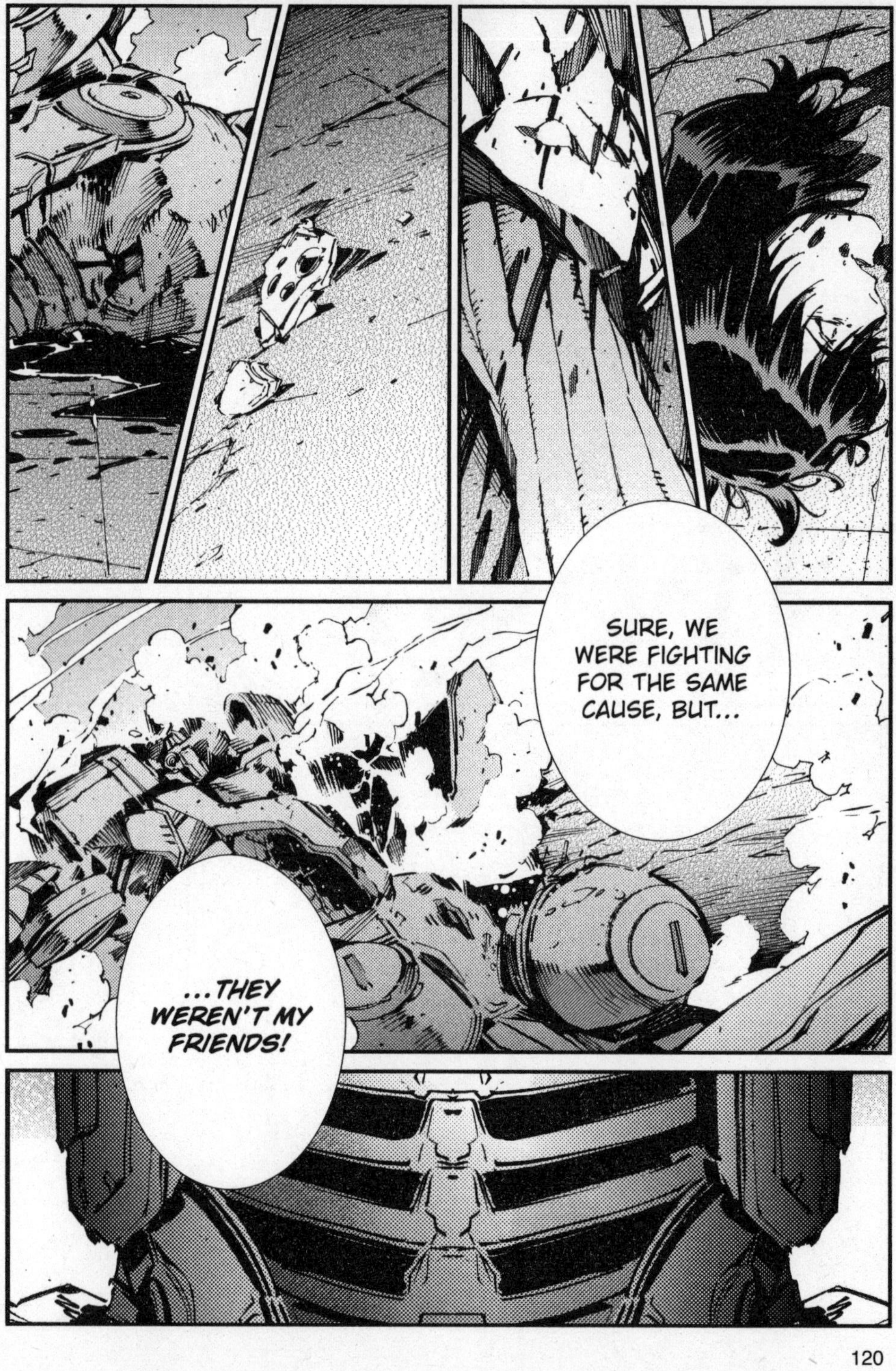
SURE, WE WERE FIGHTING FOR THE SAME CAUSE, BUT...
...THEY WEREN'T MY FRIENDS!

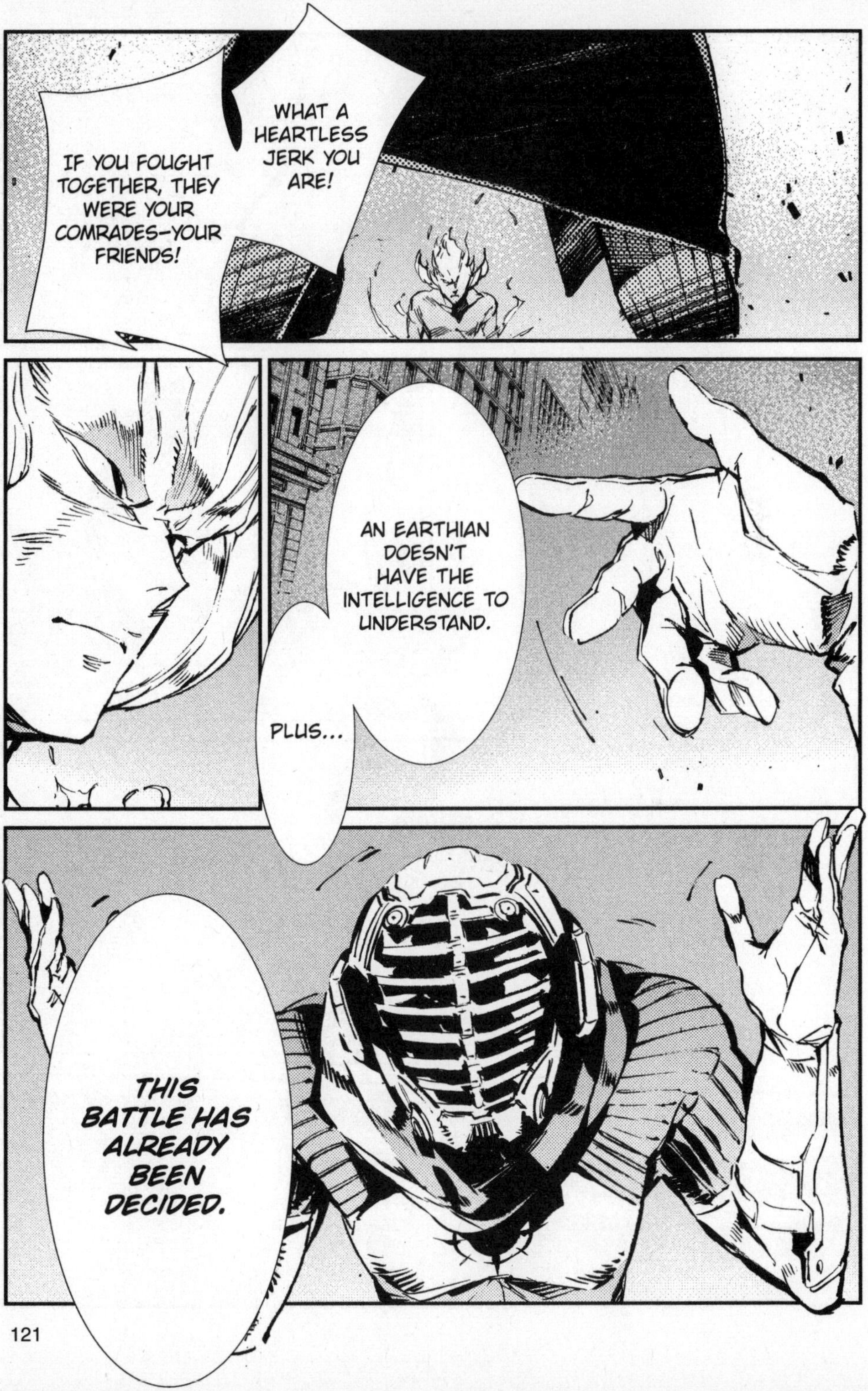
WHAT A HEARTLESS JERK YOU ARE!
IF YOU FOUGHT TOGETHER, THEY WERE YOUR COMRADES—YOUR FRIENDS!
AN EARTHIAN DOESN'T HAVE THE INTELLIGENCE TO UNDERSTAND.
PLUS...
THIS BATTLE HAS ALREADY BEEN DECIDED.

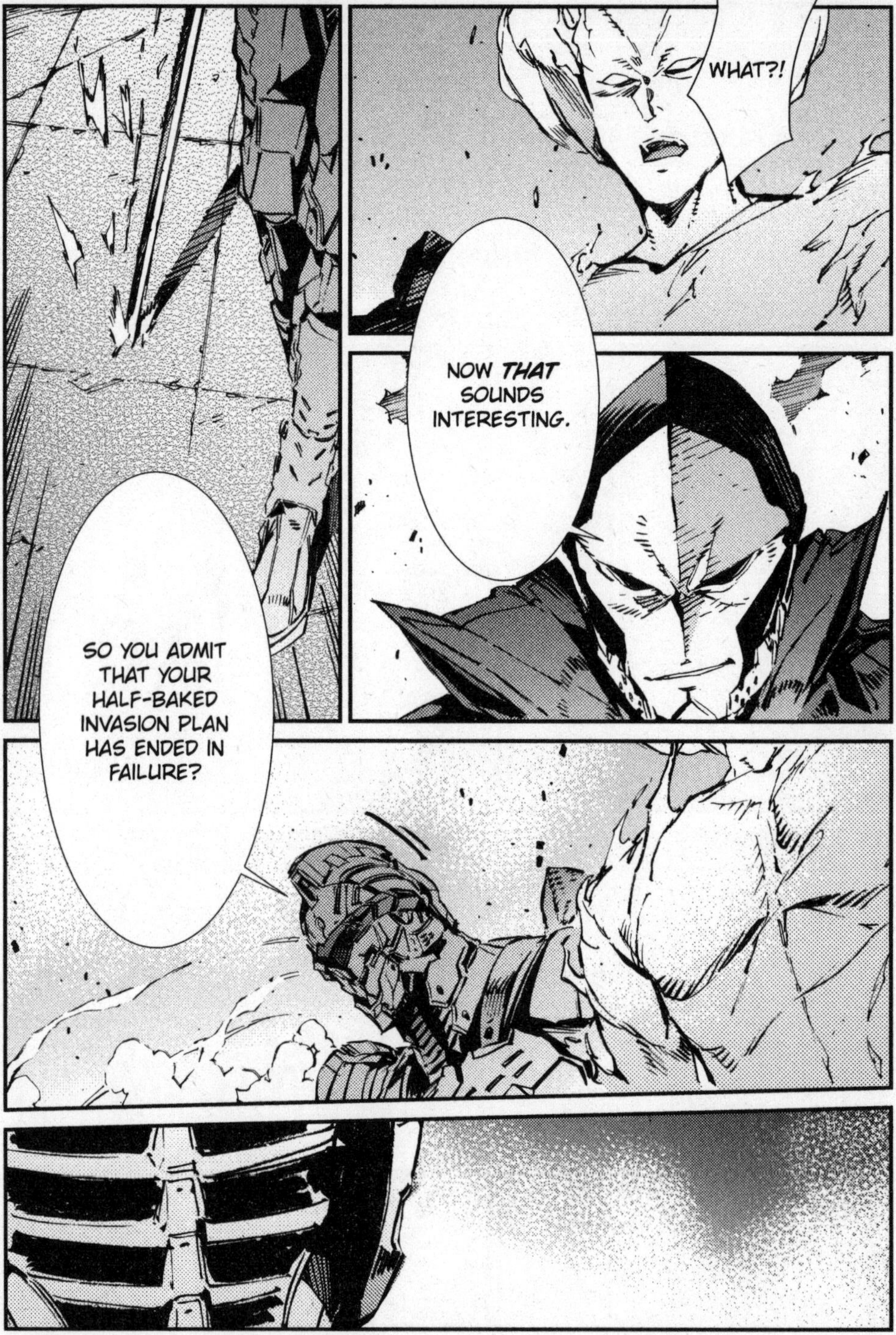
WHAT?!
NOW *THAT* SOUNDS INTERESTING.
SO YOU ADMIT THAT YOUR HALF-BAKED INVASION PLAN HAS ENDED IN FAILURE?

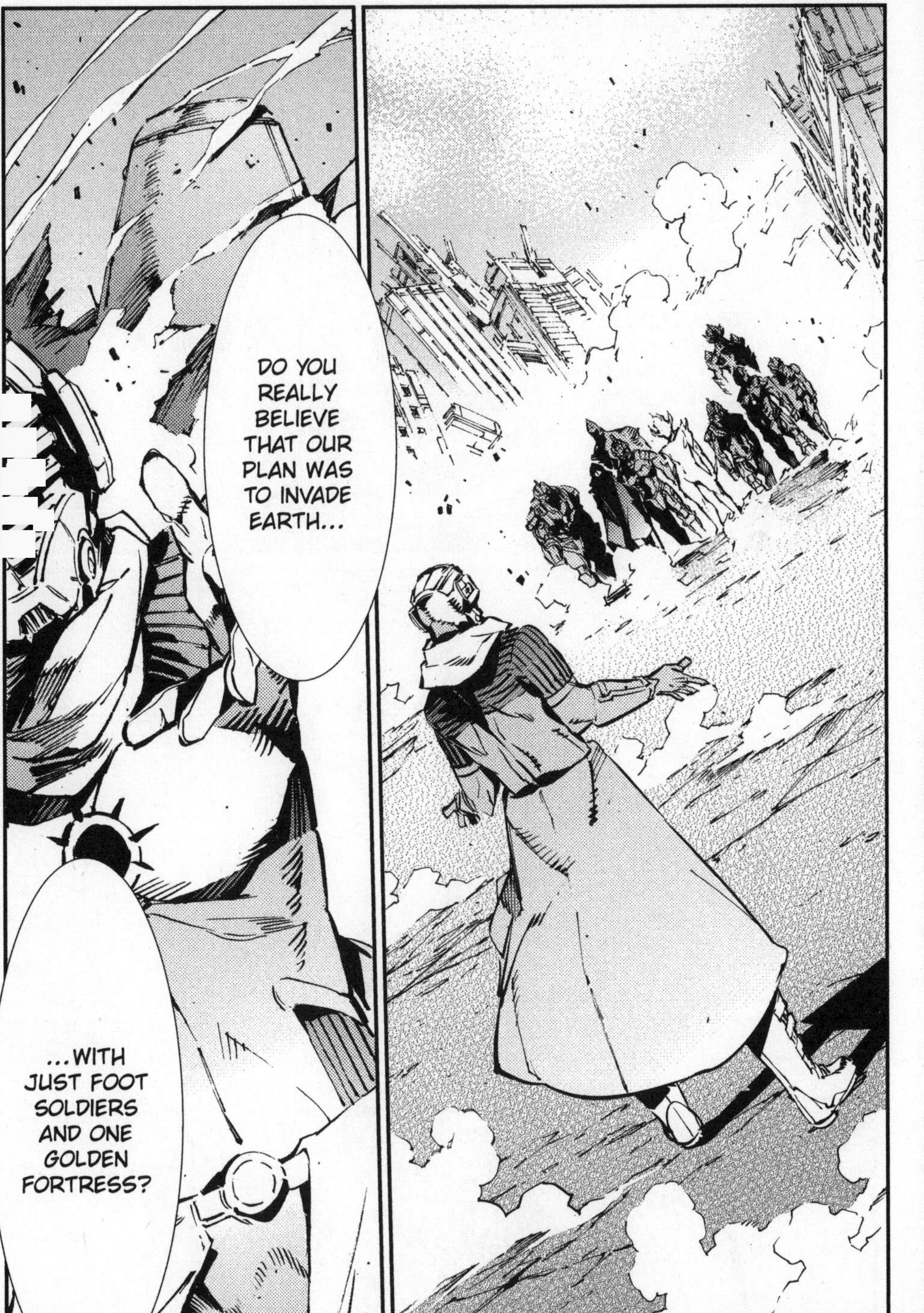
DO YOU REALLY BELIEVE THAT OUR PLAN WAS TO INVADE EARTH...
...WITH JUST FOOT SOLDIERS AND ONE GOLDEN FORTRESS?

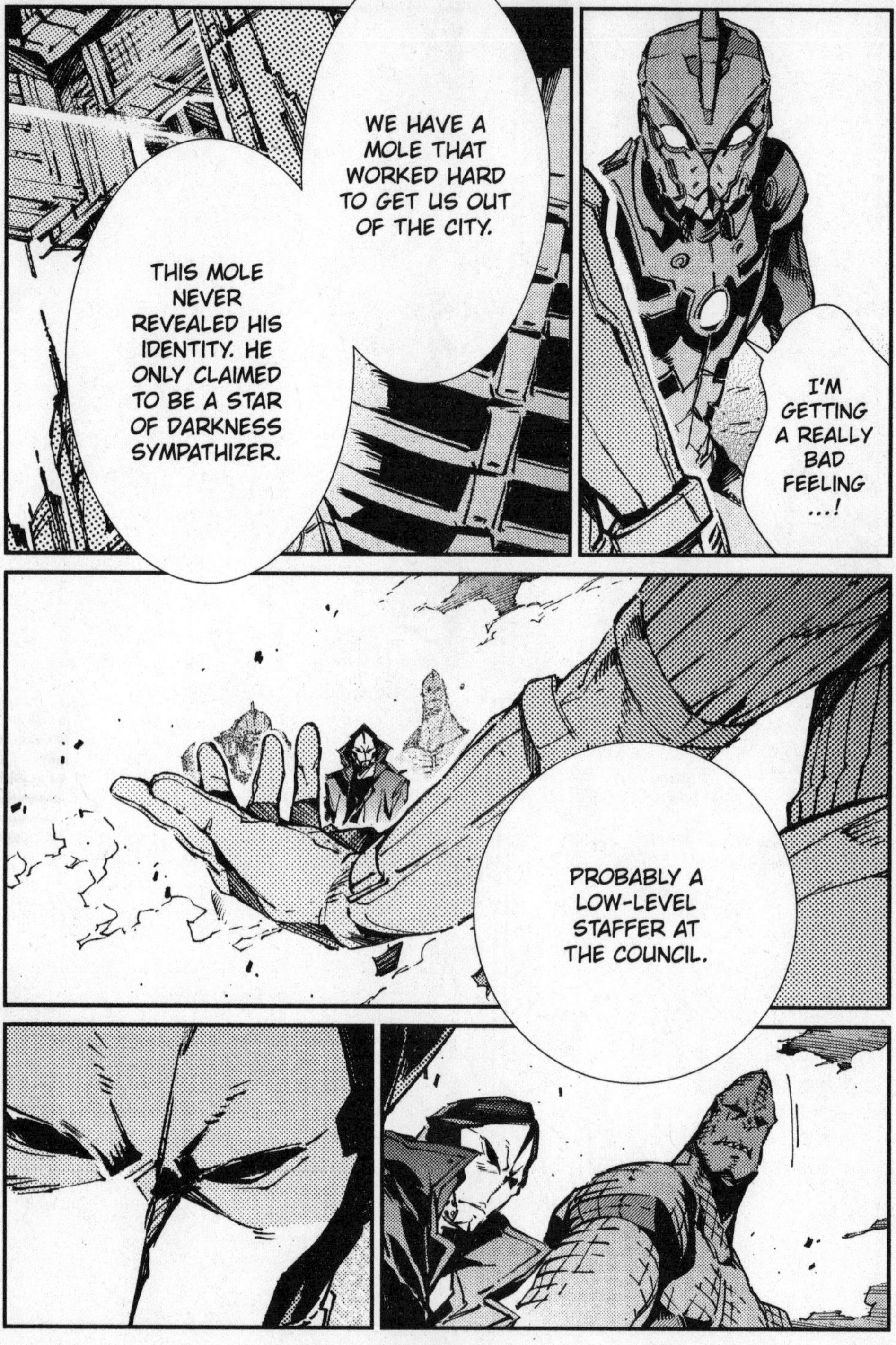
I'M GETTING A REALLY BAD FEELING ...!
WE HAVE A MOLE THAT WORKED HARD TO GET US OUT OF THE CITY.
THIS MOLE NEVER REVEALED HIS IDENTITY. HE ONLY CLAIMED TO BE A STAR OF DARKNESS SYMPATHIZER.
PROBABLY A LOW-LEVEL STAFFER AT THE COUNCIL.

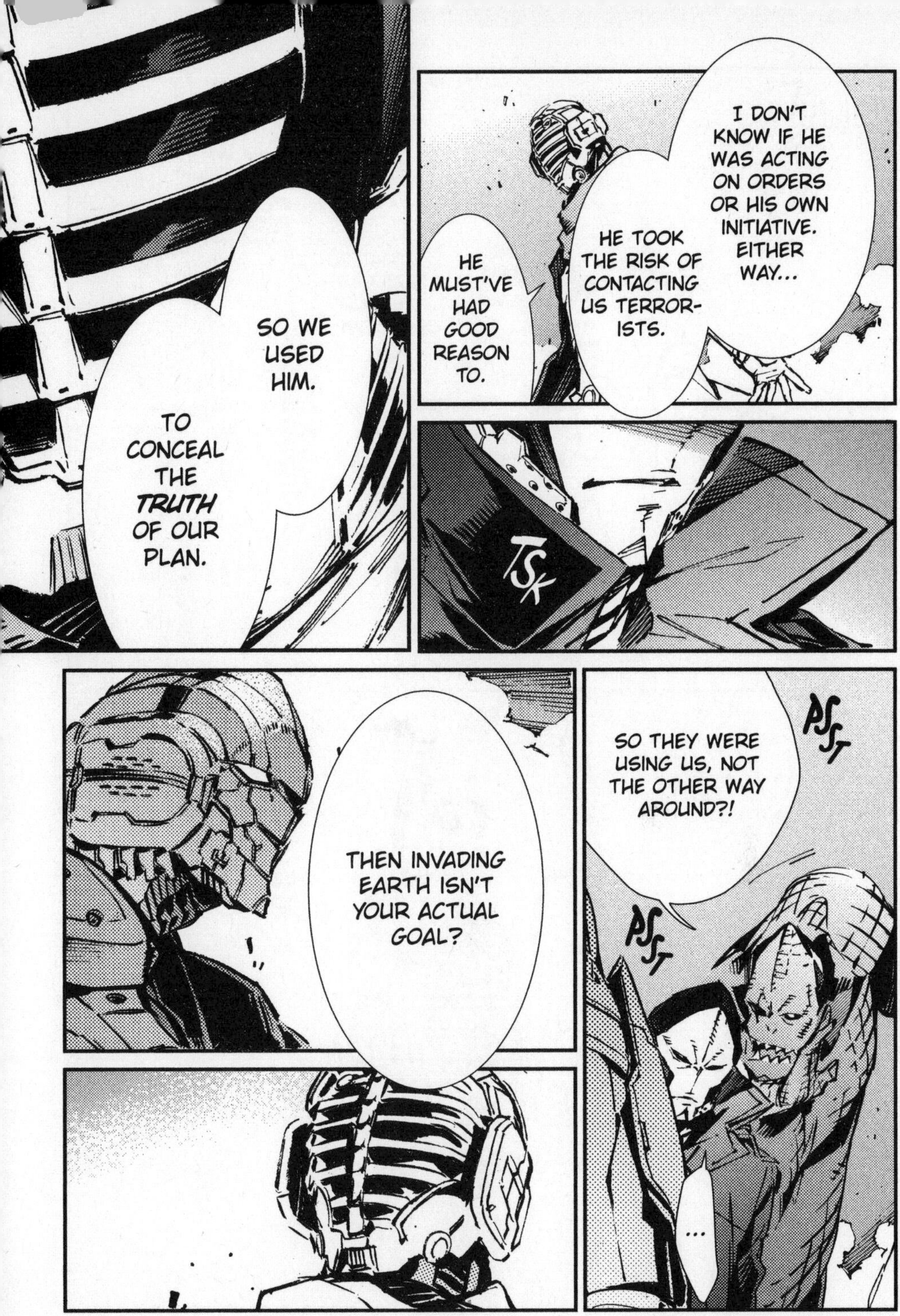
I DON'T KNOW IF HE WAS ACTING ON ORDERS OR HIS OWN INITIATIVE. EITHER WAY...
HE TOOK THE RISK OF CONTACTING US TERROR-ISTS.
HE MUST'VE HAD GOOD REASON TO.
TSK
SO WE USED HIM.
TO CONCEAL THE *TRUTH* OF OUR PLAN.
SO THEY WERE USING US, NOT THE OTHER WAY AROUND?!
PSST
PSST
...
THEN INVADING EARTH ISN'T YOUR ACTUAL GOAL?

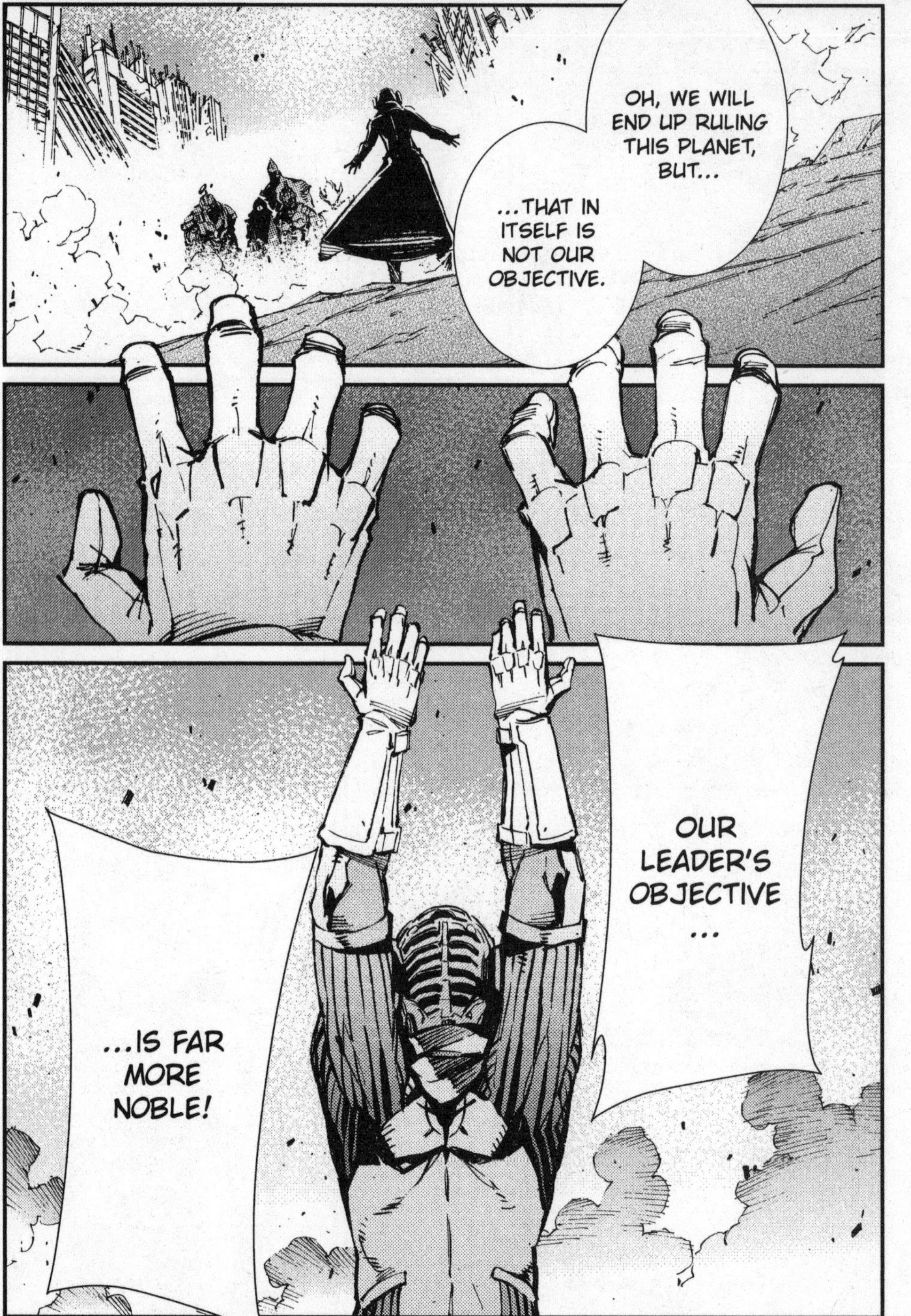
OH, WE WILL END UP RULING THIS PLANET, BUT...
...THAT IN ITSELF IS NOT OUR OBJECTIVE.
OUR LEADER'S OBJECTIVE ...
...IS FAR MORE NOBLE!

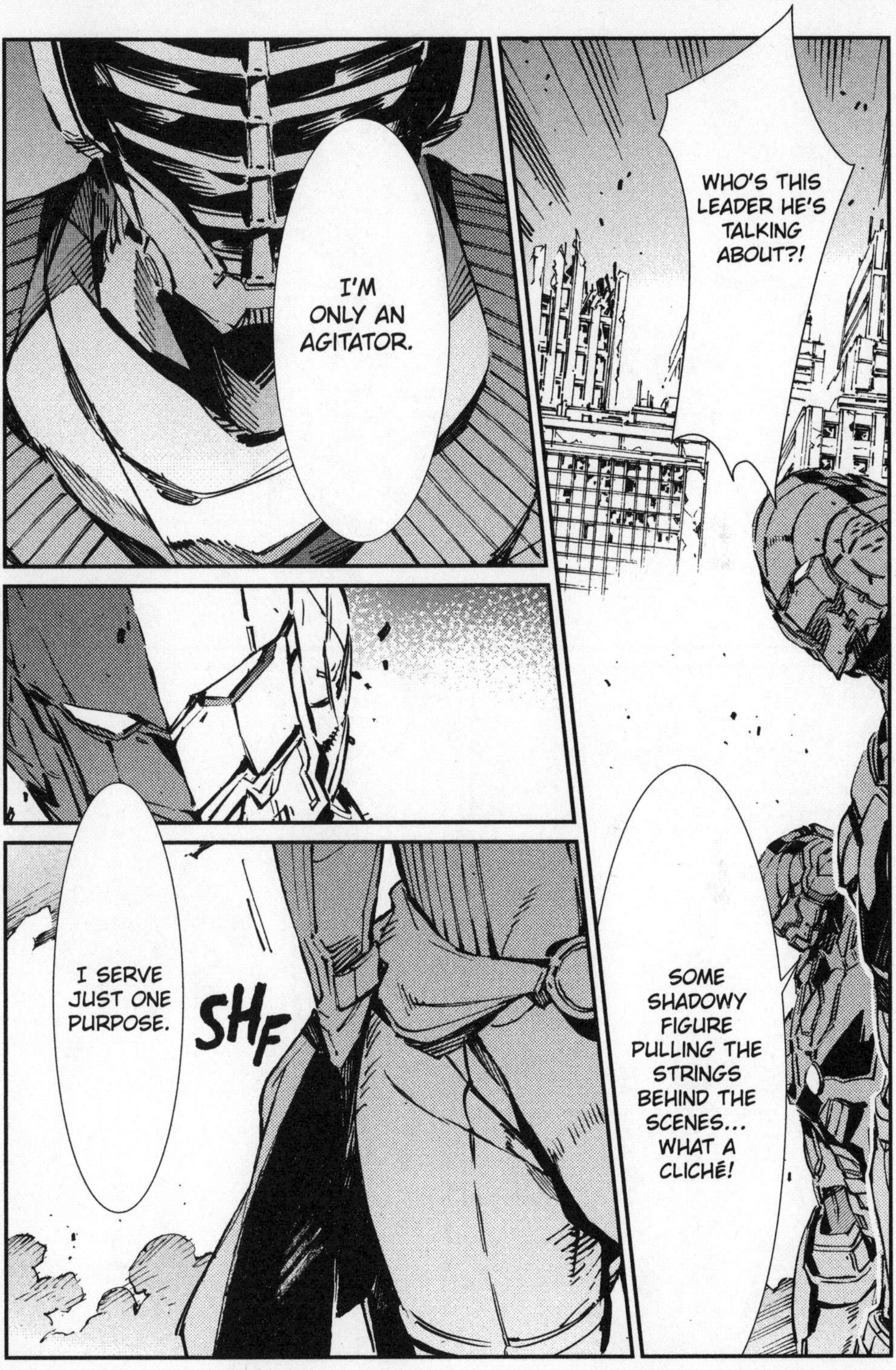
WHO'S THIS LEADER HE'S TALKING ABOUT?!
SOME SHADOWY FIGURE PULLING THE STRINGS BEHIND THE SCENES... WHAT A CLICHÉ!
I'M ONLY AN AGITATOR.
I SERVE JUST ONE PURPOSE.
SHF

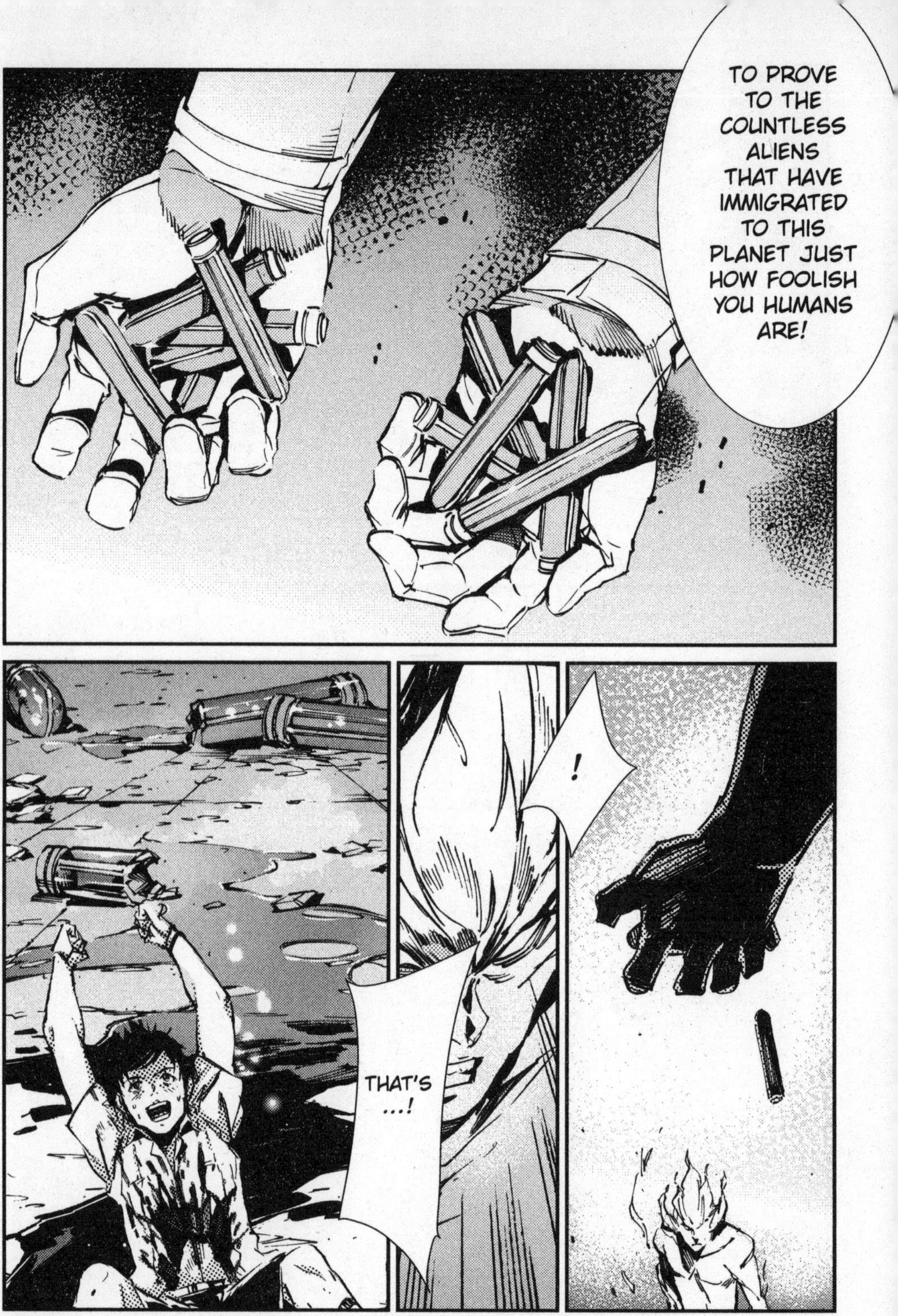
TO PROVE TO THE COUNTLESS ALIENS THAT HAVE IMMIGRATED TO THIS PLANET JUST HOW FOOLISH YOU HUMANS ARE!
!
THAT'S ...!

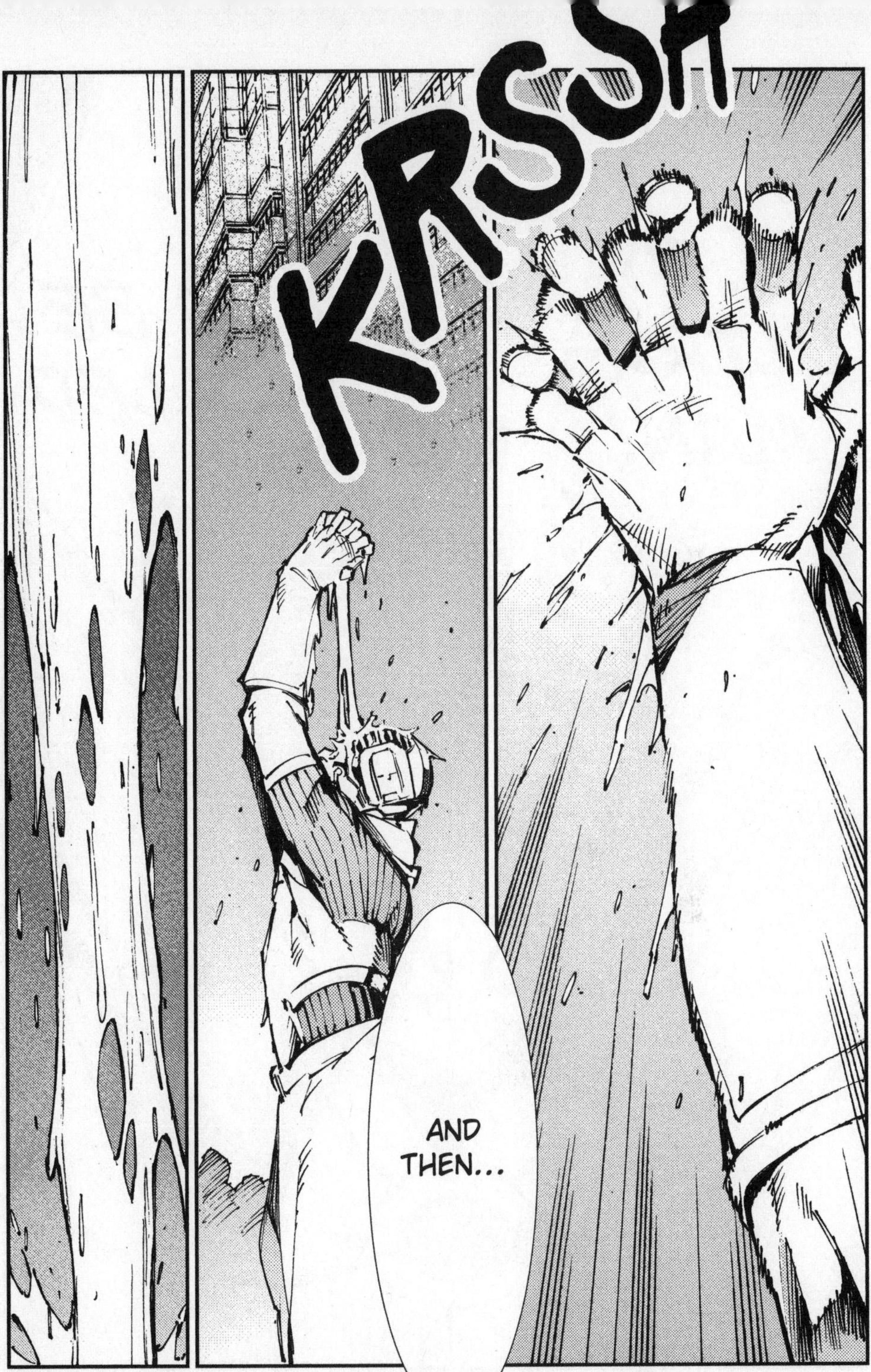
KRSSH
AND THEN...

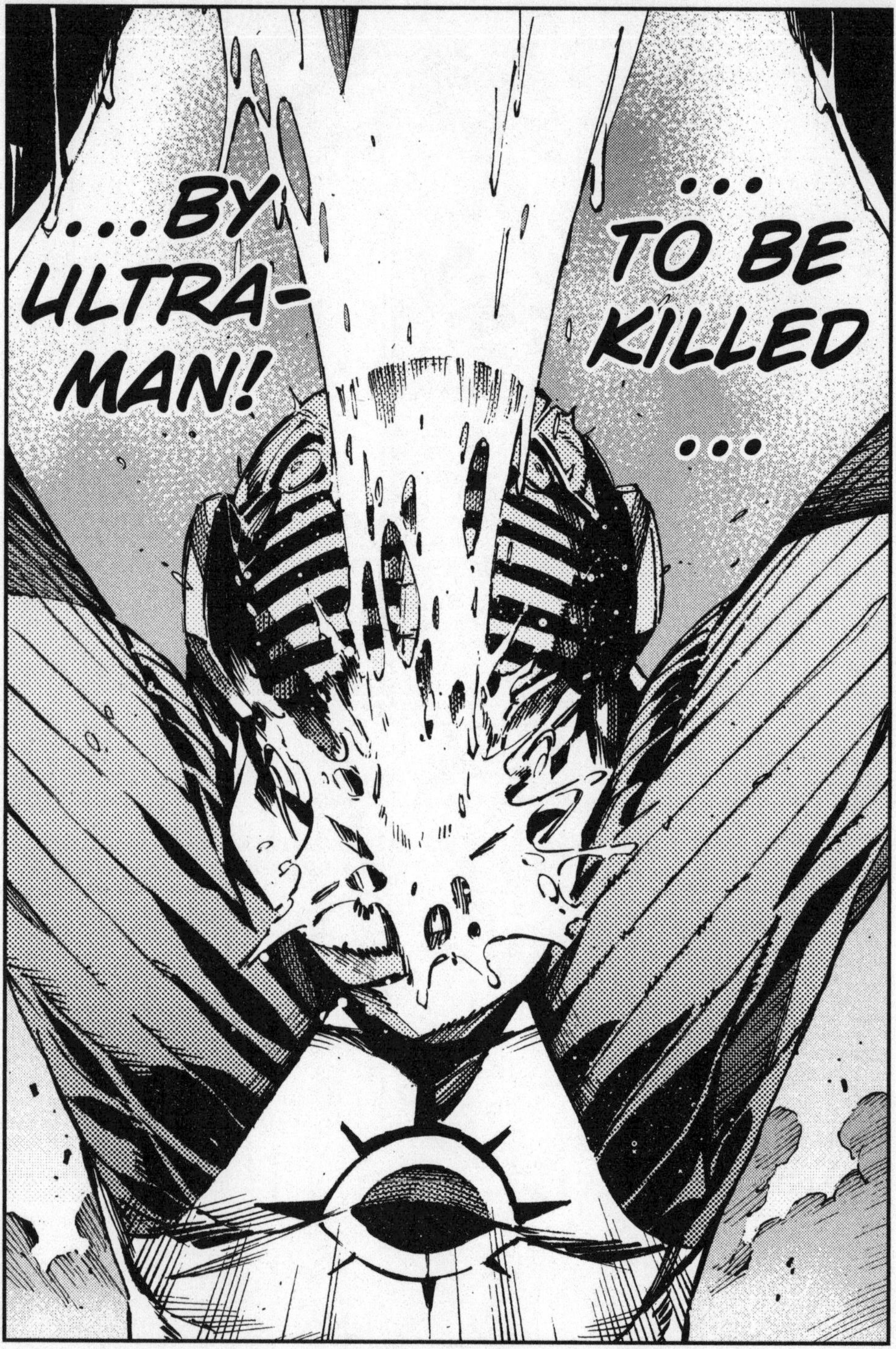
...TO BE KILLED...
...BY ULTRA-MAN!

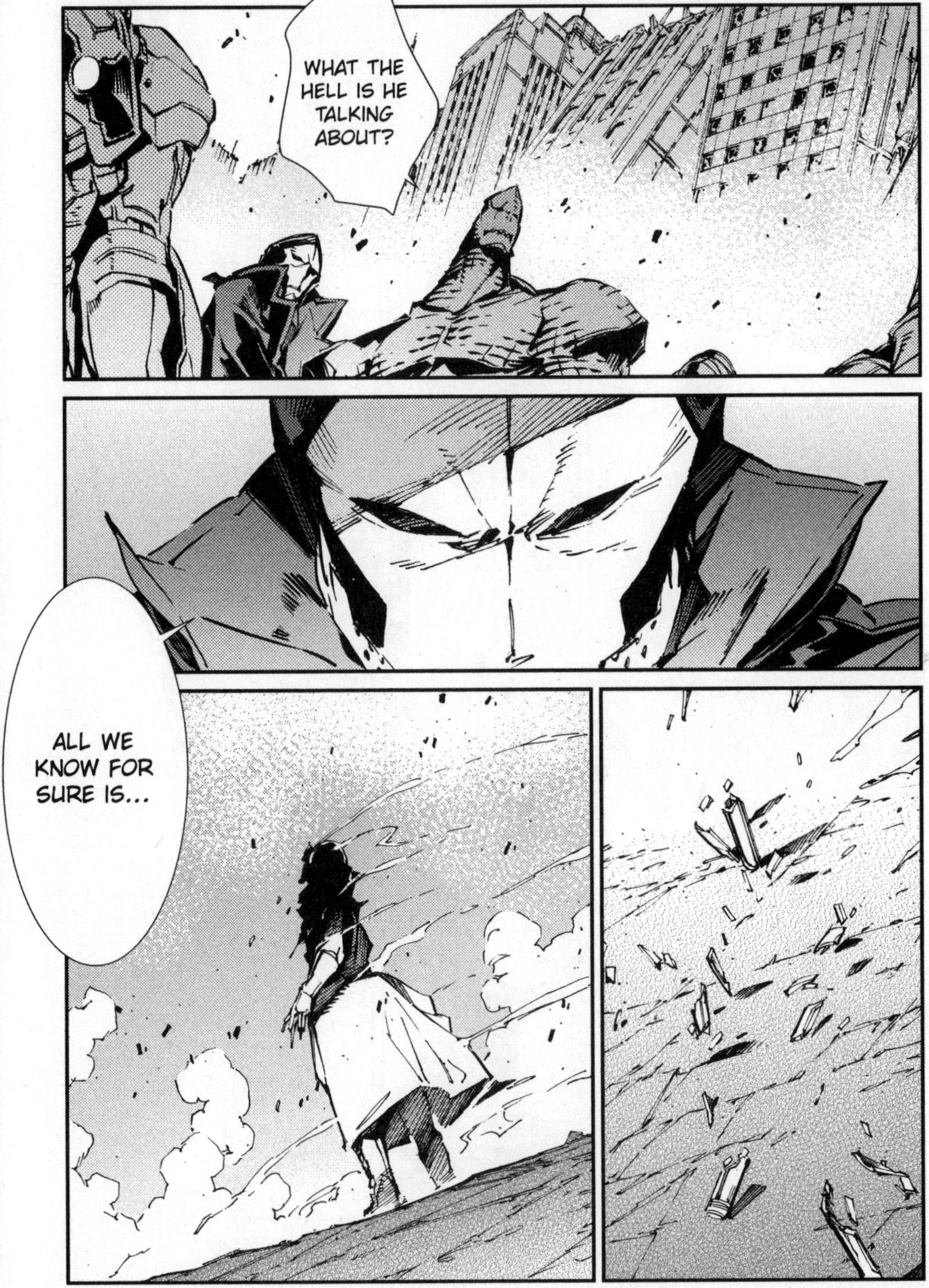
WHAT THE HELL IS HE TALKING ABOUT?
ALL WE KNOW FOR SURE IS...

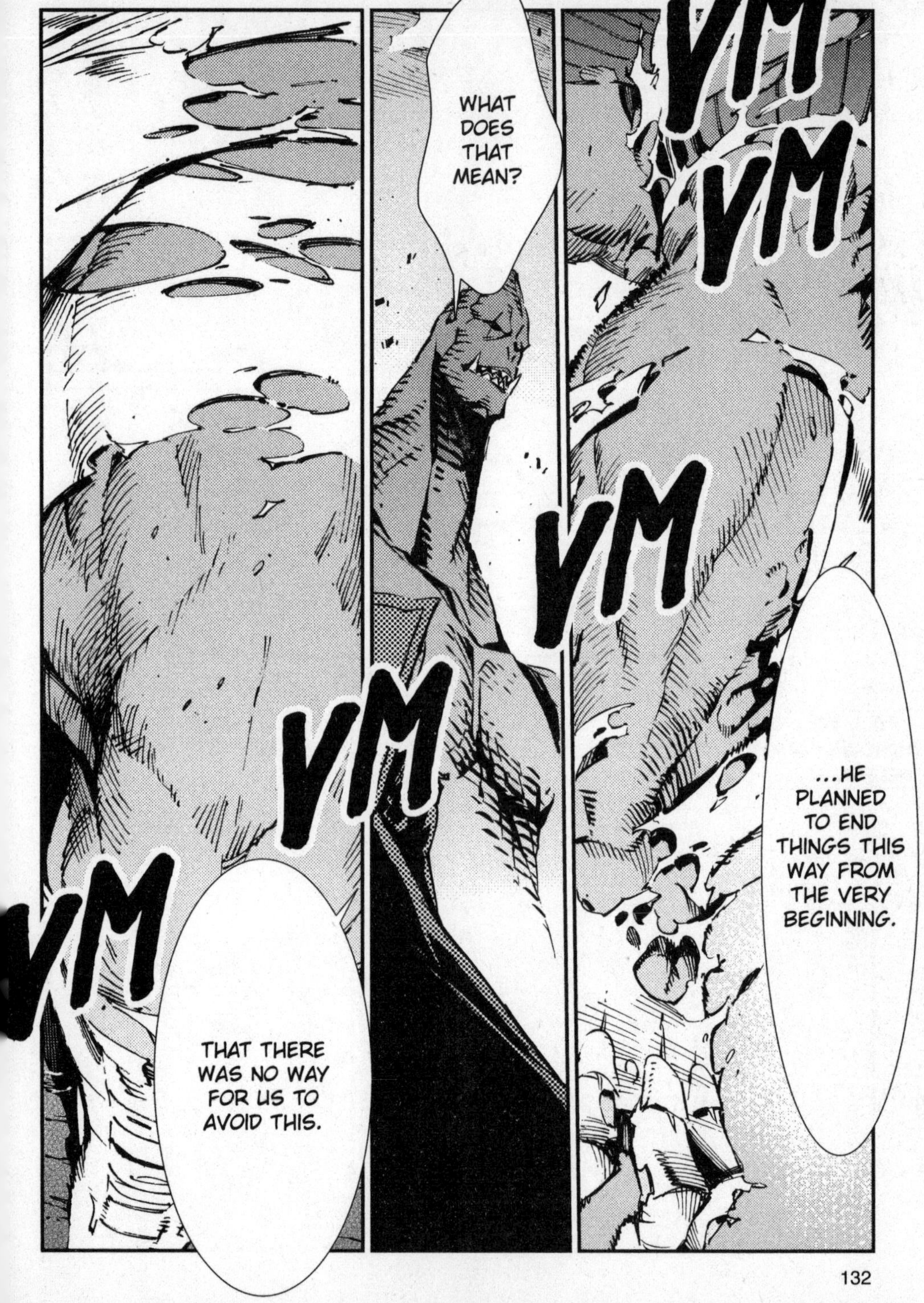
VM
VM
VM
...HE PLANNED TO END THINGS THIS WAY FROM THE VERY BEGINNING.
WHAT DOES THAT MEAN?
VM
VM
THAT THERE WAS NO WAY FOR US TO AVOID THIS.

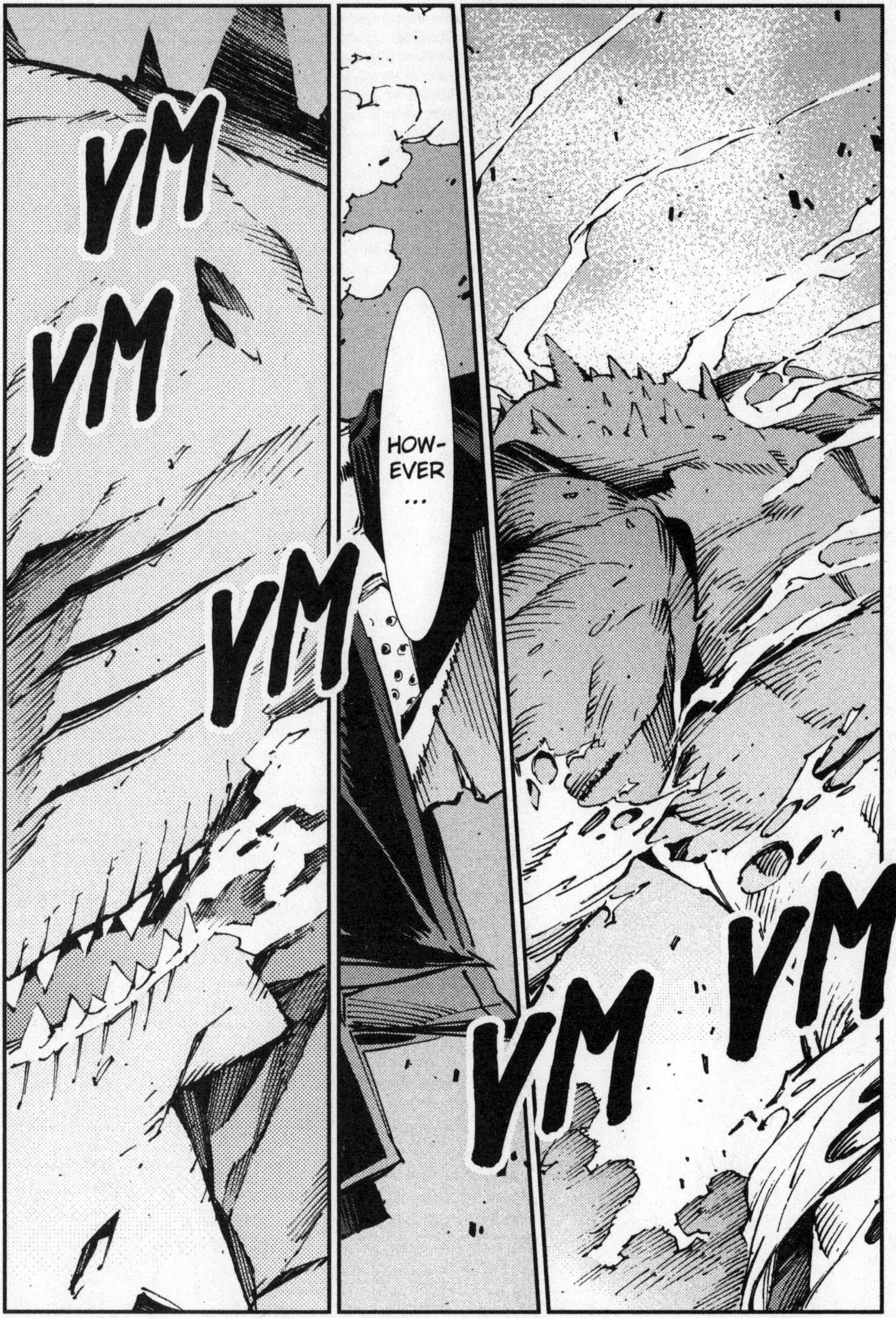
VM
VM
HOW-EVER...
VM
VM
VM

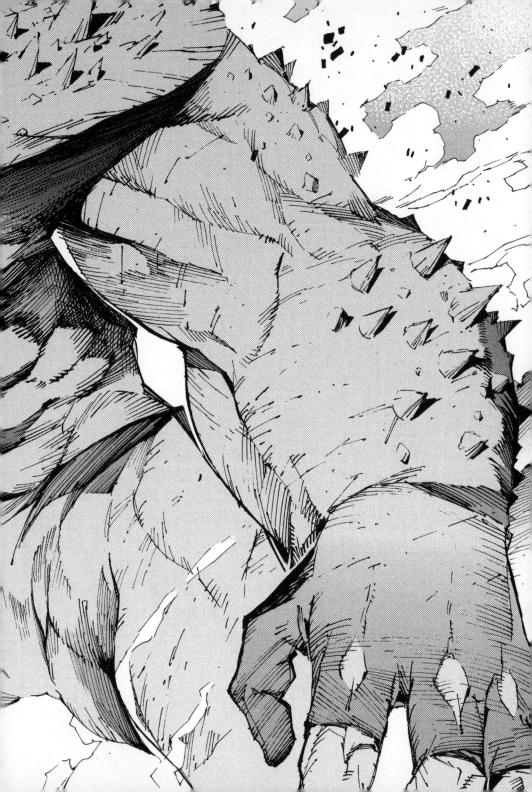

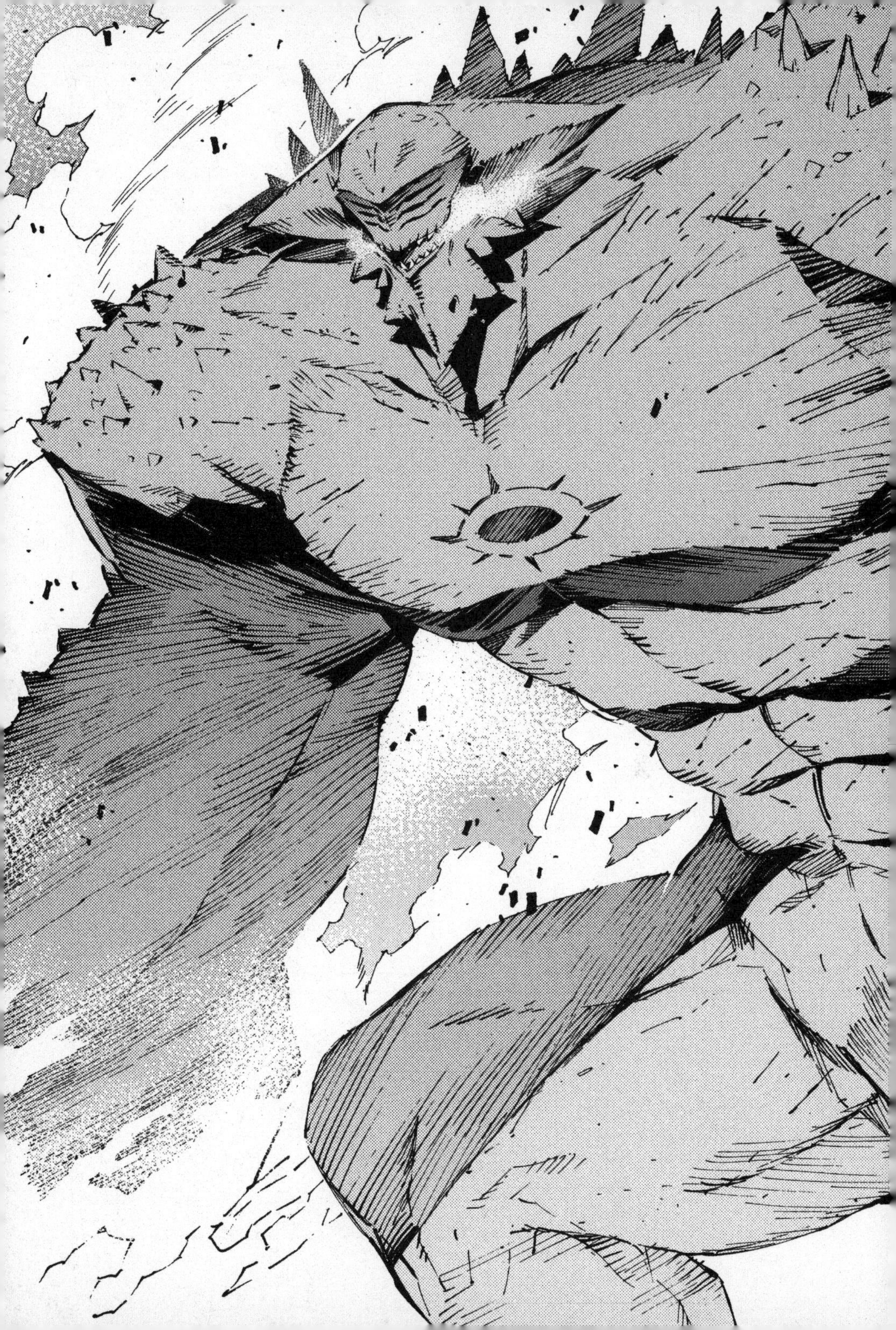

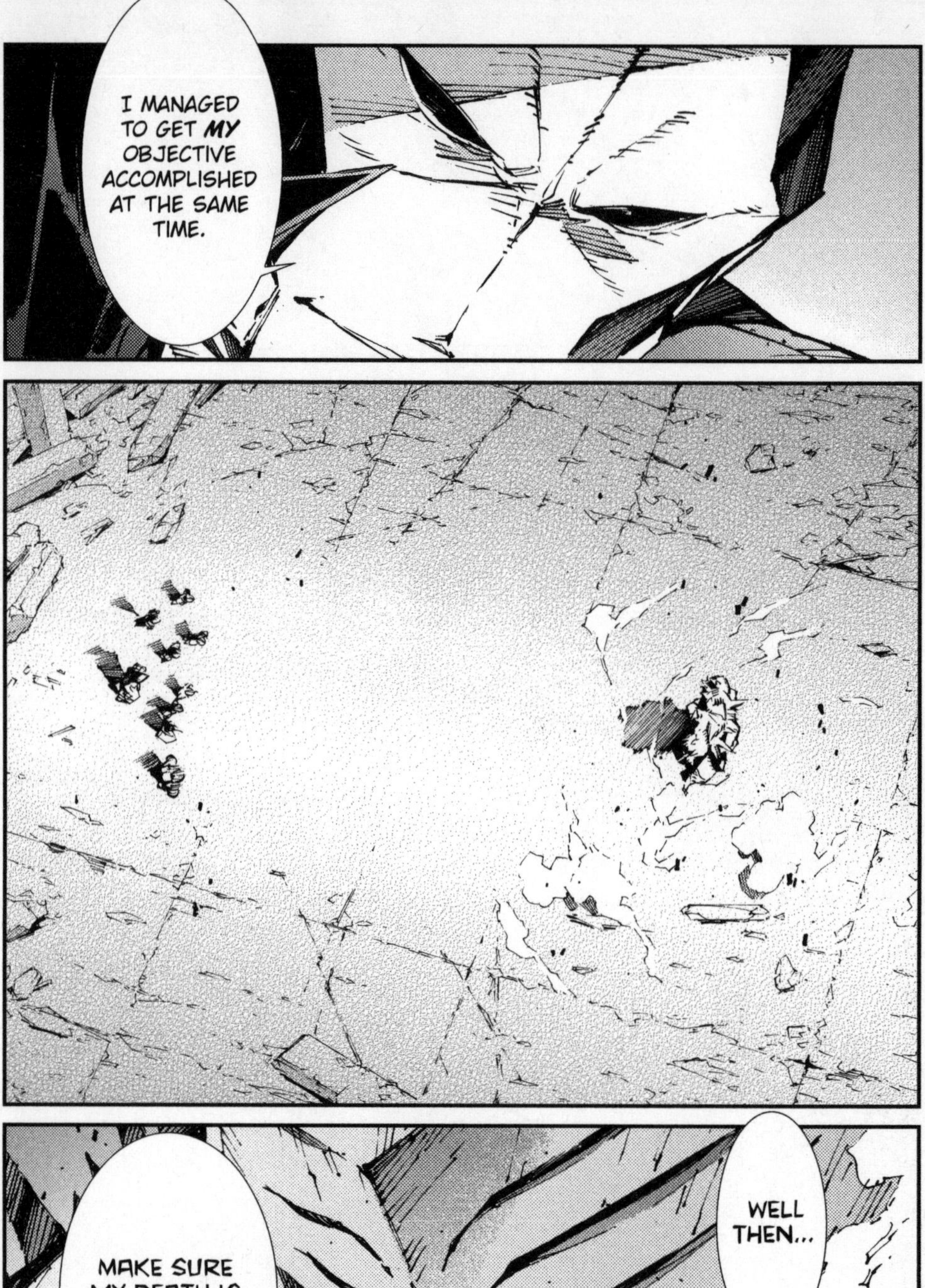
I MANAGED TO GET **MY** OBJECTIVE ACCOMPLISHED AT THE SAME TIME.
WELL THEN...
MAKE SURE MY DEATH IS GLORIOUS!

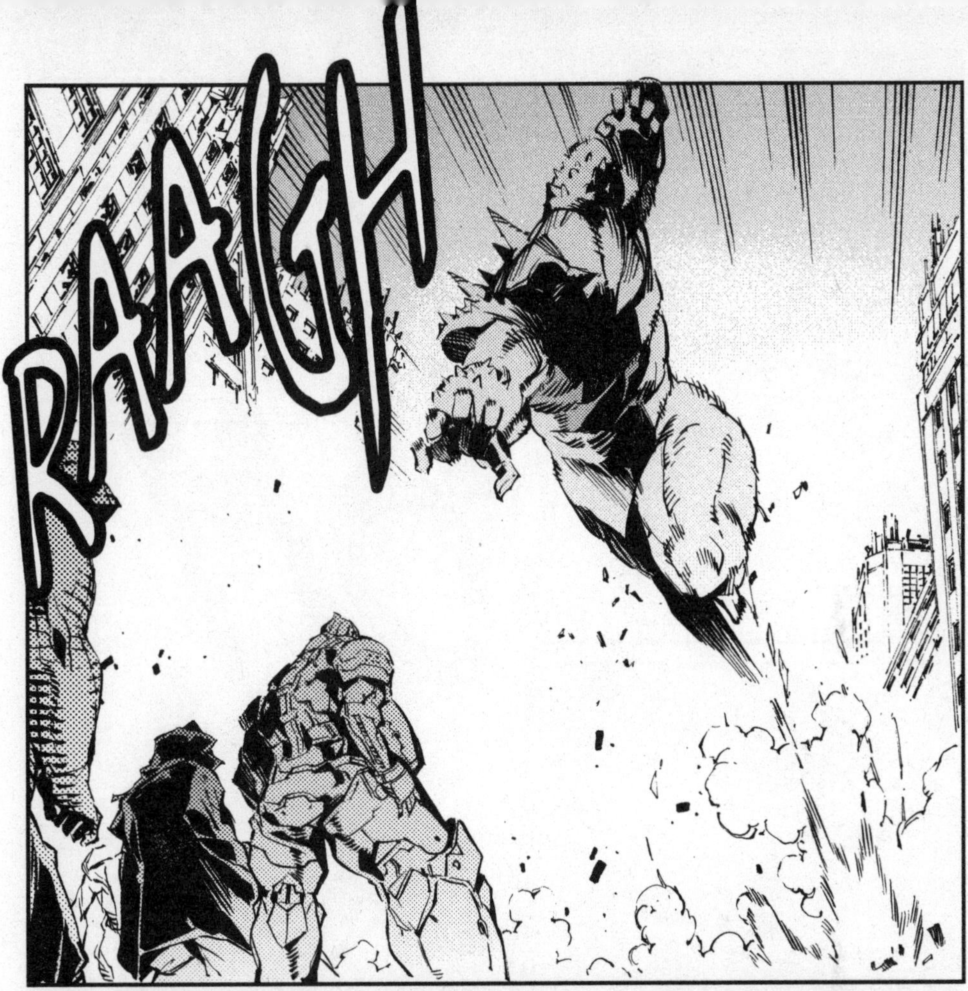
RAAGH
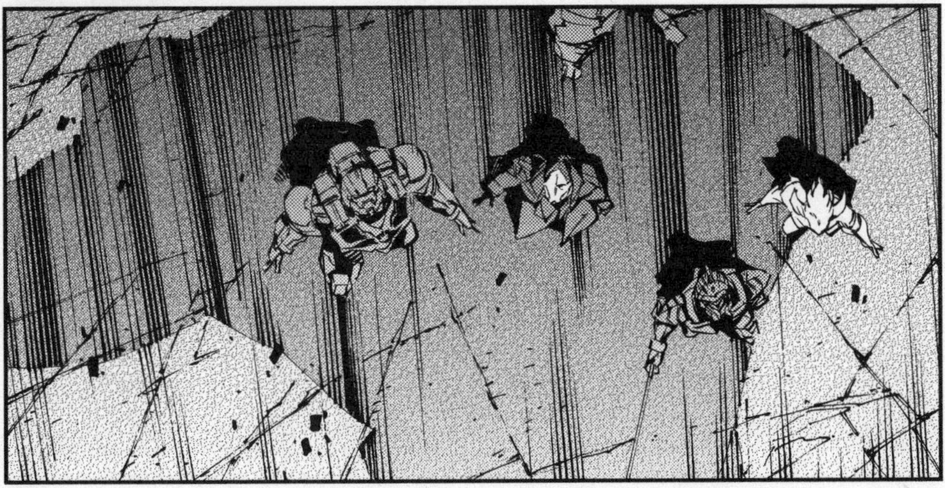

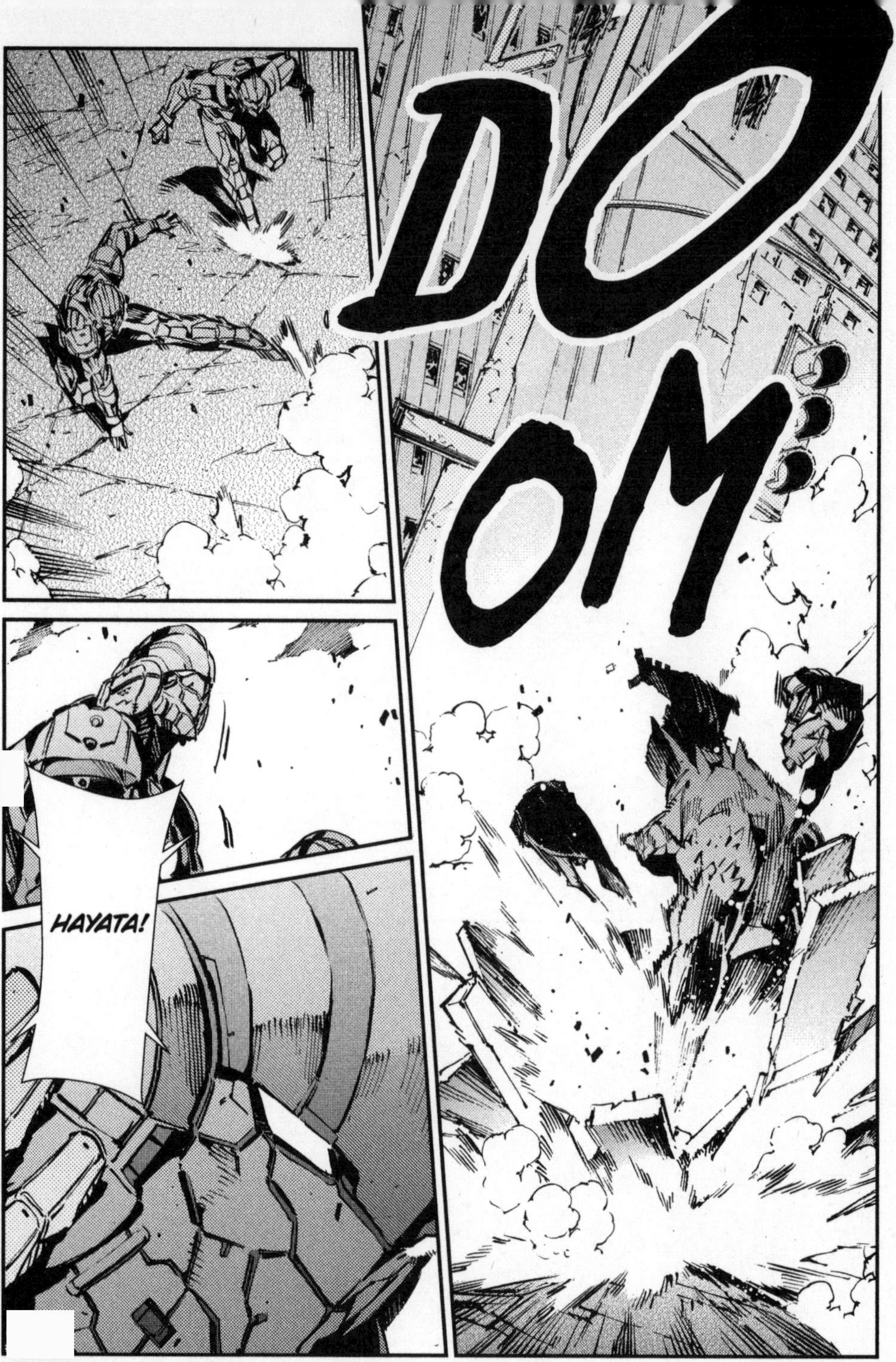
DOOM
HAYATA!

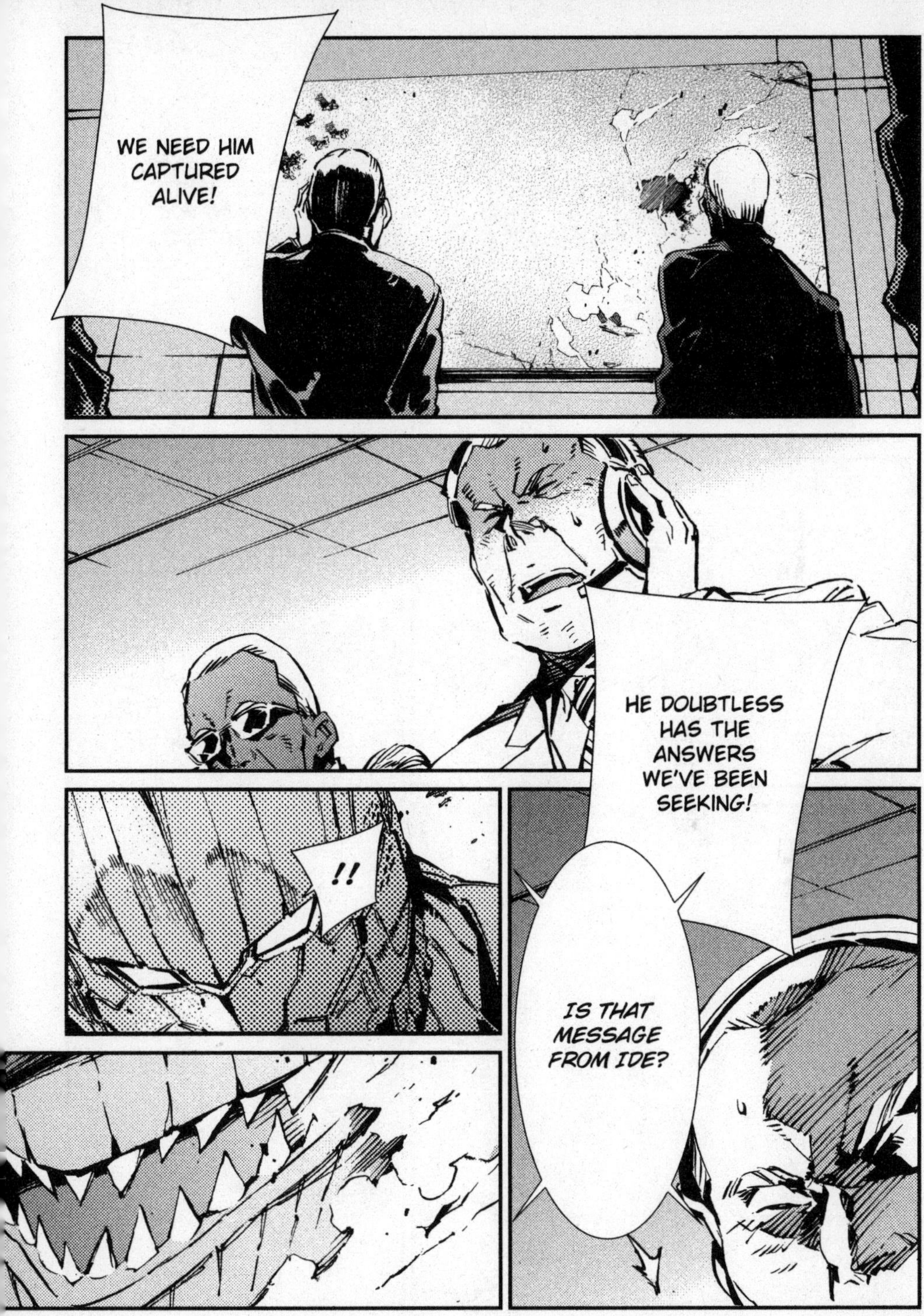
WE NEED HIM CAPTURED ALIVE!
HE DOUBTLESS HAS THE ANSWERS WE'VE BEEN SEEKING!
IS THAT MESSAGE FROM IDE?
!!

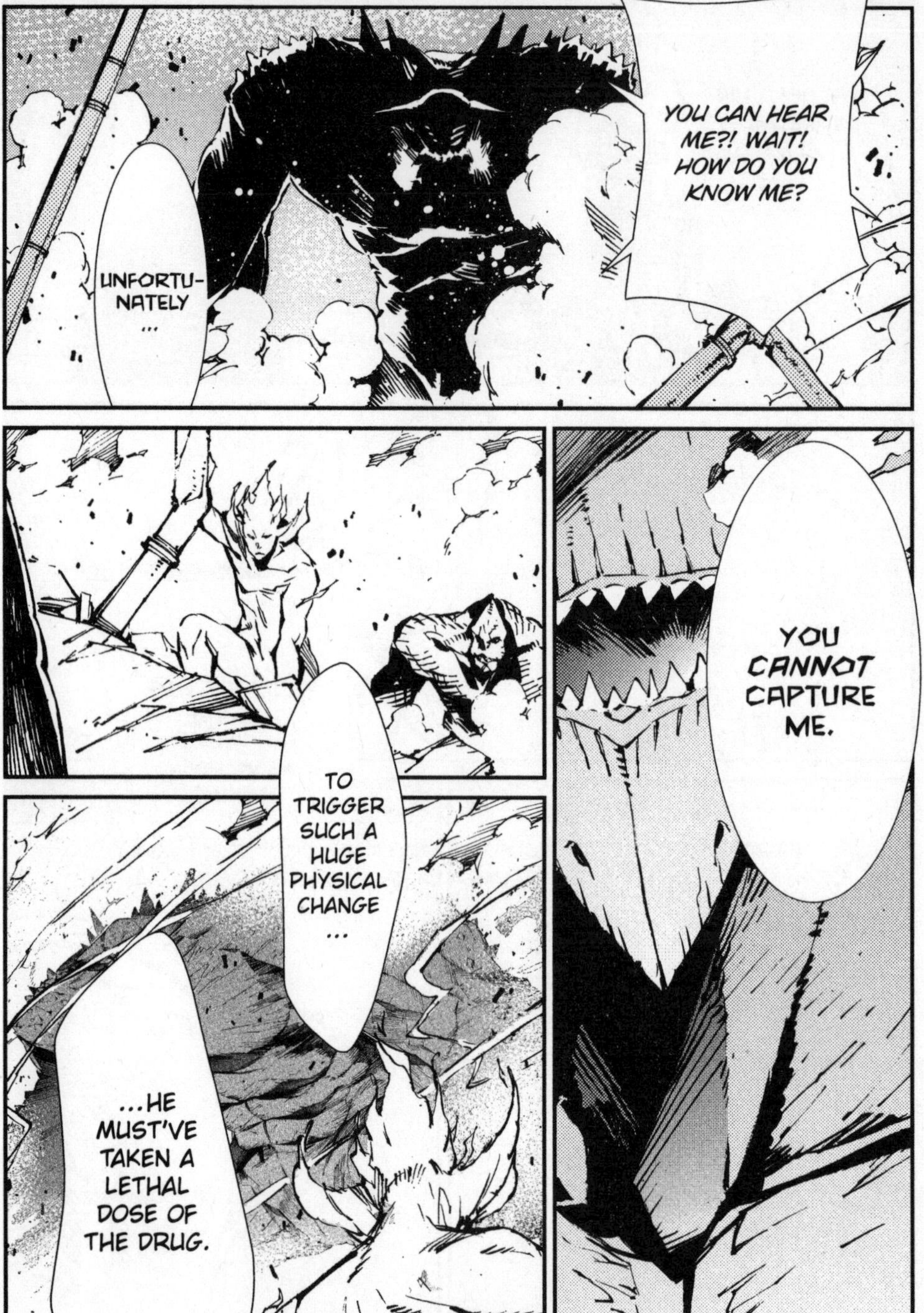
YOU CAN HEAR ME?! WAIT! HOW DO YOU KNOW ME?
UNFORTUNATELY...
YOU CANNOT CAPTURE ME.
TO TRIGGER SUCH A HUGE PHYSICAL CHANGE...
...HE MUST'VE TAKEN A LETHAL DOSE OF THE DRUG.

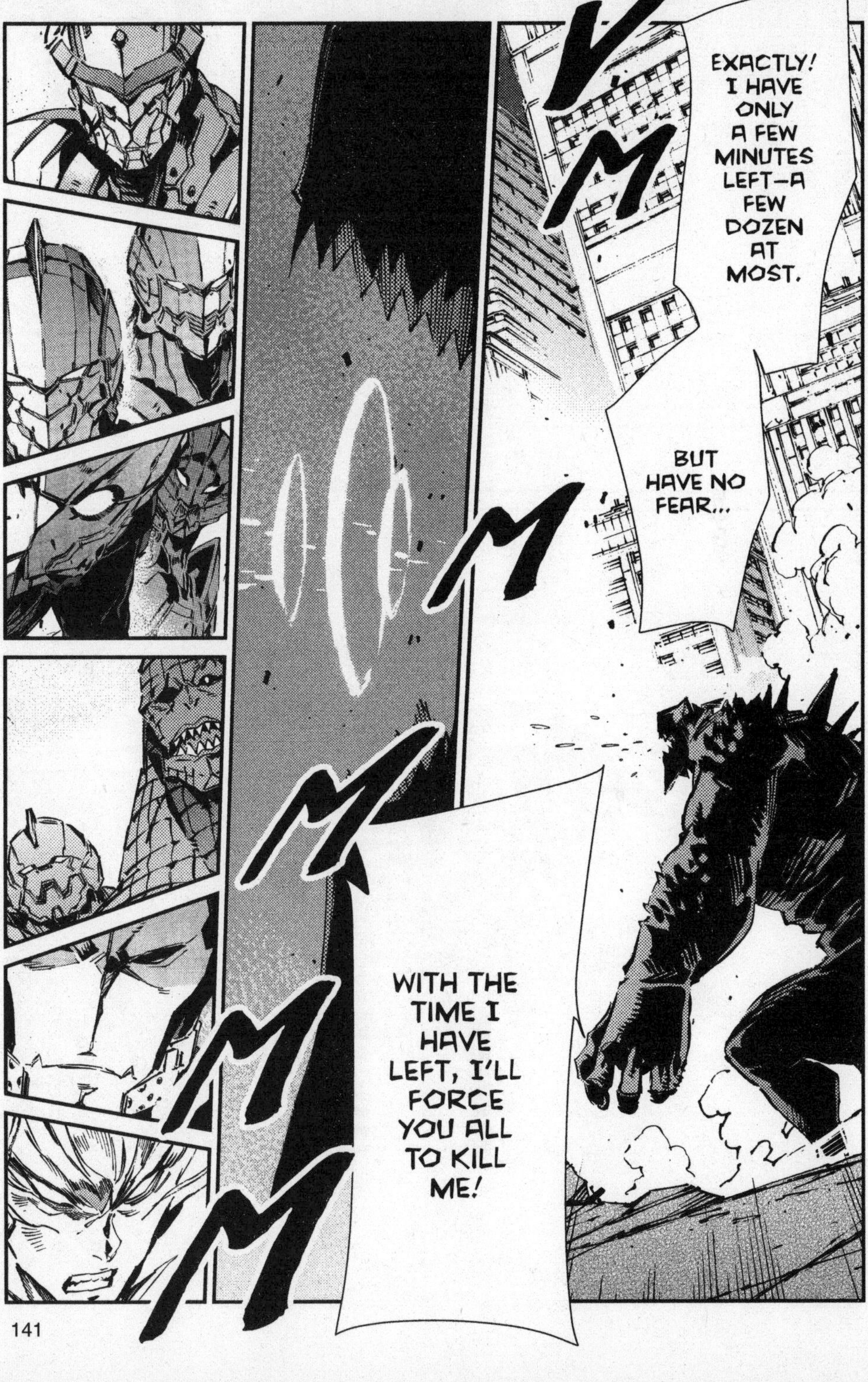
VMMMMMM
EXACTLY! I HAVE ONLY A FEW MINUTES LEFT—A FEW DOZEN AT MOST.
BUT HAVE NO FEAR...
WITH THE TIME I HAVE LEFT, I'LL FORCE YOU ALL TO KILL ME!

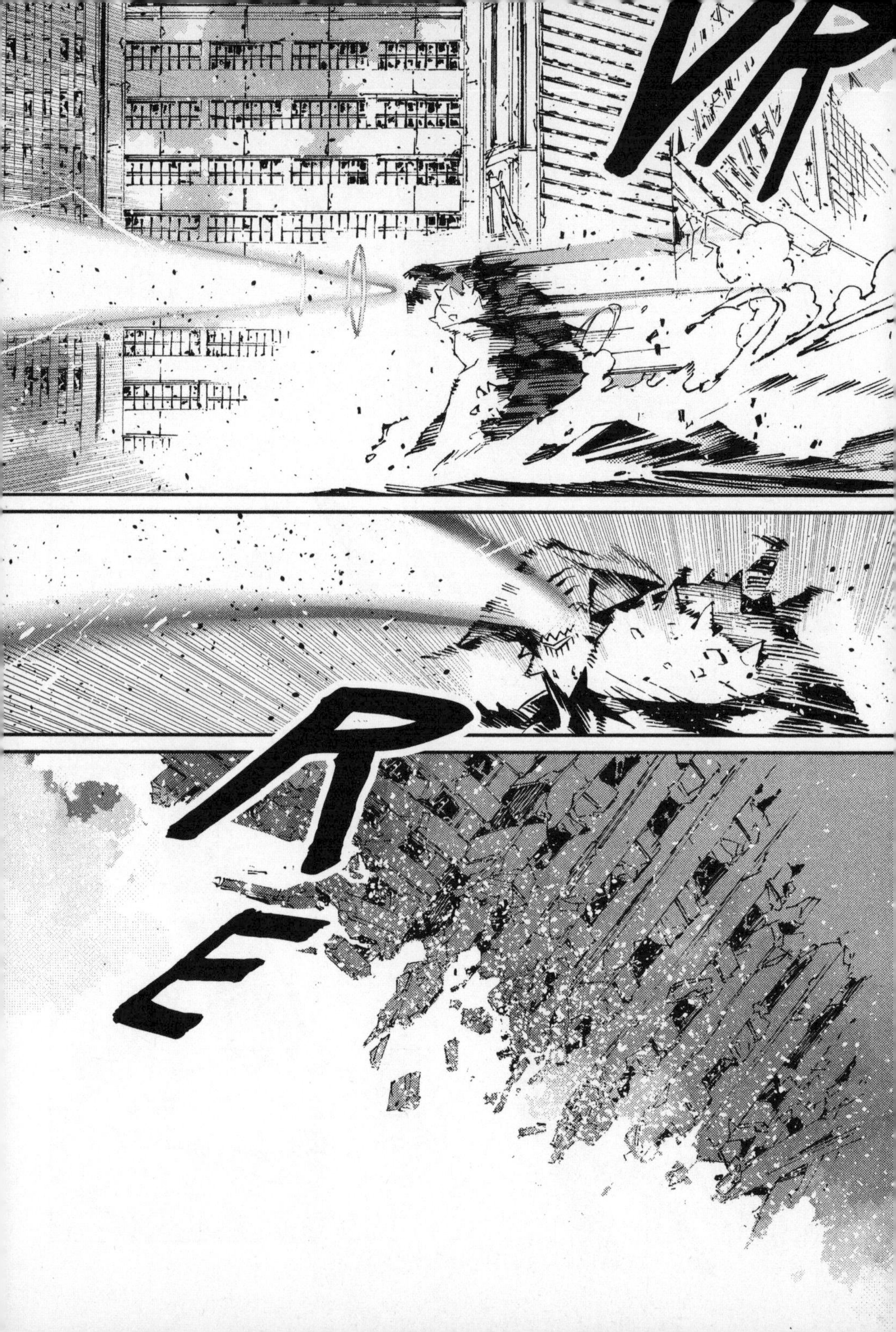
VR
R
E

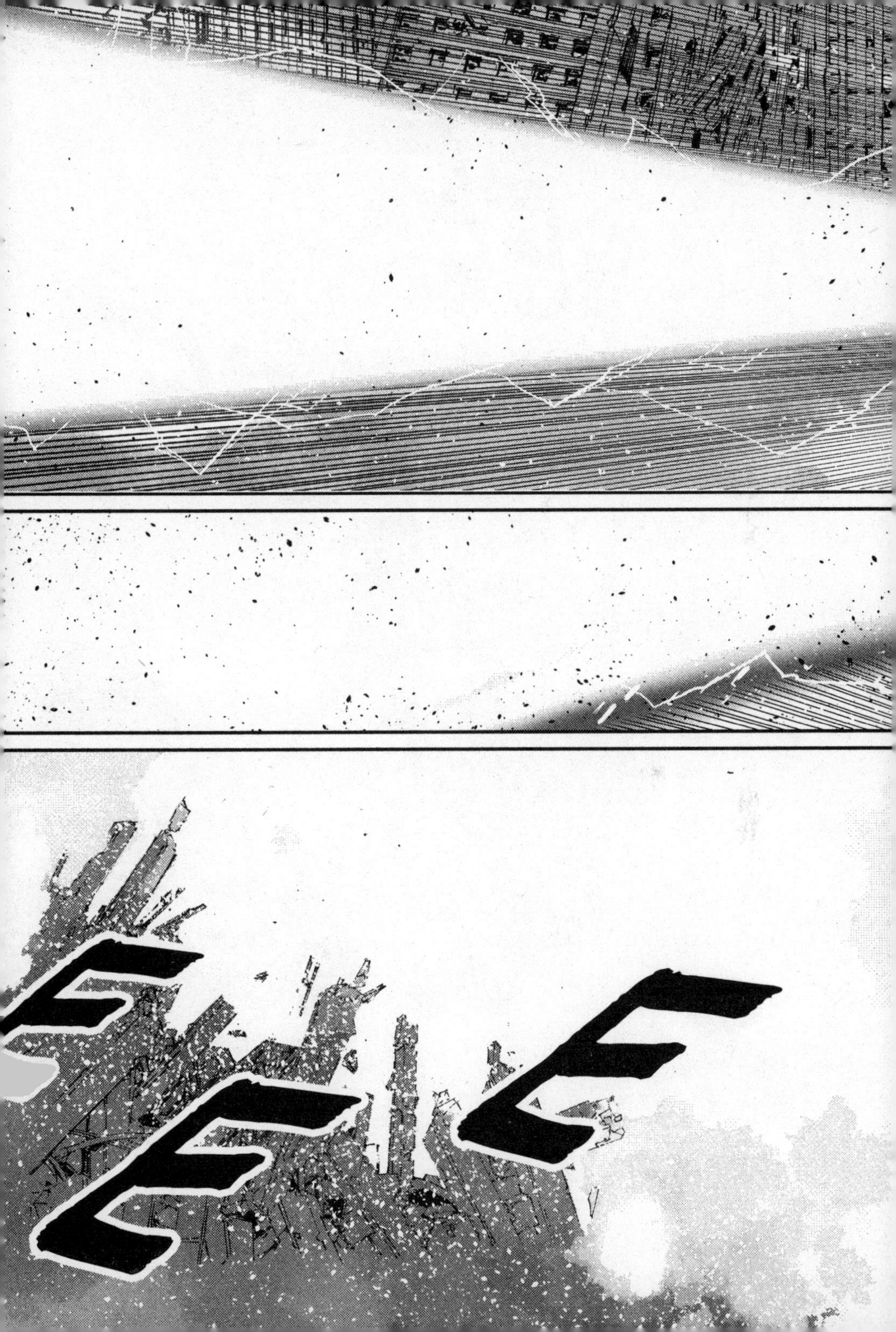

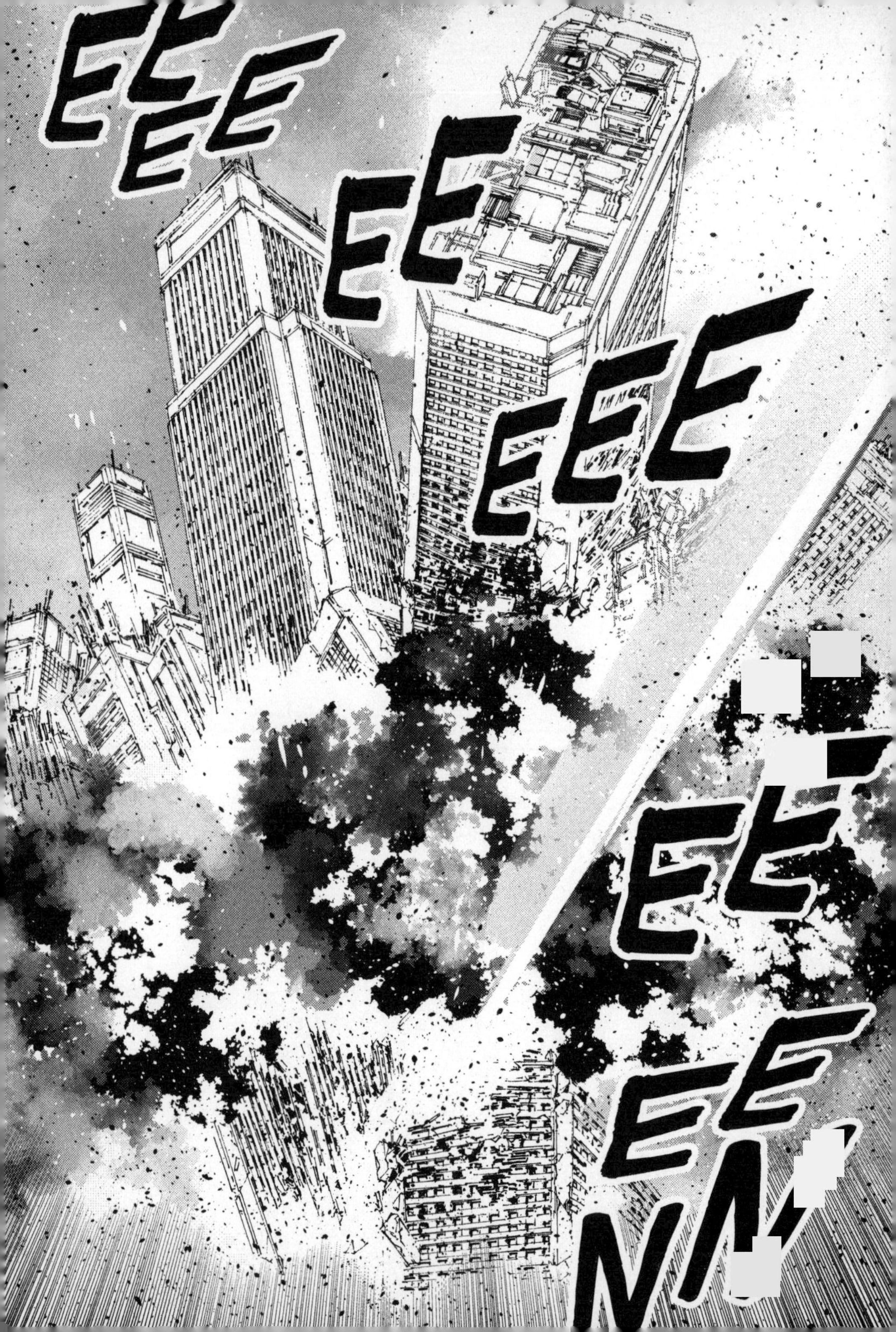
EEEE
EEE
EEEE
EE
EE
N

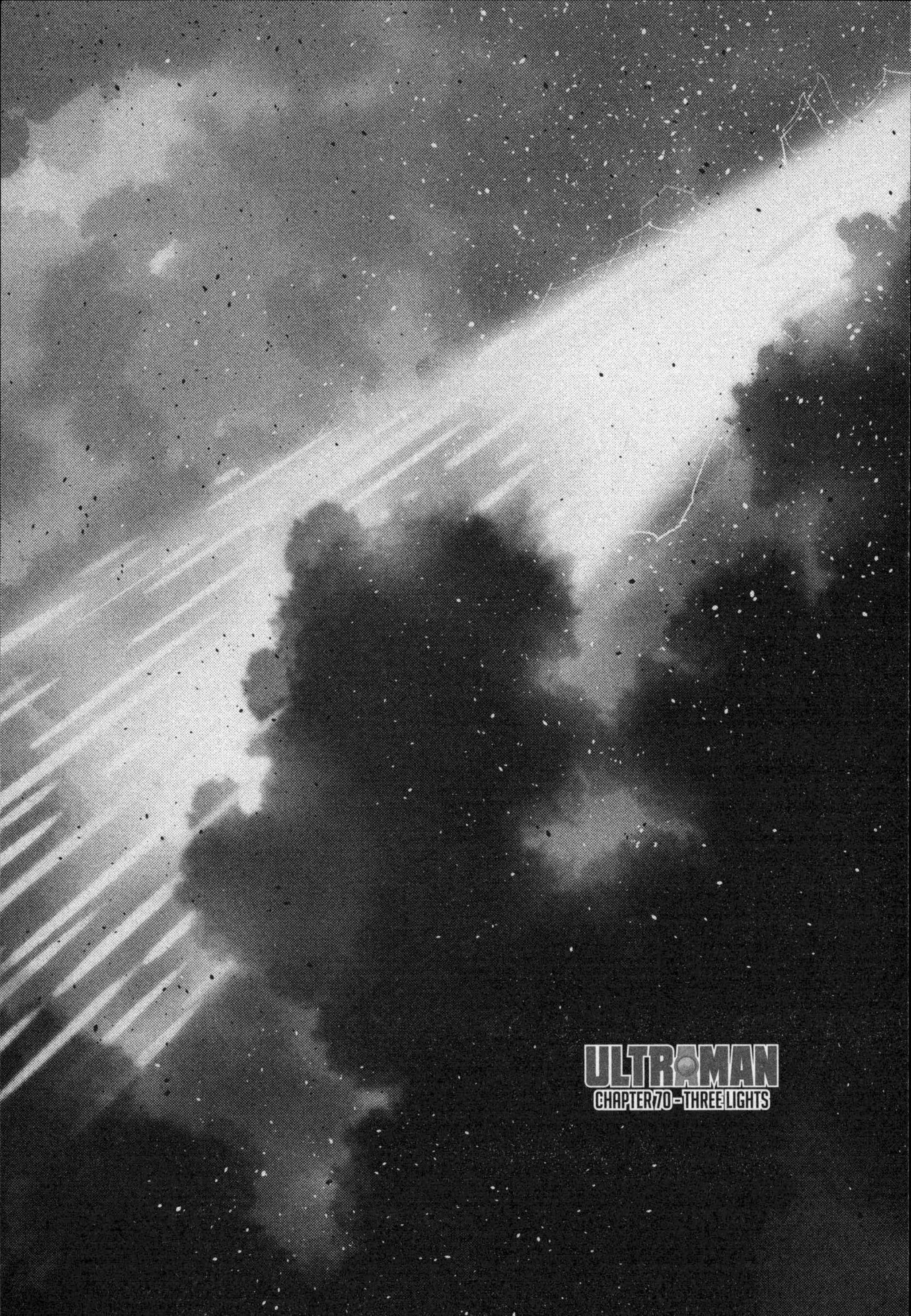
ULTRAMAN
CHAPTER 70 - THREE LIGHTS

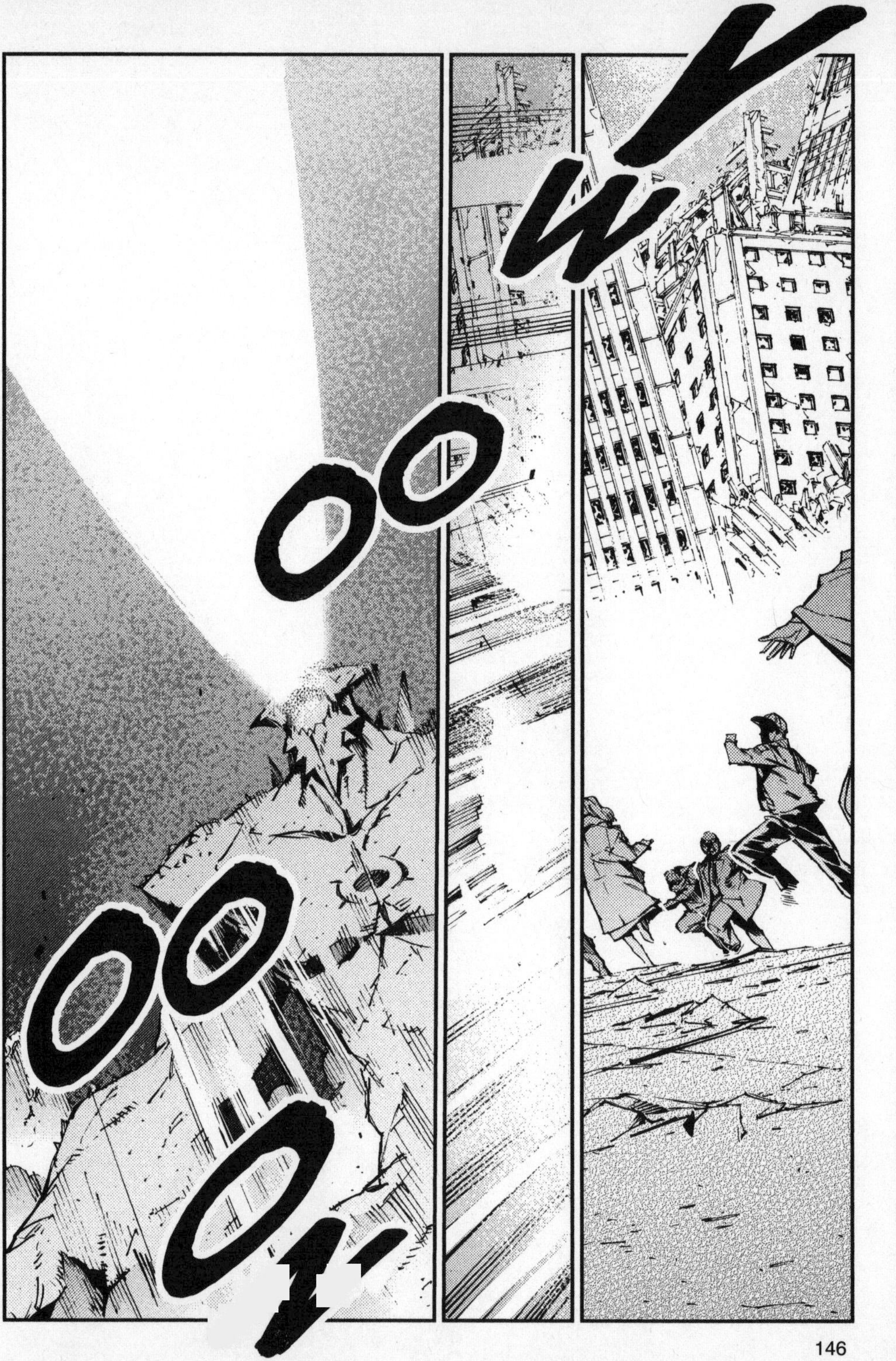
VWOOOOO

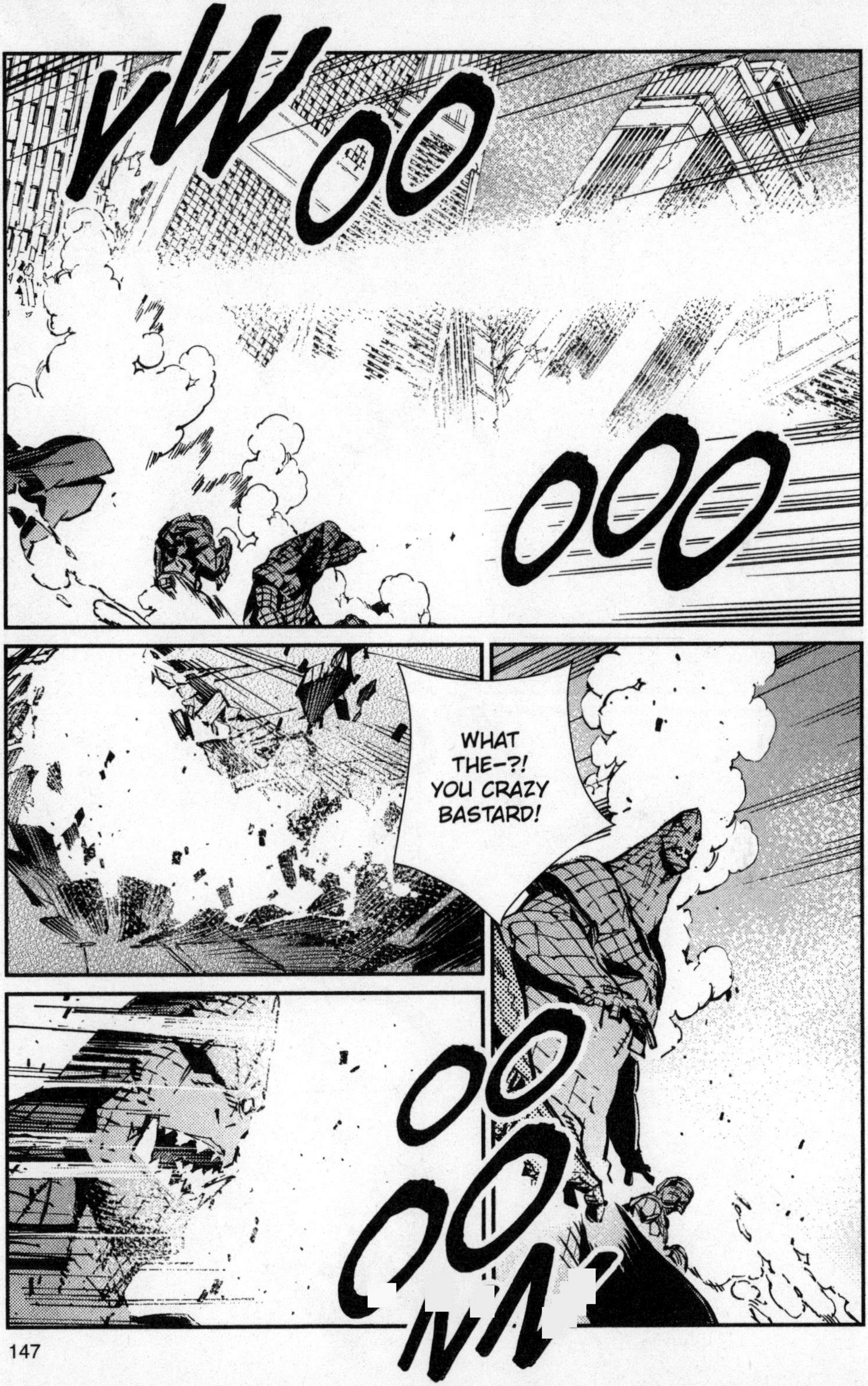
VWOOOOO
WHAT THE-?! YOU CRAZY BASTARD!

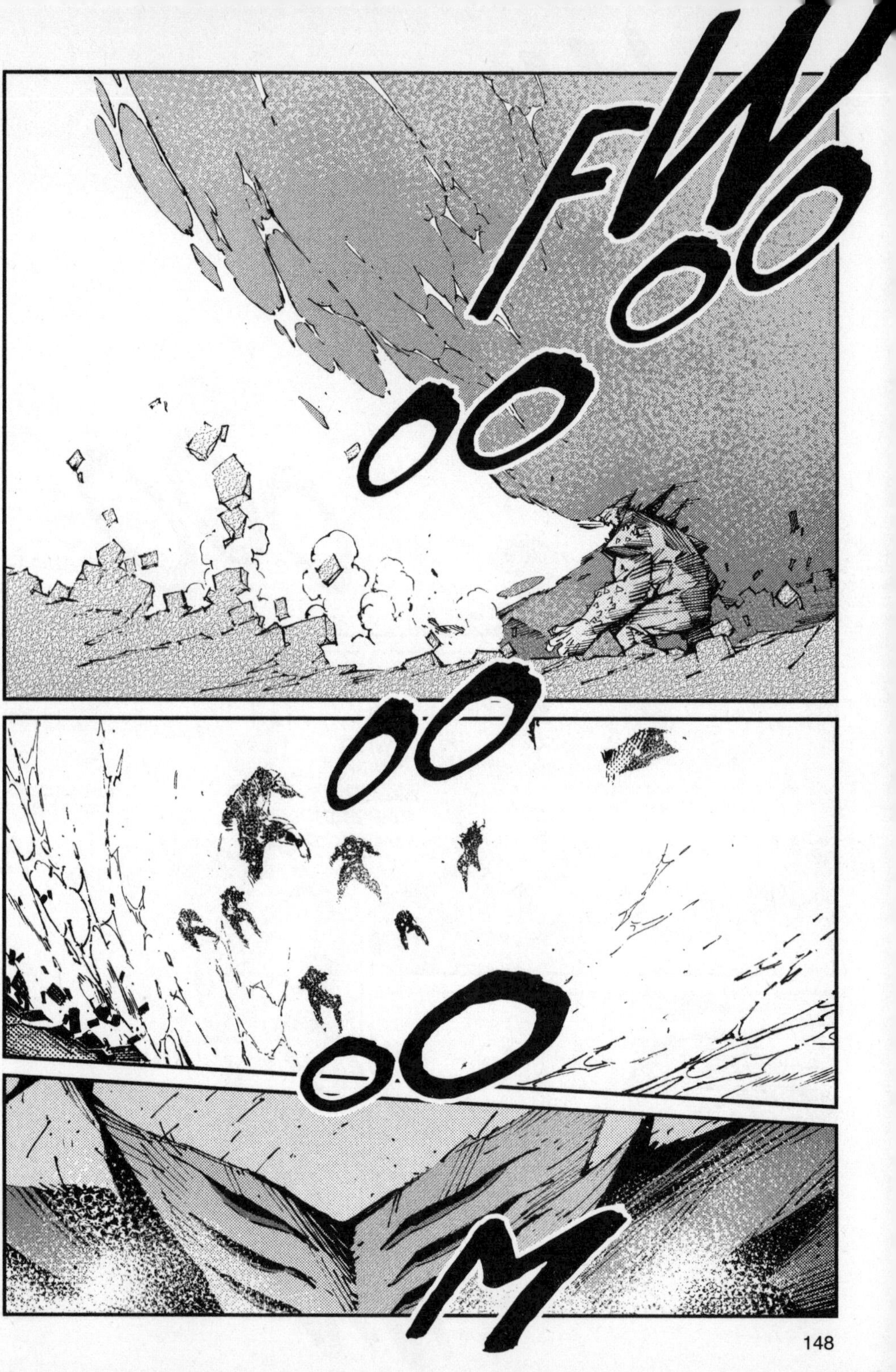
FWOOOOOOOOOM

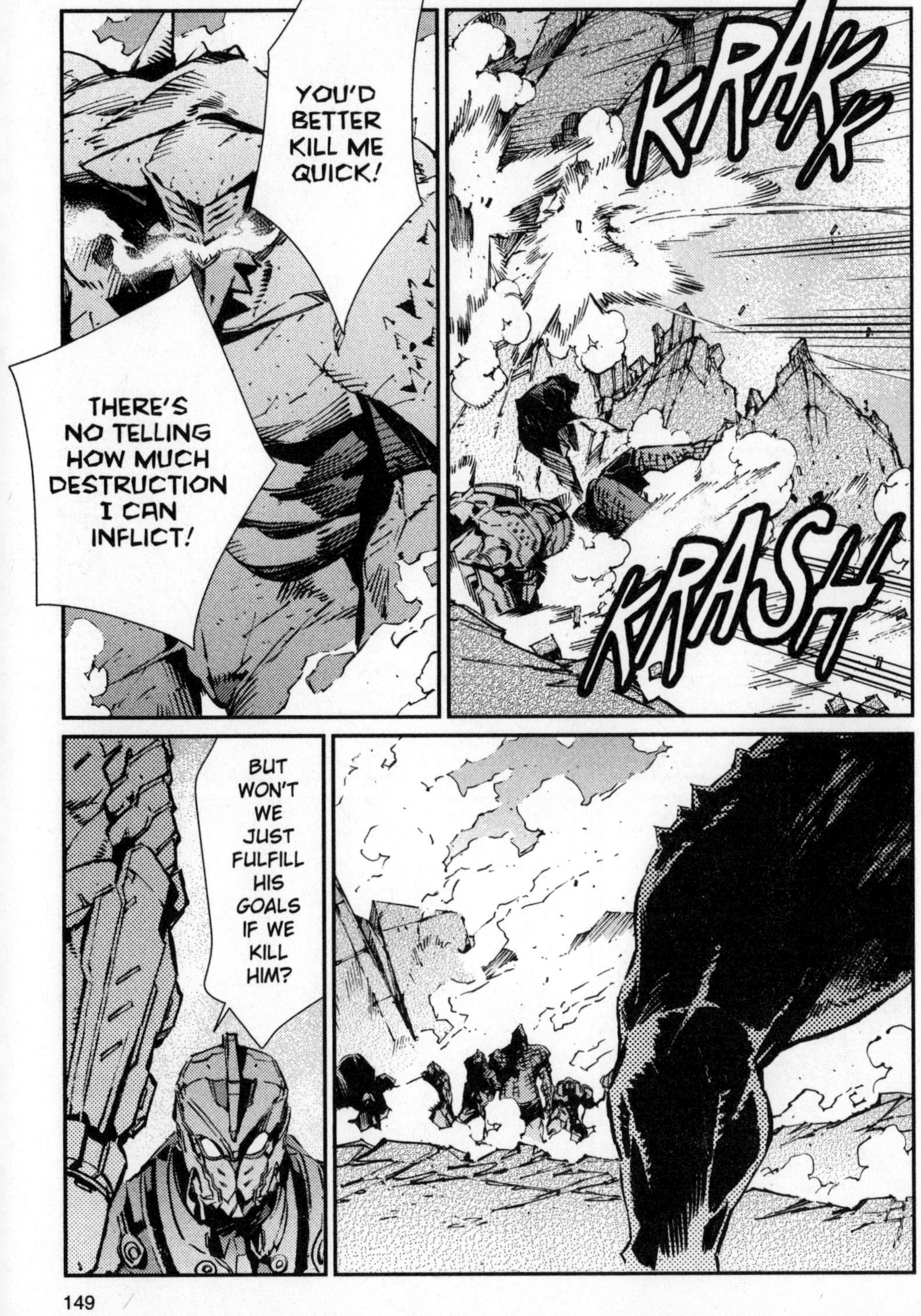
KRAK
KRASH
YOU'D BETTER KILL ME QUICK!
THERE'S NO TELLING HOW MUCH DESTRUCTION I CAN INFLICT!
BUT WON'T WE JUST FULFILL HIS GOALS IF WE KILL HIM?

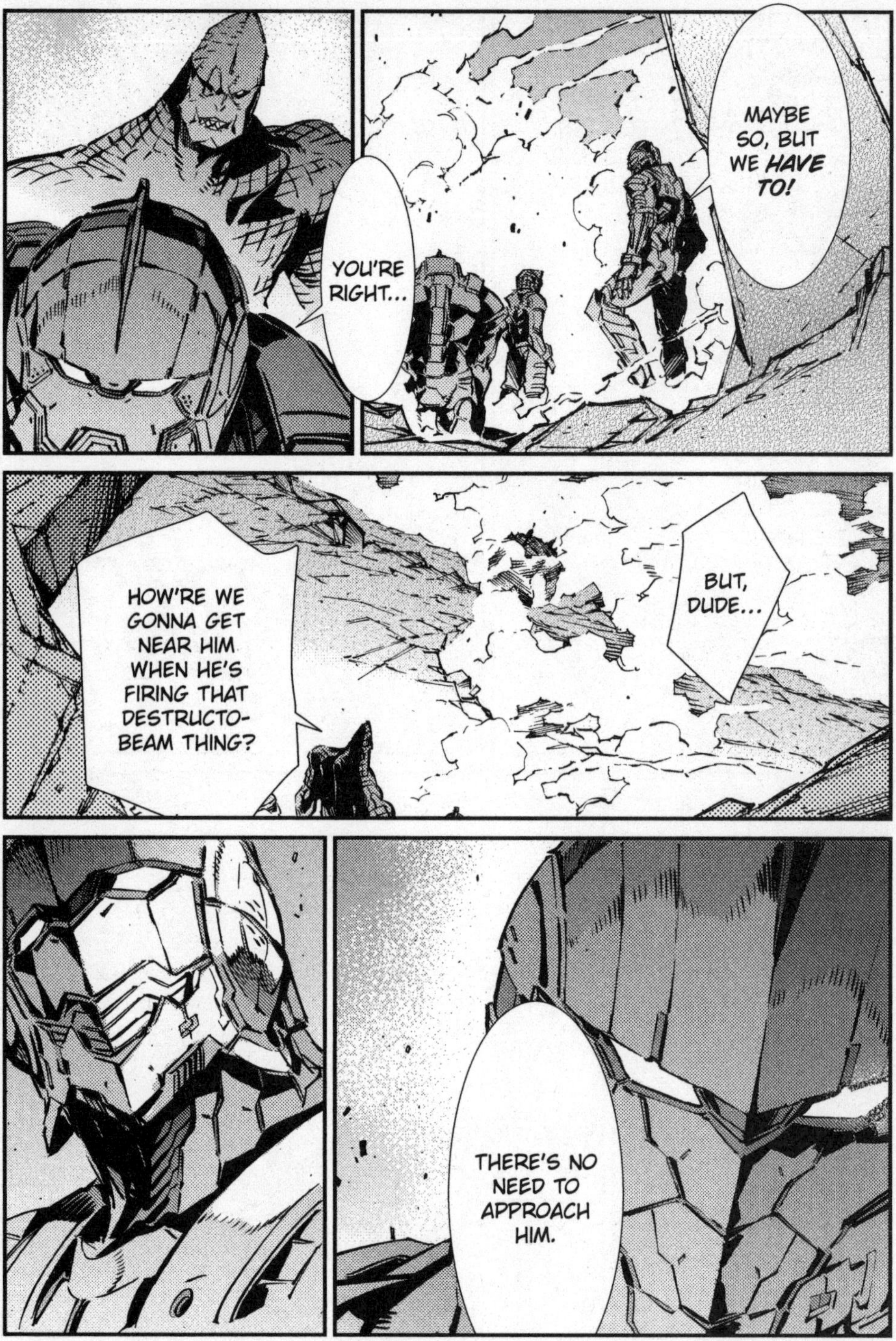
MAYBE SO, BUT WE HAVE TO!
YOU'RE RIGHT...
BUT, DUDE...
HOW'RE WE GONNA GET NEAR HIM WHEN HE'S FIRING THAT DESTRUCTO-BEAM THING?
THERE'S NO NEED TO APPROACH HIM.

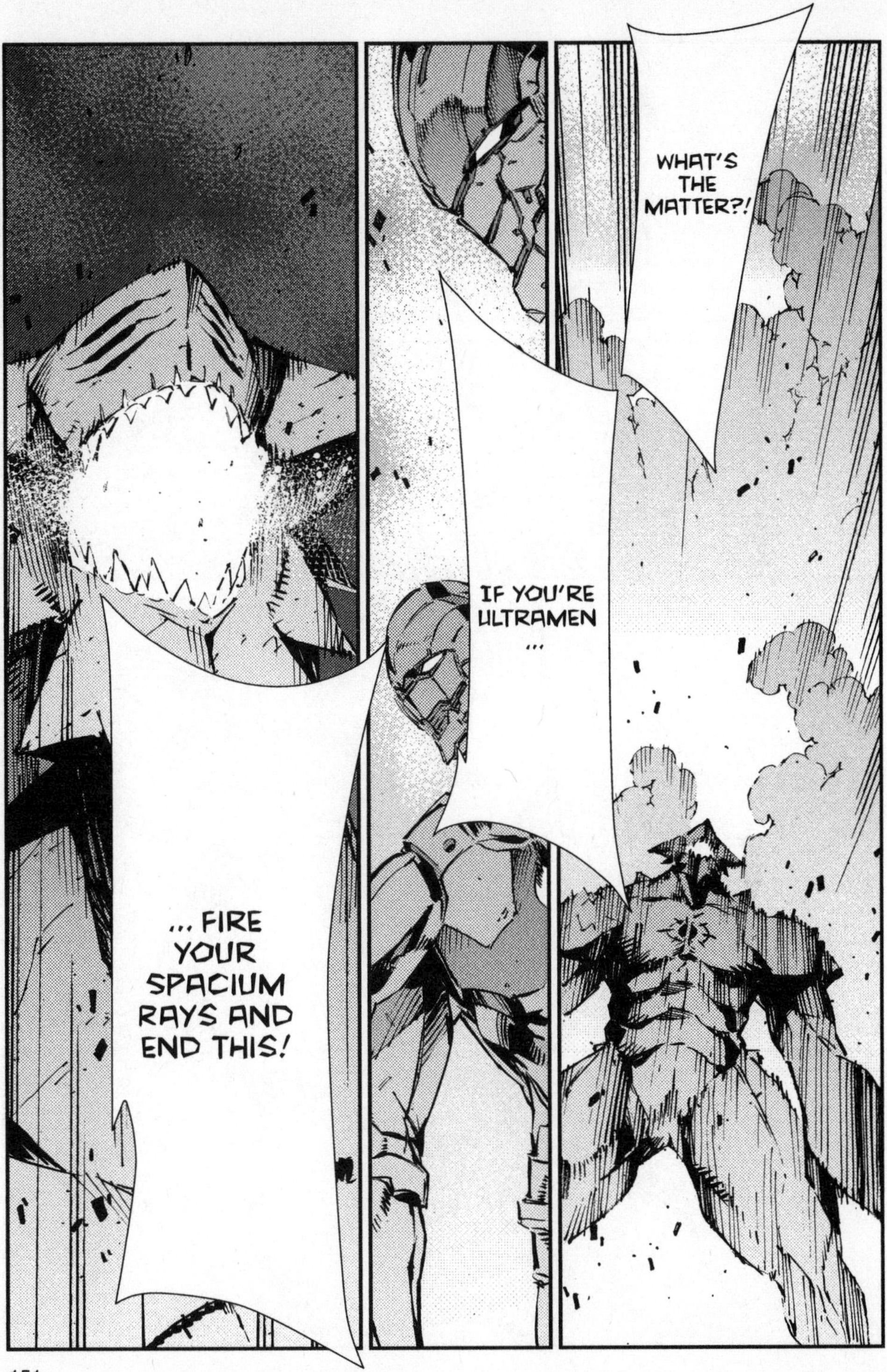
WHAT'S THE MATTER?!
IF YOU'RE ULTRAMEN ...
... FIRE YOUR SPACIUM RAYS AND END THIS!

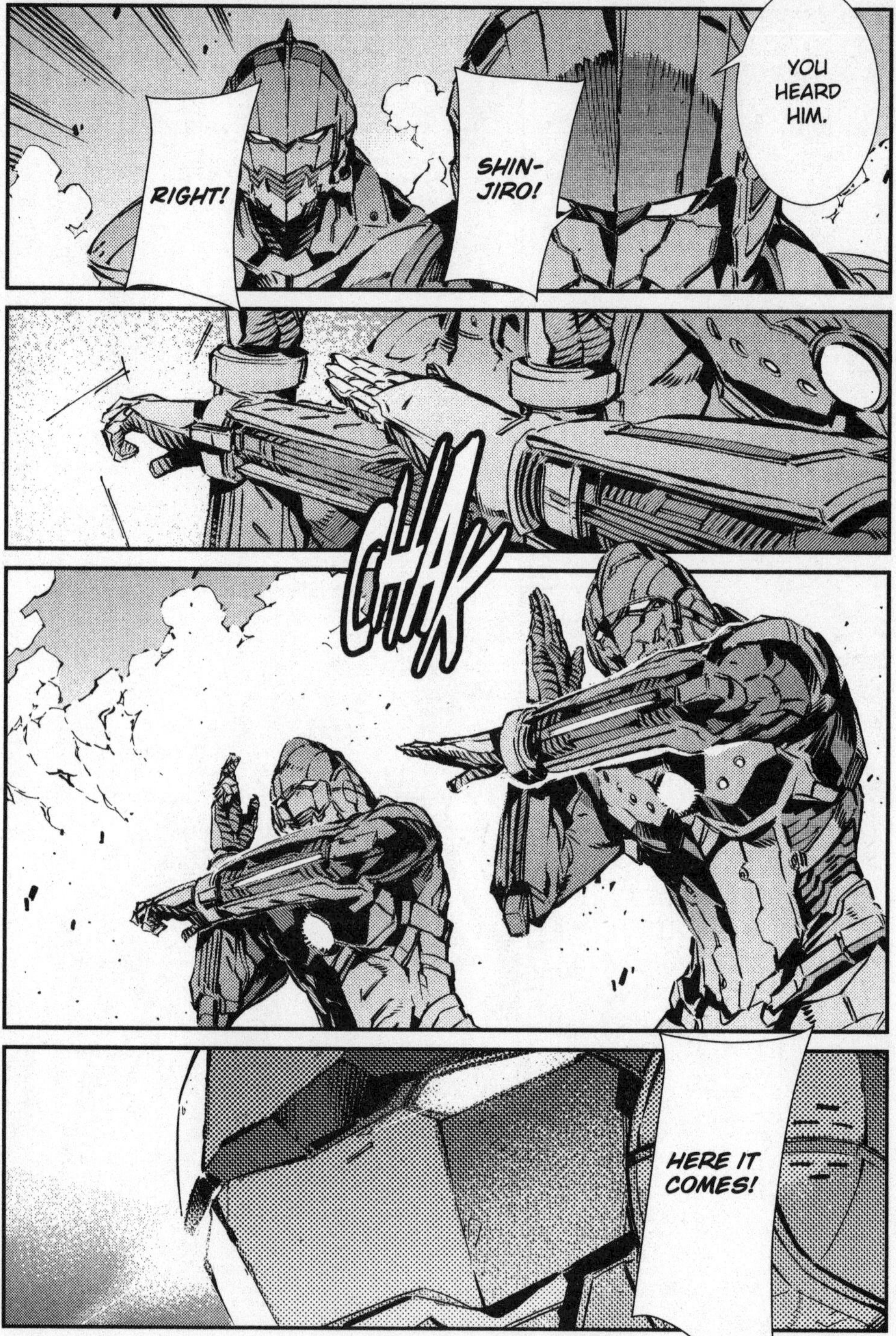
YOU HEARD HIM.
SHIN-JIRO!
RIGHT!
CHAK
HERE IT COMES!

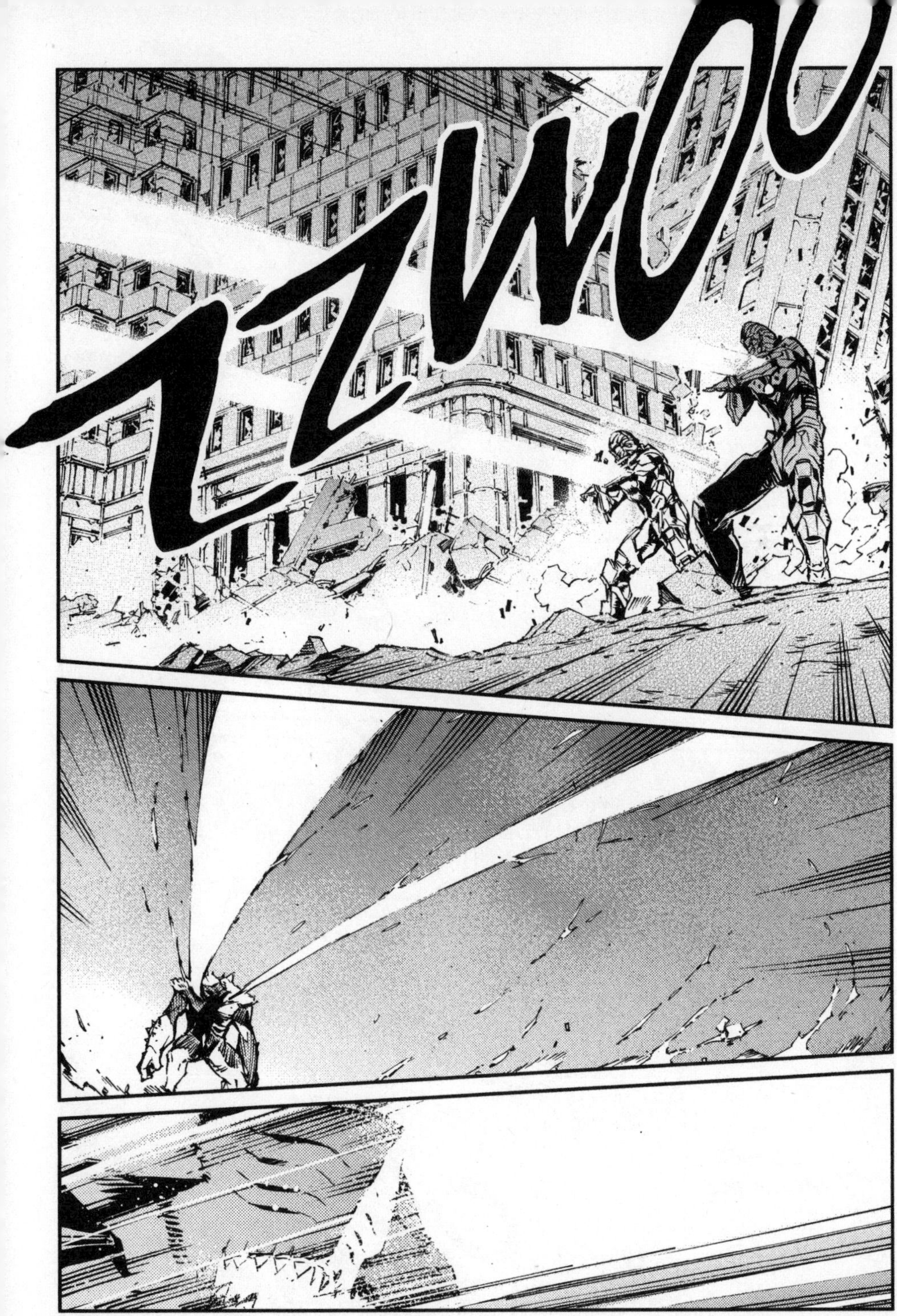
ZZWOO

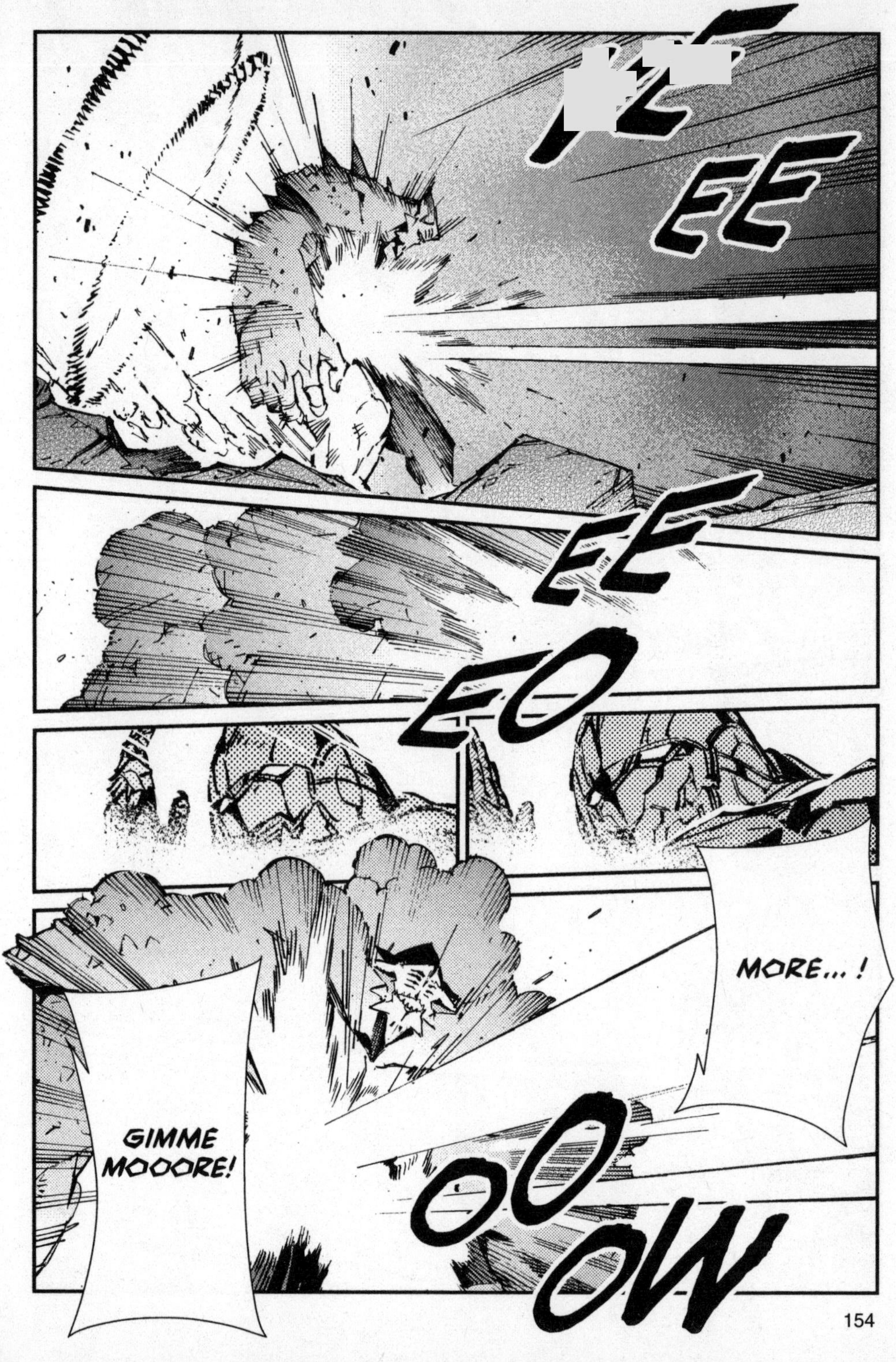
EE
EE
EO
OO
OW
MORE...!
GIMME MOOORE!

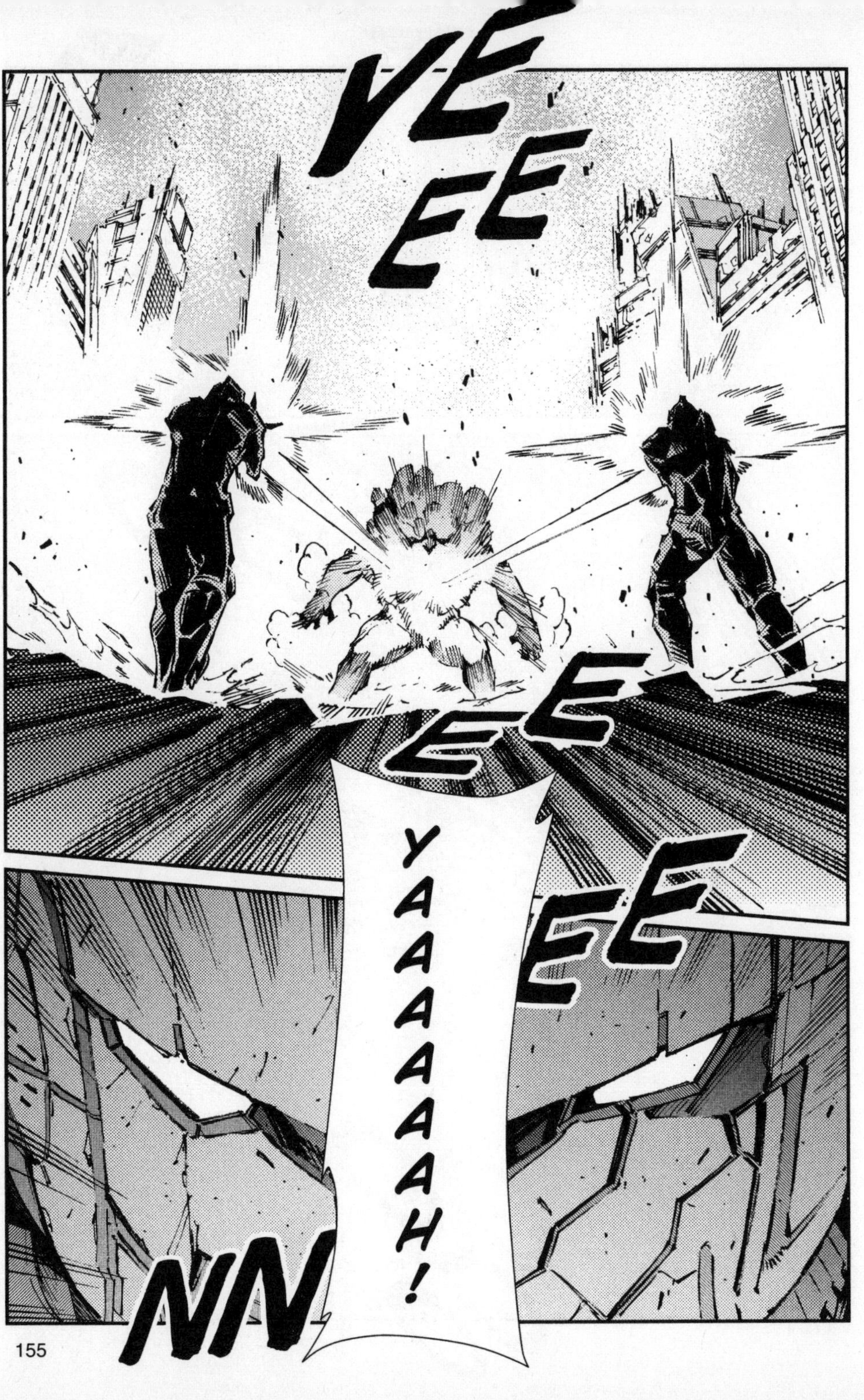
VEEEEEEEEEENN
YAAAAAAAH!

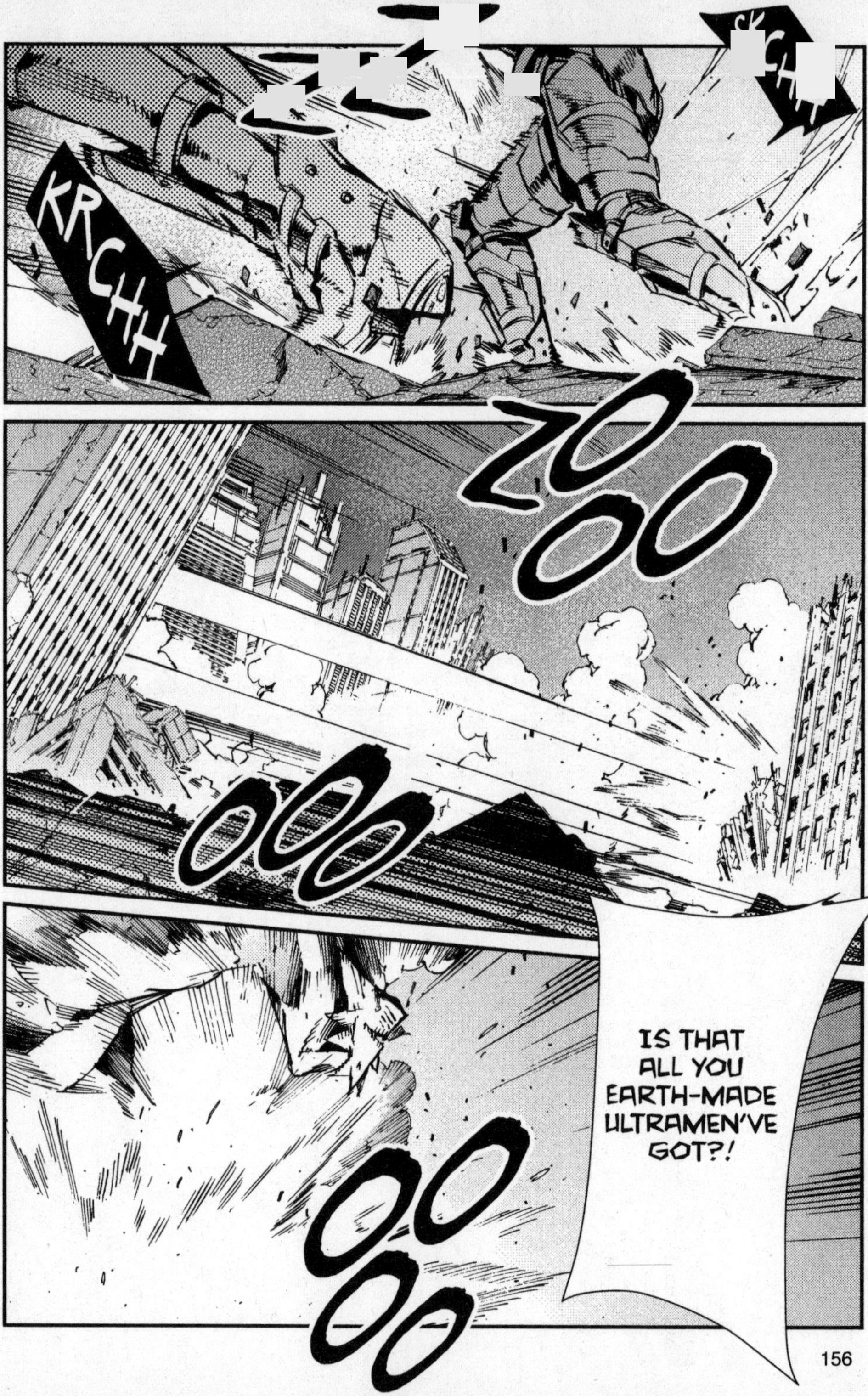
KRCHH
ZOOOOOOOOOO
IS THAT ALL YOU EARTH-MADE ULTRAMEN'VE GOT?!

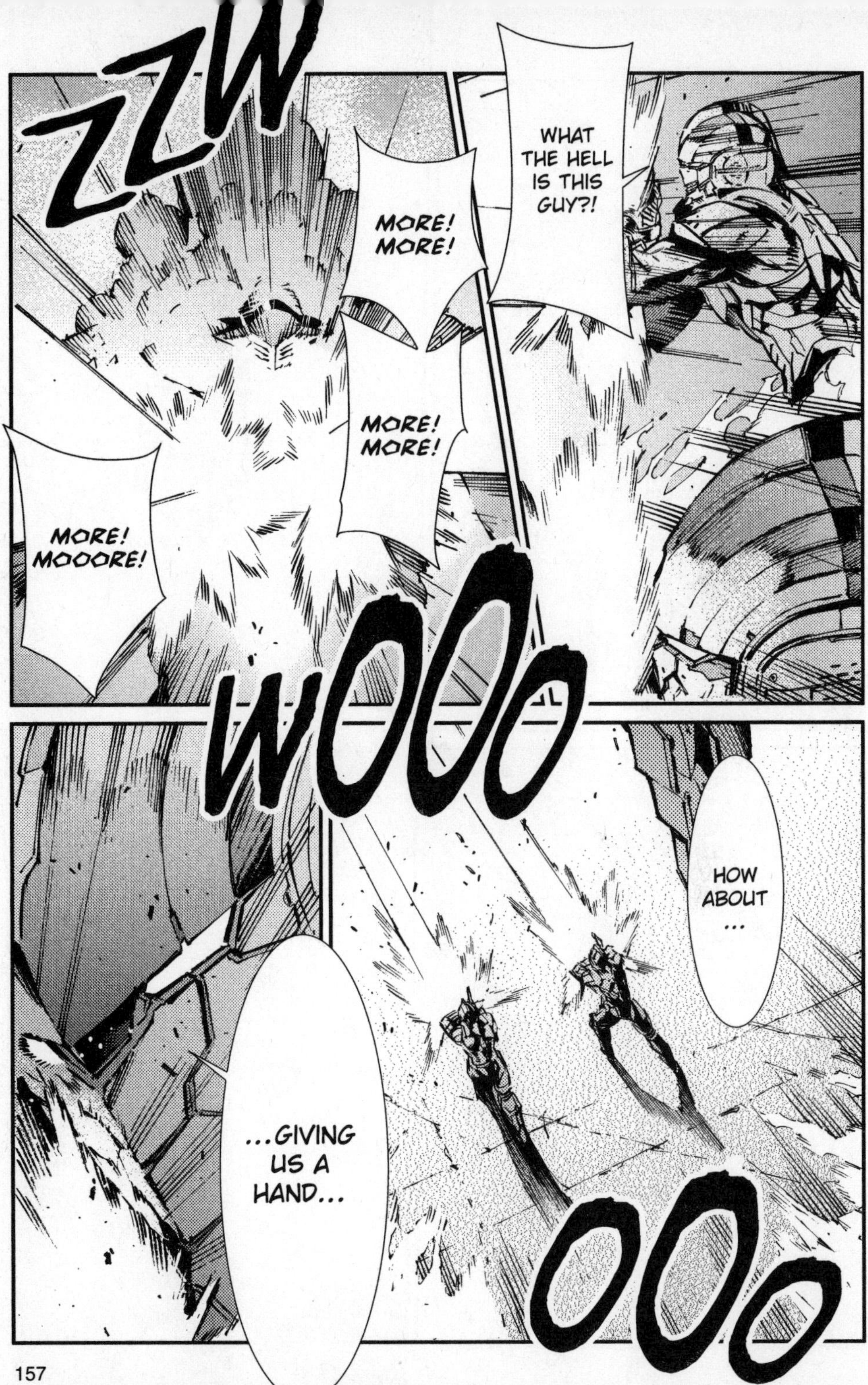
WHAT THE HELL IS THIS GUY?!
ZZW
MORE! MORE!
MORE! MORE!
MORE! MOOORE!
WOOO
HOW ABOUT ...
...GIVING US A HAND...
OOO

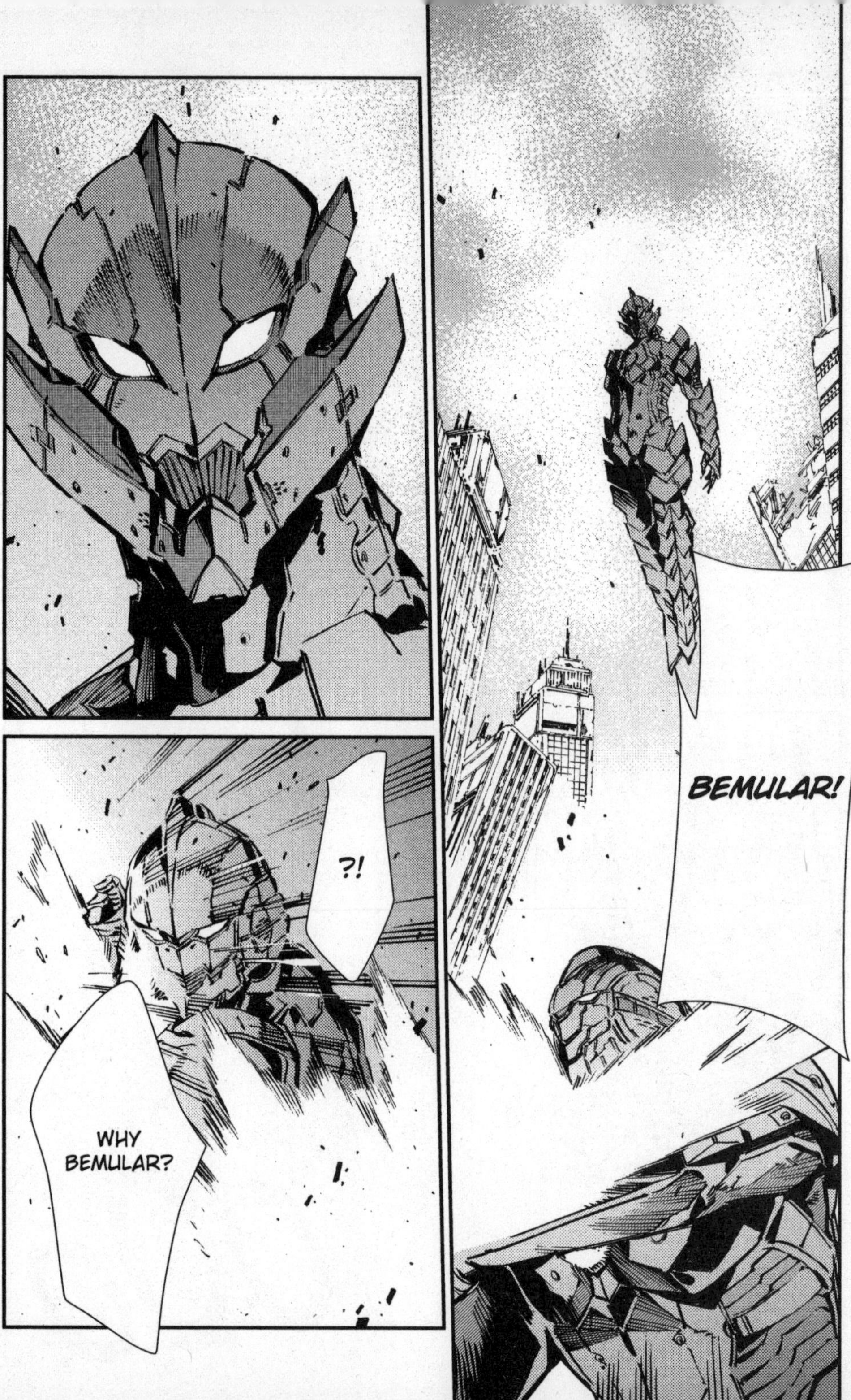
BEMULAR!
?!
WHY BEMULAR?

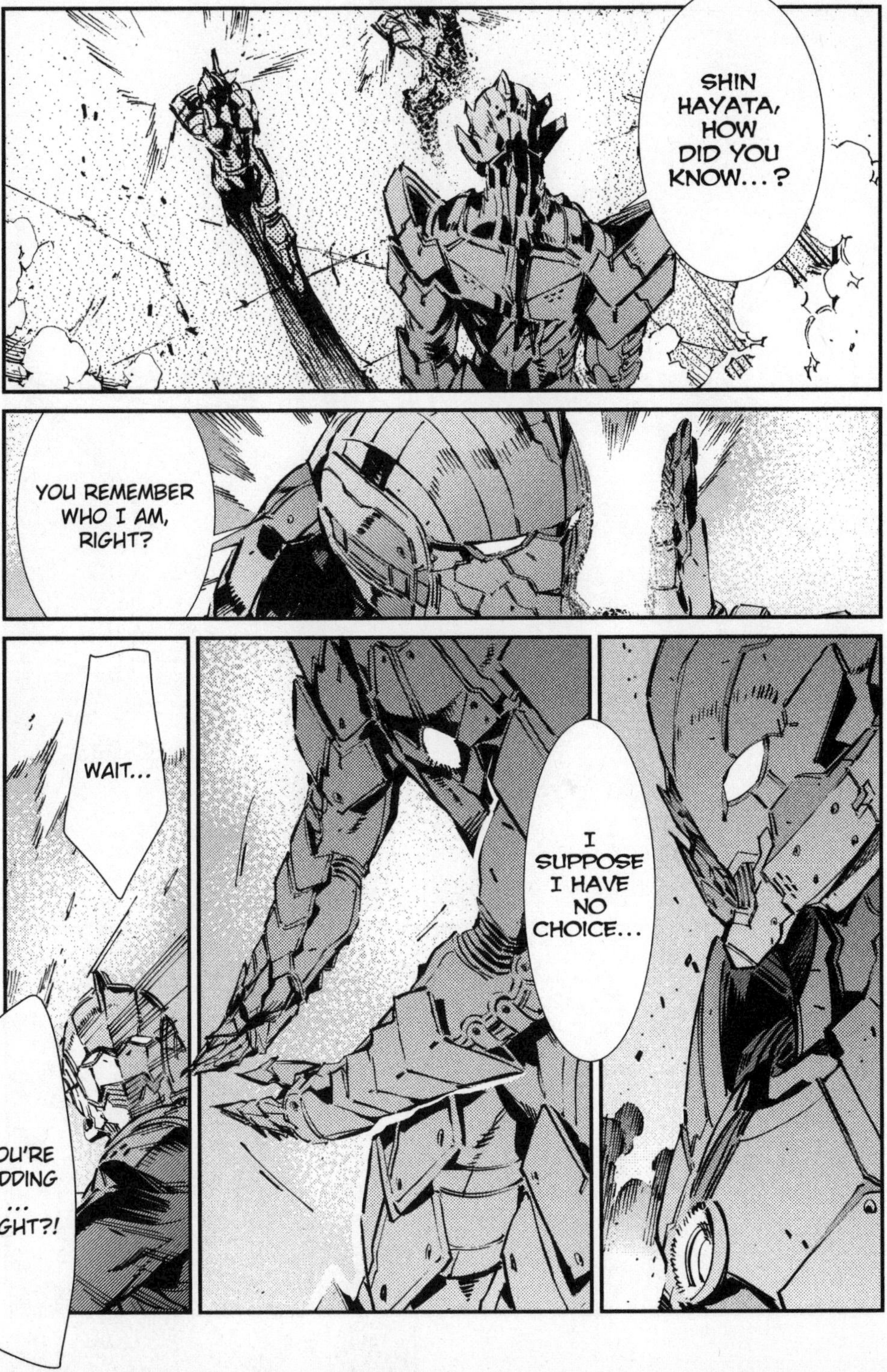
SHIN HAYATA, HOW DID YOU KNOW...?
YOU REMEMBER WHO I AM, RIGHT?
I SUPPOSE I HAVE NO CHOICE...
WAIT...
YOU'RE KIDDING ... RIGHT?!

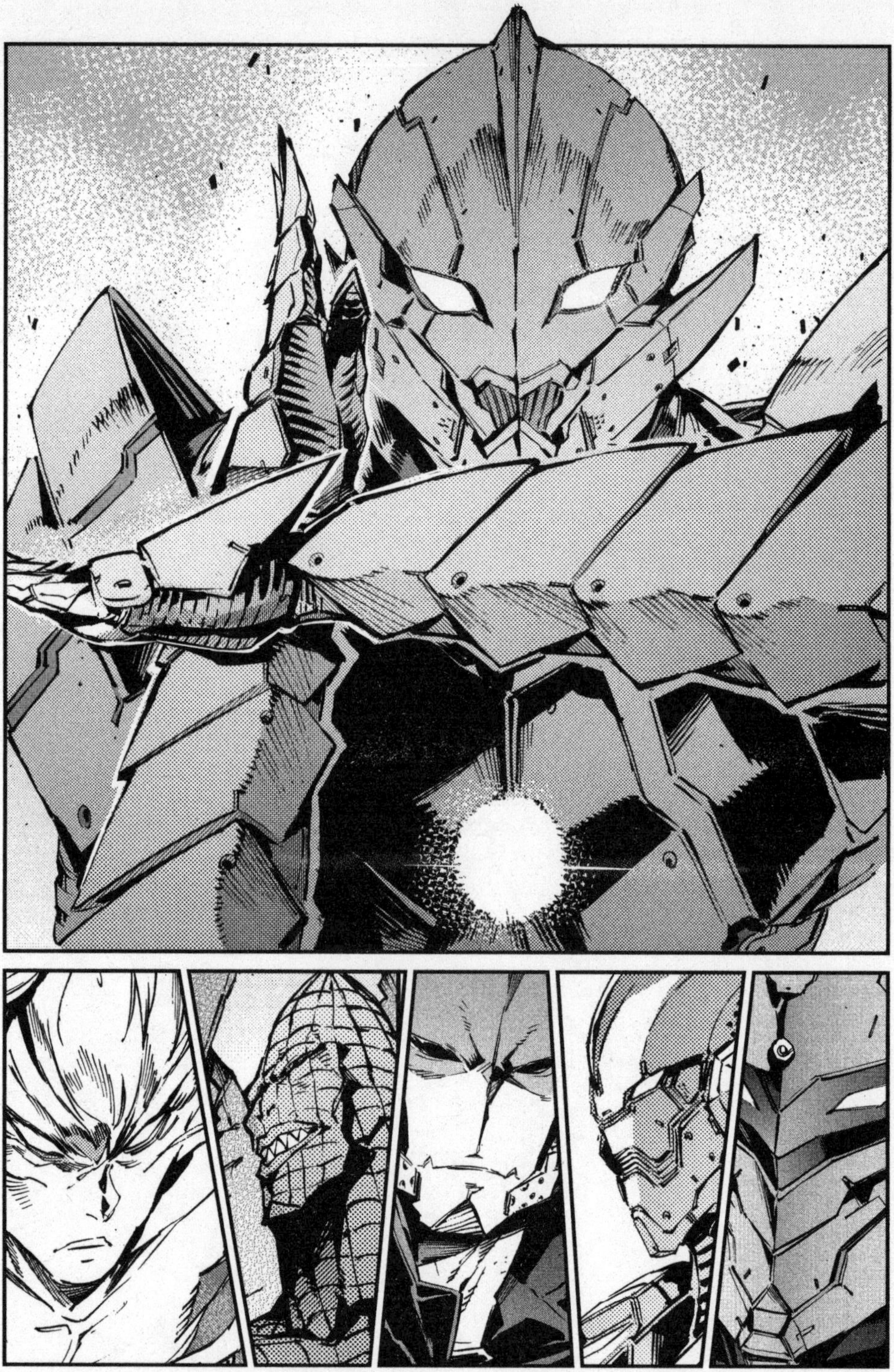

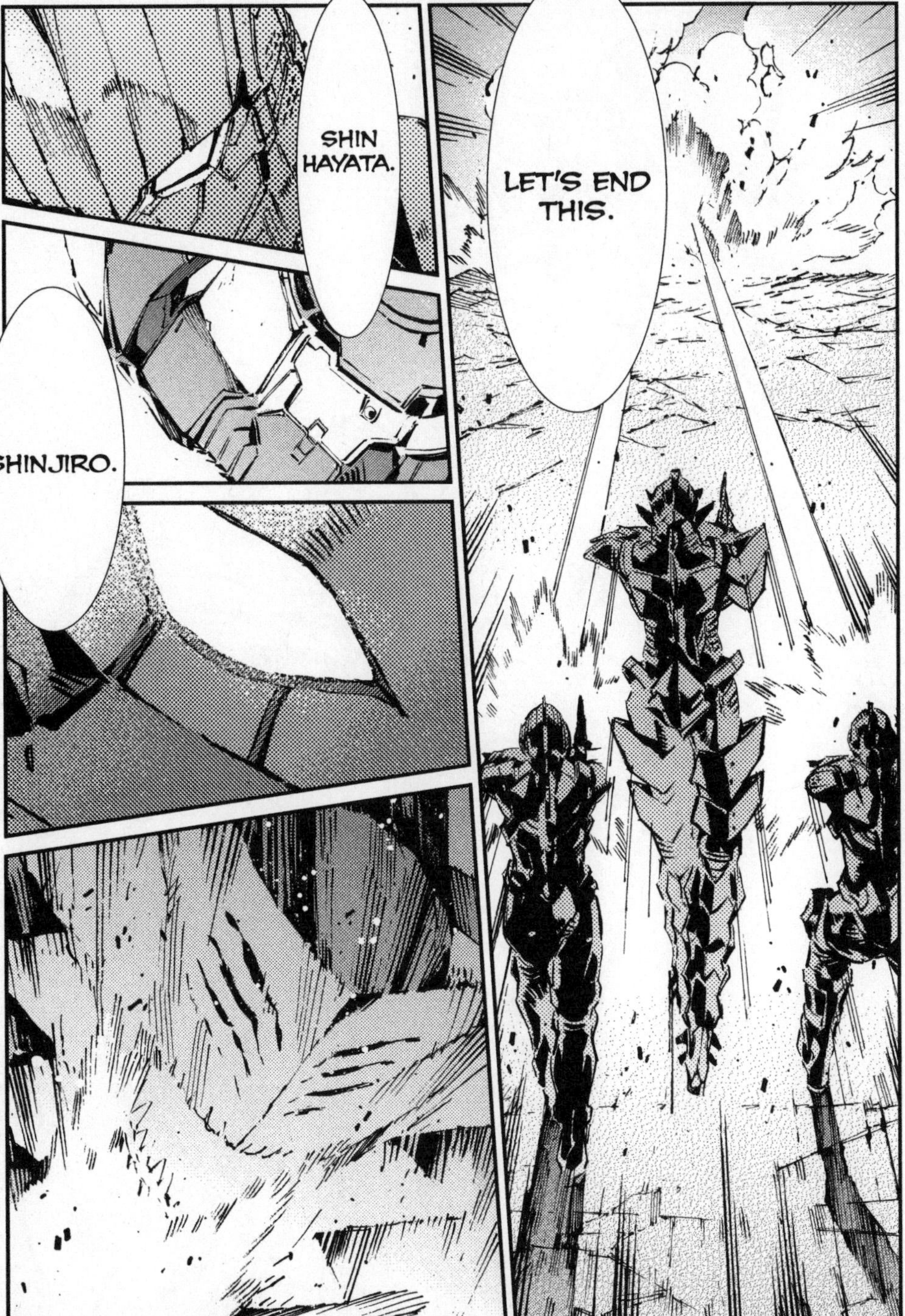
LET'S END THIS.
SHIN HAYATA.
SHINJIRO.

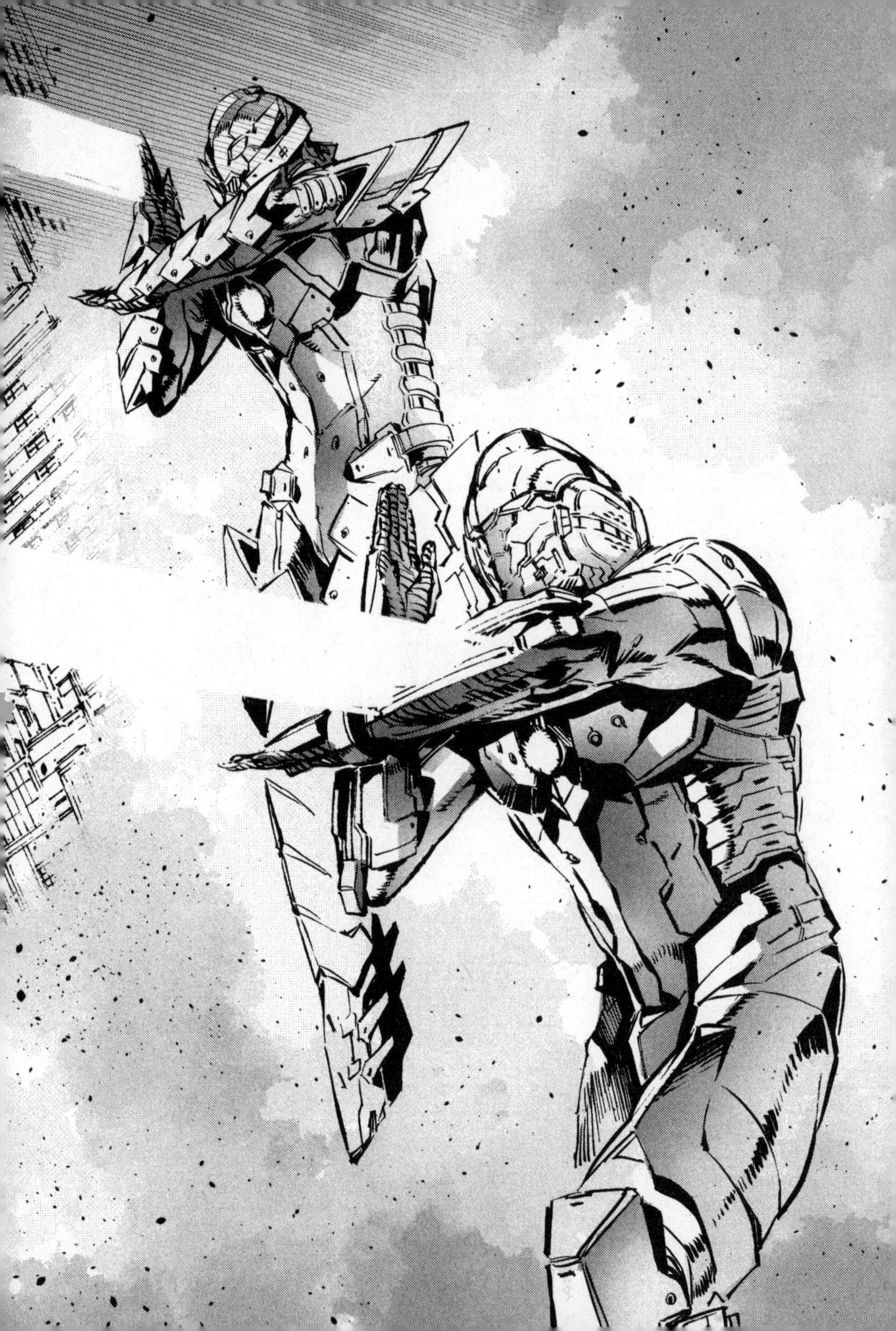

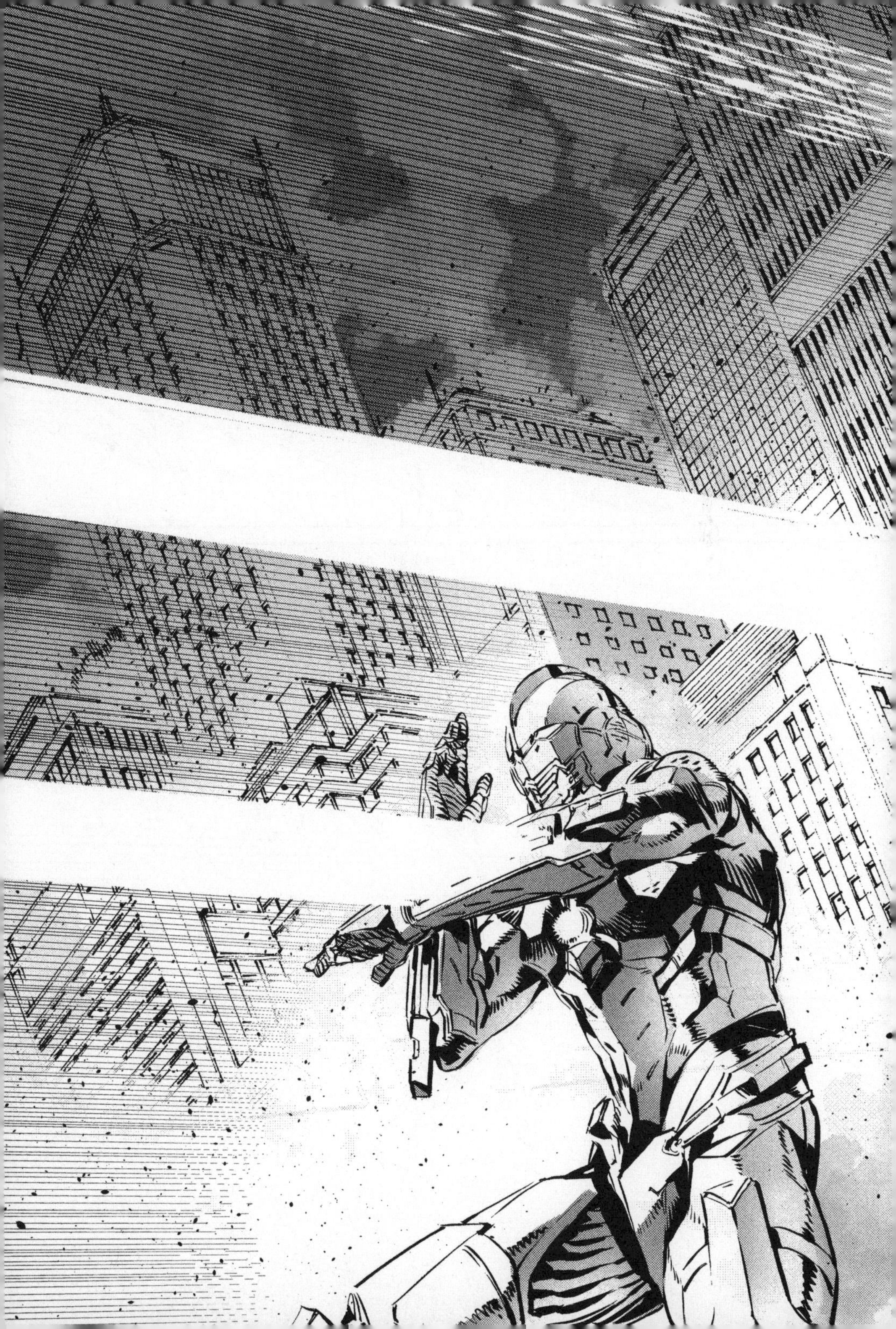

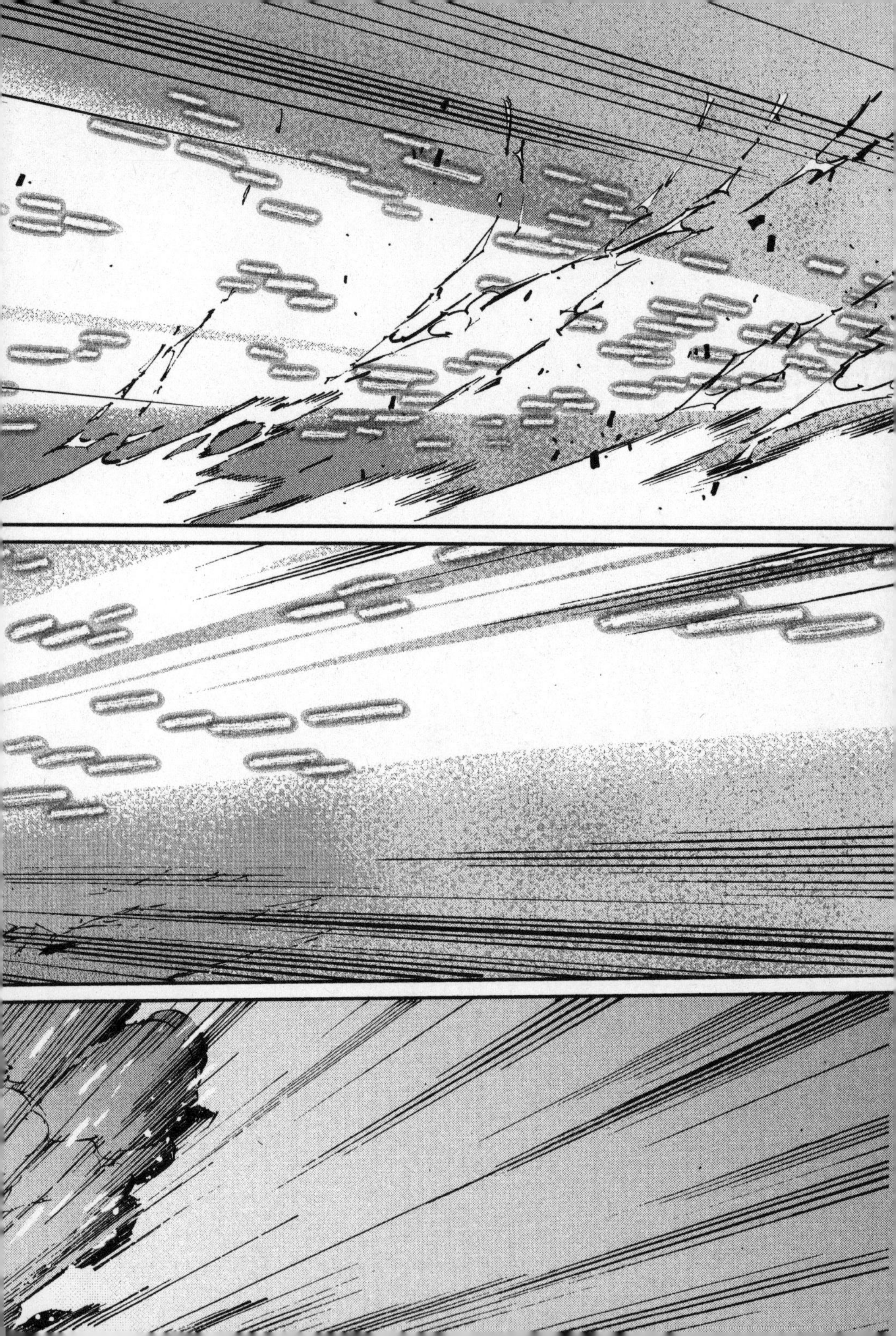

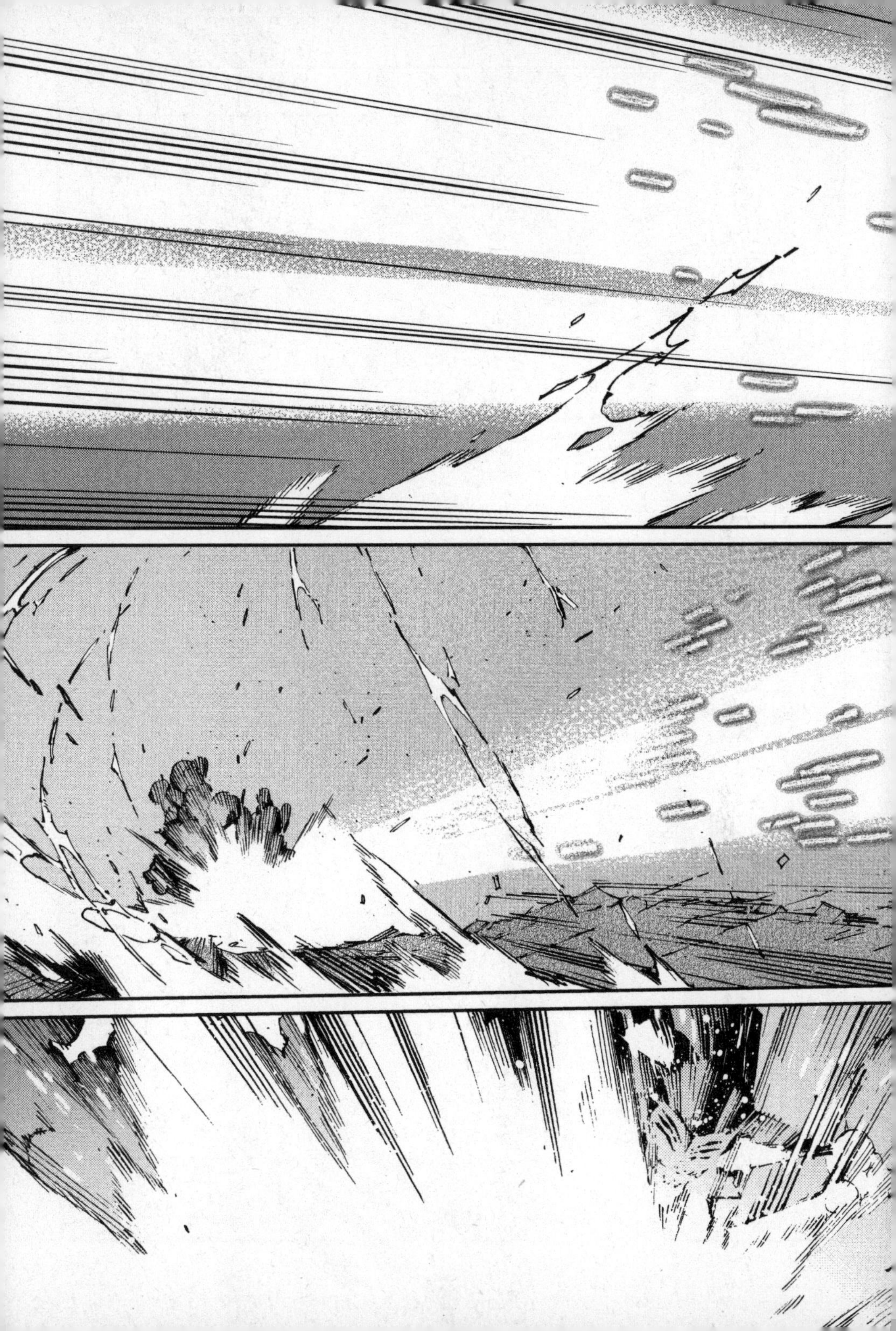

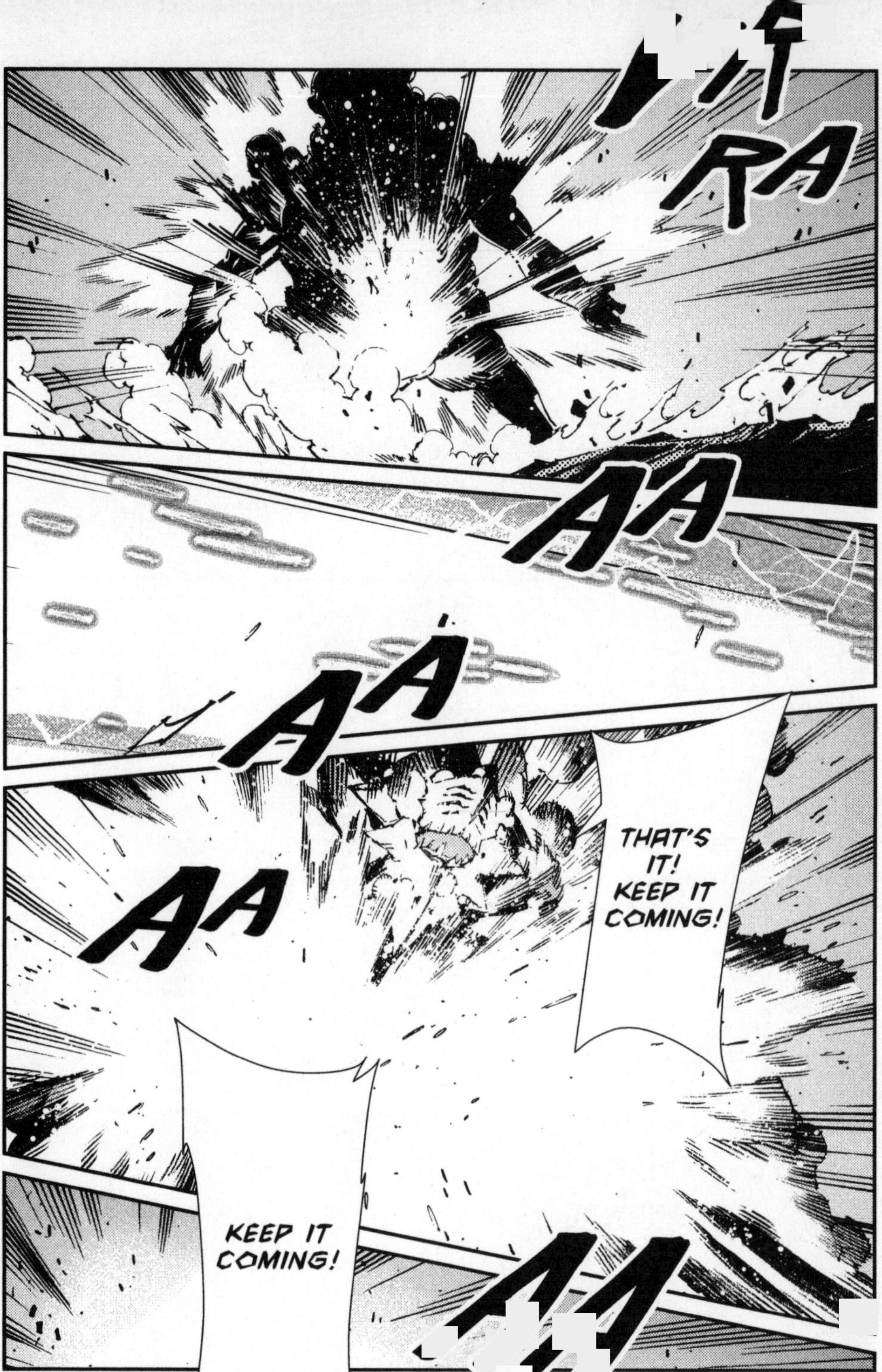
RA
AA
AA
THAT'S IT! KEEP IT COMING!
AA
KEEP IT COMING!
AA

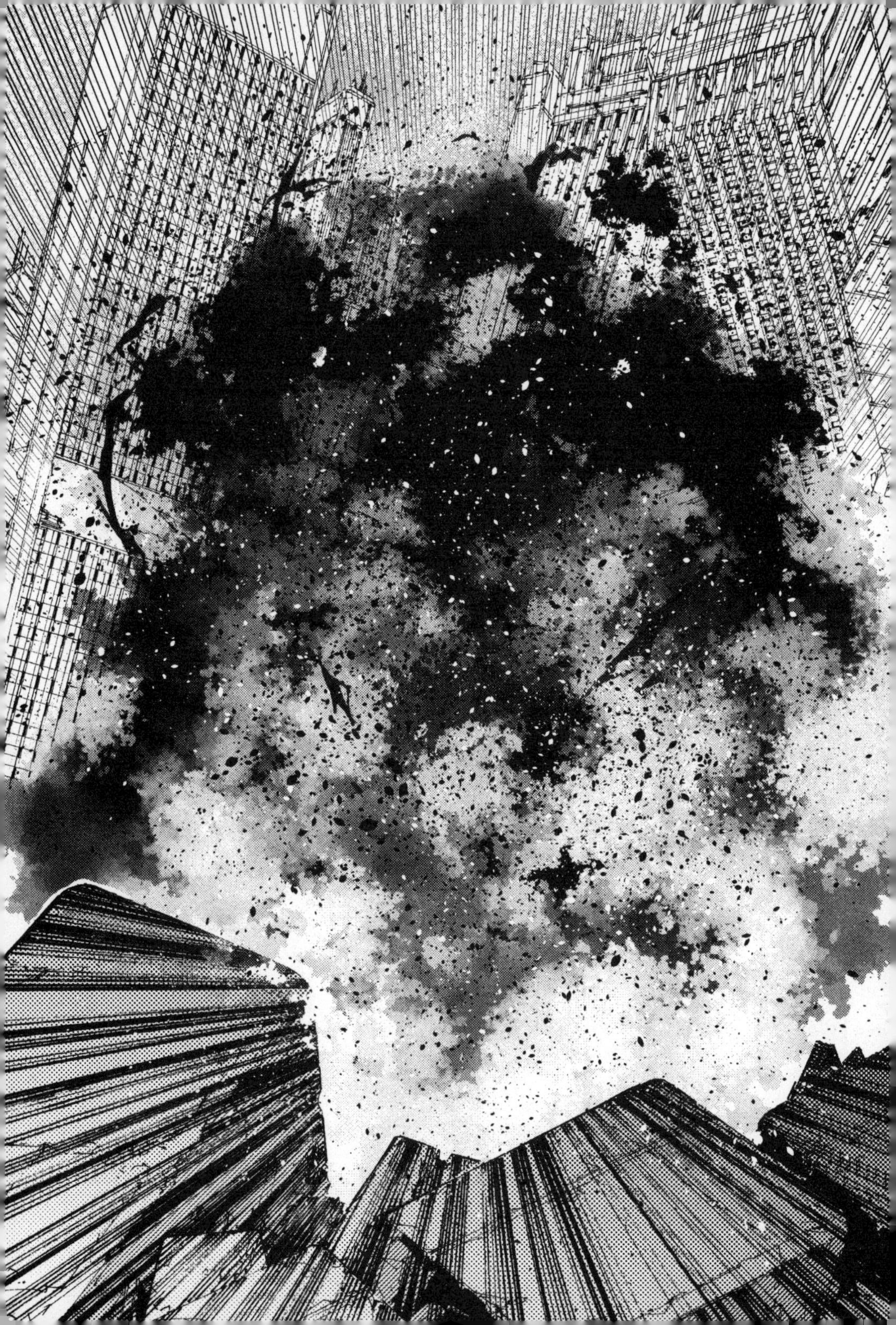

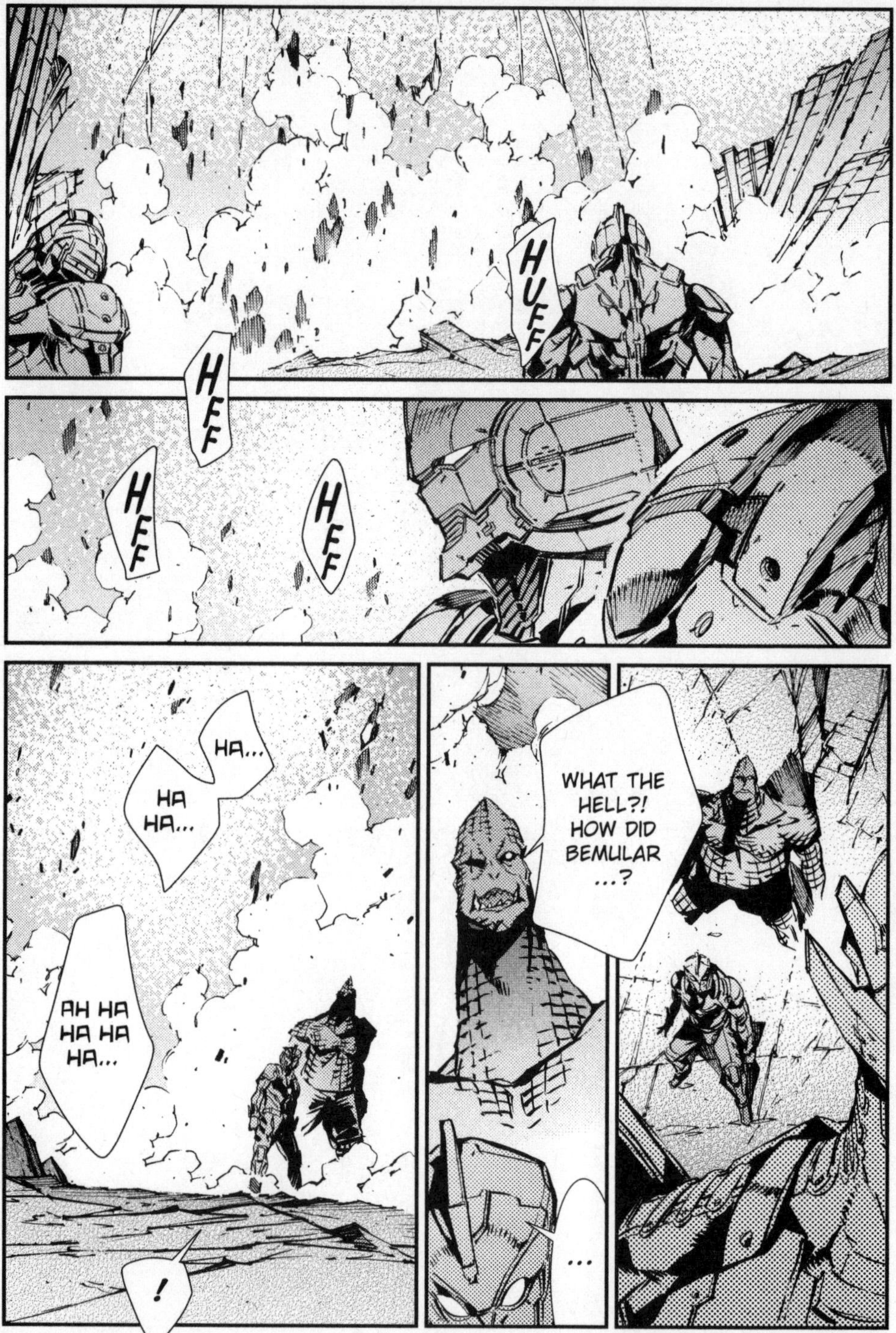
HUFF
HFF
HFF
HFF
WHAT THE HELL?! HOW DID BEMULAR ...?
...
HA...
HA HA...
AH HA HA HA HA...
!

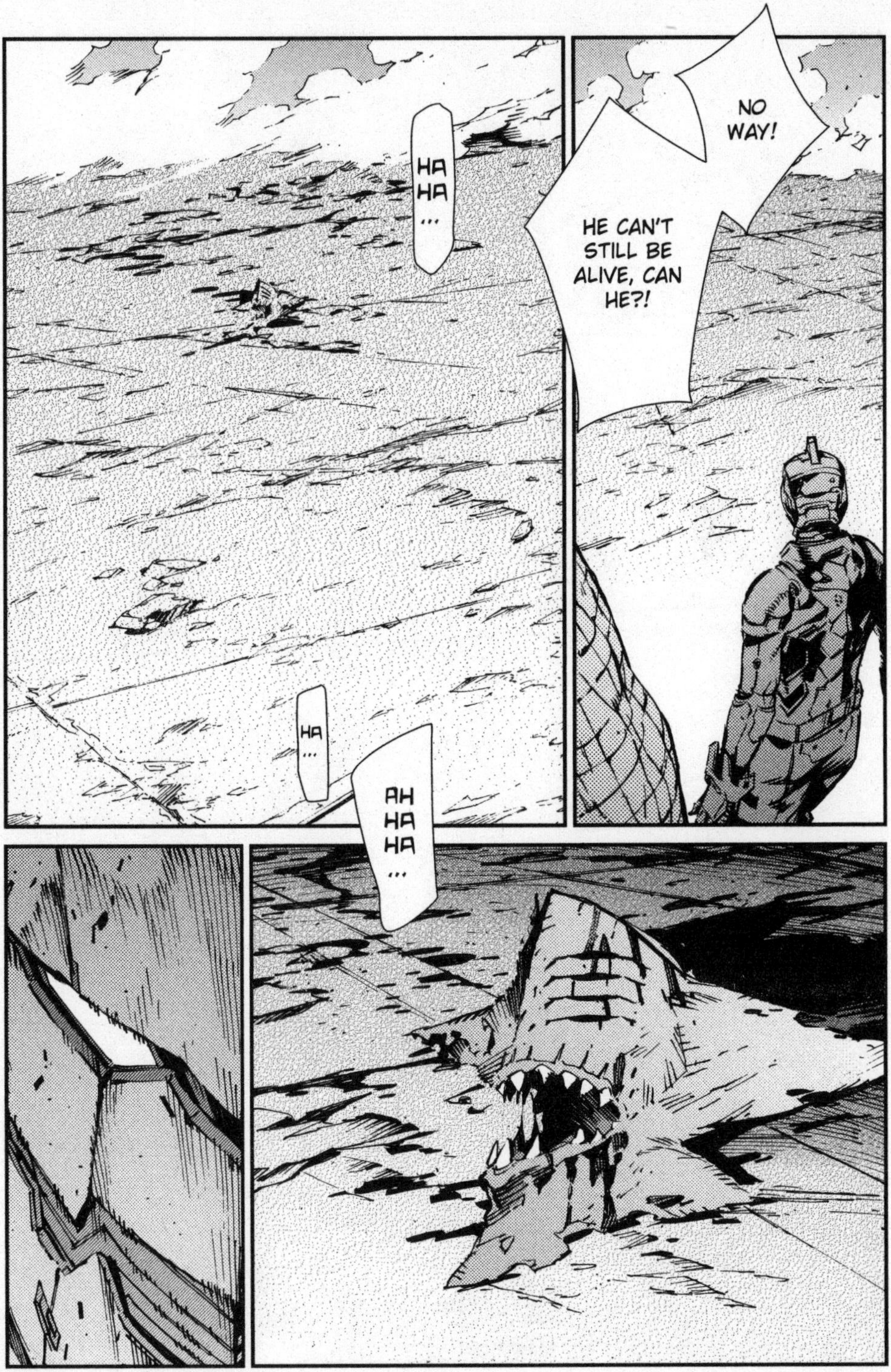
NO WAY!
HE CAN'T STILL BE ALIVE, CAN HE?!
HA HA ...
HA ...
AH HA HA ...

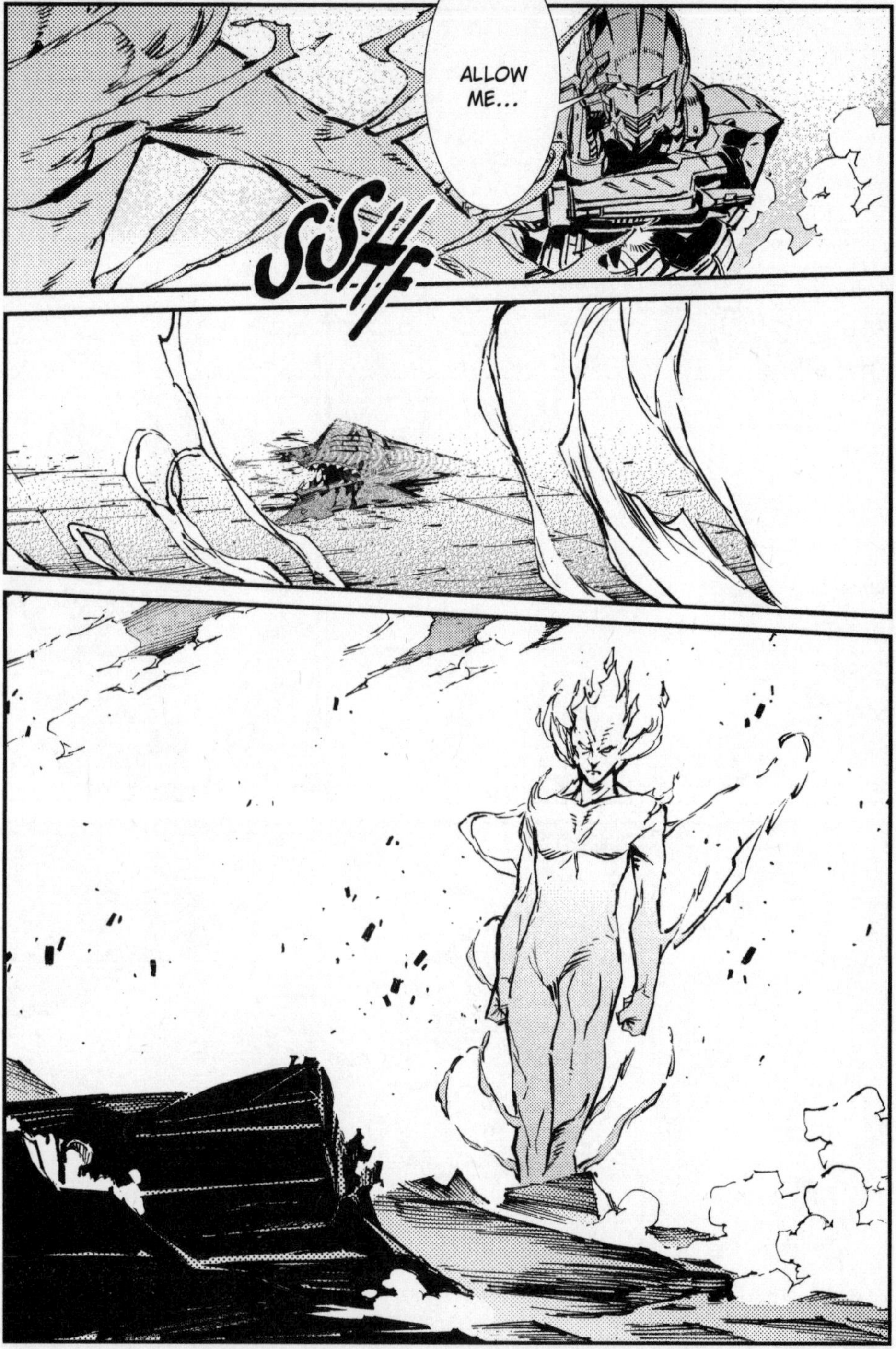
ALLOW ME...
SSHF

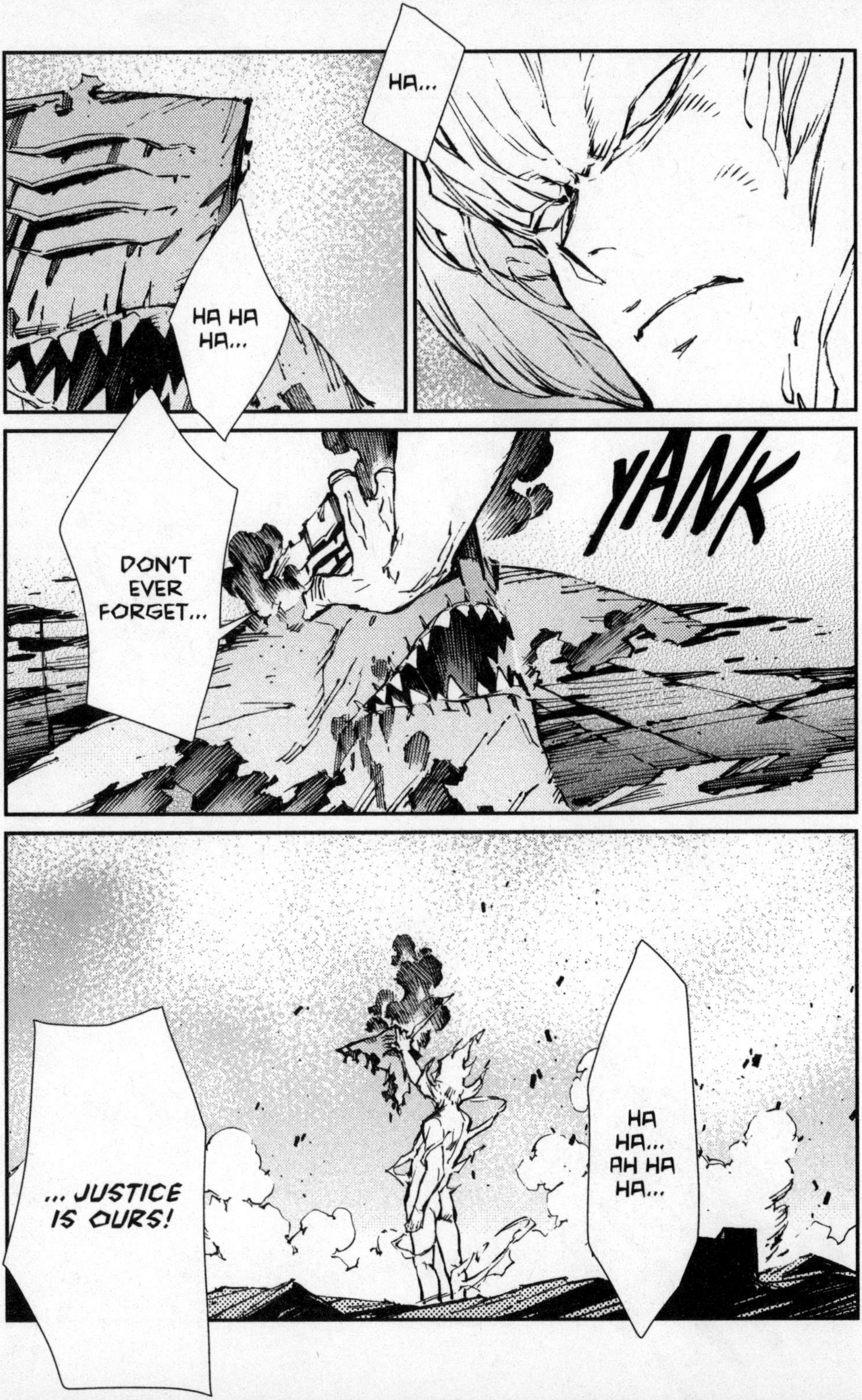
HA...
HA HA HA...
YANK
DON'T EVER FORGET...
HA HA... AH HA HA...
...JUSTICE IS OURS!

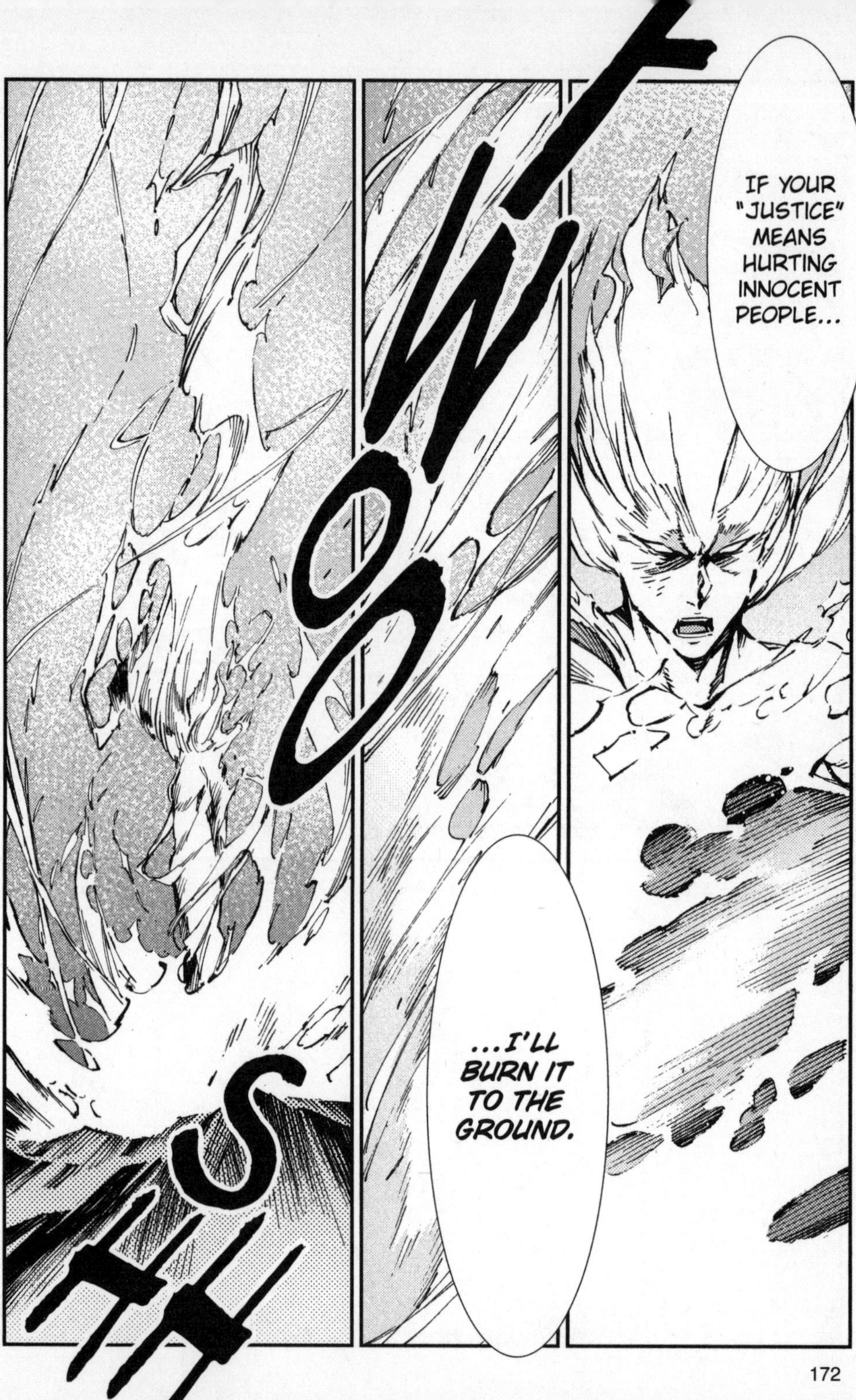
IF YOUR "JUSTICE" MEANS HURTING INNOCENT PEOPLE...
...I'LL BURN IT TO THE GROUND.
FWOOSHH

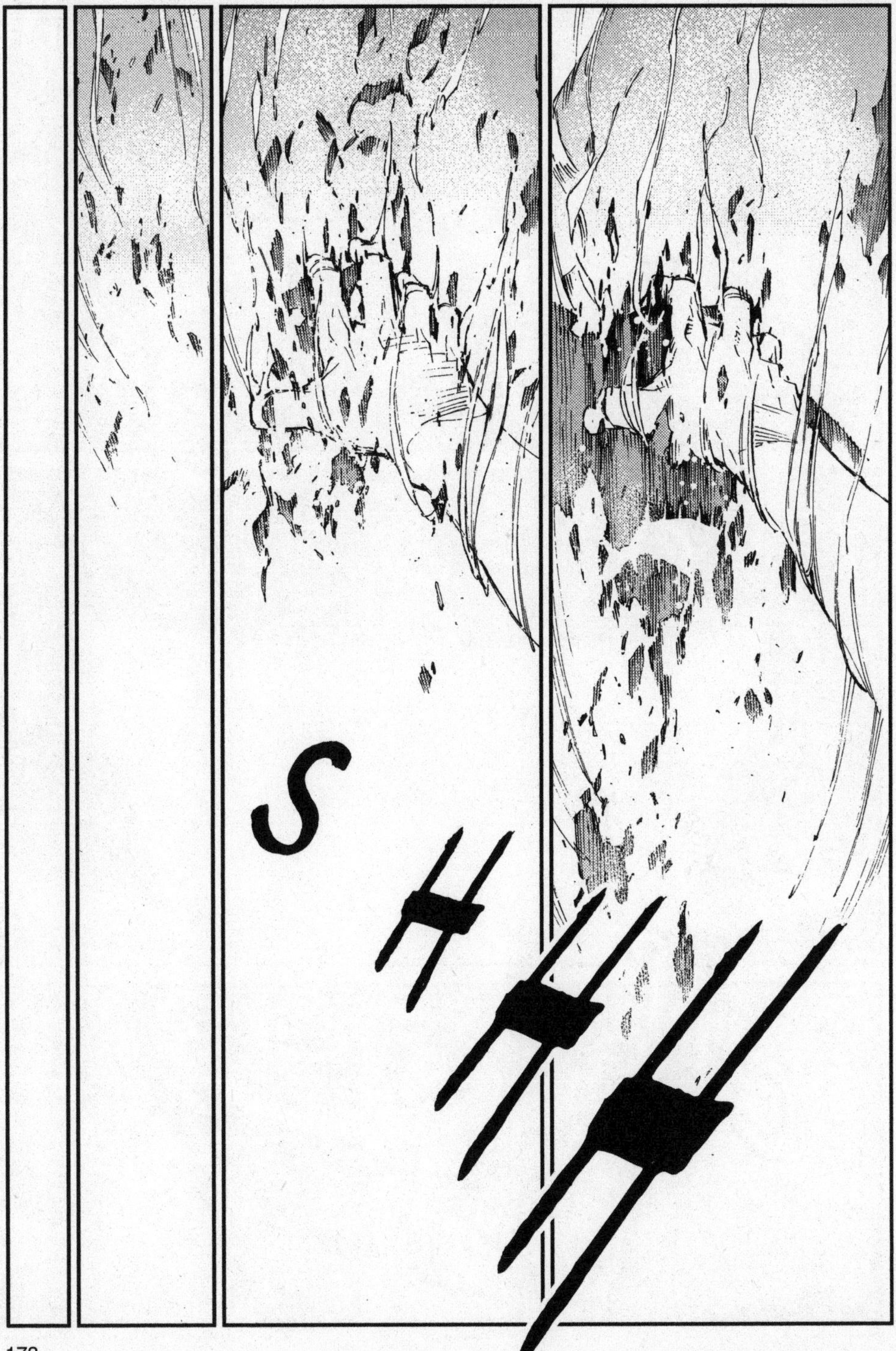
SHHH

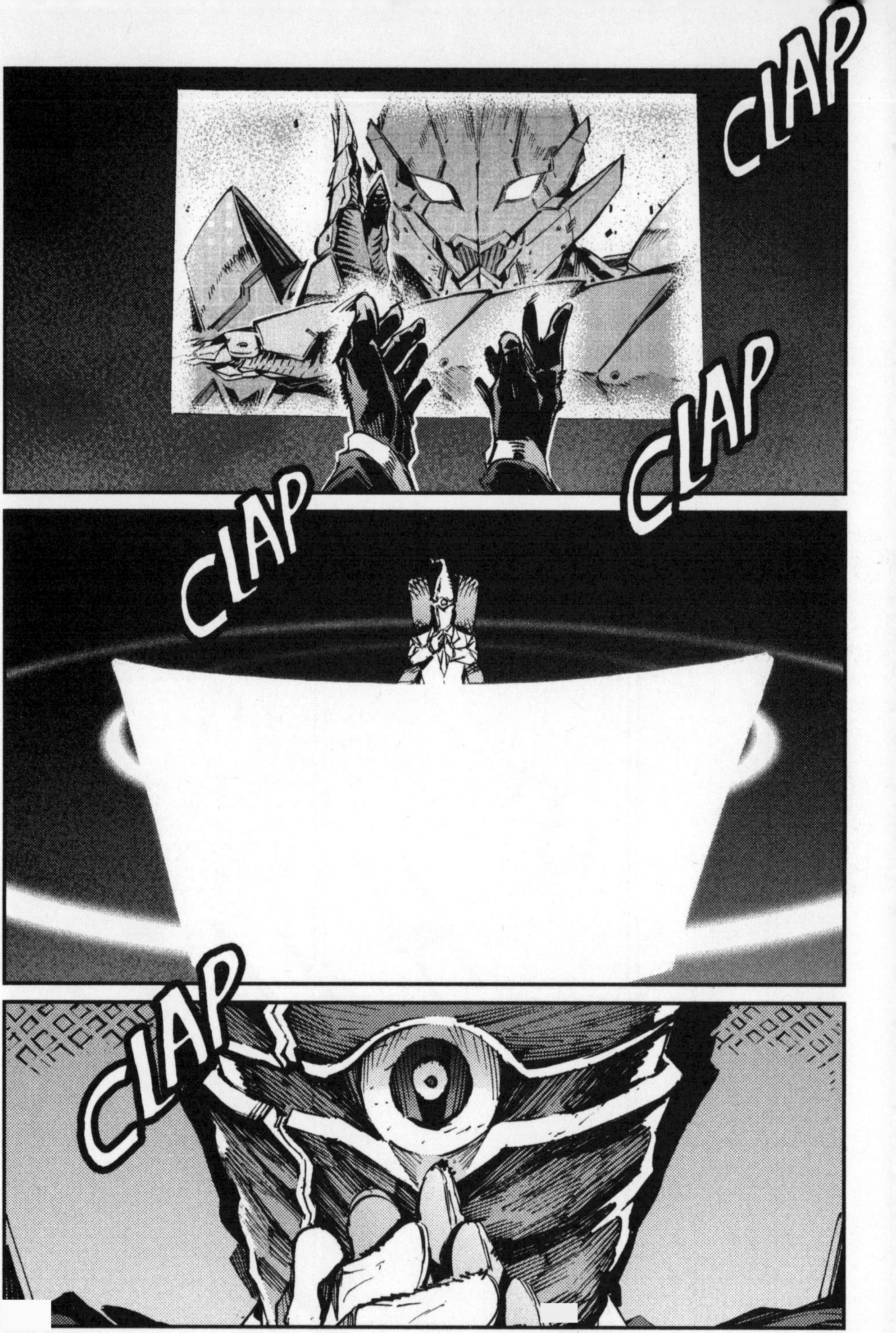
CLAP
CLAP
CLAP
CLAP

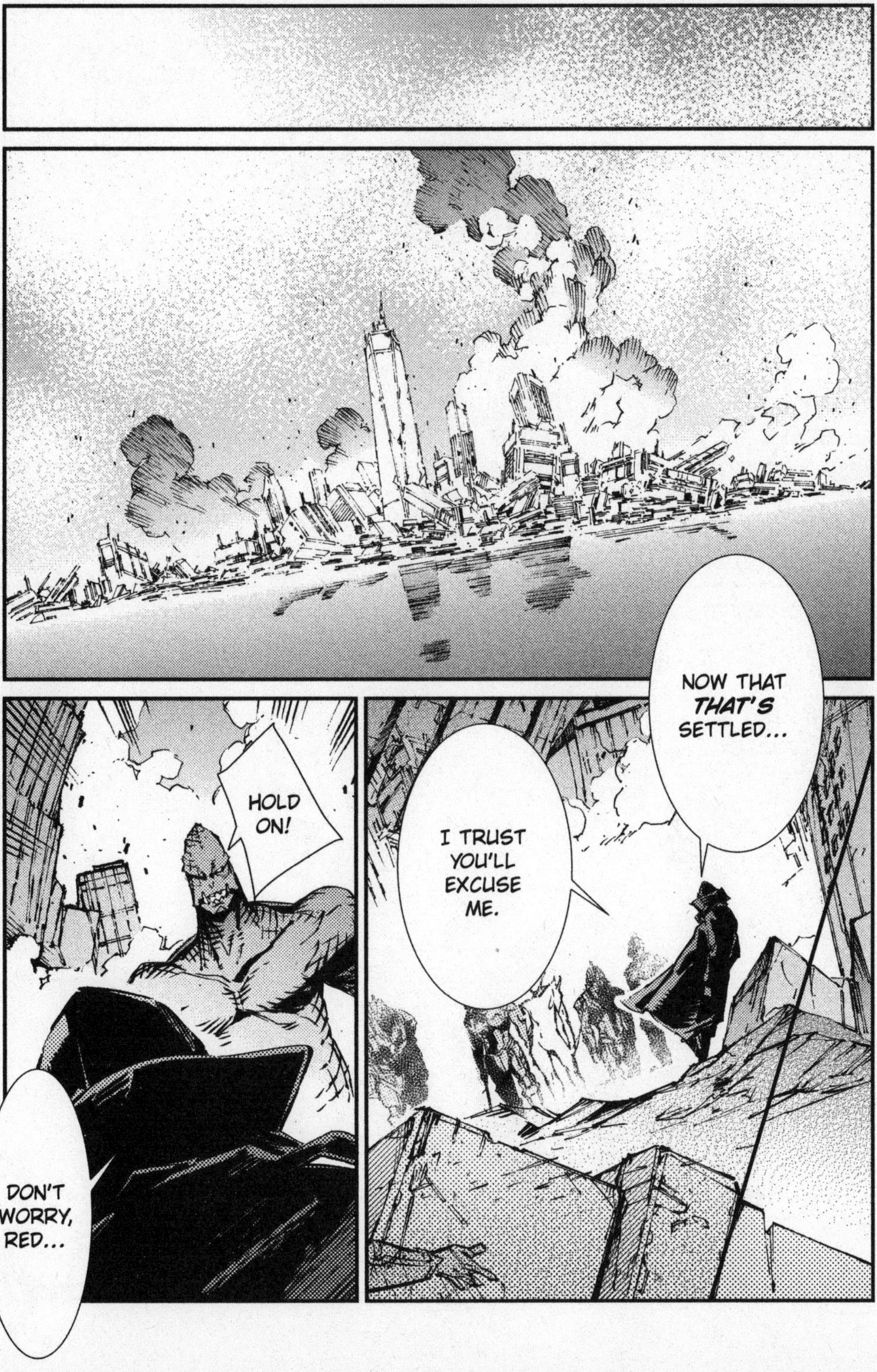
NOW THAT *THAT'S* SETTLED...
I TRUST YOU'LL EXCUSE ME.
HOLD ON!
DON'T WORRY, RED...

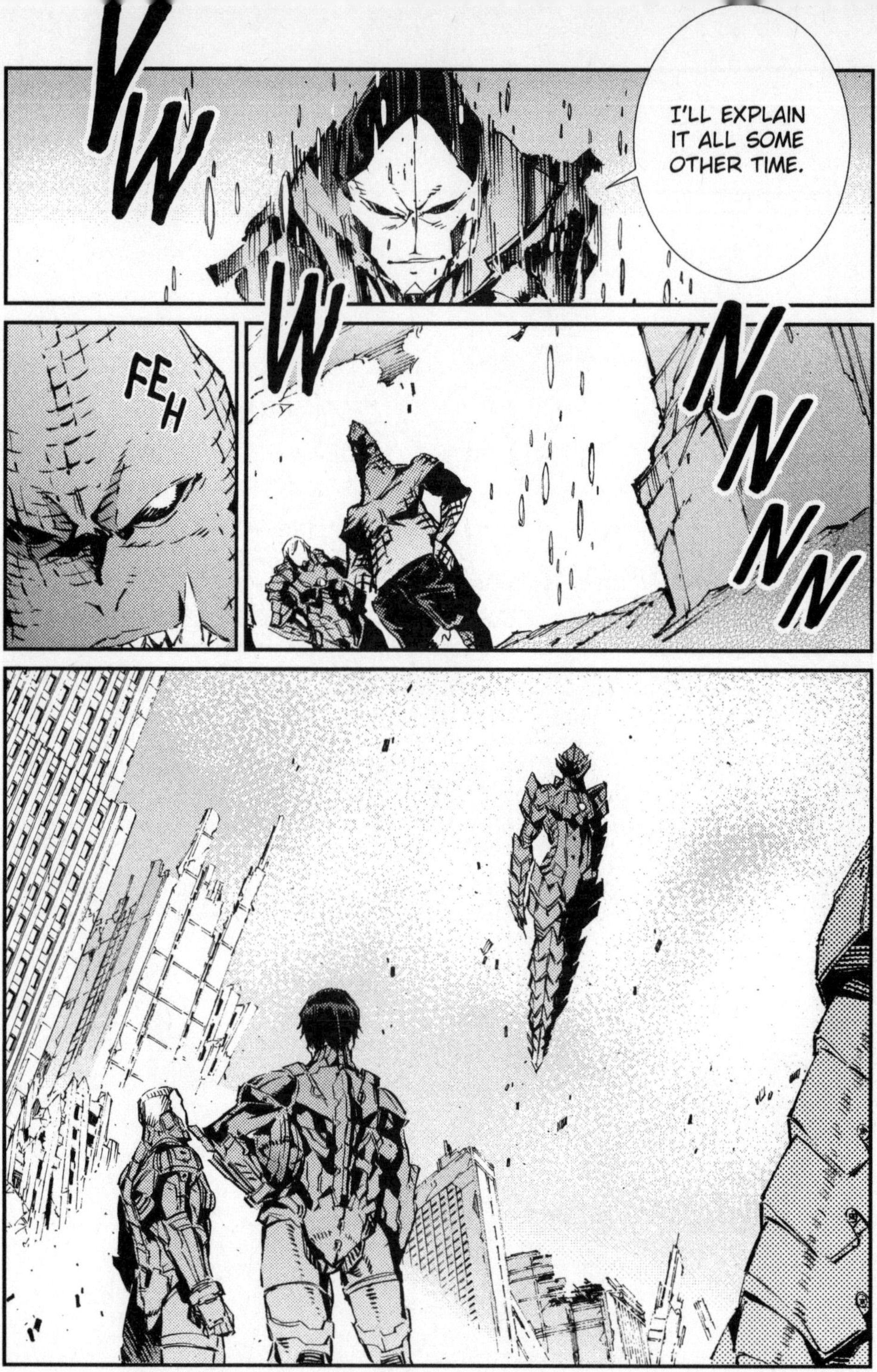
I'LL EXPLAIN IT ALL SOME OTHER TIME.
VWWNNNNN
FEH

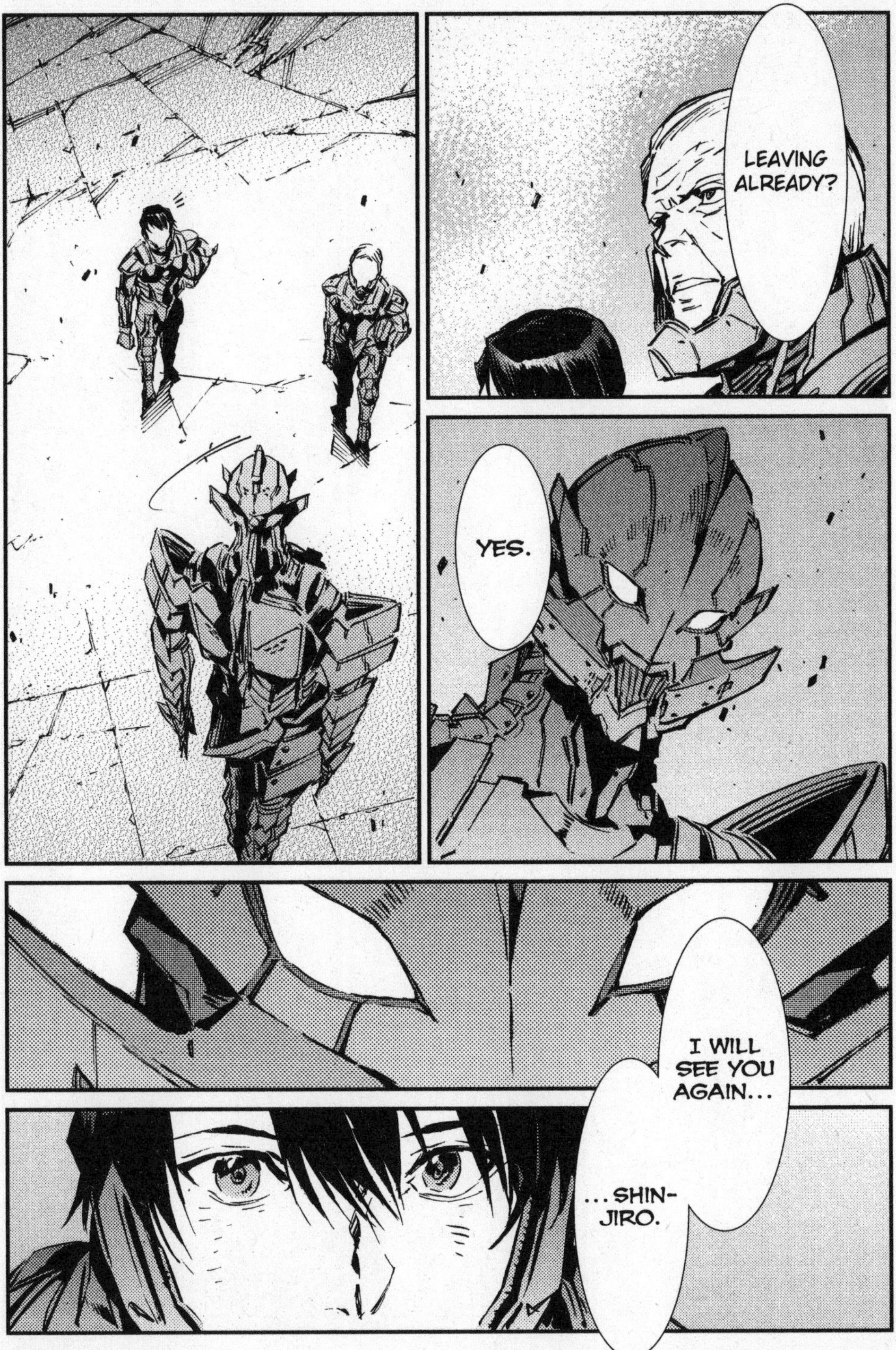
LEAVING ALREADY?
YES.
I WILL SEE YOU AGAIN...
...SHIN-JIRO.

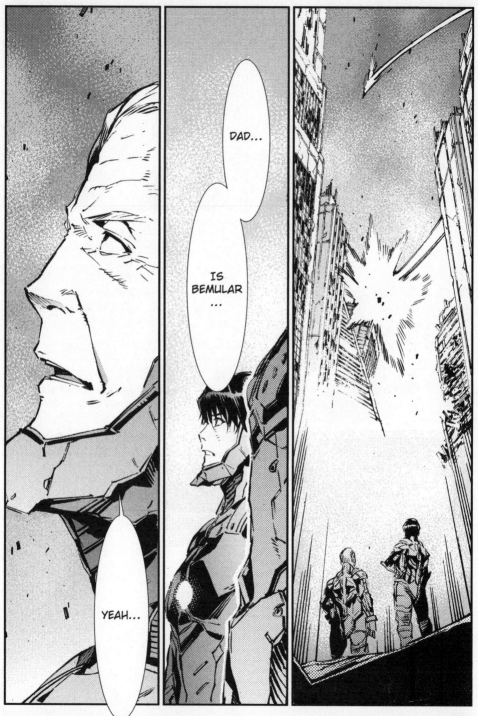

DAD...

IS
BEMULAR
...

YEAH...

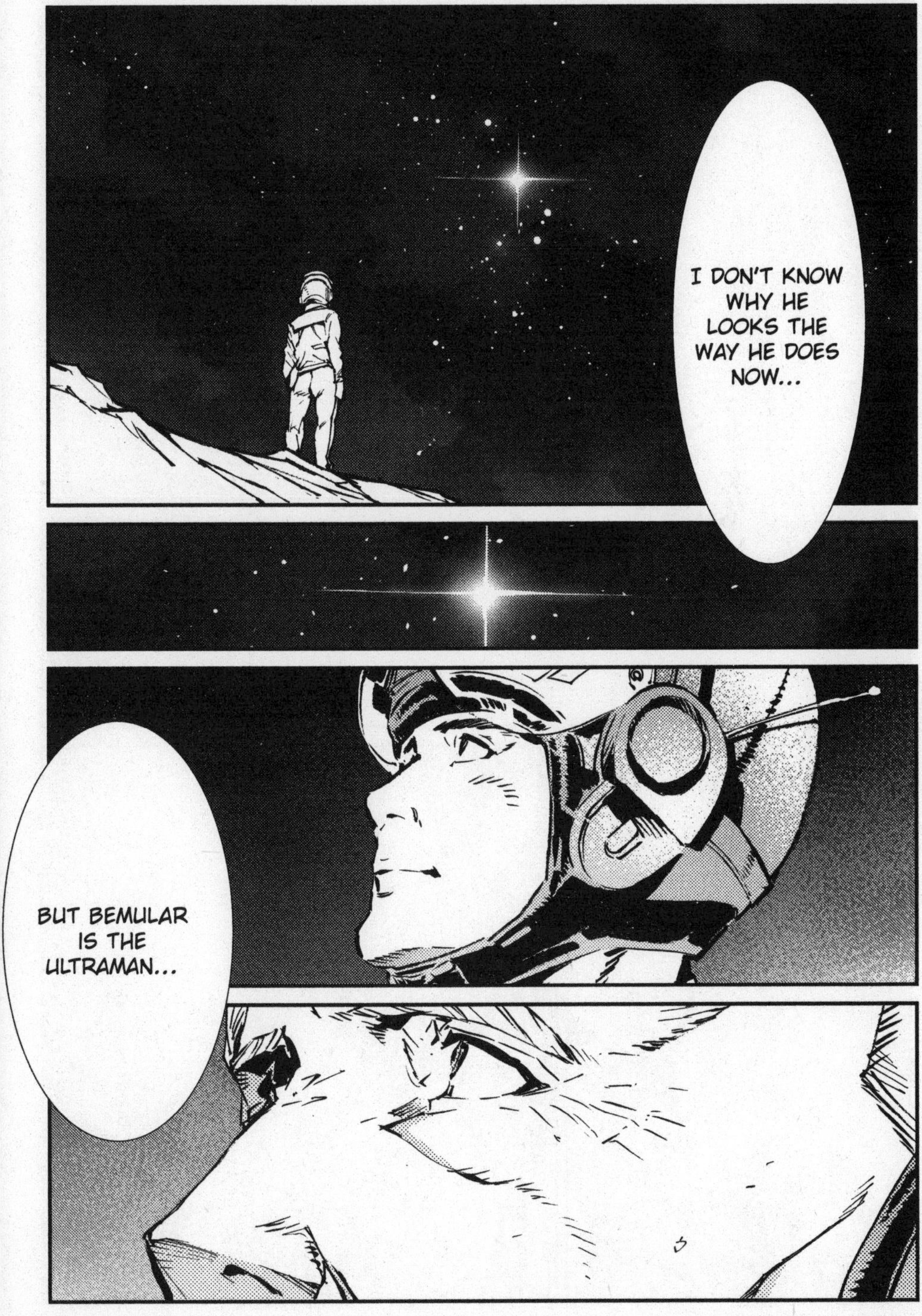
I DON'T KNOW WHY HE LOOKS THE WAY HE DOES NOW...
BUT BEMULAR IS THE ULTRAMAN...

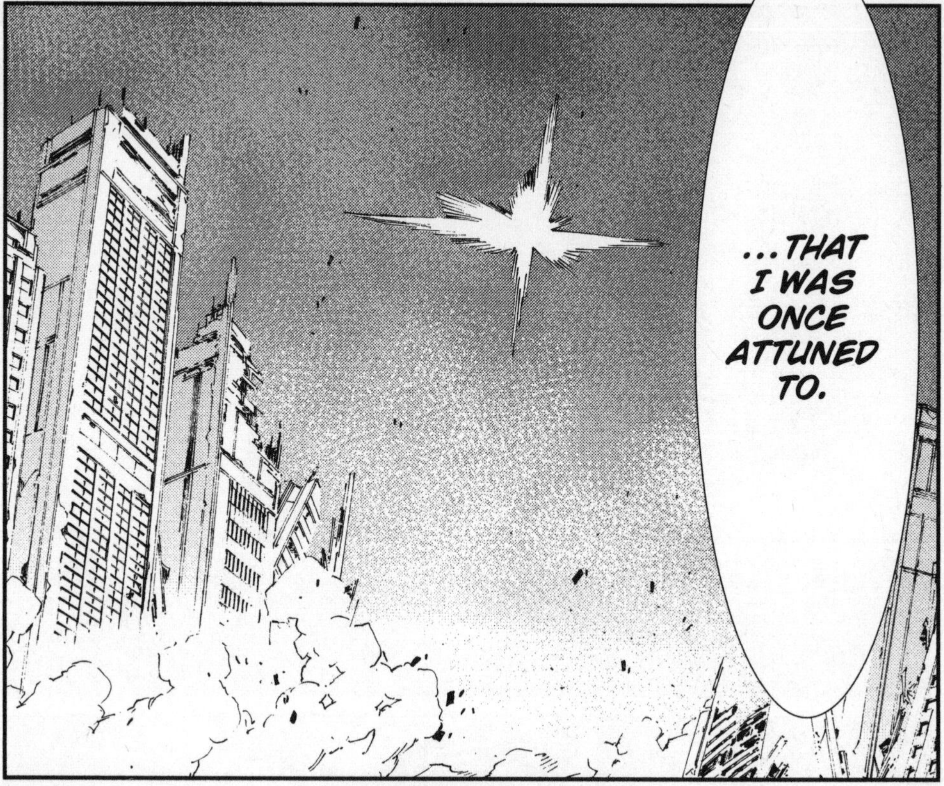
...THAT I WAS ONCE ATTUNED TO.
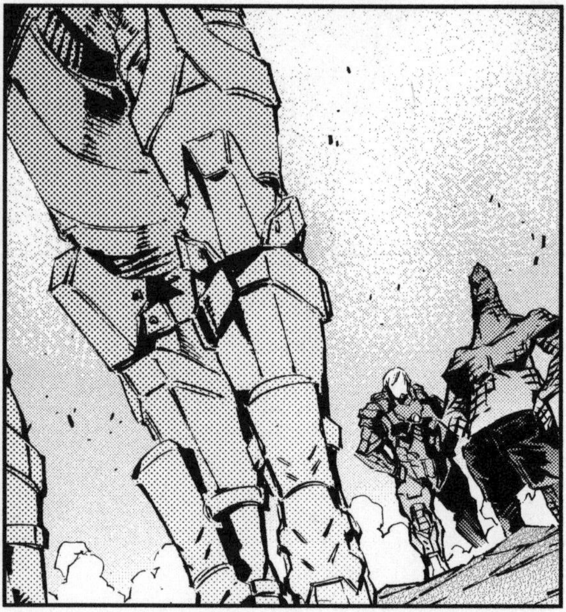
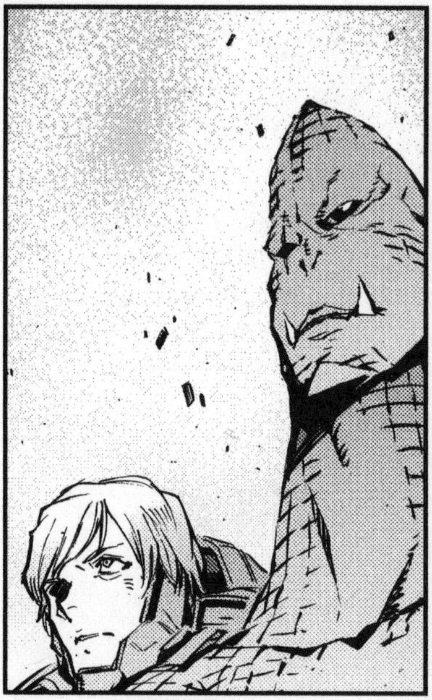

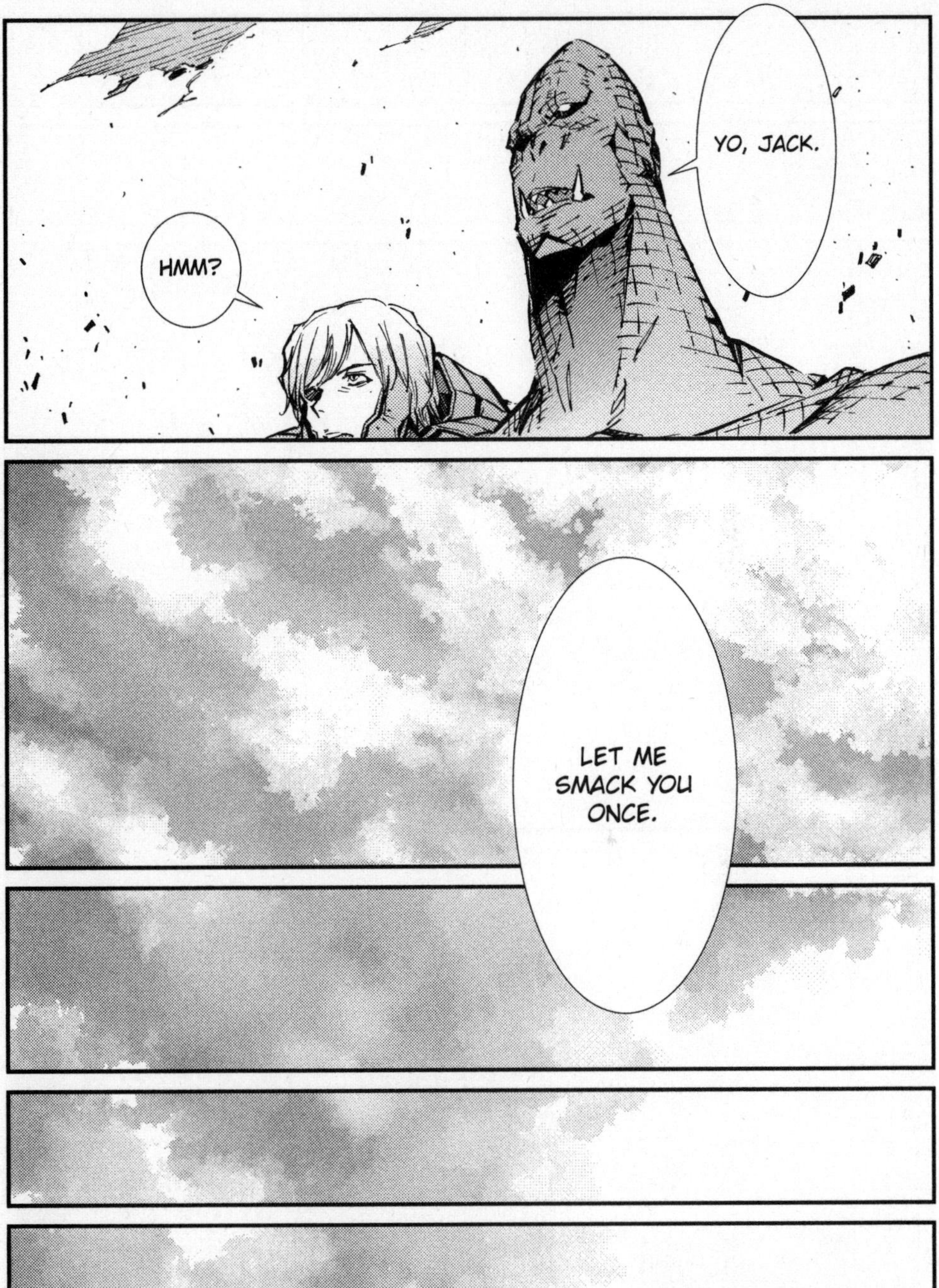
YO, JACK.
HMM?
LET ME SMACK YOU ONCE.

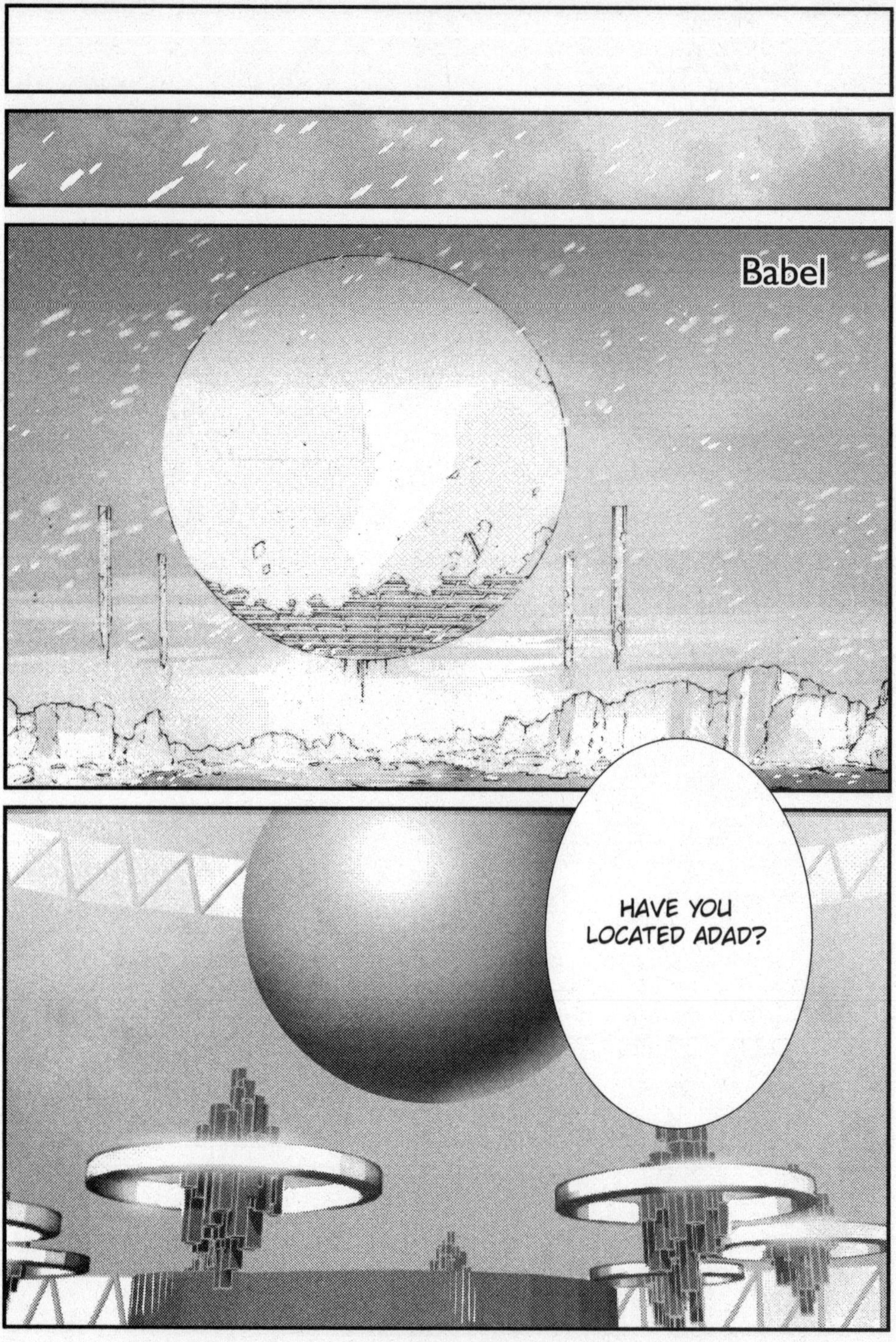
Babel
HAVE YOU LOCATED ADAD?

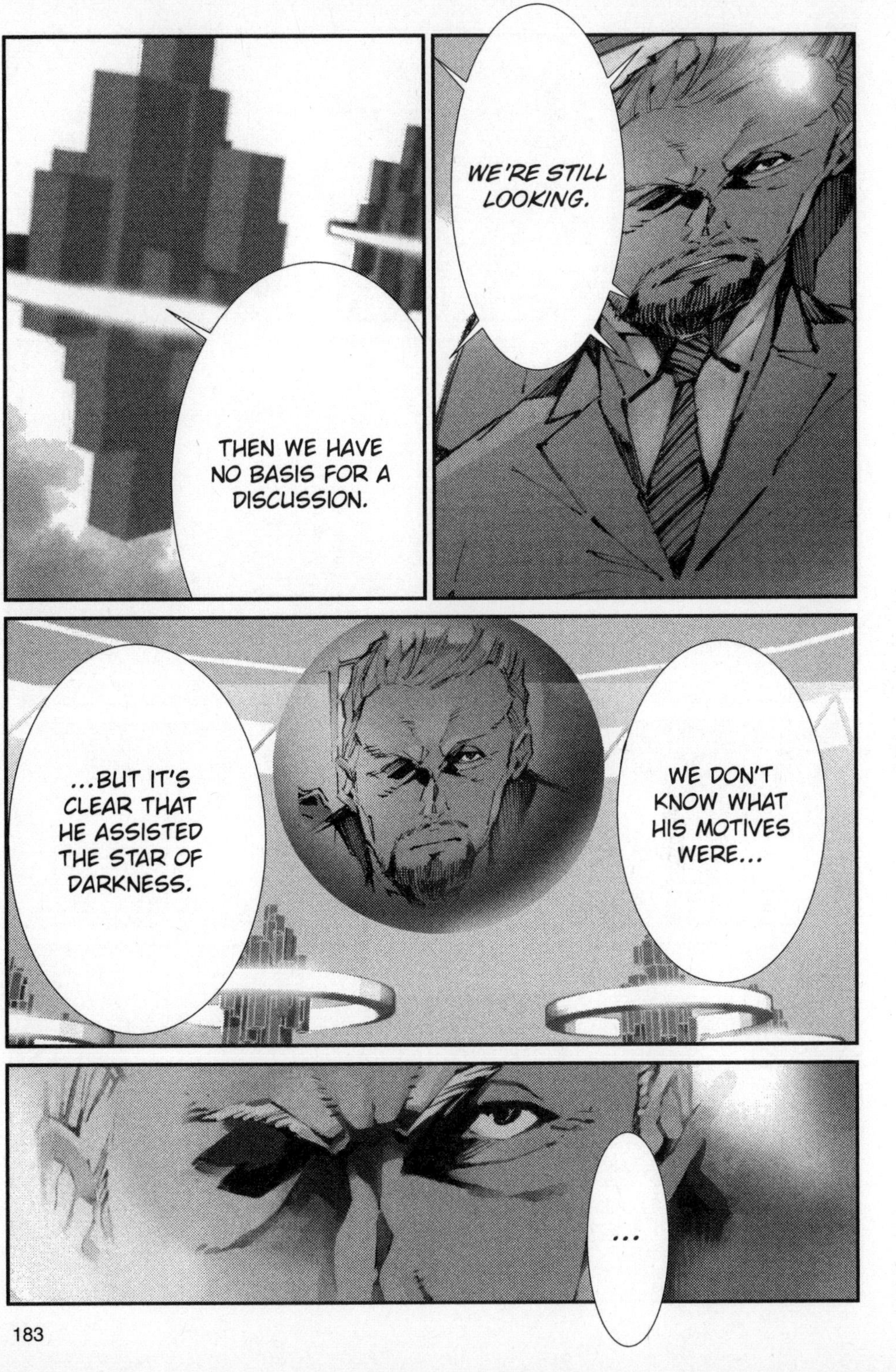
WE'RE STILL LOOKING.
THEN WE HAVE NO BASIS FOR A DISCUSSION.
WE DON'T KNOW WHAT HIS MOTIVES WERE...
...BUT IT'S CLEAR THAT HE ASSISTED THE STAR OF DARKNESS.
...

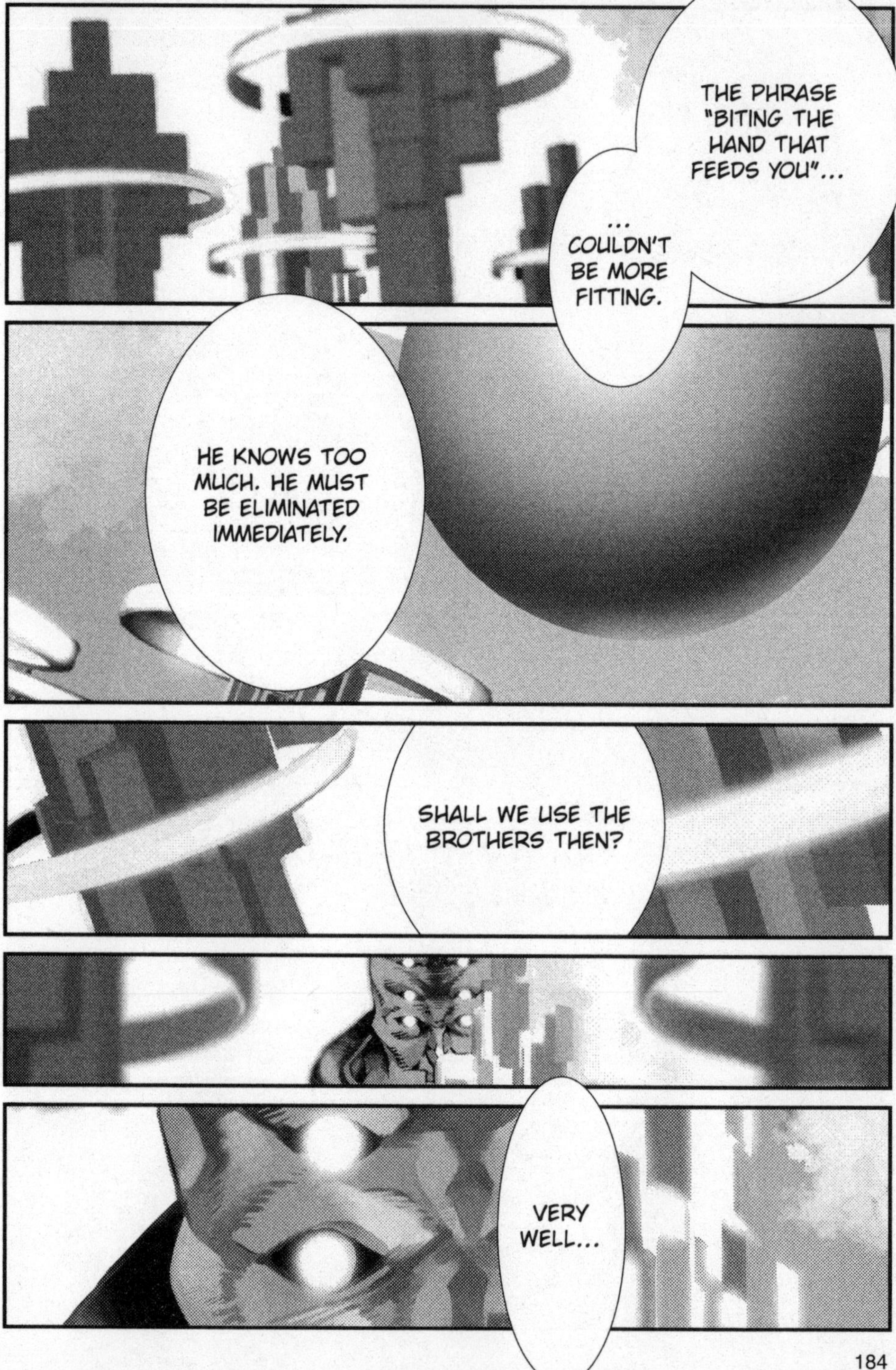
THE PHRASE "BITING THE HAND THAT FEEDS YOU"...
... COULDN'T BE MORE FITTING.
HE KNOWS TOO MUCH. HE MUST BE ELIMINATED IMMEDIATELY.
SHALL WE USE THE BROTHERS THEN?
VERY WELL...

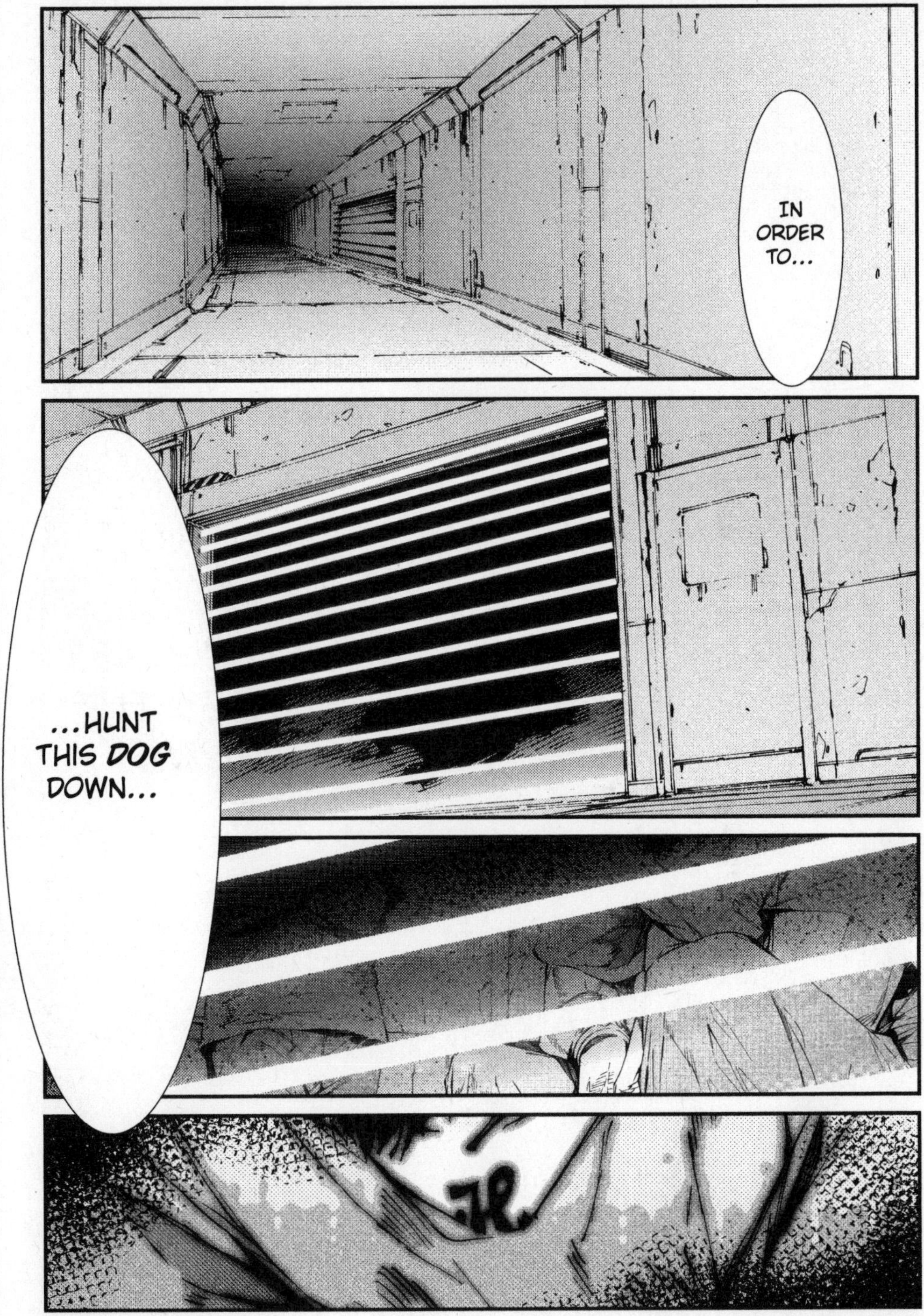
IN ORDER TO...
...HUNT THIS DOG DOWN...

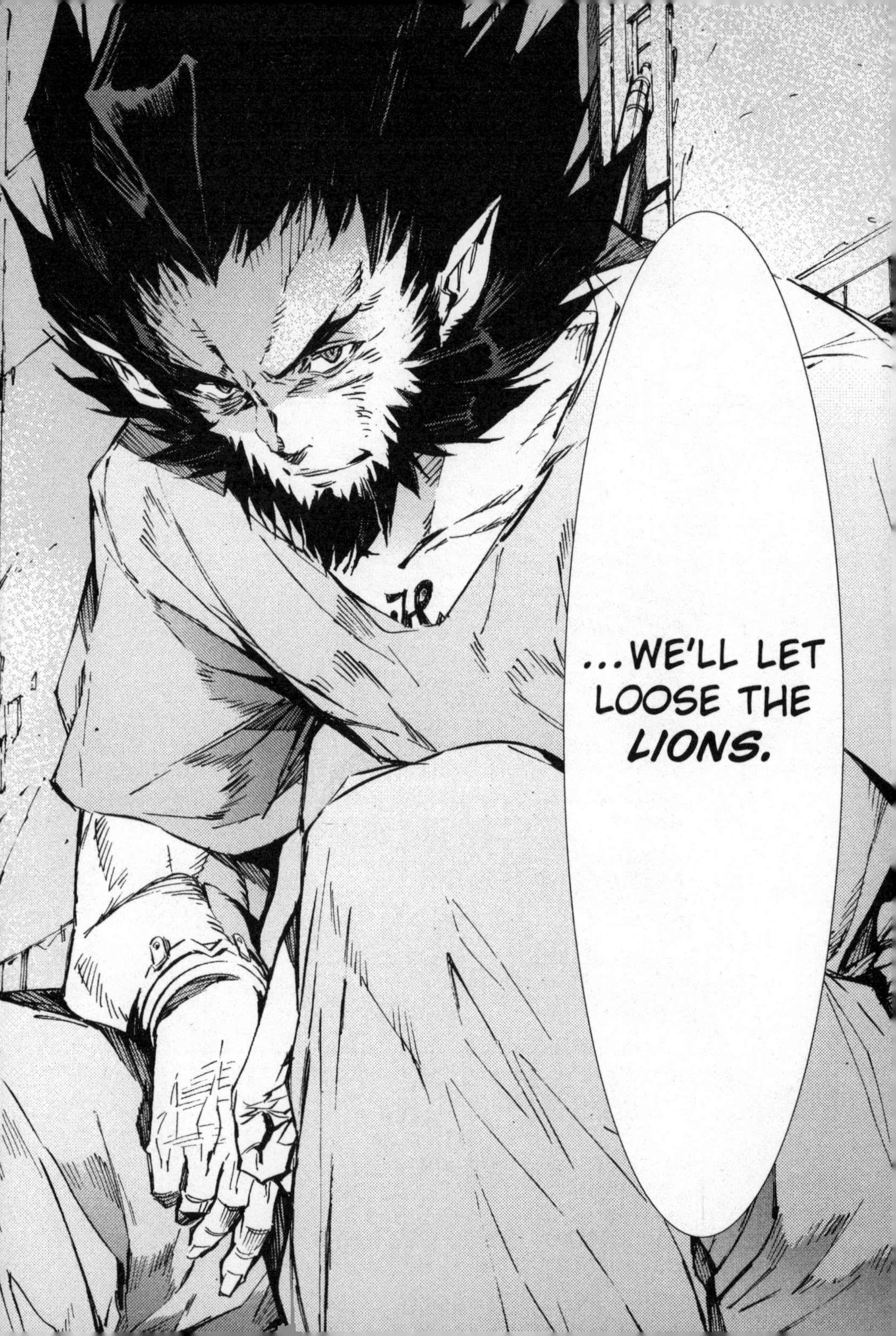
...WE'LL LET LOOSE THE LIONS.

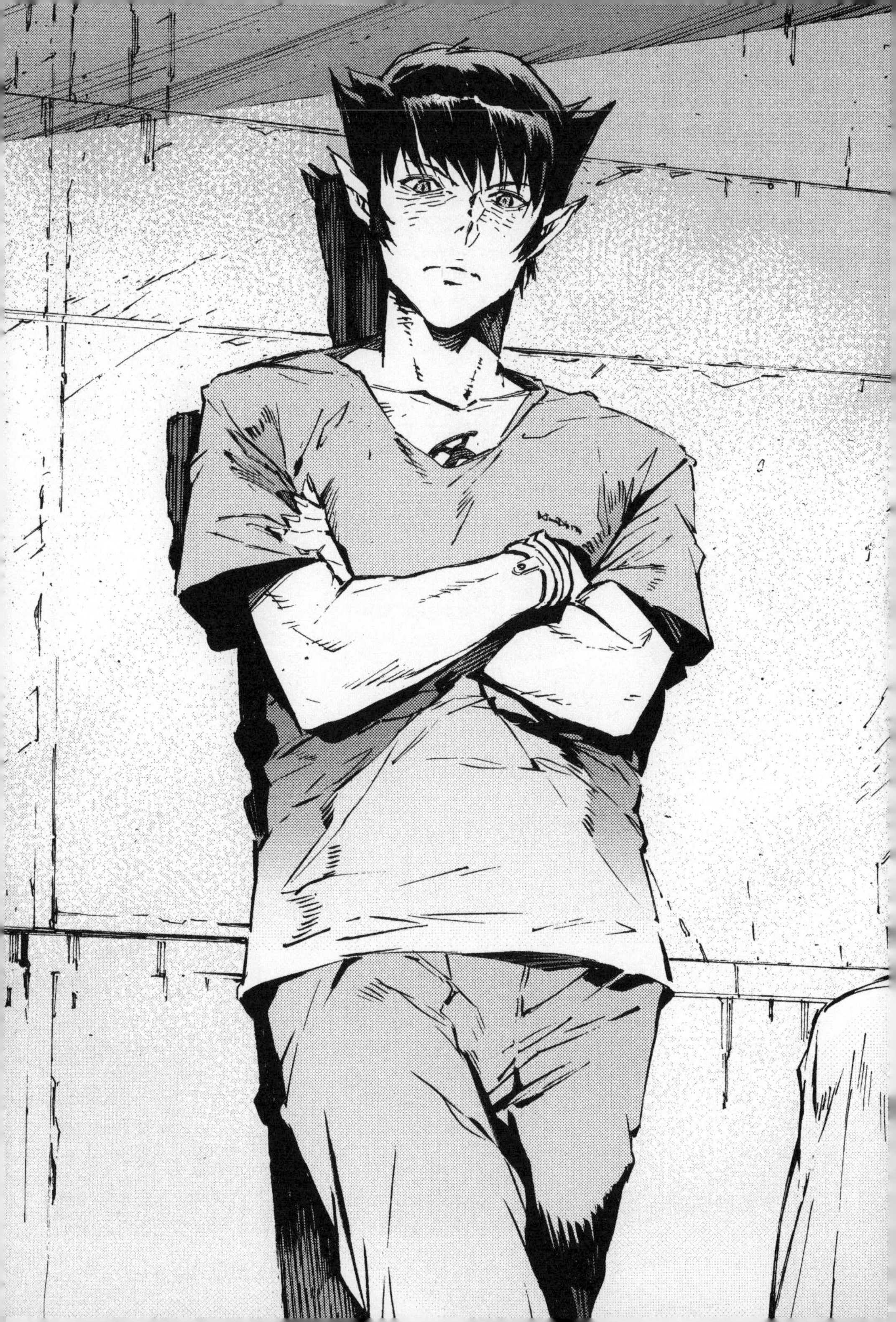

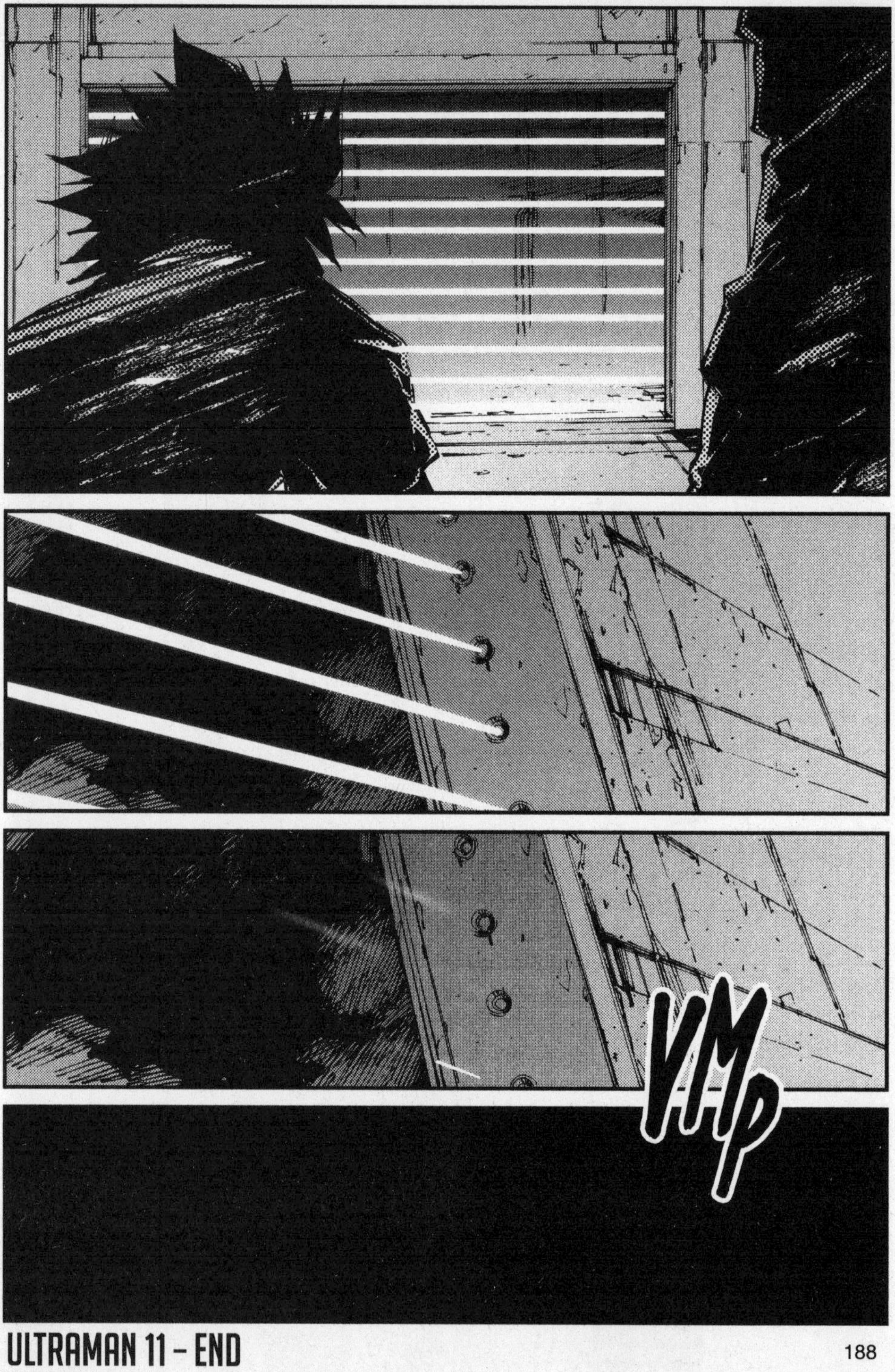
VIMP

ULTRAMAN 11 – END

THIS IS THE BEGINNING OF A NEW AGE

■ The combat exoskeleton worn by Jack (real name unknown), an agent for a classified division of the U.S. National Security Agency that specializes in hostile extraterrestrials. Named the Jack Suit based on the nickname given to it in the City. Two other suits exist, with simplified heads and chests. They were used in the Battle of New York alongside Jack (worn by agents from the same division).

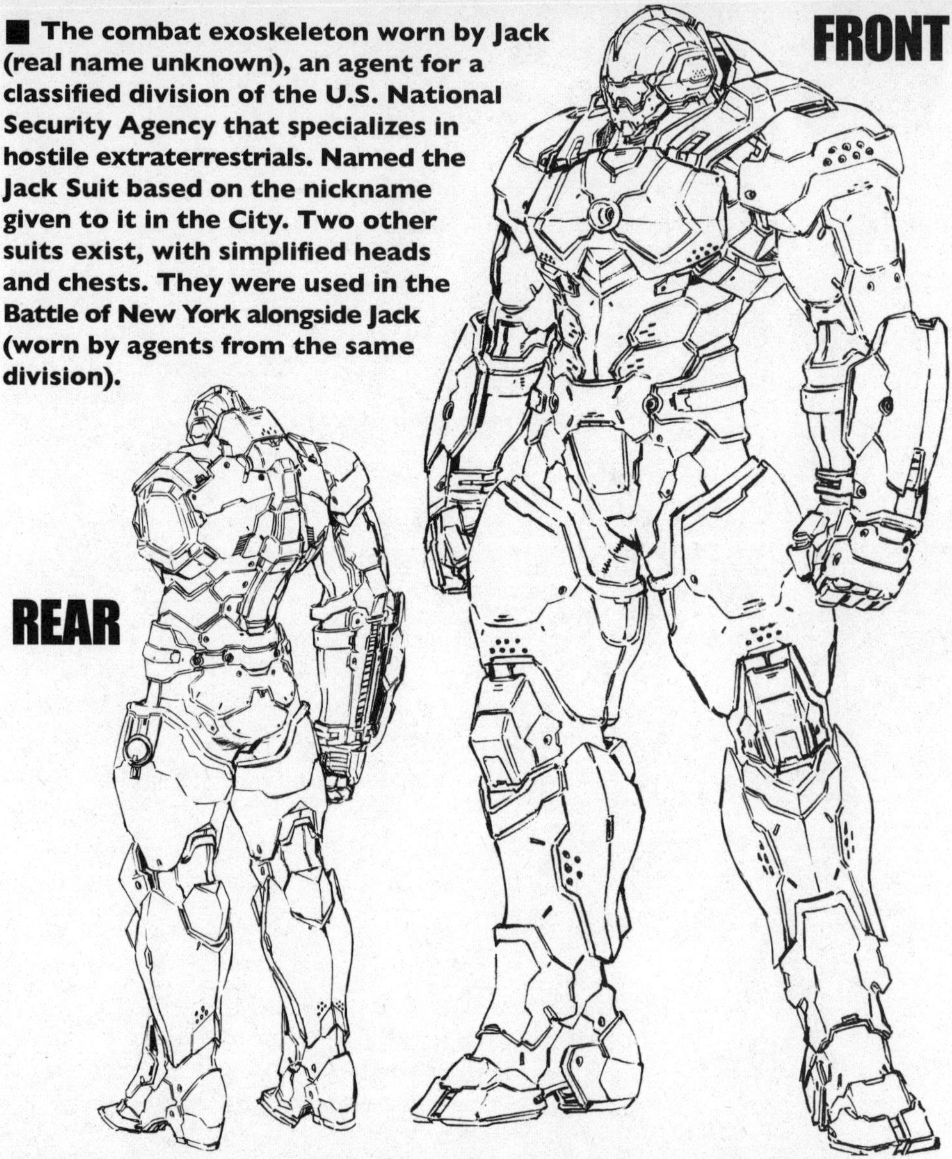
FRONT
REAR

■ The Jack Suit was created by Yapool, the renowned engineer who created the Ace Suit. The Americans requested features to help preserve the wearer's life and to create an imposing appearance, which resulted in a rugged, heavy-duty exterior that is quite different from the Ace Suit. However, the rugged exterior is not just for show. Its bulk covers many features (an invisible field that can be deployed at will, forearm weaponry, etc.).

■ The Jack Suit's mask can separate and be completely housed in the back armor. A receiver arm extends out of the back armor, requiring the wearer to face forward when the mask is being donned or removed.

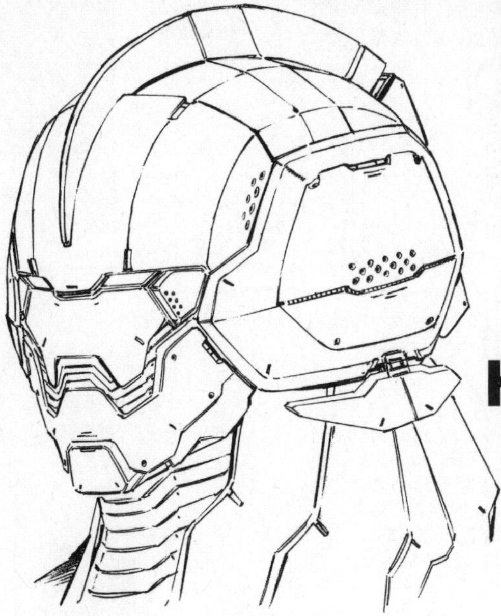

HEAD

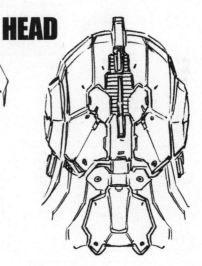

ARM

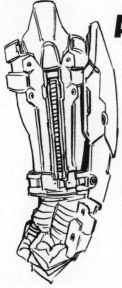

■ The Jack Suit's forearm is currently equipped with a collapsible sword and a railgun. Basic features of the suit had been completed in time for the Battle of New York, but its weaponry had not. It was designed to be equipped with energy weapons. Nevertheless, producing three exoskeleton suits (including the simplified versions) in such a short period of time was quite an accomplishment—Yapool's engineering skills should be lauded. In addition to a forearm energy weapon, a teleportation device (to allow for immediate emergency response) is currently under development.

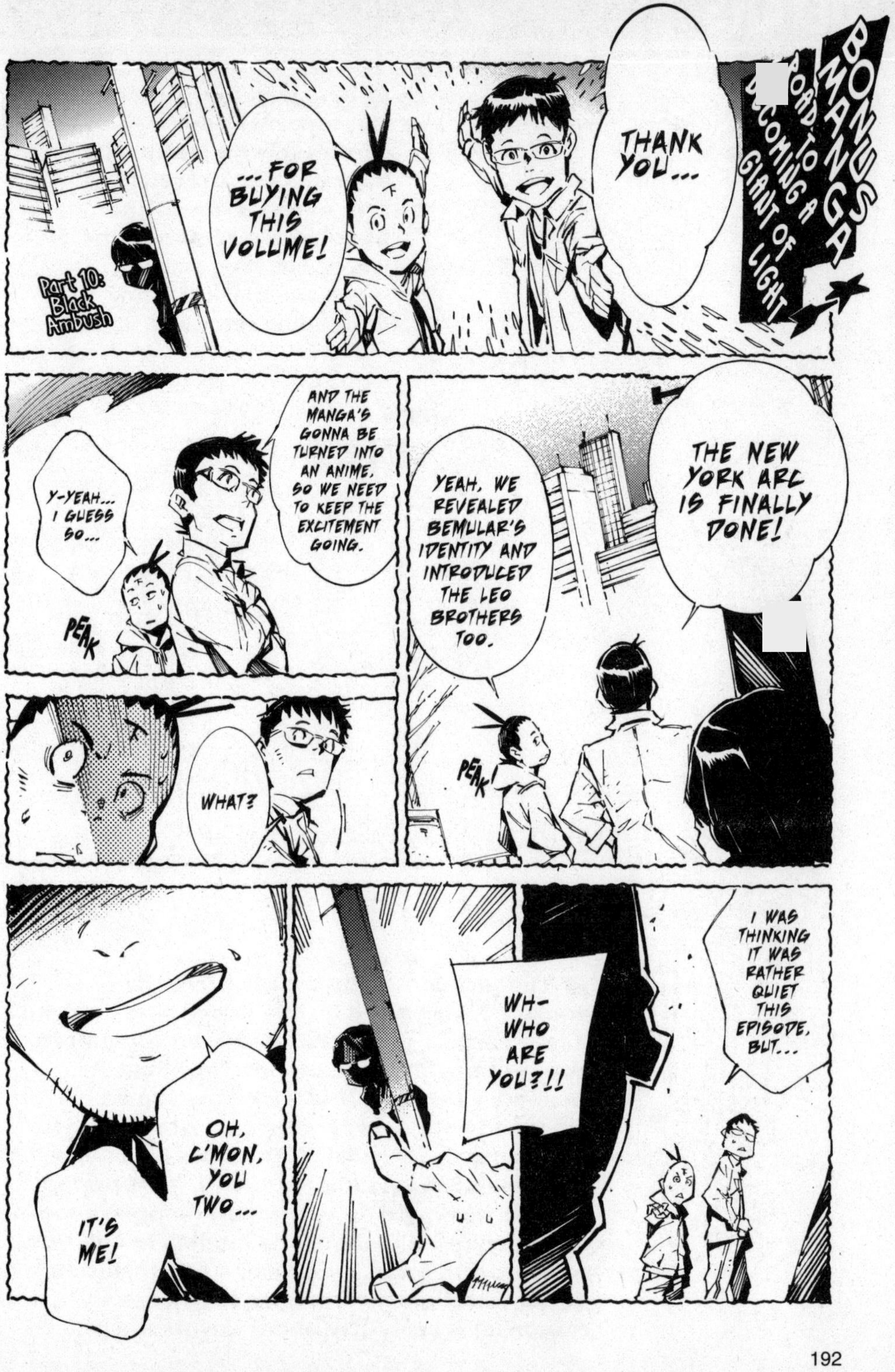
BONUS MANGA
ROAD TO ECOMING A GIANT OF LIGHT
THANK YOU...
...FOR BUYING THIS VOLUME!
Part 10: Black Ambush
THE NEW YORK ARC IS FINALLY DONE!
YEAH, WE REVEALED BEMULAR'S IDENTITY AND INTRODUCED THE LEO BROTHERS TOO.
PEAK!
AND THE MANGA'S GONNA BE TURNED INTO AN ANIME, SO WE NEED TO KEEP THE EXCITEMENT GOING.
Y-YEAH... I GUESS SO...
PEAK
WHAT?
I WAS THINKING IT WAS RATHER QUIET THIS EPISODE, BUT...
WH-WHO ARE YOU?!!
OH, C'MON, YOU TWO...
IT'S ME!

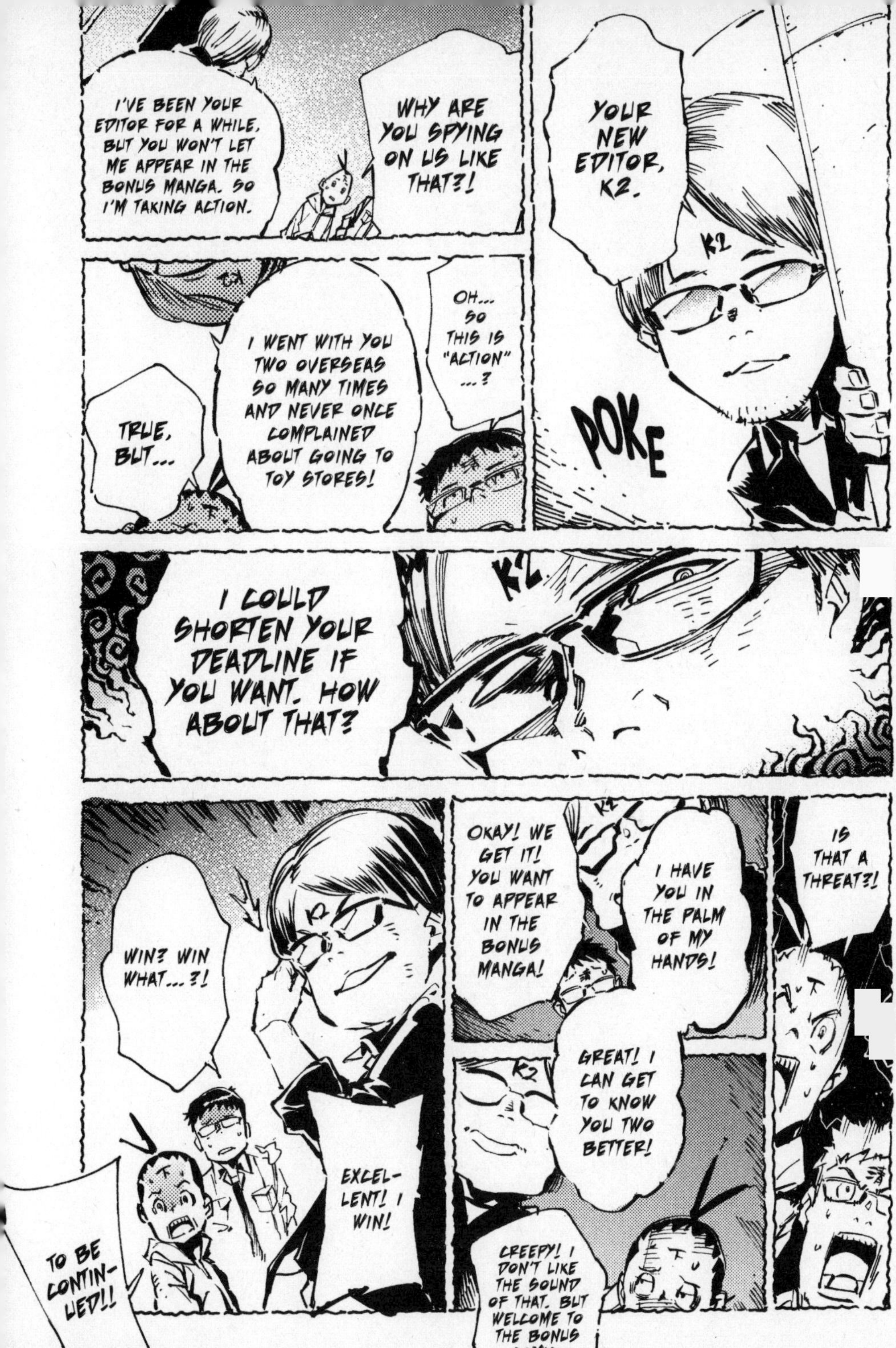
YOUR NEW EDITOR, K2.
K2
POKE
WHY ARE YOU SPYING ON US LIKE THAT?!
I'VE BEEN YOUR EDITOR FOR A WHILE, BUT YOU WON'T LET ME APPEAR IN THE BONUS MANGA. SO I'M TAKING ACTION.
OH... SO THIS IS "ACTION" ...?
I WENT WITH YOU TWO OVERSEAS SO MANY TIMES AND NEVER ONCE COMPLAINED ABOUT GOING TO TOY STORES!
TRUE, BUT...
K2
I COULD SHORTEN YOUR DEADLINE IF YOU WANT. HOW ABOUT THAT?
IS THAT A THREAT?!
K2
I HAVE YOU IN THE PALM OF MY HANDS!
OKAY! WE GET IT! YOU WANT TO APPEAR IN THE BONUS MANGA!
K2
GREAT! I CAN GET TO KNOW YOU TWO BETTER!
CREEPY! I DON'T LIKE THE SOUND OF THAT. BUT WELCOME TO THE BONUS COMIC.
K2
EXCEL-LENT! I WIN!
WIN? WIN WHAT...?!
TO BE CONTIN-UED!!

EIICHI SHIMIZU ✕ TOMOHIRO SHIMOGUCHI

This is really inconsequential, but Shimoguchi tends
to disappear when we go out. He simply gets lost. Yet
he insists that isn't the case. According to him it's
everybody else who disappears.
That's right.
Shimoguchi has always believed that it was other
people getting lost.
I thought that was a rather radical way of looking at it.

ULTRAMAN

VOLUME 11

VIZ SIGNATURE EDITION

STORY/ART BY EIICHI SHIMIZU AND TOMOHIRO SHIMOGUCHI

TRANSLATION JOE YAMAZAKI
ENGLISH ADAPTATION STAN!
TOUCH-UP ART & LETTERING EVAN WALDINGER
DESIGN KAM LI
EDITOR MIKE MONTESA

Printed in the U.S.A.

Published by VIZ Media, LLC
P.O. Box 77010
San Francisco, CA 94107

10 9 8 7 6 5 4 3 2 1
First printing, January 2019

ratings.viz.com RATED T TEEN

PARENTAL ADVISORY
ULTRAMAN is rated T for Teen and is recommended for ages 13 and up. This volume contains realistic and fantasy violence.

VIZ MEDIA
viz.com

VIZ SIGNATURE
vizsignature.com

HEY! YOU'RE READING IN THE WRONG DIRECTION!

This is the END of the graphic novel

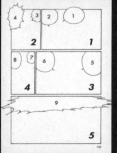

Follow the action this way.